# The Story of
# Billy Young

Anthony Hill is a multi-award-winning, bestselling author, and his books include works for both adults and children. His novel *Soldier Boy*, about Australia's youngest-known Anzac, was winner of the 2002 NSW Premier's Literary Award for Books for Young Adults.

Anthony's most recent book, *Captain Cook's Apprentice*, won the 2009 NSW Premier's Young People's History Prize. It follows *Soldier Boy*, *Young Digger* and *Animal Heroes* as further testimony to his remarkable ability to extensively research historical material and, from wide-ranging sources, piece together a moving and exciting story.

He is also the author of two novellas, the beautiful *Shadow Dog*, and the award-winning *The Burnt Stick*, illustrated by Mark Sofilas, as well as the picture book, *Lucy's Cat and the Rainbow Birds*, illustrated by Jane Tanner.

Anthony lives in Canberra with his wife, Gillian. Their daughter, son-in-law and grand-daughter, Emily, live in Melbourne.

# ANTHONY HILL

# *The Story of*
# Billy Young

*To my dear Brenda & Bob.*
*With much love*
*As ever.*
*Tony.*

*Anthony Hill*
*2012*
*First Edition*

VIKING
*an imprint of*
PENGUIN BOOKS

VIKING

Published by the Penguin Group
Penguin Group (Australia)
250 Camberwell Road, Camberwell, Victoria 3124, Australia
(a division of Pearson Australia Group Pty Ltd)
Penguin Group (USA) Inc.
375 Hudson Street, New York, New York 10014, USA
Penguin Group (Canada)
90 Eglinton Avenue East, Suite 700, Toronto, Canada ON M4P 2Y3
(a division of Pearson Penguin Canada Inc.)
Penguin Books Ltd
80 Strand, London WC2R 0RL, England
Penguin Ireland
25 St Stephen's Green, Dublin 2, Ireland
(a division of Penguin Books Ltd)
Penguin Books India Pvt Ltd
11 Community Centre, Panchsheel Park, New Delhi – 110 017, India
Penguin Group (NZ)
67 Apollo Drive, Rosedale, North Shore 0632, New Zealand
(a division of Pearson New Zealand Ltd)
Penguin Books (South Africa) (Pty) Ltd
24 Sturdee Avenue, Rosebank, Johannesburg 2196, South Africa

Penguin Books Ltd, Registered Offices: 80 Strand, London WC2R 0RL, England

First published by Penguin Group (Australia), 2012

1 3 5 7 9 10 8 6 4 2

Design by Cathy Larsen © Penguin Group (Australia)
Front cover photos: Billy at age 15, courtesy Billy Young; Liberated prisoners at Changi, AWM 019192
Back cover photos: Barbed wire and background texture, Shutterstock; Author portrait courtesy John Feder
Typeset in 11/16pt Sabon
Printed and bound in Australia by McPherson's Printing Group, Maryborough, Victoria

National Library of Australia
Cataloguing-in-Publication data:

Hill, Anthony, 1942–
The story of Billy Young : a teenager in Changi, Sandakan and
Outram Road/Anthony Hill.
9780670076178 (pbk.)
Includes index.
Young, Bill, 1925–
World War, 1939–1945 – Prisoners and prisons,
Japanese – Biography.
World War, 1939–1945 – Personal narratives, Australian.
Prisoners of war – Australia – Biography.

940.547252092

Supported by

This project has been assisted by the ACT Arts Fund supported by the ACT Government.

penguin.com.au

FSC
www.fsc.org

MIX
Paper from
responsible sources
FSC® C001695

For the Dead End Kids
and the POWs of Sandakan 1942–1945

*Not a day goes by that Billy Young does not remember you
For he loves you all.*

Author's card left at the Sandakan Memorial
Anzac Day, 2009

Sometimes when crimes have been committed,
it is necessary to go back and mark the spot ...

Bill Young
*Return to a Dark Age*

# CONTENTS

The lines at the head of each chapter are from Bill Young's *My War in Pictures, My Thoughts in Verse*, and also his *Return to a Dark Age*.

# AUTHOR'S NOTE

I first heard the amazing story of Bill Young from one of his relatives, Mrs Win Adams, who came to my bookstall one Sunday morning at Canberra's Old Bus Depot Market. Browsing through my military books, Mrs Adams remarked that I should write a book about her husband's cousin Bill, who'd joined the army at 15, was sent to Singapore, and spent the rest of his teenage years as a prisoner of war of the Japanese forces.

A number of people have said I should write about their cousin Bill or Jack. One of the great joys of the market stall is meeting my readers and listening to their stories. But this cousin Bill stayed in my mind. And nearing the end of writing my previous book, *Captain Cook's Apprentice*, it seemed ever more important to try to find him.

Following leads from Win Adams, I tracked Young Bill to Sydney and, with heart in mouth, made the first phone call. There is always some trepidation. Will the subject respond favorably – or tell you to go to hell? I needn't have worried in this case. For the next three-quarters of an hour, Billy regaled me with tales of growing up around Paddy's Market during the Depression, of his father who was killed in the Spanish Civil War, of lying about his age when he enlisted in 1941 (the fictitious aunt in whose name he signed the consent form still appears as his official next of kin), of Changi, Sandakan and Outram Road prisons.

Finally, as we ended that first conversation, he said, 'Do you know what the older blokes called me in the prison camp? "Billy the Kid".'

And I knew I had a book.

I bought Bill Young's self-published war memoir, *Return to a Dark Age*. It is raw and powerful. It makes public the pictures that Billy taught himself to draw, and many of the poems he taught himself to write. But as a largely self-educated man, Billy is the first to admit that, for him, spelling, grammar, punctuation and syntax are 'foreign vegetables' – and I felt his story should be accessible to as many readers as possible. So armed with a digital recorder I went to see him, and thus began the first of what turned into more than 60 hours of interviews as Bill relived events from long ago – sometimes in painful detail, always with humour, intelligence and compassion – as we probed his memory of happenings and the substance of half-forgotten conversations. For that confidence, I am deeply grateful.

Where I've been able to test Bill's version against the written record, his memory on matters concerning himself has often been remarkably accurate. For example, he still quotes many lines from the verses scratched on the walls of his prison cell, and comparing those printed in his book with the published poems I was surprised how close to the original Bill's rendering was. The reports in the *Workers' Weekly* of the 1938 Christmas party after his father's death corresponded exactly with Bill's remembrance. And the material relating to Captain Pieter van Hemert, discovered in the Dutch archives by my friend Anny de Decker, tallied reasonably well with Bill's recall of what his dying cellmate had told him of his background.

For these reasons I have felt confident in generally relying on Bill's memory of events where he was personally involved. For the broader historical narrative, of course, I looked to the authoritative references: principally Alan Warren on the war in Malaya, Lynette

Silver on Sandakan, and Bob Christie on the 2/29th Battalion, as noted in the References and Chapter Notes. My friend Shuji Yamazaki generously advised on Japanese words and culture. And while Bill Young naturally is the source of his own story, I'm aware the human mind is fallible and partial. Where possible I have checked his story against other versions and recollections from his comrades who survive, and it will be found that certain sequences and participants differ somewhat from *Return to a Dark Age*. Even so, it is possible that adjustments will need to be made to this text in the light of further knowledge; I can only plead in mitigation where I have erred that every book like this must be considered a work in progress. As is every life.

Having said that, however, I believe – as I did when I first heard it – that the story of 'Billy the Kid' stands as an extraordinary tale of adversity and survival. It is a testament to the youth growing up barely educated around Paddy's Market – though well-enough schooled in the wisdom of the streets – and the indomitable optimism of the market stallholder, for whom the next lucky customer is always just around the corner. The trader in me has long wanted to write a story about market people, and this is it. It is the story of the circumstances that led to Billy's enlistment, captivity and incarceration in some of the most barbaric Japanese prisons, of the tragic effects of war and its aftermath on Bill Young's personal life, and his salvation through the power of art and self-expression.

This is the tale of an Australia that has almost gone. It is one that should be told to a wider audience while there are still people alive who can remember it.

Anthony Hill
Canberra, 2012

# SOUTH-EAST ASIA

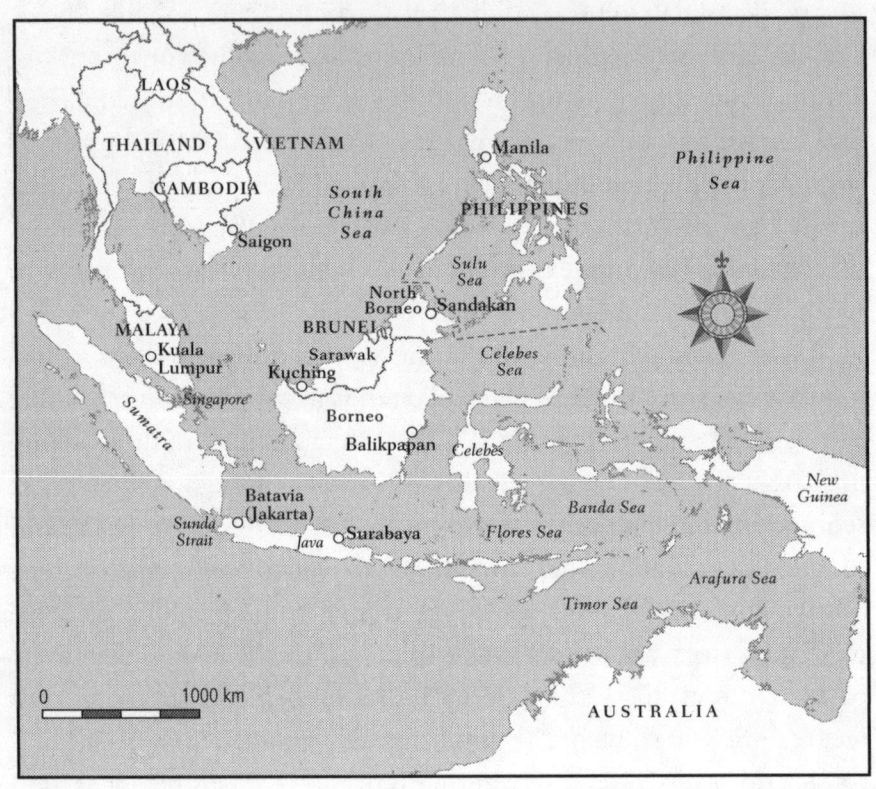

# MALAY PENINSULA AND SINGAPORE

# SINGAPORE

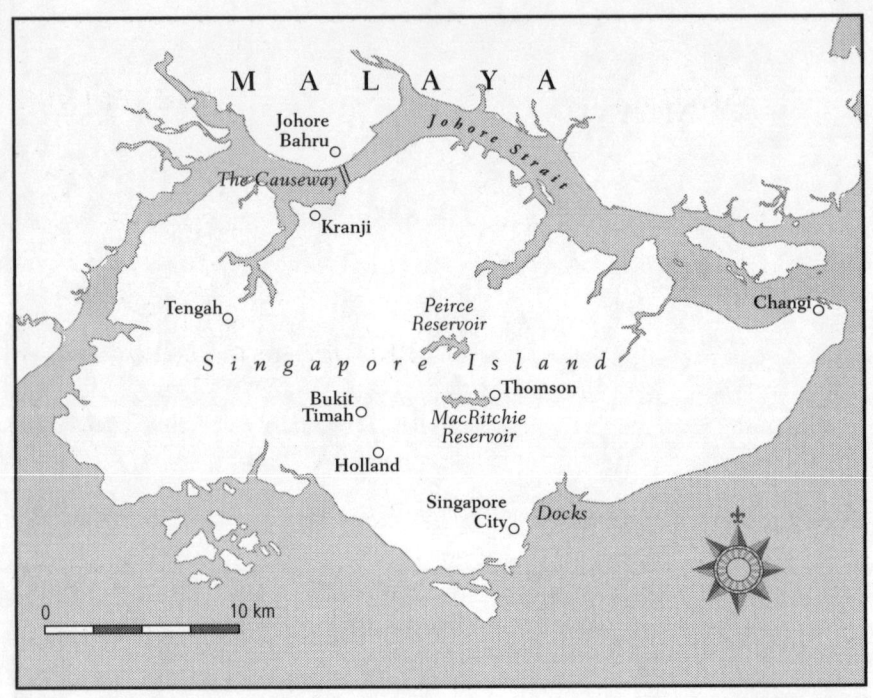

# BORNEO

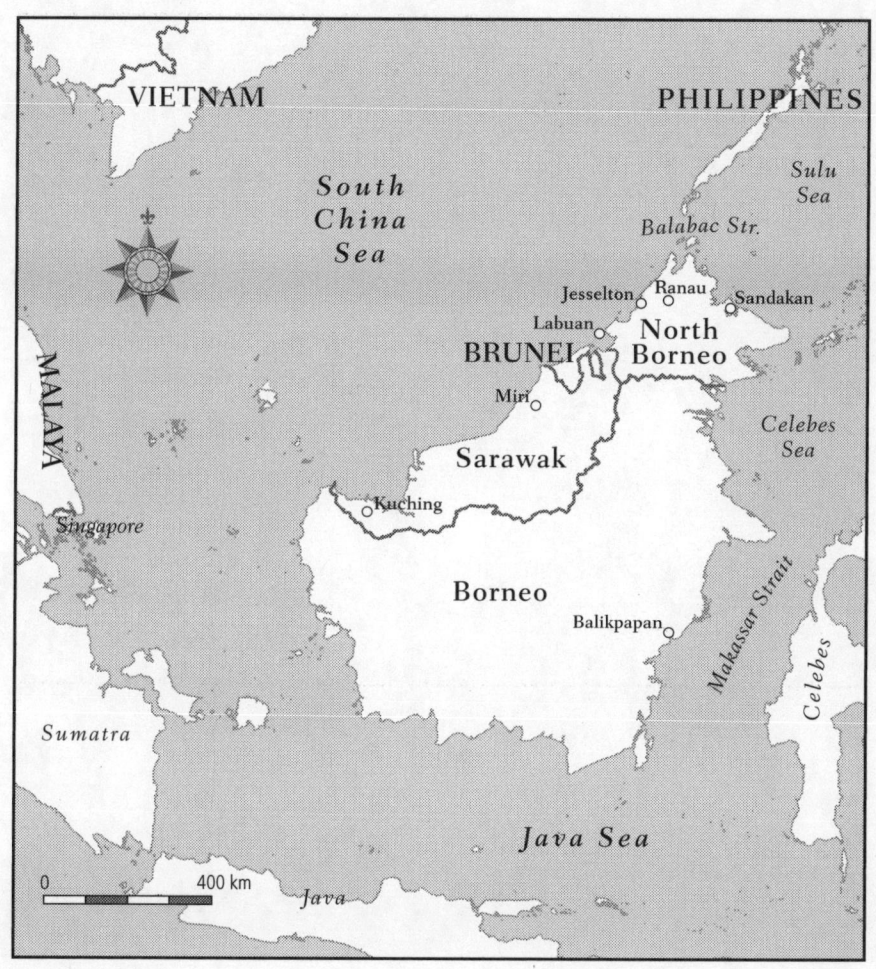

VIETNAM

PHILIPPINES

*South China Sea*

*Sulu Sea*

*Balabac Str.*

Jesselton  Ranau
Sandakan

Labuan  **North Borneo**

**BRUNEI**

MALAYA

Miri

*Celebes Sea*

**Sarawak**

Kuching

Singapore

**Borneo**

Balikpapan

*Makassar Strait*

*Celebes*

Sumatra

*Java Sea*

0  400 km  *Java*

# 1

# OUTRAM ROAD

*Grim house of travail*
*Where ghostly inmates wail*

Billy the Kid was only 15 when he joined the army in July 1941. It wasn't wartime patriotism or adventure or a misplaced sense of mateship that drove him; nothing like that. He was hungry and broke, with nowhere to sleep. Homeless. An orphan. And the army offered him a feed, a blanket and five shillings a day in his pocket.

Now, two years later in Singapore, jolting towards jail in the back of a canvas-covered truck, Billy Young knew the army couldn't even offer him that. For he was a prisoner of the Japanese military police – the dreaded Kenpeitai: Nippon's version of the Gestapo. And he was still a kid. Still starving. He still owned nothing except the rags he wore – a soiled and bloody pyjama top and a pair of filthy shorts cut from a canvas kitbag. And his greatest treasure was a pencil stub, clutched in his fist.

Sleep, moreover, was something the Kenpeitai had stolen months ago when Billy first came into their possession, an escaped prisoner of war from the labour camp at Sandakan in North Borneo. He had been beaten, his body broken, kept like an animal in a cage by the interrogators. Chained. Tried. And shipped with seven other Sandakan men in a horsebox across the sea to Singapore, sentenced

1

to four years solitary confinement. Sleep – the peaceful slumber of content – had long gone. All that remained was the pulse of life: an individual human will to survive that still beat, with the naïve certitude of youth, even through Billy's bleakest hours. That, and the call of mateship, which, after all, is the same response reaching out to one's fellow journeymen in suffering.

The truck suddenly braked and lurched, throwing the eight prisoners together on the floor. A tangled mass of humanity indeed: thin bones and bodies, barely cushioned with flesh, aching from the knock. As they heard the Jap guard and driver shouting from the front seat at some unfortunate coolie on the road, the men in the back began to sort themselves out. It was lucky their hands were not manacled. Taking advantage of the diversion, they quickly reassured themselves.

'You all right, kid?' This addressed to Billy the Kid, as the older men often ribbed him.

'Yeah. You too, Brownie?' Billy's partner in escape, Myles Peace Brown, though nobody ever dared call him that. Peace? In the middle of a war? The 24-year-old timberman would have flattened them. He'd been born on Armistice Day, 11 November 1918, hence the middle name. But it was always 'MP' or 'Brownie'. 'You okay?' Brownie's shins had swollen dark as eggplants where the Sandakan guards beat him with wooden swords, his eyebrows had been split and the bloody skin draped across his face. Even now his wounds were only half-healed.

'I'll feel a lot better when you get your flaming elbow out of my back,' came the reply.

'Jimmy?'

Jimmy Darlington was in some ways the worst affected of them, his body still scarred from the torture of wet ropes and burning sun, splintered stakes to kneel upon and merciless bashings after he dared hit a Sandakan guard who attacked an older POW. The incident had led directly to the attempt by Billy and MP to escape – and the three had been together through the four harrowing months since then.

'In the pink, mate.' A stifled snort. Darlo, a part-Aborigine, was still red raw from his injuries.

It was all very surreptitious in case the guard heard his prisoners breaking the iron law against talking and vented more anger on them. As the truck staggered into motion again, swaying and complaining as it climbed a hill, the eight Australian soldiers fell silent once more, energies bent on trying to steady themselves and conserving their strength in the stifling heat.

Like all of them, Billy the Kid felt quite disoriented, tossed about in the khaki half-light, not knowing where he was going or what would happen to him, except that it was bound to be unpleasant. Sight and sensation – even passing time – seemed dislocated, and had done from the moment the ship docked earlier that day.

The horsebox, in which the prisoners were incarcerated on a troop deck, was shut. The upper door had been open during the voyage, allowing a little light, air and food scrapings to enter – though it also exposed the POWs to the constant taunts of Japanese soldiers. But in port with the door bolted, the eight were left in darkness amid the stench of rotting straw, horseshit and three days of their own bodily wastes.

For hours, it seemed, they waited, confused and anxious, until at length a cable was attached and the ship's crane began to lift the horsebox up through the ship's bowels. Higher above the deck and superstructure, the crate with its human cargo was dangling and slowly twisting in the air.

'Jesus, don't let it fall!'

They swung out over the side. Hung there a moment. Then with a jerking, sea-sickening motion, the cable suddenly ran out. The horsebox descended rapidly, paused, and without ceremony they were dumped on the wharf.

'Any bones broken?'

There were hurried consultations as it landed. All were intact, yet a guard, hearing the forbidden sounds of speech, banged the wooden crate with his rifle butt.

*'Damare!'* Shut up!

In the silence that followed they heard a truck being backed up to the horsebox. The door was unbolted and swung open.

*'Koi!'* Come!

Guards, armed with swords, stood on either side as the prisoners emerged from the horsebox and climbed into the enclosed truck. The Kenpeitai would permit nobody to see them entering Singapore. The men themselves had only the merest glimpse of sky and sunlight after days below decks before the canvas was laced tight and the truck moved off.

In one of those ironies of war, the vehicle was in fact their own: part of that vast dump of Allied supplies captured by the Japanese when Singapore fell in February 1942, and 130 000 British, Australian and Indian troops became their POWs.

'How considerate of our side to provide the transport to convey us to prison!' MP muttered. And not for the first time Billy cursed the folly that ever tempted him to propose an escape with Brownie.

'We should have stayed in Sandakan,' MP had said over and again. And Billy was now forced to agree. 'We'd have been safe there.'

Yet the kid was only 17 and invincible – and consequences were something to worry about later. Until, that is, they eventually caught up with you...

Still, he had to admit that the truck was better than the horsebox. It was reasonably clean (though their own pressing bodies stank), and they could at least see in the camouflaged light. Heat continued to run in tropical streams down human flesh, however, as the sun turned the canvas into a sweatbox. Billy's pyjama top was wet as a dishrag, mopping up perspiration. And it was a pity about the lousy driver! His vehicle bucked and shuddered up the hill, gears grating constantly.

'Where are they taking us?' Billy asked. It was curiosity really, not fear. They had all got beyond that. Or thought they had. 'Where are we going?'

'Luna Park, kid. That's what it feels like.'

'Dodgem cars.'

'Switchback railway, more like.'

The prisoners laughed. Softly to themselves, in case the guard heard. It was a feeble joke, but prompted a laugh nonetheless. Then they grew quiet as other memories intruded: of summer nights in St Kilda with girlfriends; of pink, sticky lips and fairy floss; of coloured lanterns and sideshows, wheezing merry-go-rounds and the wide, grinning mouth of home...

'D'ya think they'll take us out to Changi again?'

'The Changi Hilton? That's home to us now, son. That's where the battalion is, in the POW camp. And they aren't taking us home.'

'Don't you remember, Billy? The judge at Kuching?'

*Because of your youth, His Majesty the Emperor of Japan in his leniency reduce sentence from eight to four year.*

How sweet those words had sounded. Especially when he'd just heard sentences fall sharp as an executioner's sword upon the bowed heads of five local prisoners beside them in the dock – and they were next! *That* was fear. When death is the alternative, the love of life fairly throbs. Anything is embraced.

'No holiday camp for us, Billy boy.'

No, indeed.

The truck shortly ceased its groaning and came to a halt. Doors slammed. There was the sound of feet stamping, and orders shouted in high Japanese.

This was it – wherever they were going.

'Look after yourselves, fellers.'

'Good luck.'

The canvas flap was unlaced. Shafts of sunlight pierced the gloom, through which appeared the head of the guard as if in a halo.

'*Kotchi koi!*' Come here! He indicated that they should get down.

One by one the prisoners edged to the rear and eased themselves to the ground, half-blinded by the sun. After the horsebox and covered truck, the light slashed Billy's eyes like razors and at first he couldn't see where he was.

'*Korakora!*' Hey you! Now! The guard pushed him into line with the others as he shuffled and fumbled his way.

'*Bango!*' Prisoners will number off!

The orders were all given in Japanese, but after four months with the Kenpeitai, where numbering off was a daily ritual, these ones at least were familiar to the Australian captives.

'*Ichi, ni, san, shi, go…*'

A pause. Billy realised he was next.

'*Roku…*'

Then came a jab, fierce as sunlight.

'*Ojigi!*' Bow when you number off!

The kid folded a little at the waist.

*Don't upset them! Don't be a fool!* Billy admonished himself more severely than the guard. For he had treasure – the little stub of pencil – to smuggle inside. *Don't draw attention to yourself!*

'*…nana, hachi.*'

He'd been letting his eyes get used to the sun – clamping the lids, then gradually allowing the silver-white rays to creep beneath his lashes and the pupils to dilate. As the numbering finished, Billy began to look about him.

Curiously, his vision at first wandered along the road they'd just travelled, down the hill towards Singapore town and the harbour, as if not yet ready to see what lay ahead. Not far away he noticed a group of men – POWs like himself, Billy supposed – watching the new arrivals from a vegetable garden where they laboured in a school ground. And that was strange, because Billy had spent much of his time running away from school when he was a kid, a little kid, growing up in Sydney.

No escape from here, though! His eyes wandered back and rested on a large sign by the roadside: OUTRAM ROAD PRISON. Nearby, the guard was handing over his charges to the Kenpeitai officers with voluble ceremony. Beyond them, the grief-stained, whitewashed walls of their jail loured like a yet-undreamed nightmare. And the heavy, green gates yawned open to receive them.

It was not Luna Park.

Outram Road had been built by the British a hundred years before to enable them to impose their colonial will upon recalcitrant subjects. Just before the Second World War, it had been replaced by a new model jail at Changi, on the north-east coast, eight miles from the city. In 1942 the Japanese victors had obligingly used Changi and the nearby barracks to intern the British Empire's own civilians and soldiers as POWs. Outram Road became the Kenpeitai prison, and the sum of human misery its brick and stone walls had already witnessed was as nothing compared to what followed. They had every reason to be known as 'the devil's Kenpeitai'.

Thousands of men and women were to die as their victims in Outram Road during the three and a half years that remained of the war. It's as well that Billy the Kid and his companions didn't know it on that first afternoon standing in a line at the entry: but all the whitewash in the world couldn't efface the horrors of that place. While the two-storey gatehouse was elegant enough with its late Georgian fanlights and corbel stones, it was only the welcoming smile on the face of a torturer.

キヲツケ!

The handover ceremony complete, the new squad of three guards marched across to their prisoners and began shouting orders.

キヲツケ! *'Ki-o-tsuke!'*

What the heck did they want? Billy hadn't heard the word before. What did it mean? The guards weren't offering anything by way of English translation, and the kid looked uncertainly at MP for a clue. Brownie was clever, and knew a smattering of Japanese words. Perhaps he could guess.

*'Bakayarou!'* Idiot! It sounded like 'Bugger you!' Which of course meant the same in their own language. A guard unclipped his long brown metal sword sheath, preparatory to bashing them with it for defiance and stupidity.

*'Wakaru?'* Understand?

They'd learnt that too.

*'Ki-o-tsuke!'*

It was all being done with much military display. And luck being a fortune, these Australian soldiers-turned-prisoners of war guessed correctly and came to attention, as if on parade at Changi itself.

*'Ah! So!'*

*'Zentai susume!'*

Their luck held. A second correct guess. The party began to quick march after a fashion towards the evil green gate.

It was a pathetic spectacle. The eight captives – bemused, bedraggled, reduced after months of confinement and hunger, yet trying to maintain a soldierly bearing out of a sense of self-respect and not wanting to draw attention. The CO might not have approved their style, though he would have admired their spirit...

Alan Minty and the four who'd escaped with him from Sandakan and spent months hidden in the jungle before the Japs caught them: Corporal Bill Fairy, Bruce McWilliams, Normie Morris, who were all only 23 or 24, and 'Pop' New, the eldest of them at 40. These five were all from Billy's own 2/29th Battalion. MP, still limping with damaged shins, was from the 2/26th.

*Left, right, left, right*...Their bare feet sought comfort in rhythm on the roadway, arms swinging straight – all except for Jimmy Darlington of the 2/18th, whose welts from the torturers' rope were still scarlet and blistered on his limbs, and whose arms would now always hang somewhat loose and forward, like a wrestler. And that was also strange, because Darlo had the makings of a champion boxer. When he hit that Sandakan guard, Jimmy had known what he was doing...

Billy glanced at the guard beside him in a jungle-green uniform: peaked cap, sweat staining the armpits of his short-sleeved shirt, and the creaking of his sword scabbard held beside a well-fed trouser leg.

*Left, right, left, right*...The kid's own legs were skinny and pale, sticking out through two holes cut in the bottom of his kitbag shorts. His arms were tensed and fists balled tight beneath the thumb, as per the drill book, as if marching off the parade ground...

Out of the sunlight.

Entering the gate.

And into the shadow of a long tunnel that ran, like a sewer draining all humanity, through the guardhouse of Outram Road prison to the cesspits inside.

Darkness fell upon them as rapidly as night does in the tropics, and eyes, which had just got used to the glare of daylight, were suddenly unfocussed again. Billy stumbled, trying to see.

'*Kora!*' Hey you!

The guard was shoving, his sword threatening. And the gate was closing behind them.

*Left, right, left, right* . . . They continued through the tunnel, office doors and windows on either side, until they emerged into a courtyard and the afternoon sun looked down on them once more. A thinner sun, diffused within such high, man-made walls and fears. But just as confusing to the senses.

ゼンタイ トマレ!

Another gate shut behind, enclosing them.

ゼンタイ トマレ! '*Zentai tomare!*'

*What?*

The guard's face next to Billy was screwed up and screaming.

'*Tomare!*'

*What did they want?* None of the prisoners knew what the words meant.

'*Kora! Wakaru! Tomare!*'

Swords were unclipped.

A few men stopped. A few kept marching. And then it was on for them all.

A heavy scabbard smashed Billy across his back, his brittle bones crying out to the stars. Another blow fell on the kid's shoulders, bowed and burdensome too soon.

'What do you stupid bastards want us to do?' they cried.

Voices could no longer be suppressed, reason no longer denied.

'We don't understand you! We no bloody *wakaru*!'

But speech drove the guards to greater fury, and they laid into the eight with their scabbards, belting them with all the might of practising samurai – Jimmy Darlington's arm, Brownie's legs, Alan Minty and Pop New in the guts.

'*Yame! Damare!*' Stop! Shut up! '*Bakayarou!*'

So it went until by force they imposed their will. The men shut up. Any semblance of military order had collapsed, however. The line was in disarray and the eight huddled together for self-protection, Billy trying to save an arm that had already been busted once by Sandakan swords.

Still, the guards had their *zentai tomare!* The soldiers had come to a halt. They'd stopped outside a small building like an office – the quartermaster's store apparently, because another guard appeared with a bundle of clothing: Japanese regulation prison-green shorts and shirts. With much gesturing of scabbards and yelling of commands, it was made known to the Australians that they should remove their reeking garments and put on these new ones.

The kid undid the button of his pyjama top, still caked with the blood of countless bed bugs squashed as they tried to eat his flesh in the cages at Kuching. It was his own blood, in truth. He untied the cord that held up his kitbag shorts. They dropped to the ground and his gaunt, naked body responded to the touch of the humid atmosphere, almost as if he were having a bath. How good it was just to *feel* a little cleaner! He dawdled as he rolled up his clothes, reflecting that they were his last earthly possessions, save the pencil stub. But then he remembered his tattered army haversack. He'd carried it everywhere, until it was taken from him that afternoon he and Brownie were arrested. The kid had scarcely thought of it since. But now he realised it held his only other treasure and wondered what had happened to it: a Log Cabin tobacco tin containing the one-inch piece of shrapnel that had wounded him during the battle for Singapore, extracted by a doctor from his right thigh.

'You're lucky it didn't get the middle stump!' Billy could hear his mate Paddy O'Toole saying it now, making light of it, like an older brother, even as he dressed the wound under a rubber tree in those awful last days before the island was lost.

Paddy…and Bob Shipsides, the Corp, who knew everything and would see them right, as he always did. Paddy had stayed behind in Singapore when the labour force left for Borneo, but Bob was still waiting safe at Sandakan…

'*Kora!*' Hey, you!

The kid's daydream vanished. He pulled on the prison shorts, patched and darned, and struggled into the shirt. It was rather more difficult than might be supposed. Not only were his arms suffering from the bashing, but Billy only had one fully free hand. The other was still half-clenched, for it held his contraband.

When the men were dressed and reassembled into line, the quartermaster's guard took their few things and noted them methodically against the prisoners' numbers. The Japs were nothing if not bureaucratic. Every shirt had a white patch above the breast pocket with a number stamped on it in black. Indeed, as Billy gave them his clothes that July afternoon in 1943, he also handed over his name.

From then on he would be known only as number 510.

'*Go-hyaku-ju.*'

The guard shouted it. And Billy repeated it, until the number was drilled into his brain. '*Go-hyaku-ju!*'

Thus, with the new residents properly costumed and enumerated, the Kenpeitai used their swords like cattle prods to herd them in single file across the courtyard to a large building on the other side.

Of all the cellblocks Billy could see, this one seemed the biggest: tall and forbidding, matched by a similar building beside it. The thought occurred to him that the three grim storeys of barred windows looked like serried rows of campaign ribbons on the chests of ancient warriors. They'd certainly seen many years of punishing service.

The kid grinned at his wit – and as it happened he was not that far from the truth. The Kenpeitai used this particular block to hold all their military prisoners: enemy POWs certainly, those contemptible *horyo* who had compounded the dishonour of surrender with criminal disobedience to Nippon's orders; and also those of their own troops whose breach of Japan's implacable martial code deserved not just a thrashing or demotion, but correction – even execution – in Outram Road.

Every bone in Billy's body smarted from his beating. He knew it would take days for the swelling and bruises to subside. Even so, his larrikin humour still flickered. He'd told that fat guard what he thought of him! A bit more pain was worth that. The boy glanced at the man.

'Little Hitler!' he muttered.

True, he didn't look like the little Hitler that Billy had seen in newspapers and on the big screen at the pictures in those far-off days before the war came. No toothbrush moustache. No cowlick of hair. This one was small but dumpy, his over-stuffed face glistening after the exertions of swordsmanship. Yet he was just as vicious, just as dictatorial. And the kid chuckled to himself again at his cleverness. As, of course, did Little Hitler. He, too, had given expression to his feelings about the prisoners.

Another guard was waiting at the cellblock door with a bunch of iron keys that the British had thoughtfully left hanging on a hook when they vacated the place.

'*Koi!*'

The portal was unlocked and sighed a little as it opened, inviting them to step in. The prisoners also sighed as they entered, like the last breaths of hope. This place was designed to suffocate any expectation of liberty under the sheer immensity of architectural oppression. The cells extended along either side of a central passageway, perhaps 20-feet wide. How many cells there were Billy couldn't say, but there must have been at least a hundred of them on each level, one above the other, the upper two tiers reached by iron catwalks. Beneath the roof was a ventilated opening – but the light was foul and grey, and gave no hint of freedom outside to those below.

The black wooden doors to each cell stared vacantly like the eye sockets in the skulls of the prisoners locked behind them. Rather, Billy supposed they were there. For the thing that struck him was the utter silence. Not a sound. At first he wondered if they were the only people there, until he heard a cry in the distance. Quickly suppressed. And he could tell they were not alone.

Besides, there was the smell – the revolting spoor of human excrement hanging in the stillness from God knew how many overflowing toilet buckets. Fetid. Loathsome. Billy wanted to spew what little remained in his gut. As did all of them. The eight had known much by way of degradation from the Kenpeitai already. But this was something altogether different. Putrefaction was almost visible in the contaminated light.

'*Tomare!*'

They'd reached about halfway along the cells when the shouts of the guard once again told them to stop.

'*Bango!*'

Number off. Again.

'*Ichi, ni, san, shi, go, roku, nana, hachi.*'

'*Fuku-o nuge!*'

Strip. Another familiar order.

*Bloody hell!* Billy thought. *We've just had our clothes off already.*

But he kept that opinion to himself. *Don't draw attention!* For this was the testing time – the tricky bit where treasure had to be smuggled past the suspicious eyes of authority.

The kid felt confident enough. Never once, in all the time he'd been a prisoner at Sandakan, on the ship, in the cages of Kuching, not once had the Nips ever told him to unclench his fist during a strip search. They'd inspected his clothes, looked under his armpits and up his arse. Yet he'd never been ordered to open his palm. Amazingly. And you can secrete many riches in a closed hand: cigarette butts, food scraps. Such things were more precious than diamonds for those in the grip of the Kenpeitai.

Billy reckoned he'd get away with it again – although he knew there was always a first time...

'*Koi!*' Come!

They went through the ritual of the strip search. Shirts were removed and shorts taken off, each garment shaken and held at arm's length. Nothing fell to the floor.

'*Jampu!*'

The eight men, their bodies leached as the walls of their prison, began to jump up and down, legs and arms going as if in the exercise squad at training camp, or even (the kid's mind drifted further back) as they had at PT class on the asphalt of that school in Ultimo from which he had kept running away...

Still nothing dropped to the prison floor.

'*Yame!*' Stop!

There was one final indignity to come: the body search. The guards strutted around the prisoners in turn, contemptuously prodding them and looking inside open mouths, up nostrils, down earholes and, in case something was hidden in that other orifice, making them bend over and peering up their bums.

Somebody farted.

Who was it?

The kid couldn't tell from up the line. He stifled a laugh and wished he had the nerve to do the same. But then he heard a guard shouting, '*Kora! Bakayarou!*' as he laid into his victim with the bunch of iron keys, flogging him around the body and ending with a blow to the head.

Billy's fist was still closed.

And still nothing had tumbled to the Kenpeitai.

'*Fuku-o kiro!*'

*Same to you, chum* was the unspoken response to this order to dress, as prison shorts and shirts were dragged over scrawny frames.

Inspection over, the guard with the keys strode to the open doors of individual cells. As their numbers were called, each man was escorted forward, up two small steps, and placed inside.

Their eyes met briefly. Glances said more by way of compassion, God-speed, and the enduring bonds of fellowship than could be conveyed in a torrent of words. Brownie. Jimmy Darlington. Alan Minty. Pop New...*How would the old bloke bear it?* Billy wondered, before the door slammed shut and the turnkey locked them from the world.

'*Go-hyaku-ju.*' 510.

Billy the Kid drew a deep breath. His insides constricted to a tight core, as they had in Kuching, confronted now with consequences. One part of his mind was crowded with those 'if onlys' that were never far from the thoughts of those held at Outram Road: if only he'd stayed at Sandakan; if only he hadn't seen Jimmy Darlington being tortured; if only he hadn't talked MP into escaping, they'd have been all right.

Yet whatever else he was feeling, his dominant thought was that he must not show it. *Never let them see your fear, or they'll have you!* It was the lesson of his whole life. So Billy squeezed his fists and set his face to stare impassively at the wall.

'*Kotchi koi!*'

The boy stepped out, stomach knots hardening. Little Hitler was scowling beside him, sword at the ready. Up the two steps set in a wall arch. Above it the number 72. Through the wooden door, black as midnight. And into his cell.

It was a narrow chamber, about six-feet wide and no more than 12-feet long. A small barred window, high in a recess at the rear, admitted a little anaemic light, with a couple of air vents below, mostly cemented up by the Japs. A *benki* bucket stood in one corner for his toilet, three bed boards in the other. And that was it, apart from a wooden headrest, and a scrag of dirty cotton blanket. *Was this to be home for the next four years?* The court had indeed been lenient to his youth.

'*Suware!*' Sit down! Little Hitler motioned him to the floor.

Oh yes! Another order that was all too familiar from Kuching – the demand that, by way of extra punishment, prisoners should sit at attention all day with legs crossed, hands on knees, back rigid and upright. Movement was not permitted, except to go to the *benki*.

Billy had put that cramped servitude from his mind over these past few days, for the eight had at least been able to pace around the horsebox. Even the march through the gateway into jail got the blood going. The business of changing clothes, walking to the cell block, jumping up and down for the strip search – all helped to exercise weakened muscles and sinews. To say nothing of the bashing.

But now, as Billy lowered himself to the cement floor of his prison, his protesting mind and body knew they were in for more solitary torment. More atrophy. More deadening inactivity, which could weigh down on you worse than masonry.

The boy took up the required posture: one leg folded beneath the other, fists clenched on his knees.

'*Sokoni iro!*' Stay there!

Little Hitler gave his command and, turning on his heel, left the cell. The door swung shut behind him with a thud like a guillotine. The key turned in the lock, and was withdrawn.

Muffled on the other side of it, Billy could hear the last of his comrades being conducted to their cells, orders shouted and doors secured. Bill Fairy. Bruce McWilliams. Normie Morris, whom he'd known from the beginning, for they'd joined up at almost the same time in 1941.

His heart went out to them. *What would they be thinking now?*

He knew what MP would be thinking: *Ah, Billy, what have you got us into?*

Brownie had said it constantly during the long journey from Sandakan: not in reproach so much as wonderment at the kid's youthful impetuosity – and at his own foolhardiness in agreeing to go along with it.

*Billy boy, what have you done?* The kid asked himself that, as quiet began to settle once more like a pall over the cell block in Outram Road.

Disturbed air flurried briefly and then was still. Heat descended as a greasy curtain upon the scene. The stink of corruption seeped through ventilators and into the cells. Sallow light crept its petty pace across the wall.

Silence.

Nothingness.

All hope gone.

Except that, sitting cross-legged on the floor, Billy the Kid smirked softly to himself. The knot in his gut eased a fraction. He listened intently, eyes fixed on the prison door for any hint of sound or shadow that might betray a Kenpeitai guard lurking outside.

Then, satisfied he wouldn't be sprung, the boy slowly opened his fist and admired the bit of pencil nestling in his palm. A short, blunt pencil stub swiftly picked up from the ground at Kuching. It was a mere trifle – a worthless discard thrown away by a Jap officer – here cradled in Billy's hand, as valuable to him in captivity as any king's ransom.

And he knew it. A shard of black lead pencil connecting his fingers to his brain – and thought to the expression of self. Even in the fastness of Outram Road he still had a voice. Hope was not all gone. The kid had something that might help 510 to survive, though as yet he knew not how.

So Billy smiled at the pencil and at his own ingenuity.

'*That's* what I done,' he murmured. Brownie would know it too, eventually.

Yoking himself to the burden of the day, Billy Young as carefully closed his fist again.

# 2
# SOLITARY

*Reaching up*
*Like trees*
*Searching for the light*

Never had the kid imagined that time could be quantified by weight. In Outram Road prison the solitary hours were not measured by duration but by endurance. By density and pounds per square inch, like the atmosphere, pressing down relentlessly upon Billy: sitting, standing or lying under his cotton blanket.

Every day was precisely the same. Billy would rouse from a fitful doze, unrested, as morning lit the high window bars. There was never any sun: a sloping shade outside prevented it entering his cell. There wasn't any darkness, either. All night a globe burned behind a wire grille in the ceiling, driving away sleep and forgetfulness, attracting only phantoms and mosquitoes. And the eye of any passing guard through a peephole in the door.

There wasn't any help for the anxious ghosts who came into the boy's mind, except to let them have their say. Nothing to be done about the guard, other than to echo '*Go-hyaku-ju*' if he called Billy's number. But his blanket did at least help to protect his bare flesh from the worst insect bites. Not altogether, because malaria – like every other tropical disease – was still rife. Yet it was something, and Billy was lucky in that. Many Outram Road prisoners had nothing in which to wrap themselves.

The blanket also trapped body heat wonderfully, until Billy was in a veritable steam bath. It was always a choice between that and the mozzies. Blanket on. Blanket off. Half awake. Half asleep. Sweating. Scratching. Remembering. As dawn gathered – as day arrived and the night creatures departed – he'd stretch uncovered on the bed boards for a little, letting his thoughts untangle themselves into the present. Wondering, in those early days, where he was. On the bunk at Sandakan? At training camp, still? Or perhaps in his little bed on the balcony at Ma's place in Ultimo? He could hear a small bird chirping…

Billy unstuck his eyelids, the clammy light squeezing through the bars and revealing soon enough his whereabouts. Of course. He lay there, one arm for a pillow, as disordered dreams resolved into faint morning sounds at Outram Road. The squeak of a guard's rubber thong on the passage outside. A distant door opening. Shallow voices remarking, perhaps, that another soul had escaped their custody during the night and died. Another number to be allocated. The Kenpeitai didn't care about the dead, so long as the paperwork was correct. Their only concern was that the strict regimen of their jail was followed. Everything by the rule. For suddenly, into the silence came the only loud noises of the day. Near the stairs leading to the upper floors, a guard started banging a sheet of iron. Reveille. Time to get up. Metal reverberated like a gong to the furthest corner of the cell block.

Upon the alarm, Billy sat up – not too quickly, to let creaking muscles adjust. Then, for a full reach, he'd stand, yawn and step to the floor. It was no distance, for the bed boards were laid directly on the cracked cement. At one time they'd been raised on a couple of concrete supports to give a little ventilation, but these had been removed by the Kenpeitai as a punishment, and prisoners now slept on the floor.

In time to come, Billy learned to prop one end of the boards on the hateful wooden headrest, to give a bit of slope. But not at first. Like everyone else, he lay close to the dirt and any overflow from his toilet bucket. His bed was easy to make, however. First chore of the day was to stack the boards lengthways, one on top of the other against the wall. Just as the guards liked it.

Next came the *benki* bucket. He'd remove the wooden lid and piss, gagging at the smell and hoping the *benki* wouldn't fill too quickly – or if it did, that this might be the day it would be emptied. Its collection was very erratic. Several days had gone by before the guards sent round a trustie – a *benki toban* – to take and clean the wooden pail. It was why Billy tried to shit as little as possible. But it couldn't be helped when he got a bout of diarrhoea, and then the stench and spillage from the *benki* was nauseating. That, too, was part of the punishment.

He had nothing to wipe himself with. Nothing with which to wash his body or clean up his mess. No paper. No water. No soap or towel. So the kid had to squat in his own filth as he took up the mandatory sitting position on the floor for the rest of the day: legs crossed, hands on knees, back straight. The guards would be on their rounds at any time, to make sure the rules were observed. Indeed, they were busy already. For the wake-up gong was always followed by another ritual to break the habit of imposed quietude.

Billy could hear doors being opened in the cells on the floor above, orders barked with military amplification.

'*Ki-o-tsuke!*'

And on to the iron catwalk Billy heard dozens of feet stamping as the inmates emerged from their cells and stood to attention.

*Bango!* Numbering off was fairly bellowed into the emptiness.

'*Ichi, ni, san, shi...*'

Then came the orders to march. *Zentai susume!* The air

resounded to cries of '*Hi, hi, hi*'. Feet banged on the metal stairs as they descended. Halt! Form up! Quick march! Along the passage. Out the door. And off to wherever it was that they disappeared to for the rest of the day.

Who these prisoners were remained a mystery to Billy for some time. 'Phantoms of the night' he called them, remembering those stories from his old *Triumph* comic books. Unlike the voices that spoke to his imagination from days gone by – unlike Paddy or Bob Shipsides or old Ma Jepson – these ones were substantial, in the here and now. He never saw them, naturally; he hardly saw anybody. But by their voices and drill, Billy guessed they were soldiers of Nippon under sentence of court martial.

He was correct. Though in one respect these phantoms were like Billy's own: once he was awake they disappeared into the ether, and implacable silence once more enclosed the walls of Outram Road.

Then it was that the leaden mantle of time descended on Billy's shoulders again, barely supportable under the pressure of boredom and inertia. Time that had no clockwork or mainspring. Time that was not calibrated into seconds and minutes. It could be reckoned only by the snail's movement of a shadow across the wall, and the long intervals between one event and the next.

Of all the daily happenings, the only ones that counted were meals. From early morning Billy sat facing the door, waiting. Listening to his gastric juices gurgling like a gully trap. Watching the letterbox slot through which his little tin bowl of rice would be posted. Anticipating the taste. Wondering if it would come today with a bit of sweet potato on top or a few corn kernels. Ears alert, like a starving dog, for the faint sounds that told him the food trusties – the *meshi toban* – were on their way.

In truth, Billy was not starving. Not yet. But he was young, and felt he was. The kid was at that age when he was still supposed to be growing – still fattening up. But that had stopped the day

Singapore surrendered and the Allied battalions marched to Changi as prisoners of the Imperial Japanese Army. From then on, food had become scarce – something to be bartered and hoarded. After that, Billy never added anything to his height of five feet eight inches.

Yet while rations were meagre, they were at least adequate for the time being. Barely so, but enough. When Billy was sent to Sandakan with the men of B Force to build an airfield, it was in the Japs' interest to ensure the men had the strength to do the job. The rice they doled out was sufficient, supplemented by occasional treats of meat and vegetables and whatever else men could scrounge from the jungle and native villagers. Sufficient at least for those able to work. The sick had their rations halved. And halved again. Yet for those labouring on the airstrip, Nippon's supplies kept them going. They lost weight. They lost condition. But body and soul were kept together. At any rate, until the work was done.

When Billy the Kid and his mate MP Brown tried to escape from Sandakan in February 1943, work on the airfield was at its height, and the two were lean and reasonably healthy. Even at Kuching they had been fed; and with so many Nips seasick on the ship to Singapore, many leftovers were passed into the horsebox. Thus, sitting and waiting for breakfast, the boy would drool at memories of meals already eaten, of the feasts at Sandakan, and of sneaking back at night with all kinds of good things.

The 'Dead End Kids', that's what they called them – the young fellers like Billy and Joey Crome and Harry Longley, living in the last hut of the last row at Sandakan, near the wire perimeter fence down by the swamp. The dead end of the place. Often they'd creep out after dark, slipping beneath the wire underwater, and steal through the swamp into the surrounding jungle.

'You be careful, you silly young buggers!' Billy could hear Bob Shipsides, the Corp, warning them. 'The Japs will have your heads.'

'Literally,' MP added, pausing from his harmonica tune.

'Don't worry yourselves! We'll be all right,' the Dead End Kids would reply. And mostly they were. Certainly there was never any complaint from the older blokes when the Kids returned with the night's takings: yams, tapioca, sweet coconuts.

Billy's mouth was watering as he remembered such treats. He could taste them. If only he'd stayed!

There was a sound – clinks and rattles that seemed to be coming closer. Billy sat up, rigid as a carving, hands on knees in the best military manner, nerves a-quiver. All ready for inspection as a guard stepped to the door and looked through the peephole, rapped, and made his announcement.

'*Meshi!*' Food.

The boy stood and moved to the door. The guard stepped aside as the *meshi toban* – one of the Indian trusties – passed a small metal bowl through the letterbox. Billy stooped to look through the slot. Eyes exchanged looks, but the presence of the guard prevented any words.

The food bowls were on a large wooden tray with a handle at each corner, carried by two trusties – strong, well-fed men, as you'd expect of *meshi toban* who worked in the kitchen. Billy didn't blame them for eating any extra food that came their way. He was merely envious and wondered if he'd ever earn that privilege.

It was also the same tray used to carry the slopping toilet buckets outside. Disgusting, perhaps. Yet that didn't dispel the eagerness with which Billy took his dish from the servant and sat down again to eat. The bowl was only a few inches high, and never more than a third full of grey, glutinous rice. A couple of mouthfuls. Nothing on it this morning. No shred of yam. Perhaps at lunchtime…

The kid sat looking at the food, playing mind games. He breathed the aroma, such as it was, and let his fingertips respond to the lukewarm metal bowl. Remembering other meals…the enormous plate of sausages and mash in the mess that first day he'd joined the army a ravenous, lying recruit two years ago.

'*You'll regret it!*' He could hear the old hands jeering him: men who'd enlisted all of a week earlier. '*You'll be sorry!*' No, he wasn't. Or sorry only that the army didn't have such a feed to put in front of him now.

Thinking. Dawdling. Billy tried to prolong the moment when he'd eat his morsel of rice. Once started there was no stopping, and then the weary, time-laden wait for the next meal would commence all over again.

He could torment himself no longer! The bowl came with two chopsticks: little bits of twig – another Kenpeitai triumph of form over substance. The rules said prisoners should have chopsticks, but they didn't specify what kind. Like the regulation three meals a day. The bowls were delivered (except when stopped as punishment); it's just that they hardly had anything in them.

But who cared about chopsticks? Billy snatched up the twigs and began to scoop the gelid rice into his mouth.

He tried to take his time. He tried to chew it daintily: to let each portion slide across his tongue and slip around his palate, savouring the taste and texture like a gourmet, before swallowing. He tried. But failed. The food went straight down his gullet and into an empty stomach. Two mouthfuls. And before he knew it, the kid was staring at an empty bowl again: licking it clean and sucking the last skerrick of flavour from the twigs, his hunger completely unsatisfied, with nothing to recall except the succulent fat juices dripping from army sausages that first day as a rookie in the mess at Royal Park – the smell of butter and milk, salt and pepper, rising deliciously with the steam from a mountain of mashed potatoes.

Some chance! The only steam in the solitary confinement cells at Outram Road came from the rank bodies of the inmates, as the temperature rose outside and seeped through iron bars. Heating. Itching. Sweat running in rivulets of grime down faces and chests.

Pooling in pockets of loose skin. Eyes stinging from salt tears that flowed like washaways through their dirt. Wiping. Wishing. Men waiting, like shrunken Buddhas in their shrines behind black wooden doors, for something to drink.

Yes, there was always that. A meal was always followed by a sip of so-called 'tea', known as *char*. There was nothing else. So Billy sat in his sauna, thirst growing, tongue lapping saliva, eyes fixed on the door.

It got that he knew every detail of that door. Every groove and knot in the timber. The shapes of flaking paint, like islands in a sea of black. The pattern and contour of every board. The toothless mouth of the food slot in the middle. The swivelled eyehole below it, through which only the guards peered. The cast lock, encrusted with a century of grief. Iron bolts rusted to the prison door forever.

Below was an open metal grille, like latticework, designed for ventilation but which also gave brief glimpses of movement in the passage outside. Foreshadowing danger, too, should a guard try to sneak up to a cell door and catch a prisoner unawares for not sitting in the correct position.

'*Benki!*' the incumbent had to call. Toilet!

To which the guard might grunt '*Yoshi!*' All right! It was the only permissible excuse. Otherwise, there would be another bashing. Or far worse, a day without food.

The grille had one other use. Confident that no guard was nearby, Billy could bend low and look through the iron lattice to a cell door on the other side of the passage. You couldn't see anybody, for the doors were not directly opposite but staggered, like seats at the pictures. Yet you could discern shadow – even movement – across the diagonal, and wonder about the life being lived behind that door grille. MP? Jimmy Darlington? Where were they? How were they going?

Same as him, Billy supposed. Learning to bear time's solitary load.

27

'*Char* up!'

The singsong voice of the Indian *meshi toban* sounded through the food slot, reliving those days when he'd served tiffin to the English sahibs in their cantonment at Rajapur. Afternoon tea with scones and sandwiches, and perhaps a hot kedgeree.

'*Char* up!' Through the opening he passed another unclean metal bowl, barely two inches high.

Billy stood and held the dish as the trustie half-filled it with a tepid brown fluid poured from what looked like a watering can. The guard was watching and there was no chance of any further exchange. Tea poured, the kid returned to his place on the floor, where he sat contemplating the bowl as he had the food dish: trying to defer the moment when he should swallow it, letting the liquid swill slowly around to rinse his mouth, imagining what the *char* might have been like.

The kid couldn't think of anything that looked less like tea. This lukewarm water was barely coloured, and he'd be lucky to find even one leaf floating in it. Why, Billy could remember Ma Jepson pouring cup after cup from the big brown teapot in the kitchen at Bulwara Road. Milk and as much sugar as you liked, and the tea so strong it made your eyes smart. Yes, and the tea leaves were so thick at the bottom of the cup afterwards that Ma would read them to her visitors.

'Oh, Millie,' she'd say to the friend in her most mysterious voice, tilting the cup and examining the patterns in the dregs. 'Oh, Millie, I don't like the look of this.'

'What is it, Ma?' Millie would exclaim a-tremble, for she was as superstitious as they came. 'What do you see? Tell me, for God's sake!'

Both Ma and Pop Jepson had been circus performers in their youth and knew how to play an audience. So Ma, as fortune-teller, would come over all otherworldly. 'Millie, Millie, my dear, what *have* you been doing?'

Little Billy would watch them, his eyes as big as the blue china saucers they'd got as a job lot with the cups from one of Pop's stallholder chums at Paddy's Market.

But there were no saucers at Outram Road. No tea leaves. Not much future to read, in any event, for the lonely day now stretched before him interminably on the rack of time. Nothing until the next meal – exactly the same as the one he'd just eaten – when the shadow passed halfway across the wall and the deadening hush once more briefly awoke. For the rest, the Kenpeitai regime seemed calculated to destroy every aspect of their prisoners' mental and physical independence: to crush their humanity completely.

Yet Billy had a resilient mind. Growing up around Paddy's Market in the Depression years had sharpened his survival instincts – taught him a trick or two of the trade – and learning how to live *was* a trade for a working-class kid in those days. Nor was he overawed by authority. The boy who kept running away from school knew from a young age how to keep one eye open for the truant inspectors – and the other alert for any chance copper on the beat – when he was out with Pop Jepson selling fruit in the streets from an unlicensed barrow.

The Kenpeitai were just another – more grotesque – form of officialdom to be outwitted. From the very first Billy knew, with every fibre of his being, that he could not give way to the despair his captors sought to impose upon his spirit, any more than he could show them fear. To be sure, the lad often wanted to break down in tears as he had as a little fellow, crying for the mother he could never remember. But boys toughened in the Depression don't cry. Not in front of their tormentors. They fight back. And the kid was well aware that, in this fight, his most important strategy was to keep his mind active, positive, open to every little opportunity that might come his way. As anybody reared in a market would understand.

So, to relieve the monotony, Billy developed his roster of daily chores – of which the most important (after meals) was to mark his calendar. Billy might not have been able to measure the hours with any accuracy: but in this vacuum, where the laws of time and motion were suspended, the only way to keep some grip on reality was to track the passing of each day. And, as untold prisoners who'd occupied the cell before him had discovered, the only way to do that was by marking the wall.

It wasn't difficult to do. Each cell, after all, was only six-feet wide. Sitting opposite the door, Billy could reach out and touch the wall on either side. The risk was in doing it. No reaching was allowed. No writing permitted. A bashing if caught.

Yet the human will cannot be extinguished if the soul resists strongly enough. The stone walls of Outram Road were plastered with the detritus of misery: ancient limewash ringed green with decay, like tidemarks of sorrow. And whatever the rules might say, they were also scored with scratches and crosses, where generations of those they'd imprisoned recorded the slow tally of their years.

Billy and his mates had been sentenced at Kuching on Thursday 26 June. He knew that. Allowing three or four days for the voyage to Singapore in the horsebox (for they'd seen no daylight to gauge it precisely), he reckoned they entered Outram Road at the beginning of July – and fixed his wall calendar from that.

Tense as a watching cat, the kid twitched his ears for any hint of sound or movement in the passage outside, any sneaking footfall. He stared at the grille, concentrating on any change of light or shadow that might betray a guard lurking by the door to nab him. He took his time about it, for time had no meaning here.

Nothing.

At last he slowly lifted his right hand from his lap and moved it to the wall. His hand crept across the floor, his head still, every nerve alert, ready at an instant to resume his lotus position.

Safe. So far.

Once at the wall, Billy let his fingers steal along the edge, sifting the dirt, feeling for the little piece of wire buried in a crack where he'd found it not long after his arrival: a gift left to him by some former resident. He had it! The wire was sharp and tactile in his fingers. He palmed it carefully as a pencil stub and then quickly returned his fist to his knee. Where he sat like a statue again, nerves settling down.

When he first entered the cell, Billy thought he'd use his pencil to keep the calendar. But he soon realised it would be a mistake. The walls were covered in scratches: dates, initials, names and even lines of poetry engraved into the plaster over the past hundred years. The kid who'd grown up always with one eye out for the coppers – had learned to do so, quite literally, at his father's knee – quickly saw that a pencil mark on these walls would stand out as if written in lights. The Kenpeitai would know he had one in his possession on their first serious inspection of his cell. The pencil would be confiscated and he'd be beaten.

Much better to keep his treasure for more profitable use. To hide it, ever resourceful, in a crevice where a lump of rotted plaster had fallen away from the wall. And to bless whoever it was that secreted the bit of wire in the dust for him to find.

Billy gave his thanks and swiftly made his mark on the clear patch where he'd already begun to delve his days.

Saturday.

The excitement of marking his calendar occupied a good deal of Billy's thoughts – not just in its planning and execution, but also in the debriefing that followed. Assuring himself that he'd put the wire back and covered it properly. Drilling the date into his brain by rote, like his teacher at Ultimo, so he'd remember it even if they moved him to another cell. Imagining what might have happened had the Kenpeitai burst in and caught him in the act. Steeling his body for the blows – as he'd learned to do on the day of recapture at Sandakan when the guards beat him senseless – knowing that he had to save his eyes at all costs and keep his tongue pressed behind his teeth so he wouldn't bite it. Grinning that he'd got away with marking his calendar today. Wondering what would happen tomorrow and how he might improve the operation...

Such musings could keep Billy's brain active for whole slabs of the morning. Yet they'd only go so far before lassitude set in once more. His muscles would start to cramp, and have to be flexed. His buttock bones ached and sent stabbing pains up his spine, for there wasn't much by way of padding. He'd try to ease them by shifting his weight from one side to the other, but it gave little relief as time bore down and screwed him to the floor.

Lunch came and went. The shadow inched a little further. The kid sought to keep his mind flexible by reading the names and initials carved into the plaster: wondering who they were and what they'd done to deserve being shut up in this hole. Some of them must have been soldiers of the British Empire, like himself, for they'd scratched patriotic verses that clearly meant something to them:

> When you're wounded and left on Afghanistan's plains,
> And the women come out to cut up what remains,
> Jest roll to your rifle and blow out your brains
> And go to your Gawd like a soldier.

Like hell he would! Not if Billy the Kid had any other choice. He turned away and shut his eyes to the images.

Yet into the darkness came other thoughts, equally as disturbing. He fancied the walls of the cell were closing in on him, for claustrophobia was only an arm span away. And the phantom voices returned from Billy's past to speak of other days and other campaigns...

'*Go on, if you're game enough, kid...*' He could hear Paddy O'Toole daring him to prove his marksmanship by shooting at a tin near Sergeant Dobson's feet on the rifle range at Bukit Timah, along the road from Singapore.

'*Christ Almighty!*' The same Brian Dobson exclaiming not two weeks later, when a Lewis gun went off accidentally in the dark, again at Bukit Timah. But this time it brought the whole wrath of the Japanese Army down on them, and they had to run for their lives into the jungle – Billy without his boots, and his feet cut to blazes.

'*Dear Keith...*' The last letter he got from Dad, written from Spain where he'd gone to fight the fascists. Barcelona, July 1938. Hoping he was being a good boy and learning his lessons. '*I've been down to the creek for a swim and to do a bit of washing.* (Lucky dog!) *Our battalion is billeted behind the lines, but we are expecting and ready to go up to the front any time now...*' He did. And he never came back.

*Dear Keith*...It was a name from his past the kid had not used for a long time, for he never liked it, calling to him now down the corridors of memory, quietly, insistently leading him all the way back through the years to Hobart and a door at the very end of the tunnel with his proper name on it: Keith William Young.

He opened his eyes. The ghosts disappeared in the torpid afternoon, yet he knew they were still there – still hovering at the edge of consciousness, waiting to be acknowledged. Very well, then, let him try to make some sense of what they had to say. To put them in coherent order. And turning the handle of that furthest door, Billy the Kid – young Keith – opened it and stepped through...

...into the front room of the house in Hay Street, New Town, just off Tower Road below Mount Wellington, where he'd been born on 4 November, 1925. A suburban brick house with a yard backing on to the railway line: the family home of his grandfather and Nana Tot, Totty Young, Susan Young – a formidable woman, known as 'The Admiral'.

Her nickname was in part a tribute to Nana's habit of command. But it also arose from an incident in the youth of her second son, William John – Billy's father, called 'Big Bill' Young, who grew to a solid six feet three inches and became a heavyweight boxer. At the age of only 15, Big Bill had run away and signed up for the army, in all the fervour of the Gallipoli landings. He got as far as the troopship berthed at Hobart, when Nana got wind of it. She marched aboard, grabbed her son and marched him off again, ordering the protesting officers to prepare his discharge papers. An Admiral indeed: Gilbert and Sullivan's very 'ruler of the Queen's Navee'!

Big Bill's son would in time emulate his career as an underage soldier, though the kid got a lot further than Dad! For The Admiral didn't drag *him* ashore. On the contrary, he could hear Nana's voice behind closed doors at the family conference, agreeing that it might be better to let him go.

'I know he's a young larrikin. The army might just knock him into shape and help him to grow up.'

She'd been right about that. Right, too, in her diagnosis of his character. The kid was wild and undisciplined. And in that, he'd also followed his father – in contrast to the rest of his family.

The Youngs had migrated to Tasmania in the 1840s, settling in a farming and fruit-growing district with the evocative name of Sandfly, south of Hobart. It was a close, God-fearing community, where people raised large families and thanked heaven there was no convict stain in the blood (or kept quiet about it, if there were). Billy's grandfather, Douglas, was of the second generation. He and grandmother Susan moved to Hobart, where they ran a couple of hotels – sold them, and bought a shop – on the eve of Depression.

They also purchased the house in Hay Street and at the time Billy was born had six living children: Uncle Doug, Big Bill, Aunts Ada and Elsie in Hobart, Aunty Ilma married to prosperous Vince Morsello, who owned taxis in Sydney, and Uncle Harold, whom everyone called 'Cocky'. A fourth daughter, Gladys, had been killed in a motorcar accident a few years earlier.

They were a respectable, hard-working family about Hobart. Doug was employed at the Risdon zinc works, becoming a supervisor and remaining there most of his working life. Cocky was a carpenter and builder, a man of substance in his trade.

The exception was Big Bill. He was a good student with a fine brain, highly thought of by his schoolteacher at Sandfly. But then he ran off to join the army, and although The Admiral hauled him off the troopship, he never resumed his education, never settled down. Big Bill drifted into an itinerant life, moving to the mainland and taking odd jobs wherever he found them. Travelling with Jimmy Sharman's boxing troupe. Doing a bit of shearing. Cane cutting up north. Working with the fruit barrows at Paddy's Market in Sydney, which was where he first met Pop and Ma Jepson.

In Sydney he also met Adora Shaw – a young woman of only 22, who already had a small child called Kevin. The two came together and, according to Billy's birth certificate, she and Big Bill Young married in Sydney on 4 May 1925, when Adora was three months pregnant.

They went to Hobart for the birth, to be with Big Bill's family. It was an unhappy choice. Not only did Adora have a fatherless child, she was also a Roman Catholic. Such things had meaning at a time when sectarian beliefs and social morality could separate families and whole communities. Nana was Church of England, and Adora's life was not easy under The Admiral's directive.

Soon after her baby was born and baptised Keith William, whom everyone in the family called 'Keithy', they moved to a small weatherboard house near Risdon. Uncle Doug got Big Bill a job in the zinc works. Yet the domestic idyll was short-lived. Something went wrong. The kid was never told what it was – other than that his mother had died when he was a baby. At length he and his dad went back to Sydney, though he never found out what became of his half-brother Kevin.

Certainly Billy had no memory of Adora whatsoever. Of all the images that entered his mind, and the voices that spoke to him in his cell, not one was his mother's. All Keithy could remember were the iron spears on a cemetery gate, when his father took the little boy to visit a grave…and the perfume of a lilac tree in the front garden of the house in Hay Street, which, Aunt Ada told him, his 'dear mother' had planted. But that memory was from a later time – when Keithy was 11 and went back to live with Nana Tot after Dad left to fight in Spain.

The only recollections he had of his early childhood were fragmentary – and mostly to do with food. Of going down to a corner shop in gritty Redfern with Dad's black book and buying a tin of condensed milk on tick. Of the thick, creamy liquid dripping all over him as he hid behind the tenement door where they lived, licking it up (Billy salivated at the memory), and a woman who was not his mother saying, 'You silly young beggar. Look! You got it all over yourself.'

It was a precarious existence, always on the fringe of a twilight world, moving from one rented room to another. Big Bill worked for a time at a Redfern billiard parlour, as well as for a starting price bookmaker, where eyes constantly had to be skinned for the coppers. He'd be off with the boxing troupe if he wanted a quid, or spend a day with Pop Jepson on the fruit barrows.

It was a case of catch as catch can in the late twenties. And the boy could remember the police catching a large runaway bird – was it an emu or an ostrich? – that had escaped its cage. The coppers cornered it and got it down on the ground in Redfern, with the boy watching and starting to cry as they pinioned its legs. *That's what they could do to you!*

'Hello, Keithy! What are you doing here?'

He looked up and there was Dad coming back from an afternoon at the market, carrying a big paper bag of grapes. Fat, green, succulent grapes. And as Dad swung the boy onto his shoulders, Keithy sat astride, balancing the bag on Dad's head and eating the fruit like a rajah riding all the way home.

The boy adored his father! It was, and remained, the central fact of his life. And he knew it was reciprocated. Dad's sister, Aunt Ilma Morsello, who lived in comfortable circumstances at Waverley, apparently offered to adopt Keithy. From one point of view it would have been to the boy's advantage, but Big Bill refused. Love could not be measured in a material way. Keith was his responsibility. Besides, the man possessed little enough in life to part with the one certain thing he could call his own.

Still, the lad always found it strange that, when Dad went north again to cut sugarcane, he ended up in the care of the Sisters at a Catholic children's home set among the orchards and dairy farms of Seven Hills, 20 miles from Sydney. How it happened he didn't know. But Keithy was then aged about four: and it's from this time that his memory of people and places became stronger during those endless days of solitary confinement.

The home he could reconstruct quite clearly. It was a square, plain weatherboard building, raised on high wooden stilts covered with trellis, like a Queenslander house. Below was a play area that could be used in wet weather, and the place where they had lunch every day. Three long benches were set in a U shape, and the little ones had to sit as the big boys carried round a baby's bath filled with 'dodgers' – slabs of bread smeared with brown treacle. Didn't they go down well, Keithy holding one in each hand. He could taste them now – treacle oozing rich as molasses!

Beyond were paddocks with cows, fruit trees and dams. There was even a pond near the orphanage with a log bridge that Keithy used to walk across, arms spread as aeroplane wings for balance. Until he ditched into the water – cold, deep water, as much of it as he could drink! He was hauled out, taken upstairs to Sister's office, and given a smacking for that.

Then he sobbed and wondered what he was doing there. 'Just you wait till my dad comes! I'll tell him about you, and he'll take me away!' he wept.

As it turned out, it wasn't Big Bill Young who came for his child, but somebody altogether different.

One afternoon Keithy was called upstairs again to see Sister, severe in her black habit and starched wimple behind the desk. A small, rotund, middle-aged woman was with her, cloche hat encasing grey curls, and a fox fur about her neck. The room was shaded, blinds drawn against the afternoon sun; even so, Keithy at the door could see two foxy eyes – glassy, carnivorous – regarding him as prey.

*If she takes one step towards me, I'm out of here!* the boy thought.

Yet it was a pleasant, calming voice that spoke – not the predator at all.

'Hello, Keith. I'm Ma Jepson. Your dad's told me about you. He's written and asked me to take you home to our place in Ultimo.'

'Is he there?'

'He'll come to the Big House presently, when he gets back to Sydney.'

The child gave himself to her, hesitant at first. Yet the desire to see his father overwhelmed any lingering suspicions about the fox. Within half an hour the two were walking along the country road that led up one of the Seven Hills to the railway station: Ma with a parcel of Keithy's few shabby clothes in one hand, and holding the boy's trust in the other.

It was a long, hot mile in the sun to the station, where, finding they'd missed one train, they went into the refreshment room to wait for the next one.

'I'm having a pot of tea, Keith. Would you like a raspberry cordial?'

'My word I would.'

'And a slice of Chester cake?'

'Please, Ma. I've never eat one of them.'

So they sat at a table, having their afternoon tea and laughing at the posters on the railway hoardings, at the Aborigine on the advertisement for Pelaco shirts saying in pidgin, 'Mine Tinkit They Fit!' Keithy's own ragged shirt was distinctly ill-fitting.

But it was the ruby light refracted through a cordial glass that he remembered most vividly. Oh, and the sensation of Chester cake: solid, plump dough, rich as a Christmas pudding, filled with currants and moist with golden syrup; baked between pastry sheets; topped with pink icing and coconut; cut into squares and served on a thick white china New South Wales Railways bread and butter plate. Heaven!

Billy the Kid was about to sink his teeth into it when the Chester cake vanished. Refreshment room chatter faded away. He was back in Outram Road again, the late-afternoon shadows congregating in his cell.

In the distance Billy could hear those phantoms who lived on the next tier returning for the night. Feet stamping up the iron stairs. Orders shouted. Numbering off in Jap. Doors slammed shut, and the silence enveloped him once more.

He tried to recall his fantasies. To summon up the Chester cake again – and when that failed, to picture the gas lamp burning in Ma's kitchen at the Big House in Bulwara Road as evening drew on, and to smell Irish stew simmering on the stove. But his visitors had gone for the day. Besides, the *meshi toban* was due any time with his bowl of tasteless rice and sour water. Anticipation of real food drove anything else from Billy's mind.

Hunger pains gripped him, and his digestive juices ran like a drain. He could sense the food tray outside, coming closer. Any time now . . . and the guard would bang on his door for the prisoner to come to the slot.

Yet this particular evening was different. It wasn't a Jap voice that shouted '*Meshi!*' Instead, with the knock came an urgent and unmistakably Australian voice whispered through the feeding mouth.

'Hey! You! What's your name? What mob are you with?'

'Billy,' he replied in astonishment as he stooped to the opening to see another European face looking back at him. 'Billy Young – 2/29th.'

'Keep your voice down! You okay?' the man murmured as he passed through the rice bowl.

'Yeah. Me mates?'

'Doing fine. Got to go.'

And he went. The boy continued to stare after him to catch what glimpses he could of the wonder, as the man returned to his food tray, the lazy guard and the Indian *meshi toban*. They passed by to serve prisoners further up the row their evening meal, garnished with his scraps of news.

At length Billy returned to his sitting position on the floor. All through dinner – *mukin* – he marvelled at the phenomenon.

Who was this bloke? A digger? A POW like himself? Sounded like it by the way he talked – and a prisoner, obviously, by his clothes. How could an Australian con the Kenpeitai into making him a food trustie?

But then the kid reflected, and smiled to himself.

Well, of course he could! Experience had taught there wasn't a situation so grim that you couldn't find some way to talk yourself through it. Sooner or later you'd discover the trick.

Billy learned a little more when the trustie returned with '*char up*'.

'Who are *you?*' he asked *sotto voce*, hurriedly through the slot.

'Dean. Pen Dean. Lieutenant – 2/4th machine gunners.'

'I know your lot from Kranji! Youse were with us when the Nips came ashore.'

'Yes. Well, your mate Brown says to tell you he's remembering *you* in every one of his prayers!'

'I'll bet he is.'

The kid sniggered. There was no further exchange, however, for Dean had gone. But as Billy sat with his water, there was much for him to think about. Even when darkness fell outside and the ceiling light came on for the night, when the gong resonated through the cell block and it was time to spread his three bed boards and lie down, the boy's mind was spinning. An Australian trustie in Outram Road prison! It *could* be managed.

Mosquitoes returned with the votaries of the night, alive to any exposed offerings of human flesh. The boy pulled the blanket over his head. Itched. Scratched. Turned on one side in a foetal position. And looking through a tear in the cotton, concentrated all his thoughts on the prison door.

It was – still – a barrier, dark and seemingly impenetrable, sealing him in this chamber. But now, with Pen Dean, it was something more. The letterbox slot was a means by which the boy could communicate with his mates outside. The mouth not only fed him. It could also let him speak and escape with them to the world of liberty beyond.

Billy the Kid closed his eyes and for the first time in months fell into an easy sleep.

# 3

# SCABBY BATH

*Scabies are a democratic lot, I laugh,*
*In that they eat both prisoners and staff.*

For 38 days the Sandakan eight were kept in absolute solitary confinement. For 38 days Billy the Kid was locked behind the black door with only his thoughts for company, and only his strength of will and the daily routine to stop the walls from driving him insane.

His only human contacts were the shouts of the guard outside, prying eyes through the peephole swivel, and the touch of another hand as the *meshi toban* passed his food: mostly the Indians, but several times a week Pen Dean would join the rounds and season the mess with his titbits of gossip.

'Fred New's got a bad dose of shits – don't think it's dysentery yet...Darlington's arm is still bad – what did they do to him...? Brown says don't scratch too much or you'll infect yourself...Word is the Americans have landed at Penang, but they've been landing ever since I came here last year...'

Dean could only whisper his news if the guard were standing well away from the door. Everything depended upon who was on duty. Some, like Little Hitler, were inflexible and stayed with the *meshi toban* constantly to enforce the rule of silence. Others, such as the one Billy called Mopoke (bespectacled as an owl), were inclined to be lazy and dawdle, especially if no other guard were nearby. Naturally Pen Dean knew them well; and unless there was some unexpected change in the roster, he was generally able to make his visits coincide with the guards he knew could be relied upon to hang back. Indeed, it was by earning their trust in the first place that he'd become a trustie himself.

Dean and his mate, Corporal John McGregor, had escaped from Changi in March 1942, a month after Singapore fell. They spent several weeks with Chinese saboteurs in southern Malaya, before they were betrayed and handed over to the Kenpeitai. The interrogators used many tortures on them – beating, kicking, electric shocks, tearing out toe and fingernails – trying to extract confessions. At length Dean and McGregor were discarded and sent to Outram Road for two years, entering the prison on the eve of Anzac Day, 24 April.

Conditions at first were relatively easy. Men could congregate in the passage outside their cells after the evening meal. But when a Chinese prisoner tried to kill a Japanese guard during this interlude, the full severity of the Kenpeitai fell upon the inmates. Lieutenant Dean had in fact seized the assailant – but it made no difference. All were incarcerated in their cells without respite, forced to constantly kneel or squat. Rations were cut. Food was sometimes denied for days at a time. The sick were left to starve, to die alone and untreated. Bashings became habitual.

Determined to ameliorate conditions, Dean ingratiated himself with the Japanese by learning to sew prison clothes – even to mend the guards' uniforms – on a small sewing machine brought to the jail. To keep his brain active he began to learn the language, picking up new words each day from guards whose goodwill he earned through the sewing, and practising during the hours of isolation. In time Pen Dean became reasonably fluent. Guards began to compete among themselves to teach him and to use him as an interpreter. Through them he was able to voice complaints that the Indian and Malay *meshi toban* were favouring some prisoners over others: giving large servings to their friends, with little food left over for the rest.

Eventually Dean was appointed to oversee the distribution. He insisted that meals were dished in the kitchen, not served directly from a rice bucket carried on the food tray, thus ensuring that the sparse rations were at least apportioned fairly. He changed the delivery order each day to avoid charges of favouritism – although this didn't always work. Selfishness is universal; a couple of more senior Australian officers in the cell block tried to pull rank and demand that Lieutenant Dean give bigger servings to *them*! He refused, much to their annoyance. Indeed, when the officers were released and returned to Changi, they laid a complaint against him. It was dismissed. Pen Dean didn't retaliate. As he said, 'I was not interested in adding to the problems of conscience they would have to live with.'

It was months before Billy the Kid learned the full story of how Dean became the food trustie. The fact of it, meanwhile, was sufficiently amazing. Some looked on Dean with suspicion, as if he'd become a collaborator. They even blamed him for looking better fed than themselves. But not Billy. The streetwise kid knew instinctively how clever Dean had been. Even so, during those first 38 days of solitary confinement, the boy had no idea just how much his survival depended on Dean.

Two mouthfuls of insipid rice, three times a day, were little enough! No wonder he spent days dreaming of those feasts at Ultimo, when Ma would have roast chicken, carried smoking from the oven. This stuff at Outram Road was starvation diet. As the weeks went by, Billy could feel his weight falling away, and hunger gnawed like a rat in his belly. Yet under Pen Dean's system the prisoners were at least starving more or less equally. Indeed, Dean was sometimes able to sneak food to the sick who were denied it, and occasionally a Vitamin B1 tablet to those suffering the worst cases of beriberi.

Billy would have acknowledged what Dean was doing, had he known of it. As things were, he could only look forward to the trustie's occasional visits with the food tray, and those fleeting sentences through the slot that kept him connected to life and to those dear friends who languished along the corridor.

'Tell Brownie I'm scratching me flaming ribs out.'

This was true enough. For Pen Dean wasn't his only visitor. Along with the spiders, ants and mosquitoes came many other forms of insect life, including the scabies mite. The prison was infested with them.

Billy was not at first aware he was sharing his cell with scabies. His scratching came as much from mozzies, lice and heat rash. But scabies make themselves at home anywhere; and finding Billy newly arrived in their living space, the females were soon crawling out of the dirt, up his body, and burrowing into the top layers of his skin to lay their three eggs a day. Tunnelling through his flesh.

Within a fortnight, the first larvae began to hatch and eat their way back to the surface. A rash spread across his body. The itching was intense, and the only alleviation was to scratch it, which made things worse. Pimples grew between his fingers, lumps forming in the soft skin behind his knees and elbows, on his penis and balls.

It was impossible to sleep at night for the irritation. Billy lay on his boards, covered with the blanket, scratching like a mangy dog. It was all very well for Brownie to send a message through Pen Dean not to – but it couldn't be helped.

'Anyway, what are *you* doing?'

His thoughts flew back to the Big House in Bulwara Road, and the hives he had as a little fellow. And he remembered the time he fell into stinging nettles when they all went into the country to pick bracken to sell at Paddy's Market.

'Try and find some dock leaves to put on it,' Ma had said. 'They always grow near nettles, and they soothe the pain.'

There were no dock leaves at Outram Road, and they would not have assisted. The scabies itch was infinitely worse than any hives and Billy's mind became so concentrated on it that memories of childhood were quickly displaced. As even the pangs of hunger could be forgotten. For a bit.

He scratched and clawed, tearing at the rash, which broke and bled and as it coagulated began to form new lumps. These hardened into scabs from which of course the scabies got their name. The scabs in turn became inflamed, were rubbed and ripped, only to bleed again and spread more infection.

All through the night and into the next day: 38 days – at the end of which Billy's body was covered in sores. His ribs were indeed almost torn out. To say nothing of the rest of him...

On the afternoon of the 39th day, the kid heard guards approaching. Rubber thongs squelched on the floor outside, and orders were shouted. *What was happening? Surely it was too early for the evening meal?*

Billy sat rigid behind his door, every instinct at the ready. A key turned in the lock and the door swung open for the first time in over a month. A guard stood waiting.

'*Kotchi koi!*' Come here!

The boy got to his feet a little unsteadily, feeling like a toddler making his first steps. And his thoughts, which had bent inward during five weeks of solitude, now turned outwards and raced uncertainly between one extreme and another. Was he being released? Was it all over? Had we won the war? Perhaps Hirohito had pardoned him for escaping and decided to send him back to Sandakan? Or were they going to kill him? Was he going to have his head cut off like those five men at Kuching?

'*Koi!*'

Billy tottered down the steps – to see the seven mates with whom he'd entered the jail also emerging from their cells and gathering in the passage. MP Brown, Jimmy Darlington, Alan Minty...

Relief swept over them. Whatever was to happen next, the sense of emotional liberation after 38 days was as profound as any physical release might be. They looked at each other and laughed, and clasped hands – hands that were as scrawny and scabby as the next man's, bodies as thin and dirty as each other. But who cared? Pop New was looking older, but he was alive. Normie Morris, who'd been with Billy from the start, was still there. Ignoring the rule of silence, the eight cobbers began talking hastily to each other.

'Billy, you young beggar, you lost a bit of weight!'

'Reckon the cook needs to learn a new recipe.'

'How's your head wound, Brownie?'

'The scabies are doing a better job of skinning me than the Nips.' He, whose eyebrows had fallen across his face when the Sandakan guards beat him.

'Your arm, Jimmy?'

'I'm with MP. These scabbies are worse than rope torture.'

'Did you get a bit of pumpkin on your rice last night?'

They quite forgot where they were. The guards did not, however. At the wicked outbreak of speech, swords were unclipped. And with shouts of *Yame! Kora! Bakayarou!* they began laying into the eight.

'*Hanasanai!*' You will not speak! '*Binta! Binta!*' Hit! Hit! they yelled, as metal scabbards threshed pale bodies weakened after 38 days of hunger and the onset of disease. It wasn't long before the prisoners were winnowed, like grain, into single file and the submission of silence.

'*Bango!*'

They began to number off.

'*Ichi, ni, san, shi.*' Which always came out sounding like 'Itchy knees can't see.' Each number marked with its own little bow.

Satisfied there were indeed eight of them, the guards cried '*Koi!*', and the column moved off down the cell block. Through the cavernous building they marched, three tiers of black doors staring down like rows of dominoes that might fall and crush them.

On they shuffled, until they reached a door at the far end. It was unlocked and they passed into the dazzling light of a courtyard. After five weeks without sight of the sun, Billy's eyes flared and burned. He shut them tight and in the darkness could see stars wheeling – for he'd not been allowed to see the night sky either in his cell.

Sunlight gradually filtered into his vision and he was able to look on the world through slatted eyelids.

'Holy Jesus!' He heard MP down the line.

And Brownie was right. As Billy's eyes adjusted, he could see rows of men sitting cross-legged in the shade of a covered walkway through the middle of the walled courtyard. Men – if they could be called men! Prisoners like himself, undoubtedly, some with their shirts off and all wearing these flimsy green Jap shorts. But there was nothing of them! Their bodies seemed utterly wasted away.

The kid had thought *he* was thin. Billy was all fat at present, compared to these fellers. Their heads had turned into mere skulls: eyes sunk into the sockets, cheeks hollow and teeth rotting away. Necks seemed distended, Adam's apples bulging like golf balls as they moved up and down incessantly, swallowing food that existed only in their imaginations. Chests and bellies were shrunken, the skin stretched over protruding ribs, and you could count every one of the vertebrae that climbed like stairs up their spines.

'*Suware!*'

Billy sat on the ground next to one of them. The man seemed

more dead than alive: a corpse sitting there. His arms and legs were encrusted with scabs, like salt on a fish carcase. And he stank as if his body was in an advanced state of decay.

Yet his neighbour was not dead. Billy could see eyes blink and the fingers of his right hand seemed to dance with agitation on his bony thigh.

'Good'ay. What's yer name?'

A voice spoke low in the kid's ear. He looked around to see who was talking.

'What's your mob?'

No jawing anywhere.

'I'm Kenny Bird. Transport driver.'

The kid looked at the skeleton next to him and suddenly twigged that Kenny Bird – jailbird – was talking from the corner of his mouth, like a ventriloquist.

'Billy Young. Second 29th.'

*'Damare!'* Shut up!

Billy copped a jab in the back from the escort guard. The kid was no ventriloquist's dummy, though the ability to speak without lips moving was clearly a skill worth acquiring. For as he looked around him properly, Billy realised that this wasn't a graveyard of men or of hope. It was in fact full of animation.

There were perhaps 70 men sitting there, stick figures every one of them. Yet it didn't take his quick wits long to notice that their fingers were not idly fidgeting; they were tapping messages in Morse code. Dot dash dot. Some were signing in the palm of one hand with deaf and dumb language. Eyes were sending signals full of meaning. Indeed, Billy would learn that the clever ones could even transmit Morse by blinking. Silent the place might be, but it was alive with unspoken conversations. And the kid longed to join them.

'Bath time's coming up.' This from Ken Bird, the talking scarecrow again. 'Look.'

He nodded forward slightly. Out the front stood a large antique hipbath. It appeared to be made of white porcelain, inlaid with bands of terracotta elaborately decorated with hieroglyphs. A valuable object, such as Cleopatra might have known. Pop Jepson would have got a few quid for it at Paddy's Market. How had it ended up so incongruously in a prison yard? Looted, probably.

'What's it for?' Billy muttered, keeping his lips as still as he could.

'Scabies. They're eating the Japs, too. They're giving us a disinfectant bath.'

A guard appeared with a 'Swan Ink' bottle, half filled with some chemical. He was a rather tall, dark fellow for a Jap, whom Billy dubbed 'The Black Prince' after a story he'd read in his *Triumph* magazine. Others, better acquainted with his infernal qualities, were more inclined to call him 'The Prince of Darkness'. He certainly acted the showman. This Prince stood beside the bath, and with much ceremony held up the ink bottle between thumb and forefinger – showing it to his audience with a toothy smile, like a magician about to perform a vaudeville trick. He then poured the contents into the bath and stirred it with a paddle.

'Cripes,' Billy murmured.

'Don't worry. The disso's strong enough to kill any bug.'

Which was a mercy.

'All the same,' Kenny added, 'as soon as he says *"Koi"*, try to get in line before them Indians.' He glanced at two Tamils sitting nearby. 'They got syphilis.'

'Shit!'

At 17, Billy the Kid as yet had no direct sexual experience with women. He was still a virgin, although he'd never have admitted it. Well, he'd been a POW for nearly a year and a half, and sex didn't come into it. Even so, he'd heard enough barracks-room talk and listened to enough lectures from army medics to know the effect venereal disease had on a man.

'I advise you *not* to go into the brothels,' the doctor had warned repeatedly on the voyage from Fremantle to Singapore. And to show them what to expect, he'd passed around photos of a penis disfigured with syphilis blisters, and lesions clinging to the crotches of men and women. They sure frightened the kid. When Billy entered the brothel district of Johore Bahru several times with the patrol on piquet duty, the squalor so sickened him he had no desire to return as a client. And while it was all very well for the doctors to say you couldn't get VD from toilet seats or even from bath water, who could really tell? There was no certain cure for syphilis. They'd repeated that, too! And who knew what was in the 'Swan Ink' bottle?

The boy looked at The Black Prince. He looked at the hipbath. And understood that between him and the Tamils was a race to perdition.

'*Koi!*'

There was a scramble in the rows of sitting men. Shirts and shorts were cast aside, and the skeletal figures seemed to rise as one – like the naked bodies of the dead ascending from their graves on Judgement Day, as Billy had once seen in a picture book, hastening to be among the first in line for the heaven of the hipbath.

The kid was caught flat-footed. When he got to the queue, the Indians were well in front of him. His race was lost. And with each man required to spend at least a minute in the bath – soaking himself thoroughly in disinfectant – sunburn was adding its sting to the scabies rash by the time it was Billy's turn.

The water had turned to slurry, polluted with the dirt of 70 unwashed, diseased bodies, on the surface of which floated the skimmings of a great many scabs. The boy turned away in revulsion. He wasn't going to step into this! It was like bathing in liquid manure, and catching VD at the end of it. But the presence of The Black Prince with his sword made any other course inadvisable; Billy knew that. So he held his breath, gripped the porcelain sides, and got into his bath. He sat down in the muck, closing his eyes and mouth as he sluiced it over his body, trying to stop his nose and ears as the Jap made him douse his head with this stuff that stank worse than phenyl. It had better be good!

The kid wanted to throw up as the guard at last said '*Yoshi!*' and released him. He stepped onto the cement, shook himself, and made his way back to his clothes. Billy was almost dry as he dressed in the heat and sat down again. But he continued to twitch with little tremors of disgust at the thought of the scabies bath...and at the recollection of those photographs the doctors had passed around.

'Syphilis!' he murmured. 'Jesus! Your dick can rot off.'

His new-found friend, Kenny Bird, seemed to take compassion on his youth. For the ventriloquist said quite distinctly, 'It's all right, son. I told yer. That disso kills any germs. You'll survive.'

'You sure?'

'Course I am.'

'How do I know?'

'I'll show yer. I'll have another dip meself.'

Billy had been among the last in line. The bath was almost over, the magician getting ready to end proceedings, when Kenny Bird suddenly got to his feet and called out his number. The sound was almost shocking in the afternoon silence. Every head turned towards him.

Kenny repeated his number with a low bow – so low, Billy noticed, that his nose almost touched an upturned thumb.

'*Nanda?*' What? The Black Prince asked roughly. With a mixture of broken English, Malay and Japanese, Kenny pointed to himself, to the bath, and gave it to be understood that he still had an itch and would like a second scabby wash, if the Emperor of Japan would kindly permit.

There was a pause during which the guard pondered this request. His first instinct was to refuse it. But as the scabies were also attacking himself and his colleagues, and this *horyo* was offering to do more than his bit to get rid of the mites by having another bath, he at last gave his consent.

'*Yoshi!*'

Kenny took off his shirt and shorts, and picked his way among the seated audience to the hipbath, like an artist walking onto the platform. He'd spent much of his 31 years as a riverboat man in South Australia before joining the army, and had that tough, laconic self-sufficiency that's often found among river men. He also happened to be a comic of genius.

The Black Prince was standing in front of the hipbath, keeping an eye on his prisoners as Kenny approached, in case it turned out to be a diversion. It was – but of a different kind altogether. The guard missed the best of it, and this was probably as well. He fancied himself a comedian: but Kenny completely upstaged him, and he'd have turned nasty. Billy and the others, however, were spellbound.

Ken stepped up to the bath with all the leisurely aplomb of Claude Rains or some other gentleman of the silver screen about to take his ablutions. He stretched and began to mime the act of untying a dressing-gown cord. He took off the imaginary gown and hung it over an imaginary chair. The garment fell to the floor. Kenny mouthed 'Bother!' and picked it up. The gown fell down again. For a second time Ken replaced it on the chair, patting it firmly in place.

The kid had seen nothing at the Saturday pictures better than this – and he almost cried out laughing when Kenny got into the bath. For the man lifted one matchstick leg and dipped his toe into the scabby water.

'Aah!'

Too hot. He quickly withdrew his toe, and Billy could visualise steam rising from the bath in clouds. Ken leant over and turned on a cold tap, feeling the water temperature with one hand. Satisfied it was just right, he stepped into the bath and sank down, luxuriating, a look of contentment on his face. Indeed, he even added more water, turning on the tap and letting it dribble over his hand.

Bliss.

This had gone on for several minutes to the silent mirth of his audience, when Kenny came to his grand finale. He thought he'd have a smoke. As The Black Prince stood with his back to him, Ken leaned out of the bath, reached over to the dressing-gown, and withdrew a packet of cigarettes and matches from the pocket. He put a fag in his mouth, lit up, and inhaled deeply – and there wasn't a man in that smoke-free environment who couldn't smell a wonderful tobacco fragrance drifting in the air. More so, when Kenny lay back in his bath and began blowing smoke rings at The Prince of Darkness.

It was too much! Laughter rippled through the rows of men. Sensing something was wrong, the guard quickly turned to the bath – where Kenny sat calmly waving his hands to dissipate the smoke rings and explaining loudly '*Ka!* Mosquitoes. *Ka!* Mozzies.'

The curtain rang down on his act, and he went back to his place to the silent acclamation of his spectators. Kenny Bird, reduced after months to a mere framework of skin and bone – so emaciated that he almost disappeared if you looked at him side on – still had his spirit intact. The Japs had not taken his independence. On the contrary, Ken could yet take the piss out of them, to thumb his nose in contempt as he made his bow, defying them. And letting everyone present know that, whatever happened to his body, the freeborn soul was still his own.

It was a performance that stayed in the minds of all who saw it. Billy the Kid could think of little else when he was returned to his cell and locked in again. He'd seen some brave things in his life: Bob Shipsides leading them to safety under night attack at Bukit Timah; Colonel Walsh standing up to the Japs at Sandakan, even when they put him in front of a firing squad. Kenny Bird's burlesque showed the same courage. If The Black Prince had looked around, he'd have had Ken's head off. If the escort guard hadn't been of junior rank, too afraid to question his superior's apparent approval of the mockery, it might have been over for all of them!

And what resolute blokes these fellow prisoners were. Starved and degraded to the point where they looked like the walking dead, their humanity was undiminished! Whatever the rules about not speaking, their dancing fingers and blinking eyes were still communicating messages of mateship across the gulfs of silence. There was a way around everything, as the kid always knew. He was sorry only that he hadn't taken a signaller's course in the army when he had the chance. Morse code couldn't be all that hard to learn, Billy thought, and he resolved to find someone to teach him. There'd be an opportunity. Perhaps at the next scabby bath.

But that inevitably conjured visions of having to sit in that filth again, to catch God knew what. It had to be endured, of course. It even worked for a bit, as Kenny said it would, because the incessant scabies itch died down for a day or two, leaving the mind free to think of other things. And to counter the horrors of the hipbath came memories of other, more pleasant bathing parties...

The girls Billy could still glimpse, coming down to wash at a *tong* – a well – by the Labuan wharf when the eight were being shipped back from Sandakan: beautiful, laughing and all unconscious of self as they ladled water over their bodies in the evening light. Hot showers in the army – all in together, and the painful flicking of wet towels as they horsed around afterwards. But for a really long, hot soak, nothing could beat those Saturday-night baths at the Big House when Billy – young Keithy – and his Dad went to live with Ma and Pop Jepson at Ultimo.

There was a galvanised tin bath in the downstairs washhouse, with its own cold-water tap, and it was so long and deep a grown man could stretch full length in it and wallow. When he was little, Keithy often bathed with Dad, and there was no great race then to be head of the queue. Ma usually went first as mistress of the household; then maybe her young relative Cissie, who helped around the place; Pop Jepson, just in from the pub; and perhaps the family of a man called Les the Soldier, who'd been gassed in the Great War and coughed up his lungs like a consumptive.

Ma looked after quite a few damaged ex-servicemen. Les the Sailor had been torpedoed, and now kept to home waters: coming and going as his ships entered port. And the soldier they called 'Wingie', because he'd lost an arm in battle, nevertheless managed a living by making props and stick pegs for the clothesline, and selling them to neighbourhood housewives. The place was always full of people, and the thing was that you didn't throw out the bathwater each time. No. The next person to use it topped it up with hot water in a dipper from the copper. So that the last ones in had the tin bath almost filled to overflowing.

'In you hop, Keith, and soap yourself up.' Pretty strong carbolic soap it was too, and it would dislodge any dirt. They could have done with some at Outram Road.

'Ohhh, Dad. It's in me eyes!'

'Don't be such a sook, boy. Here, use the flannel.'

Come to think of it, the Big House had two bathrooms: one in the laundry and another across the yard where the stablemen washed after cleaning down the horses.

It was a large stone house, one of the first built in Ultimo they said, with an archway leading off the street into the yard with stables, lofts and upstairs rooms where the Jepson's lad Roy had a gymnasium.

Pop Jepson once had quite a business hiring out wagons and fruit barrows to the people at Paddy's Market, and the yard was crowded with carts, their shafts leaning against the sky at rest. But times were changing with the advent of motor trucks, and as the twenties turned into the thirties there was less demand for horse-drawn vehicles, much to George Jepson's dismay. He was a man who'd always worked with animals, and cared for them.

Uncle George – as Keithy was supposed to call him and got a clip on the ear if he didn't, especially when the old bloke had a few beers on board – was a small, bandy-legged Cockney, sharp as a ferret, who'd been a jockey in his youth. Racing in England was as crooked as anywhere else, and after several dangerous falls George got a job as horse-trainer and lion-tamer in a circus.

He was good at it, and travelled with the circus to Australia where he met a curly-headed trapeze artiste called Christina Aird. She was also a bareback rider, the tattooed lady (Ma could still peel the tattoos on and off as quick as anything) and the fortune-teller. They fell in love, as the crystal ball foretold, married and settled in Sydney to build up the market business.

It was therefore not just a matter of professional loss but also of sentiment, for Pop Jepson to see the horses on their way out. An era was ending. Still, as the clouds of the Depression gathered after the stock market crash of October 1929, there were always other sources of income.

Uncle George had his own fruit stall on Fridays at the market, and often took out his barrow – unlicensed – into town, with someone like young Keithy to keep his eyes peeled for the coppers. And Ma, as everyone fondly called Christina, took in boarders. So it was quite natural, when Big Bill Young mentioned his son in a letter to her, that Ma should offer to have the boy come and live with them. Quite natural that she should go in her fox-fur wrap to the children's home at Seven Hills to collect him.

'Hello, Keith. Your father's written and asked me to take you home.'

Dad wasn't waiting for them. He was still up north cane cutting. In fact he didn't arrive until a week or two later, when Keithy was already settling into his new life, sitting at the kitchen table with the others eating his dinner – one of Ma's stews thick with potatoes and fatty lamb. She was telling her friend and fellow circus artiste, Millie, some prescient story from the tea leaves, keeping the boy's mind engaged, when Ma suddenly turned and said, 'You've got a surprise coming, Keith.'

He looked up. And there, reflected in a wall mirror, he saw his father's face.

'Dad!' he cried, to their laughter. He leaped from his chair as Big Bill Young leaned down, lifted his son and held him close.

'I can see they're looking after *you*, boy.'

Indeed they were. Keithy shared a bedroom upstairs with his father; but the Big House was always so alive with such interesting people that the young fellow very quickly felt himself to be part of it.

The girl Cissie, for instance, who helped Ma with the housework, was an epileptic. She could have a seizure any time, and whoever was passing had to help.

'Quick, Keith!' Ma would shout from the washhouse where she was boiling the sheets. 'Give us a hand! Cissie's having another fit.'

The little chap ran in and assisted Ma to support Cissie as the girl's eyes rolled back in her head, face white as the bed linen, and her body twitching.

'Now, Keithy, grab a clothes peg – one of them long stick ones that Wingie makes – and put it in Cissie's mouth so she don't swaller her tongue. That's right. Now, we'll lay her on the floor till she comes good. And remember, a wad of newspaper will do just as well if there's no peg handy, next time it happens.'

The fragility of life was all around him; its fascination, and the arts you had to learn to get through it.

Pop Jepson had an older brother called Uncle Sam, just as nuggetty but not half as strong, for he lay very sick in a downstairs bedroom.

'Here, Keith, take this cup of tea into Uncle Sam,' Ma would say. 'And sit with him a bit. Cheer him up.'

So the boy would stand by the brass-and-iron bedstead, staring at the frail old man and saying not a word as Uncle Sam struggled to prop himself up on a pillow, croaking and coughing as he swallowed his tea.

'Ee, that were good!' he'd say through his whiskers. 'Ask Ma if she can't squeeze anuvver from 'er pot.'

There came a day when Uncle Sam croaked his last and they laid him out in his best suit on the dining table in the front room. The best room, where you hardly ever went, with family portraits on the wall, Ma's ribbons for her champion terriers, a photo of Pop's winning ride, his jockey's saddle and bridle. And Uncle Sam lying on the table like a wax centrepiece, hands crossed on his chest, a smile pinched on his face, and everyone crying.

'I knew something like this was gunna 'appen,' said Millie at the wake afterwards, sipping tea from Ma's best Willow pattern china (given as a present when she left the circus). 'I just knew it.'

'How was that, dear?' asked Ma, a wedge of sponge cake hesitating at her lips.

'I seen a black moth that morning, big as this cup and saucer, and I knew at once that death was wingin' its way to us.'

Everybody nodded wisely, and sucked their tea, and sighed. 'Ah...a black moth. Fancy that!'

Did they believe it? Keithy couldn't tell, but he never afterwards looked upon a black moth with anything other than dislike.

Tea and sponge cake…Always the kid's thoughts at Outram Road kept coming back to food, as the brief respite from the scabies itch allowed scope for hunger pains to twist in his stomach like dinner knives.

Going down with the billycan to the dairy in Harris Street for a quart of skimmed milk (cheaper than full cream) and watching it foaming and gushing from the tap.

'It's amazin' how much spills out when I'm bringin' it back,' he'd say to Ma, hoping there weren't too many guilty white traces around his mouth.

Sometimes she gave Keith a clean pillowcase and sent him up to the Arnott's factory for broken biscuits (threepence a half sack). He tried to time his visits for those days when they were making date slices – because out of the chute would come those fragments of sticky delight he preferred almost as much as Chester cake, and they could feast for a week on buttery biscuit filled with sweet, dark fruit.

His mind drifted to oxtail bought from the meatworks and turned into soup. Bananas and apples and boxes of cherries piled on Pop's barrow at the market. For as one of the household Keithy had his part to play in the family business and early morning every Friday he'd go down with Uncle George to set up stall just outside the gate.

'G'day, Stiffie!' the market men called, for Pop was always 'Stiffie' Jepson to his closest friends. 'How's it going?'

'Enough for a load,' came the reply, indicating that he was sufficiently cashed up to stock his barrow – depending on what was going cheap at the wholesalers.

Sometimes Pop did very well and Stiffie would roll home drunk and singing after dark, leaving somebody else – and on occasion the boy – to push his barrow. At other times he'd misjudge his market completely – buying oranges when there was a glut, or boxes of peaches that were on the turn. Then it would be everyone out hawking peaches ('Goin' very cheap today, lady') before they went quite rotten.

That's the nature of markets. And within his own terms Pop was a brilliant vendor. Keithy often stood there being educated as Stiffie served a well-heeled customer a dozen mandarins, three at a time in his hand: two mandarins into the bag, one dropped behind the counter – as the boy would later know how to palm a pencil stub. If the woman came back complaining she'd been short-changed, it was always a very proper 'Dreadfully sorry, madam. My mistake, I'm sure…' But not infrequently, out in the city streets, when the boy signalled 'Copper coming!', Pop would take off with his barrow (for they couldn't book you on the move), the customer running after him and shouting for her money. Then it became 'That's all right, luv. I'll catch up wiv yer at the next stop.' Fly as any pearly costermonger down Petticoat Lane.

The kid had good reason to be grateful for Stiffie's manner of doing business. Sometimes on a warm afternoon they'd go for a picnic into the bush around Como, across the Georges River, to cut sticks for Wingie's clothes props (which always tangled feet and upset the train conductor on the way home). They'd wander into moist gullies to gather fern and perfumed boronia (strictly illegal) and make bunches for the lad and Cissie to sell at the market. Anything to turn a penny.

Keith had done well one particular Friday and almost sold out, peddling up and down the aisles and dodging around the corner if he saw a market inspector coming, for of course he paid no stall fee.

'Fresh green fern for your flower vase, lady. Penny a bunch.'

'They *are* nice, dear,' said a well-dressed woman, stopping to admire. 'I'll take the last of them off your hands.'

'Good-oh.'

'But I've nothing smaller than a florin. Can you change two shillings?'

'Course I can!' Boasting.

The boy fumbled in his bag among the pennies and halfpennies, changed her money, and she took his remaining bunches of fern.

'How's it goin', Keithy?' asked Pop when they met.

'Real good, Uncle George.' Billy glowed with pride. 'I got a two-bob piece.'

'Give us a look at it.'

The man held the silver coin to the light. It only took a moment.

'Oh, Keithy!' Stiffie Jepson exclaimed. 'She's given you a duddie! It's painted lead. It ain't good for nuffin'!'

The kid's sense of achievement collapsed utterly as he kicked himself for being cheated like that.

'But never mind, Keithy,' said Pop, brightening at last and slipping the duddie into his pocket. 'I'll get rid of it for ya.'

And so he did – passing on his 'little bit of 'appiness' to somebody else during the course of the day's trade. Doing unto others what they did unto you.

As the tentacles of the Depression tightened their grip on the lives of working people, the popular song's injunction to 'look for the silver lining' became not just an escape but a necessity. Nobody could afford to lose what little they had.

One Easter, Stiffie bought a load of mullet cheap at the fish market, anticipating a quick sale to housewives for Good Friday's dinner. But it rained, not many people were out buying, and the fish began to smell. Never one to give up on a deal, Pop took the mullet home and packed it in ice, covered with a tarpaulin, on the back of his neighbour's truck.

'Better day tomorrer, Keithy. You wait and see.'

Stiffie was right. Easter Saturday dawned clear and warm, and the truck was out early heading for Botany Bay, the kids in the back with the fish. They reached a likely spot, hired a boat, loaded the mullet and rowed a little out to sea.

'Keep sprinklin' the catch wiv salt water, Keithy!'

Then, as the sun shone and the beach filled with people on holiday, they rowed back in again.

'Is that fresh fish you've got?' a woman asked.

'Straight out of the sea, luv. You can still smell the briny on 'em.'

'How much?'

'To you? Easter special, luv. Threepence each.'

'I'll have a couple for the family's tea.'

'Me, too. Fancy! Fresh fish for Easter!'

'I'll take a shilling's worth.'

So it went on. Such a bonza day! Stiffie sold every last one of his mullet. He bought everybody an ice-cream and a packet of boiled lollies for the kids in the back. And even after a visit to the pub, he still went home to Ma with a pocket full of money, where, it being Saturday night, they all had their baths in the laundry.

Billy the Kid glowed with a deep sense of satisfaction at the memory. Stretching himself full length on the Outram Road bed boards, he filled the tin bath with a dipper from the copper and sank up to his neck in steaming hot water.

And the scabby wash could go to hell.

# 4

# THE TALKING WALLS

*Which makes it hard to put a price,*
*Not knowing the worth of words.*

Some nights after the scabby bath, Billy became aware his prison walls were trying to communicate with him. He was lying on the bed boards, starting to itch again and sweating under the cover, when he heard a soft tap through the wall by his ear, followed by a muffled scratch.

The kid turned his head towards it, wondering if it was some new tropical bug come to add its torments to the scabies. While the disso in the absurdly beautiful hipbath deloused the men, the Japs did nothing to disinfect their cells; and it wasn't long before the mites were making themselves at home once more in the flesh of their human hosts.

*Tap. Scratch.* The little buggers were burrowing through stone to get at him!

No. There it was again. *Scratch. Tap-tap-tap.* A distinctly ordered, man-made noise. And through Billy's midnight drowsiness came a realisation that the bloke next door was trying to make contact using Morse code.

*Scratch. Tap. Scratch. Tap.*

If only he'd gone on the signals course.

*Scratch. Tap-tap.*

If only he knew what these dots and dashes signified.

The boy slowly turned again under the watching eye of the ceiling light, and focused his mind on the door. Was there any hint of a Kenpeitai shadow through the grille? Was any unwanted presence looking through the peephole?

Satisfied that all was clear, Billy rolled back to the wall.

*Tap.*

And with a bare knuckle he cautiously answered. *Rap.*

Which hurt like the dickens, for he skinned himself on the rough plaster.

'Shit.'

But the feller next door must have heard, because through the wall came a distinct *Tap-tap-scratch-tap.* A brief pause. *Tap-tap-scratch-tap.*

Billy's fingers felt along the floor to a corner; he knew a few bits of rubble were lying there below the crack where he'd hidden his pencil. He picked up a pebble and, straining for any sound outside, gave his responding *Tap-tap-scratch-tap.*

Much better than knuckles. But the raps seemed like pistol shots in the blanketed silence and he hastily curled up, pretending to be asleep should any guard come bursting in. None did. And it was with a sense of increasing confidence that he received and answered his next message: *Scratch-scratch-tap.*

The varying dots and dashes obviously stood for different letters of the alphabet. But which ones? The kid had no point of reference. Even supposing the first sound he'd heard was an 'A', he couldn't remember what the code for that letter was. *Scratch-tap? Tap-tap-scratch?* And then what? It was very confusing: more so when a string of taps and scratches suddenly echoed through the stone as his neighbour turned these separate parts of speech into words – and then into a whole sentence.

Billy felt as if he'd been struck both deaf and dumb: unable to understand what was being said to him or to make any sensible response. The best he could do was to reply with some meaningless scratching and tapping of his own, like infant's babble, to make his presence known but incomprehensible.

As luck had it, they were taken out for another scabby bath a few days later, where Billy was able to question Brownie about Morse.

'A is dot-dash.' Through lips that were becoming more practised at not moving. 'B is dash-dot-dot-dot.'

'And C?'

'Dash-dot-dash-dot.'

The problem was remembering more than a few letters at a time. Billy the Kid wasn't stupid. He had the wisdom of the streets – but no habit of regular learning: of training his mind through the discipline of school. He dared not write the letters on the wall with his pencil, for the Japs would spot them at the next inspection; and he was too uncertain anyway to carve them into the plaster with his wire. Besides, Kenny Bird warned that the Nips had a habit of shifting men from one cell to another without notice, to prevent any accumulation of treasure.

'Always have yer stash ready for a sudden move, kid.'

So for quite some time Billy's efforts at sending Morse through the talking walls were restricted to the first few letters of the alphabet. Any conversation confined to words like CAB, BAD and BED becomes rather limited – although FEED and FED are redolent with meaning to malnourished men. But even there the boy was unsure of himself.

'Is F dot-dash-dash-dot?' whispered from the corner of his mouth to MP when next they sat beside each other in front of the hipbath.

'That's P, numbskull.'

'Oh. Right.'

And the kid realised he'd told his neighbour last night that he wanted a good pee – instead of a good feed.

At such times he'd watch the fingers dancing to silent music across the courtyard telegraphing their songs without words, or lay awake at night imagining the discussions being tapped through other walls. And Billy would regret not just the signals course, but wish he'd paid a lot more attention to his schoolteachers – and less to avoiding the truant inspectors in the streets of Ultimo.

Yet it was a cow of a school, overcrowded as a workhouse, with sometimes 50 kids in a class ranged in desks before a succession of teachers. Poorly paid and poorly trained for the most part, they relied on their canes to keep discipline as they struggled to teach the elements of writing and number to unwilling pupils.

'Hold out your hand, Keith Young.'

Swish!

'And again.'

Swish.

'You will learn not to keep talking in my class, Keith Young.'

The wretched teacher – a large, ill-humoured woman who needed a shave – managed only to instil in her pupils the knowledge that learning seemed always to be accompanied by pain.

Much easier to avoid school altogether, and the boy sometimes played truant for days at a time. Well, Pop and Ma Jepson needed him at the Friday markets; and if they were left with boxes of fruit and vegetables, the boy had to help sell them in the streets before they went rotten. As the Depression deepened, every penny counted.

Ma gave up the lease on the Big House, and they moved along Bulwara Road to a cheaper terrace near the White Rose Flour Mill and a vacant block of land, where the kids played cricket and lit bonfires on Guy Fawkes Night. There were tips to be earned keeping lookout at Thommo's two-up school under the railway arches at Wentworth Park, where Keithy got to know every copper and police car about the place. Threepence for a tin of cigarette butts picked off the footpath and sold to the battlers – 'And make sure you pack 'em down tight!'

Gleanings at the wool stores: for after a good day at the sales the buyers would throw their small change in the air and the kids would cry, 'Up for a penny, down for a crown!' Two bob's worth of fun to see the youngsters scrambling after coins. There were less reputable earnings on offer, too. As buyers arrived in their limousines, Keithy might get a sixpence by approaching them with a polishing rag in one hand – and half a brick in the other.

'Clean your car for you, mister?' A smirk on his face.

In such ways did the boy make his contribution to the household income.

Yet authority catches up eventually; and tired of trying to nab the boy on the streets, the truant inspectors at length spoke to Ma. Who spoke to Dad when he returned from one of his boxing tours. Who spoke severely to his son.

'There's going to be trouble, boy. You've been put on probation. They'll fine me, and send you to reformatory school if you keep wagging it. There's nothing wrong with study, Keith. It's the only way to make something of your life.'

Big Bill Young was not exactly a shining example of his own precept. He'd done well at school until he ran off and tried to enlist for Gallipoli, and was still a reader with a shelf full of books in the bedroom. But to this point his life had been pretty aimless, and he was still stuck in the rut of an itinerant day-labourer. Not that this was to be scorned at a time when one man in three was unemployed.

However that may be, it was around this period – when Keithy was seven or eight – that somebody took his education in hand. Whether it was his grandmother Tot and the family in Hobart, or his rich aunt Ilma Morsello at Waverley, the boy never knew. But he was removed from the Ultimo state school and sent to the posh private school at St Barnabas's Anglican Church on Broadway.

The kid felt like a brown carp among the goldfish: the rough-speaking, bare-footed scamp, walking straight from a game at the tallow works to take his place at a desk beside the well-mannered, well-shod offspring of the middle class. They sat at one end of a hall, at the other end of which was a stage and curtain. He retained very little of the lessons; but Keithy didn't forget the concert held under lights on the platform... with some young bloke all dressed up in long pants, wearing make-up and singing to this girl: *Madam, will you walk? Madam, will you walk and talk with me?*

Pretty sissy, the kid thought it. Not like Pop Jepson when he'd come home rolling drunk, regaling them all in the kitchen with his Cockney music-hall ditties.

*Hi diddle-ee Barlow! Cock-a-doodle-do!*

Yet the concert stayed with him: the music expressing something to which Keithy responded. Not that he remained long enough at St Barnabas's to recognise or nurture it. Within a few months he was taken out and whisked across the road to the Catholic school at St Benedict's, where the only things he remembered were the black cassocks of the brothers fastened with heavy leather belts and a gold crucifix on the priest's chest glittering reproachfully like the eye of God upon him.

A struggle for the boy's soul seemed to be waged between his mother's Catholic and his father's Protestant relatives – as it had when he'd been placed in the home at Seven Hills. And it ended in much the same way. When Dad returned from the bush again, he removed Keith from St Benedict's and he returned to the Ultimo school. Life resumed its accustomed course: the kid receiving his education by virtue of the cane, the streets, and the invaluable lessons of the market trader.

Sometimes, when a barrowman had enough for a load but not sufficient to hire a set of scales, the boy set off with him down George Street: one eye open for a copper, the other watching with admiration as Les or Wingie weighed a pound of potatoes on imaginary scales behind the counter. Popping an extra spud into the paper bag, taking one out, carefully calculating the supposed ounces with all the pantomime skill of Kenny Bird in his hipbath at Outram Road...

Memories of a past when Billy the Kid ran too free crowded now into a mind too trapped inside his cell: unable to understand what messages the talking stones were trying to convey from his mates. Nor could he ask them, except on those rare occasions when they were taken out for an increasingly useless scabby wash.

'Is H dot-dot?'

'Dot-dot-dot-dot.'

'Well, what's dot-dot?'

'I. For Idiot.'

'I'll never remember it.'

Kenny Bird never repeated his performance at the bathtub. But like every good artist he had more than one act in his repertoire to entertain an audience.

One afternoon, when they were sitting in the shade of the courtyard's covered walkway, Kenny was suddenly seized with a terrible fit. He began to jerk and moan, to thrash and throw himself about. Blood foamed from his mouth, and his eyes rolled like marbles into their sockets.

'Quick! Grab 'im.'

Billy had seen this many times before with Cissie's epilepsy, and knew exactly what to do. He and Brownie laid the convulsing Kenny Bird on the ground, holding him down firmly while the kid cast around for something – anything – to put in the man's mouth to prevent him swallowing his tongue. Pity there were none of Wingie's clothes pegs handy!

In this predicament, the guard they called Mopoke came over. He took one look at the stricken prisoner, and with grunts and gestures indicated they should carry Ken back to his cell.

It was a hell of a job. For all that he looked a corpse, there was still plenty of fight in him. Kenny kicked and groaned as the pair struggled to lift his legs and shoulders and convey him back to the cell block. After several months in the prison, Brownie and the kid were themselves much weakened. Indeed, Billy was no longer shocked by the skeletons in the courtyard. He was becoming one of them, and could almost slip a hand around his wrist.

The two were therefore exhausted by the time they manhandled bloody Kenny Bird to the cell and wrestled him up the steps. They were about to lay him on the floor when Ken suddenly stopped his writhing and said quite clearly, 'Where's that guard? Where's old Mopoke?'

Billy looked out through the doorway.

'Don't worry. He's on his way back to the other blokes.'

At these words, the dying patient sprang to his feet and began dancing around his cell. Kenny laughed out loud, and cavorted, and broke into song. *'Happy birthday to you, Happy birthday, Hirohitoo!* Oh, you little beauty!'

It seemed that on the Emperor's birthday and other important celebrations, the Kenpeitai doctor inspected the prisoners of war held at Outram Road. Those considered sick enough were sent as a special treat to the POW's own hospital at Changi barracks. If they died, at least they were off the Kenpeitai books. And if they recovered they were eventually sent back to the jail to complete their sentences.

A spell among comrades and medics who cared at Changi,

however sparse the food and facilities, was a respite from the horrors of Outram Road greatly to be desired. The inmates tried many stunts to achieve it – of which biting the tongue until it bled profusely was a favourite!

'It hurts a bit, cobber,' Ken explained, 'but it makes a good show. There's lotsa blood for the Nips to see. And the pain actually helps. If you act it up well enough, she'll sometimes do the trick.'

Certainly it did in this case. When the prison doctor next visited, Kenny Bird, the epileptic scarecrow, was sent out to Changi where, with the doctors' help, he managed to remain for a couple of months. And when at length he returned it was with some decent nourishment in his belly and a little meat on his bones.

Billy the Kid looked on, and learned. The whole of life was a lesson in the strategies necessary to out-manoeuvre authority. It always had been. And the rights and wrongs of it depended entirely on the point of view. Morality was quite relative.

Next door to the terrace house in Bulwara Road lived an unmarried mother with a boy called Reg, about the same age as young Keithy. Whenever word flashed down the street that the welfare officers were coming, there was inevitably a scramble over the side fence to put Keith's clothes into Reg's chest of drawers and to carry in cabbages and fruit from Ma's pantry. Why? To satisfy welfare that Reg was being properly fed and dressed and not have him removed from his mother's care.

Then again, Ma had a policy of keeping her rent receipts in bundles, as evidence she was a good tenant who paid on time. They came in useful for other people as well. With queues of men for every job, their families reduced to poverty, neighbours threatened with eviction often came to Ma to borrow her rent receipts.

'We got to look for a new lodgings, see, and they'll help with the landlord.'

'Well, don't you lose 'em and make sure you bring 'em back!'

Precariously as the Jepsons lived with their toehold on the ladder of commerce, people who came to them in need rarely went away with nothing. It may only have been a plate of rabbit stew if Wingie had skinned a couple, or a Friday morning at the market barrow for a few bob. But at least Pop and Ma tried to see their pals right – even if the rest was a mug's game. And this sense of solidarity with his own also became very much part of the kid's consciousness.

His father's, too. For it was around this time, in the mid-thirties, that Big Bill Young at last found a purpose in life. He joined the Communist Party and began to proselytise with all the fervour of a religious convert. The upstairs bedroom became filled with political magazines predicting the imminent triumph of socialism. Big Bill started taking his son to evening meetings at the Left Wing Bookshop in Pyrmont, which he helped outfit, and where he listened to many speeches denouncing the capitalist system and praising the virtues of the proletarian revolution in the Soviet Union. So far as the kid was concerned, they had to be endured for the spaghetti supper that followed.

And certainly, when one looked at the human suffering caused by the collapse of credit, the country in thrall to foreign banks, and the government's policy of economic contraction, it must have seemed the class struggle was entering its final stages. Nor was Bill Young alone in his radicalisation. The Communist Party itself was only very small. But the Unemployed Workers' Union, which it backed, claimed 68 000 members by 1934 and was at the forefront of many a militant demonstration: the hunger marches from the New South Wales coalfields; the strikes in Victoria to increase 'Work for the Dole' payments; and the anti-eviction battles in Sydney. At Newtown in 1931, 40 police armed with truncheons and revolvers fought it out with 18 Communists in a house barricaded by sandbags and barbed wire. They were watched by a crowd numbering thousands whose hostility to the coppers, the *Sydney Morning Herald* reported, threatened to become out of hand.

It was one of many such conflicts in those years. And the Communist struggle was not just against the police and landlords – but also with rival factions, the militantly right wing New Guard, and opponents within the Trades Hall and the governing Australian Labor Party (at least until Premier Jack Lang was dismissed from office for withholding certain loan interest repayments).

In all of this, Big Bill Young's reputation as a bruiser stood him in good stead. The man was still very handy with his fists.

'You've heard of the upper cut?' he said to one bloke after he'd floored him with a double whammy to the guts. 'Well, that was the short cut!'

With Bill in attendance, Communist Party meetings were generally free of too much disruption by the New Guard, whose uniformed members modelled themselves on those fascist organisations – the Brown Shirts, the Black Shirts – spreading out of Europe like an infection borne by the Depression.

Bill Young had another reason for those evenings at the Left Wing Bookshop. He'd met a woman there: Marie Barker, younger than himself, with a melodic laugh. Marie was well educated, for her father had been a headmaster, and she worked as a secretary in town. She also shared Bill's political opinions with similar intensity, and the two were attracted. They even took young Keith out with them from time to time, the kid bored to sobs in a dreary hall, as another edifying drama of class warfare was acted out upon the stage. One, he remembered, involved a lot of dead soldiers who refused to lie down and stop talking! Bill and Marie, of course, were enraptured.

Yet, while he frequently visited Marie at her house up the hill in Glebe, Big Bill rarely took her to Ma and Pop Jepson's place. Those two parts of his life he kept quite separate. This seemed more a matter of romantic choice than shame, because Bulwara Road gave a man of his sympathy and commitment much fertile ground for social action. Indeed, the spectre of eviction came very close to home.

The kid returned from school one day to find that several families had been forced out of their houses just along the street. There'd been threats and fears that this would happen, but nobody quite believed it because the Church owned these houses. Yet here they were – men and women Keithy knew, the kids that he played with, their aunts, uncles and even grandmothers – put out on the street with nowhere else to go.

It was Big Bill Young who met their immediate needs. He obtained a tent and pitched it on the vacant land next to the White Rose Flour Mill. The people at least had a shelter for the night, somewhere to put their bedding and sticks of furniture. Naturally the police arrived and tried to move them on. But Dad had enough physical presence and sufficient gift of the gab to convince the cops to let the families stay for a little. Besides, a large crowd of neighbours had gathered in support, and the police no doubt wanted to avoid a repetition of the Newtown scenes.

Dad's powers of persuasion had other benefits. He'd made Keith a small billycart – not much more than a banana box on wheels – to which the man attached handles, and he took it around the shops seeking donations of food and other necessities for the homeless.

'Come along, comrade,' he'd say to the butcher, 'you can spare a bit of meat and a few soup bones for the evicted people...' And to the baker, 'Those stale loaves of bread would feed a few hungry mouths, mate.'

Big Bill was rarely refused. There was fruit and veg from the Jepsons, and whatever others could spare. Food was cooked over fires on the vacant land, which also gave warmth and a little companionship for the few days the evicted ones were allowed to remain in Bulwara Road.

They went eventually: some into temporary accommodation found by the Salvation Army and welfare organisations; others into camps for the unemployed; and a few men went bush, out on the wallaby track, as they said, looking for casual work. It was the nature of the Depression that many families were split altogether. Even the Jepsons had to move again – to an even smaller, smellier place in Bulwara Lane, opposite a tannery. But at least the household was intact.

Some were driven to more desperate measures. Ma's superstitious circus friend, Millie the bareback rider, came crying one day that she couldn't continue – and was going to cut her throat with a razor.

'Not on my clean kitchen floor, you're not!'

So Millie went into the backyard and did it there. Or at least made an attempt, starting from well behind the ear. She hadn't got far before Pop Jepson ran out and stopped her. Perhaps it was just another performance – a plea for help by a woman who no longer seemed to have any role in life. But there was plenty of blood. They took Millie away in the ambulance.

The ambulance came again a few doors up when a despairing housewife drank from a bottle of Lysol and was discovered choking in the laundry. While they saved her life, she never afterwards spoke in more than a rasping whisper.

More lethal was a police raid on the tenement house next door. Such things were not uncommon. They even raided Ma's place during one of the Red scares, seizing a bundle of Big Bill's Communist Party magazines from the bedroom and a number of the political comics he'd given to Keithy – though the boy had never found them particularly readable. On this occasion, though, the police had a tip-off about a counterfeiting machine next door that was making lead two-shilling pieces, like the duddie passed in the market. As the coppers burst in the front door, the machine was hurled over the back fence into the Jepson's yard. And in all the confusion, one of the lads jumped off the front balcony, impaling himself on the iron railings below.

The kid could still see his corpse slumped across the fence, its spearheads as deadly as the rails of a cemetery gate behind which, in memory, his mother lay. He could never visualise her, yet the look of surprise and incomprehension on the lad's face stayed in his mind. It wasn't at all like that undertaker's false smile on old Uncle Sam, laid out on the dining table.

Since then, Billy had become all too familiar with death. It seized men suddenly on the battlefield or crept wretchedly by degrees upon the sick at Sandakan and the starving at Outram Road. The kid was still young enough to believe death wouldn't reach him. Not yet, anyway – even if he also knew it sometimes arrived deliberately, as an agent of human vengeance.

One evening when Pen Dean came with the *meshi toban* to deliver the meal, he whispered through the food slot a message too important to be left to the garbled conversation of the prison walls.

'Bad news. They're going to execute Eric Hatfield...Sergeant Hatfield.'

'When?'

'Don't know. Soon. He's for the chop.'

The boy sat digesting the news, like his rice, with a sense of both sadness and detachment. He thought of the five local men convicted at his own trial, and of the courage they'd shown knowing that they were to be beheaded immediately they left the courtroom. Was Sergeant Hatfield, Billy wondered, able to be as brave as them, in his lonely cell down the row from Billy's own?

He grieved for the man. Yet he couldn't help feeling relief that it wasn't himself. For Eric Hatfield was also an escaped prisoner of war. Billy had seen him occasionally at the scabby bath, although he didn't really know him. The time outside was so brief and precious, you kept to your own cobbers. But he'd picked up enough jail gossip to know that he might so easily have shared Hatfield's fate.

Eric Edward Hatfield was with the 2/30th Battalion. Sydney-born, unmarried, and at 42 rather older than the others, he'd been a journalist when war broke out. A literary man and a good soldier, Eric Hatfield had fought in Malaya, was wounded in Singapore, and was said to have been promoted to sergeant in the field for his qualities of leadership. He was certainly always called Sergeant Hatfield at Outram Road, out of respect and admiration.

Hatfield became a POW when the island fell – but escaped from Changi with two mates late in 1942. They were hiding out in jungle on Singapore, when news of them reached Sergeant Peter Picozzi, of the Royal Corps of Signals, fighting with a band of Chinese guerrillas in southern Malaya. He crossed to the island, contacted Hatfield's party, and took them back to his camp.

For the next five months Eric Hatfield joined their irregular operations, colourfully dressed in blue Chinese three-quarter-length trousers, a Japanese shirt, with a bandana around his head, like one of the brigands from Billy's *Champion Annual*. He wore a knife in his belt and carried a revolver and Tommy gun as they raided Japanese installations, gathering much intelligence on enemy troops and airfields. Without communications, however, they were unable to pass it on.

In May 1943, Hatfield tried to escape by sea with his information; but he was betrayed. The Japanese seized the boat, and arrested Hatfield, Picozzi and two others. They were taken to Kenpeitai headquarters. Tortured. Sent to Outram Road. And on 30 November tried for armed escape, espionage and sabotage – on which charges the rather full diary kept by Eric Hatfield, the journalist, provided ample evidence.

Now, with he and Picozzi sentenced to death, their fellow

prisoners at Outram Road waited to know if it had been carried out. In Sergeant Hatfield's case the news came quickly enough. On 6 December, only a few days after Pen Dean whispered his message, word was tapped through the walls that Eric Hatfield had been taken to an open pit behind the jail, and beheaded. Indeed, it was said that the guard who'd done the deed returned to Picozzi's cell to inform him that he would be next – though as the senior man, Hatfield alone was executed.

Anger at the barbarous nature of Hatfield's death. Gratitude for their own deliverance. Such emotions fed the inmates in their solitary cells that day. For Pen Dean, it was even more personal. He'd been with Eric Hatfield just before he was led away, and carried messages for his family.

Told that he was about to die, the doomed man asked to see a priest. This was refused, but the Kenpeitai did allow their trustie, Dean, to spend 15 minutes with him. However distressed they were, both bore up manfully. Eric Hatfield spoke a little of his life at home, and in particular said he wanted to make a new will. There was no ink or paper; but Dean promised that if he survived the war he would swear an affidavit testifying to Hatfield's last wishes. There was little else he could do.

'I felt utterly useless,' Pen said afterwards, 'but I think it gave him some comfort to know that a fellow Australian knew exactly what happened to him.'

He spent much time that night praying for Eric Hatfield, hoping that those responsible would pay for the death of a man who had done what all good soldiers were expected to do: what John McGregor and Dean himself had done, no less. To be sure, Sergeant Hatfield was armed when they caught him.

'But he was a brave man, who died bravely on his own.'

Billy the Kid soon discovered just how courageous Hatfield had been.

Not long after his execution, the prisoners were moved to different cells. The Kenpeitai did this randomly every four or five weeks, as Kenny Bird had warned. The walls usually conveyed a hurried alert, however; and while Billy didn't understand the words, he was smart enough to know that something was up. Wise enough to smuggle out his pencil and bit of wire in his fist again, when the guard arrived.

This time he was placed in the cell that had been occupied by Eric Hatfield. It was the same as every other cell: cramped and sunless, the rotted plaster scratched with calendars and forlorn messages from prisoners over the many years. What made this chamber so memorable was the fact that Sergeant Hatfield had used his remaining time to engrave two poems of hope and consolation on the walls. They were not his own, but had obviously meant a great deal to him.

> Not understood, we move along asunder,
> Our paths grow wider as the seasons creep
> Along the years; we marvel and we wonder
> Why life is life, and then we fall asleep
> Not understood.

There was more than just this one verse evoking the human tragedy. The whole poem was written out – or had been, until lumps of plaster broke off and the work fragmented. Yet enough lines survived to incise themselves into the kid's mind. Sergeant Hatfield had scratched the second poem onto a more stable section of wall beside the black studded door.

> When you're lost in the Wild, and you're scared as a child,
> And Death looks you bang in the eye...

For three long verses it went, as high as the man could reach.

> Just have one more try – it's dead easy to die,
> It's the keeping-on-living that's hard.

Below it he'd written his rank and name: E. E. HATFIELD. And sitting cross-legged on the floor day after day, facing the poem, Billy the Kid memorised these lines until they became a very part of him. They seemed more than just an epitaph written by a gallant man to maintain his spirit in the presence of imminent death: a death that he could face with dignity and honour. The words also spoke from the walls to the living – like an order from the sergeant to the men who came after him, to keep up their morale and their sense of human worth, however bestial the circumstances in which they found themselves. Words that did not have to be rapped out on stones, and from which everyone could take their own meaning.

Thus, among the faces that entered Billy's cell during the lonely hours came the image of an old lady in black, carrying a book as a gift for him. The boy never knew her name, yet it was the most important present he ever received. For it was she who'd first shown him the power of words to touch his inner life, as music did; how they could move him as profoundly as the poems carved by Sergeant Hatfield on the wall.

Each Saturday morning Stiffie Jepson took his fruit barrow into the nearby suburb where he had a regular stand by the footpath. It was young Keithy's job to wait with the fruit boxes in a side lane, looking after the full ones and stacking the empties. Not hard work – but tedious, when he'd rather be off playing.

One particular Saturday, this old lady was returning up the lane to her back gate, a floppy hat on her head and carrying a bag of fruit, when she stopped by the boy.

'Would you like a glass of lemonade, sonny?'

'My word!'

She went indoors and returned with the drink and a slice of Madeira cake. Buttered! She also had an English *Triumph* story magazine for boys, with a picture on the cover of an airman in his little biplane chasing some rotten crook.

'You can have this,' she said. 'It was my son's. But he's grown up now, and gone away.'

Every Saturday after that she would come out of her gate bringing Keith something to eat and drink, and a story paper to nourish his mind. Sometimes *Triumph*. Sometimes the *Champion*. Sometimes both together. And sometimes, near Christmas, one of the bumper *Annuals*, filled with stories of adventure from the war, cops and robbers, cowboys and Indians, heroes of the sporting field and racing cars.

Here at last was something worth reading! Away from the strictures of the schoolteacher's cane or his father's political tracts, the boy discovered a love of words and of story that remained with him.

By that time they'd moved with Ma and Pop into the down-at-heel little house in Bulwara Lane, near the tannery and tallow works. So cramped that, at the age of 11, Keith was sleeping on the upstairs front verandah. It was rather cool in winter with only a canvas blind to protect him from the weather. But it had one advantage: right by the kid's cast-iron balcony was the only electric light in the street. And every night it illuminated his reading.

'Keith!' Ma calling to him from downstairs. 'Are you in bed?'

'Yes, Ma.'

When in fact the canvas blind was pulled up, and by the light of the street lamp the boy was absorbed in tales of G-Man Gregg, Rusty Coles the daredevil ace, Fats Worby and his school chums, or Running Fox's last fight. Stories from the British Empire: of Dr Livingstone, and Captain Cook who'd sailed into Botany Bay.

Useful articles in *Champion* on how to wind wireless coils (if you had a wireless) and repairing and maintaining your bicycle (if you had a bike). Advice on how to perform magic tricks, like the disappearing coin or the changing ace of spades, which Keith would practise on Ma as she sat playing cards at the kitchen table.

Even the weekly visits to the Left Wing Bookshop became a good deal more interesting. For as Dad and Marie sat voting on resolutions to condemn the seizure of Abyssinia in early 1936 by the Italian dictator Mussolini, the kid was lost among the bookshelves. Finding his first novels. Discovering the power of even better words in the pages of *Treasure Island* and *Forty Thousand Leagues Under the Sea*, which they'd sometimes allow him to borrow and take home, to read under the street lamp.

Words had the ability, of course, not only to light the inner self, but also to stir the outside world into action. Big Bill Young the radical knew all about that. Returning one late winter evening, Keith noticed his father was carrying a paint pot and a bundle of sticks.

'What are they for, Dad?'

'You'll see, son.'

They were crossing the bridge into Ultimo near the Powerhouse in Harris Street, when Bill suddenly stepped into one of the pedestrian bays. He tied the sticks together to make a long pole with a paintbrush at the end and, leaning over the bridge, began to paint a slogan onto the Powerhouse wall: HANDS OFF ABYSSINIA.

Only three words, but a lot of letters. And the kid was freezing. He had no coat and his clothes were threadbare. Even his shoes were worn through, for Dad had bought them second-hand at Paddy's Market – had tossed for them, in fact, and lost.

'Hurry up, Dad. I'm hungry.'

'Wait a bit, boy. And watch out for the cops. I've got to do this properly.'

And he did, too. The sign stayed there for years – though Abyssinia was soon forgotten, the cause swallowed up by other events and more urgent calls to arms.

In July that year, the violence, anticlericalism and social upheaval in Republican Spain erupted into civil war when the military under General Franco rebelled and attempted to seize power. Socialists around the world mobilised support for the leftist Republicans, largely through the International Brigades organised by the Communist Party, for the Soviet Union solidly backed them and was sending material aid to the retreating Spanish government.

THEY SHALL NOT PASS. Another sign painted by Big Bill Young, this time on the road near the dog track at Wentworth Park, warning against fascist Fifth Column collaborators. While Britain, France and Australia applied policies of non-intervention and an arms embargo, this only assisted the Nationalist rebel Generals: the more so when Mussolini and the Nazi dictator Adolf Hitler sent thousands of troops to fight with them. Indeed, when the German *Luftwaffe* bombed Spanish towns like Guernica in April 1937, it seemed to many that another world war was in the making – and the ranks of the International Brigades began to swell.

It's been estimated that some 30 000 individual men and women from foreign countries went to help the Republican cause as soldiers, nurses and relief workers. Perhaps 50 or 60 of them came from Australia – of whom one was Big Bill Young. Quite unknown to his son, arrangements were being made that autumn through the Party for him to stow away on a ship bound for England, and from there to contact the underground network smuggling volunteers into Spain.

For a man who, at 15, had boarded a troopship for Gallipoli, it was perhaps the fulfillment of a youthful ambition to sail off to war. Yet there remained the question of what to do with young Keith? Big Bill wouldn't be earning any wages to continue paying rent to the Jepsons, and it was unlikely the boy would stay with Marie. She and Bill planned to marry, but decided to postpone the wedding until after he returned from Spain. In retrospect it was a mistake, but at the time it seemed the sensible thing to do. He therefore turned to his family in Hobart, with whom he'd had little contact since the unhappy visit home with Adora at the time Keith was born.

His mother, The Admiral – Nana Tot – came up to Sydney. If she could no longer march her son off the troopship, she could at least salvage her grandson. She stayed with her daughter, Aunt Ilma, at Waverley; and with Big Bill in attendance they fitted the boy out for his journey with her back to Tasmania.

They bought him a new overcoat, the first he ever had, and a new suit to go with it. A suit with short pants.

'But, Dad, I want long trousers. I'm big enough.'

'You're a big enough larrikin.'

'Dad...'

'Keith, you're only 11. Wait till you grow up a bit more. Then I'll get you long trousers.'

There were new shoes and socks, and a shirt as well. It was not until the day before Keith and Nana Tot were due to sail for Hobart that they told him Dad was also going on a sea voyage. To Spain, to fight the fascists.

'How long are you going for?' he asked.

'I'm not sure, boy. You can't always tell with wars. But it won't be too long before I'm home and married to Marie, and you can come and live with us.'

'Yeah.'

'You'll like Hobart with Nana and Uncle Cocky, Uncle Doug and your aunties. Look at it as a long holiday.'

And certainly it was with a sense of anticipation that the kid went aboard the passenger ship *Zealandia* and waved his farewells to Dad and Marie on the wharf at Pyrmont. The two of them stood together, growing smaller and fainter as if disappearing down a telescope while the ship pulled away, until the boy could no longer distinguish them at all.

Under the Bridge they went, and down the Harbour, and then at last they were through the Heads into the open sea. Salt wind flicked his face and the waves rolled across the ocean to bear him afloat on the promise of a world beyond. The tides carried him onward, and the gulls sang of unknown possibilities.

Very early next morning, with The Admiral still asleep on her lower bunk, the boy got up, dressed in his new suit and overcoat, and went on deck. There he watched dawn break over the coastline of New South Wales: light touching the horizon, and the highest clouds tipped with grey. Here and there on the darkened land Keithy could see the glimmer of fireflies as farmhouse lamps were lit and life awakened to a new day. And he stood, hands in pockets, opening himself to the beauty and the wonder of it all as he'd never known before.

Down in the docklands, his father was hiding himself in the coal bunker of a European cargo ship – from which he would emerge like a blackened apparition during the voyage, to the crew's astonishment...

While on the walls of a prison cell in Outram Road, those lines scratched by another soldier under sentence, were singing their lament:

> And thus men rise and fall, and live and die
> Not understood.

# 5
# STRANDS OF HEMP

*When you haven't anything at all*
*Anything at all will do.*

Not long after Sergeant Hatfield's death, rumours seeped through the prison that better times were coming. Tapped in soft staccato on stone, whispered through door slots or at the scabby bath came a simple message: 'The Japs are sending us to work.'

Simple – yet carrying all kinds of aspirations. For work meant liberation from those numbing hours of solitude, cross-legged on a concrete floor. Release for stultifying minds. An opportunity for men to express themselves by doing something useful, albeit for an enemy. Billy the Kid was buoyed by the hope it might even lead to an increase in his food ration. And into his imagination came visions of steaming rice bowls topped with meat and vegetables, running with spicy Singapore sauce.

As it turned out, the rumours were half right. By early 1944 the tides of war had turned against the Japanese in the Pacific and their fleet was increasingly putting in for repair at the old Empire Dock down the hill from Outram Road. In particular, a new hawser was needed for the largest battleships; and with 80 POWs in their custody, the Kenpeitai had just the labour force to make it.

'*Koi!*'

The cell door opened late one morning. A guard motioned Billy to his feet and into the corridor to join his companions. Where, after the customary greetings and shouts for silence, the men were marched outside, past the hipbath and into a yard that ran behind the three cell blocks at the rear of the prison. The other side of the yard was enclosed by a retaining wall and terrace cut into the hill, on which the British had dug air-raid shelters and planted pawpaw trees. Beyond that was the stepped outer wall of the jail itself, topped with broken glass and barbed wire.

On arrival at their workplace, the men were marshalled into four lines as if on a parade ground. Upon the command '*Suware!*' they sat down. Cross-legged. On hard concrete again. With the sun beating down for additional discomfort.

Once they were settled, a Kenpeitai officer arrived in full uniform, who watched as a subordinate addressed them in rapid Japanese.

'What's he saying?' the kid muttered to Brownie.

'Something about the honour of the Emperor...we're to make him a rope.'

'To hang himself?'

A snort.

'*Damare!*' Shut up! From the guard.

'How are we gunna make a rope?'

'He's showing you,' Brownie replied as the instructor reached into a sack and pulled out a wad of hemp, tangled as any fishing line. With all the concentration of an angler, he picked away at the skein until he held up one strand between thumb and forefinger.

'*Ah, so!*'

It was about two-foot long, the size of a bit of fine wire: the first thread of untold thousands the men would unscramble over coming weeks. Next step, he produced from his pocket a bunch of 20 such strands, thick as a pencil, bound at the top with yet another length of hemp. This, too, was held up for inspection. Satisfied that the men understood what was expected of them, he laid it on the ground.

'Now what?' the kid wanted to know.

'*Bakayarou!*' (*Bugger you too!*) He got a jab in the back for his trouble.

The question had been anticipated. For the sergeant pointed to a rope-making machine near the retaining wall and explained how it worked. None of the prisoners understood his precise words, but the principle was clear enough. One part consisted of a handle and turning mechanism; the other of the spindles on which the threads would be spun into string – the string into cords – the cords extending into rope – and the rope into a cable the thickness of these emaciated men who were to make it.

With some final words concerning the glory of Nippon, the officer departed, leaving them to it. A couple of Indian trusties began dragging the sack along the ranks, from which each man pulled a handful of scrambled hemp.

'Looks easy enough,' Billy murmured.

Yet he quickly discovered the work wasn't as simple as it looked. Equatorial heat turned the yard quite literally into a sweatshop. Perspiration dripped into his eyes and oozed from his slippy hands, making it hard to concentrate and pick the bloody threads. Billy thought he'd become used to working in the sun at Sandakan. But after months of incarceration, his tongue turned to salt every time he licked his lips – with nothing much to drink and only his filthy shirt to wipe himself.

Besides, the boy's fingers were not as nimble as they used to be; nobody's were. With scabies, filth and malnutrition came more disease. Pellagra, for instance: red rash flaring and itching in the sunlight; inflaming the mucous in eyes and mouths; bringing more diarrhoea and secondary infections.

Every morning when Billy woke, his hands were stiff and swollen with eruptions of pus. The rims of his palms and fingers became covered during the night with small, hard pimples – so sore he could barely flex his hands. Billy's first job – even before pissing in the *benki* bucket – was to manipulate his precious bit of wire, and prick these little boils until the pus ran and his mitts became more pliable.

They lost much of their dexterity, all the same. Scabby fingers with broken nails fumbled in the knotted twine, and it needed all Billy's attention to separate the strands. If he sought escape in the web of memory, or by trying to recall the words of that Hoagy Carmichael song *Lazy Bones*, he'd lose the thread altogether.

A snarl brought him back to the present. And there was no end to it. With one swatch of strands tied and laid on the ground, the kid started on the next: teasing fibres from that blasted ball of hemp that never seemed to diminish. No opportunity for dawdling, either. The guard counting the bundles in front of each man, ready for collection by the rope makers, could easily see if he was keeping pace with the others.

Whump! A scabbard laid across his shoulderblades.

'*Kora!*' Get on with it!

'I'da been better off stayin' in me cell.'

Yet as Billy formed the words, he knew they were nonsense. Anything was better than that. Here, he was occupied in the company of old mates – whose shared contempt for the Japs he could read in their hunched bodies and the language of lidded eyes. He could see the sun and the sky. Watch the afternoon shade creep across the yard. Hear thunder as monsoon clouds gathered. Feel rain washing his skin and matted hair in the first showers before the deluge drove them inside.

In such ways the promises of work were fulfilled. Hopes that it would also lead to better food, however, were not. The same miserable portions of rice slops remained. And yet for those, like Billy the Kid, willing to seize any break, rope making offered a chance to supplement their diets wonderfully.

A *benki* bucket stood out front. If you needed to piss (or the excuse for a stretch), the ritual was always the same. Stand. And call your number.

'*Go-hyaku-ju.*' Followed by a bow, in which the nose always touched an upturned thumb, as Ken Bird had shown. When the guard grunted permission, you made your request. '*Shoben.*' Same when you finished. Number. Bow. '*Shoben owarimashita.*' 'I've finished my piss.' – although it came out sounding like 'You're a whoring bastard.' Funny that. Morale soared even higher when the guard agreed. '*Yoshi.*' You could sit down with a sense of real achievement.

With so many people using it, the *benki* was constantly having to be emptied down a covered drain around the corner. Even so, the bucket began to stink so badly that the guard eventually ordered Billy and Alan Minty to move it further away. And they knew exactly where to put it.

Well to the rear of the rope makers, the Japanese had built a pig pen near the middle cell block – the death house, where prisoners awaiting execution were held in barred cells like animal cages. It was an appropriate place for a sty, because the pigs were also marked for the chop – though their meat was destined not for the prisoners but the Kenpeitai. Indeed, the porkers were always much better fed than the human captives. All the scrapings, peelings and leftovers from the kitchens were emptied into their trough, and the animals grew sleek and fat.

It was to the pig pen, then, that Billy and Alan Minty took the *benki* bucket, placing it carefully. And they were soon making hogs of themselves. Skinny arms reaching between the wooden rails. Rummaging among the swill. Grabbing a fistful of dirty rice. Sweet potato scraps. Shoving these delicacies into their mouths, and fighting off the protesting swine. Why, the kid even found a half-eaten cabbage leaf.

'Jeez, that were good!' he proclaimed – once he'd wiped the pig mud off it. Certainly better than any feast conjured up in his cell. Alan didn't argue – and the pair returned with self-satisfied grins on their faces.

News of their banquet quickly spread, and before long most of the workforce was seized with a need to go to the lavatory. Rise. Number. Bow. '*Benki.*' And with all middle-class inhibitions shed, they scrounged in the pigsty for whatever gleanings might have been missed. Fruit peel. Fish heads. A chewed shred of bacon rind from some previous occupant of the sty...

Early afternoon was always the best time to forage, because the kitchen trusties filled the trough with lunchtime leftovers: not just the rice fed to the prisoners, but also the meat and vegetables served to the Kenpeitai. It was then that bladders became especially weak, and a procession formed to the *benki*. The ruse worked well for a while, provided men used a bit of common sense. Didn't rush the bucket all at once. Allowed decent intervals between visits so as not to draw the guards' attention.

Yet there is always someone able to spoil a good lurk by trying to take the lot.

There came a day when Billy slipped his hand between the rails and felt about in the trough for something to eat. There wasn't much left and he was about to give it up as a bad job when he touched something long and soft. A bit of sausage? He tried to pull his treat through the rail, but nothing happened. The boy gave another tug. Still nothing. He could even feel the delicacy resisting. It wasn't a pig because he couldn't hear any grunting. One more sharp pull. The sausage jerked itself out of his fingers. There was a scrambling. And above the enclosure rose the scrawny figure of an English gentleman, covered in muck and roaring at him.

'How dare you pull my nose! Scoundrel! What d'you think you're doing?'

The kid could only look with astonishment and say, 'Jesus!'

It wasn't Jesus, although the man had been venerated in his previous life as a colonial administrator. He'd probably confirmed the sentences of those condemned to Outram Road: been the sort of authority figure that lesser folk like Billy spent their lives circumventing. Now, reduced to the same level as every other prisoner, he'd no idea how to break the rules. As the Japanese guards ran towards them, carrying echoes of laughter from the rope makers, he realised his folly.

'I'm sorry...I forgot...' Full of confusion, the gent began to clamber out of the sty. 'I was so hungry...I couldn't help myself...'

'You made a meal of it, mate. And now look what you done. You've given the whole game away!'

And he was right. The guard ordered Billy to move the bucket well away from the pigsty and all chance of a hasty snack via the *benki* came to an end.

Yet hope was not a commodity that Billy ever ran out of. Others might find it in short supply: never the kid. It was the lesson taught by Pop Jepson and the market people. When the door of one selling opportunity slams in your face, you look around to open another, as with the Easter fish. He was always alert to scrounge anything that might come in useful. A few strands of hemp were smuggled back to his cell and hidden among his treasures. And while he couldn't feed with the pigs any more, lunch gave Billy a chance to capitalise on the best stroke of fortune that was to fall his way.

To save time, the midday meal was served at trestle tables in the main corridor of the cell block – Broadway, as the kid called it. There wasn't any extra tucker, but it always gave another opportunity for human contact and furtive conversation. The guards may have enforced the rule of silence, but lunchtime still buzzed with whispered exchanges and messages passed by tapping fingers. Just like the scabby wash.

The Japs had persisted with the bath long after it became obvious it wasn't helping to eradicate the scabies. It was a question of face: of not wanting to admit they didn't know what else to do about the disease. Every week or two, therefore, the prisoners had to repeat the grotesque performance at the hipbath.

Billy was sitting in the disso one afternoon, the guard known as Fatgut beside him writing in a small notebook, when there was a stir at the gate. Down the steps came a Kenpeitai officer, brisk in his colour patches. Afraid of punishment were he to be caught writing on duty, Fatgut hurriedly tossed his notebook behind the bath.

The lieutenant might not have seen it – but Billy did. An ordinary, plain notebook between cheap cardboard covers, here transformed into treasure-trove. As he leaned over the hipbath, the kid saw that the notebook had fallen with the pages open. Better still, some of the glue had come unstuck and a few sheets were loose.

'By golly, I'm gunna have a bit of that.'

He rubbed his hands through his hair to dry them and waited for the lieutenant to approach Fatgut with his orders. Their attention engaged, Billy got out of the bath on the wrong side. He bent down and tore three pages from the notebook. Still stooping, he rolled the paper like a fag to hide snugly in his fist. Stood. And with heart pealing like a church bell, Billy strode back to his place and put on his clothes.

'What's up?' murmured Brownie, for the kid couldn't entirely keep the grin off his face. 'You look like the cat that got the cream.'

'I did,' he replied. 'Ali bloody Baba. Ya wouldn't believe it!'

Even back in his cell, it took some time for the boy to realise the magnitude of his riches. Open Sesame, indeed. There was the pencil stub he'd had from the beginning. And now, he had paper. Two small things that, together, were of more value to him here than 40 sacks of thieves' gold.

The first thing to decide was where to hide the precious sheets. It was no good secreting them in the wall crevices, for the lime wash was damp and mouldy and the paper would quickly disintegrate. Where then?

On either side of the shallow window recess was a narrow air vent let into the inner wall with a bar through it. Originally these vents extended like slits a couple of feet from the floor, to allow a faint cross-current of air. But the Kenpeitai considered this too generous and they'd had all but the top few inches cemented up.

Still, it meant there was now a gap behind the cement – well ventilated and secured with an iron bar. A bar to which, secretly in the night, a strand of hemp could be tied at the top – its bottom weighted with a pencil and three sheets of rolled paper. The tell-tale hemp Billy hid under bits of dank wall plaster, soft as putty and pressed into the cement. And it would be a bloody good guard who ever found it!

Safely hidden, the next question was how best to use his find? One thing was for sure: pencil and paper gave their possessor a voice that could help him communicate with others. Thus, one lunch break, Billy got himself a seat next to Chris Neilson, a 30-year-old Queenslander and brilliant signaller, who could convey whole sentences merely by fluttering his eyelids to a mate. He'd already taught Morse to Pen Dean's mate John McGregor, and also to Herb Trackson, who'd escaped from Sandakan in the early days. He knew Billy Young was no great talent. And finding the kid beside him, Chris was forced to whisper, 'What do you want?'

'Can you do us a favour?'

'Keep your flaming voice down.'

Billy began to cough. Loudly. As if he were choking. It was a trick learned at Sandakan. You could say much between splutters.

'Will ya write out the Morse for me?' His coughing fit became more violent and Chris started thumping his back.

'With what?'

'I got a bit of paper.'

'And pencil?'

'Yeah.'

Neilson was impressed. 'Well done! All right.'

'I'll bring 'em tomorrer.' Billy's choking as quickly subsided.

That night, when all was still, he reeled in his line from the vent. With the catch safely landed, the boy hid his pencil and paper under the blanket away from the sight of any peephole guard. Then he carefully folded one page. Rubbed the crease with his thumb to weaken it. And gingerly tore the sheet in half. Two-and-a-half pages were rolled up again, tied and dropped back into the vent. The remaining half sheet and pencil were kept under the blanket for Billy to smuggle out and palm across to Chris Neilson at the lunch table during another attack of coughing.

'And for Chrissake don't lose the pencil. It's all I got.'

'I'll have it for you in the morning.'

Chris was as good as his word. In two columns on one side of the paper, he carefully transcribed the code beginning with A *dot-dash* and ending with Z *dash-dash-dot-dot*, together with the numbers from 1 to 0. The other side he left blank for some future use. When the kid returned to his cell he had the key that opened the Sesame of language. All those messages conveyed by tappings and scratches, by dancing fingers and blinking eyes, could now be understood. And answered.

It took much time and practice, for Billy was like a child just learning to form his letters. In fact, the first thing he did was to copy the code onto the wall with his wire, as his teachers used to write the alphabet in chalk across the blackboard in school. And as he'd spent as much time wagging it as he had in class, the business of learning Morse was as painfully difficult.

*Scratch-tap-tap-tap tap-tap tap-scratch-tap-tap* . . . The messages would come rapping through the wall at night with barely a pause between words to distinguish them. Even with the code as a reference on the wall, it took the kid a desperately long time to decipher the letters, and he'd have to signal the sender to slow down.

His skill was limited not only by lack of speed, but also by his inability to spell properly. Some simple words were reduced to phonetic sounds. 'Are' became R. 'You' was just U. But with many other words, the kid was constantly thrown by the inconsistencies of English spelling. Words like *bough, tough, ought* and *dough* had similar letters but were pronounced quite differently. And other words that sounded the same, like *would* and *wood,* had different spellings. Even *bow* had two meanings, depending on how you said it.

Billy could recognise such things on the printed page. Those story magazines given by the old lady in black began a habit of reading that stayed with him – even though, when he graduated to books like *Oliver Twist*, the kid had skipped the more difficult passages. But words tapped singly through a wall were robbed of their context, and he was often left floundering.

Here they could not be evaded – and they added more delays to the business of deciphering individual letters and words, stringing them into a sentence and memorising it long enough to transmit to the feller in the next cell, or to compose his reply. Practice. Patience. Regret once again that he'd spent so much of his youth playing truant. And a wish he'd paid more attention to those trying to school him . . .

Of all Billy's teachers, the only one who made any real impression was Mr Leslie: the only one who'd been able to nurture an interest in history and geography from seeds sown by *Champion Annual*. But that was at Corrimal, near Wollongong, in his last year. He'd been the last in a succession of teachers at a succession of schools during the last, unhappy years of boyhood, before Billy turned 14 and legally departed forever.

As for the rest, the green shoots of his intellect were left to straggle as best they could. Even in Hobart, where Keithy spent nearly a year with Nana, his education didn't flourish. There was no escaping New Town School under The Admiral's commanding eye. But the lessons that stayed had more to do with social acceptance than learning.

Miss Elliot's class, for example, had a fancy-dress parade that Christmas. He could see the kids now: a pirate king... Cinderella...Keith wearing the cut-down racing silks of a trotting driver who'd married one of his relations. The boy, in his boots and colours, got a minor placing, and the glow of that remained. As did the unexpected pleasure of singing for the first time in a choir at the school concert.

Until then, he dismissed anyone who sang in public as a poofter, like that kid in long pants and make-up on the stage at St Barnabas's (though Keith never forgot it). In Hobart, the simple harmonies of *Log Cabin Lullaby*, taught by Miss Elliot, wove their way into the boy, and he responded with joy – as he would with the choir at Sandakan – finding beauty and recognition in the music making, so that he could hear their voices ringing still among the shades in his Outram Road cell.

In this it reflected his broader experience of Hobart – at least to begin with. It was a time when Keith was getting to know that family of whom he'd heard from Dad, but had never met. The only relations he knew were Aunt Ilma, Uncle Vince and cousin

Wilhelmina in Sydney, with whom he sometimes went to the pictures. Now there was Aunt Ada and Aunt Elsie, his cousin Irene, Uncle Doug and Uncle Harold – a builder and carpenter known as 'Cocky', who still lived at home with Nana Tot and to whom the kid felt especially close.

Harold had stayed with Dad in Sydney during those early years at the Redfern billiard parlour and the SP bookie's, and Keith would press Uncle Cock for stories – of skinning rich toffs for a quid or two in hard times.

'Bill was always up to some con or other. But he was my big brother and could do no wrong in my eyes. Well…I knew it was wrong, but I didn't mind.'

Then the boy became all serious. Whatever Uncle Cocky said, Keithy knew that Nana Tot and the rest of the family would not approve. They'd purse their lips and call it disgraceful; and the kid would immediately feel defensive.

It was the same when Dad's occasional letters arrived from overseas, saying that he'd reached England…and then Spain. He'd make brief inquiries about the family's health – hoping Keith was being a good boy and doing what Nana told him. But then he'd launch into paragraphs of political argument about the world's Big Issues, as if he were addressing the mob from his box in the Domain: *The men of the International Brigade…have only one desire and that is to stop here and assist to drive out these barbaric fascist sadists…*

Until Nana and the family would roll their eyes and laugh at his obsessions. Which only made the kid feel more protective. Even more so when their laughter turned to criticism and he'd overhear them wondering when Big Bill would turn from the Big Issues to such minor matters as looking after his son.

Keith wondered that too. Privately. Not in so many words, but in a growing resentment at anyone trying to take Dad's place. The boy missed his father dreadfully. He was the only person he'd ever known how to love – the only authority he'd ever recognised. And here was Dad on the other side of the world saving the people of Spain! To be sure, Keithy submitted to The Admiral's discipline – but only because he had to. Even then he came close to mutiny when Nana wouldn't let him train for the football team after school because he had to help with the chores.

'But, Nana . . . no! They won't let me play unless I go to training.'

'You'll do what you're told, young man. "No" is not a word I'm used to.'

It wasn't a word the kid was used to either, after the free and easy life at the Jepsons. Here in Hobart, resentment turned to anger – and thence to rejection as the boy tried to put a distance between himself and his family. Becoming an outsider, like his father. So that when Dad's fiancée, Marie Barker, came for a holiday that Easter of 1938, he was quite happy to return to Sydney with her.

At first he stayed with Marie at her flat in Glebe, off Purves Street. Purves Lane! What a name for a boy going through the embarrassments of puberty to say. No pervert he! She enrolled him at Glebe school; but as Marie wasn't married to Dad, in the boy's eyes she had less authority over him than Nana. Back in familiar haunts, just up the hill from Ultimo, Keithy reverted to familiar ways.

He played truant for days at a time: cadging down at the woolstores or, a favourite pastime, playing on the log rafts moored near the mill at Blackwattle Bay, unconcerned he might slip and drown. It reached the stage where he once spent nearly three continuous weeks wagging school. Even Keith became alarmed by that. He got the old bloke who ran a snack shop in Glebe Point Road to write a note for the teacher. *Keith has had mumps and the doctor kept him at home. Mr Young.*

It cost Keith a penny, which the boy thought far too cheap for taking such a risk. But a penny it was – which he earned by nicking empty beer bottles stacked in a hotel yard (slipping a noose of fishing line around their necks, like a strand of hemp, hauling them over the back fence and reselling them to the publican at his own front door). As for the real Mr Young, Big Bill was in Barcelona that July, getting ready to go to the front. He had time to write home and to enclose a page for his son: *We are camped out in the lovely Spanish hills among the grapevines and nut trees* ... A letter for his mother in Hobart where, among the politics, he expressed the fond hope: *Have you heard from Marie and Keith lately? I bet you have. Marie would see to that* ...

In truth, Marie could not see to much that the boy was doing. Working in the city all day, she had little control over Keith; and after talking to Party comrades and sympathisers, two local families agreed to share the burden of looking after him. Sometimes he'd stay with a Mr and Mrs Field. Sometimes with a young couple, Harry and Diana Gould, before going back to Marie for a bit.

It wasn't a very stable existence, but at least it kept Keith from falling under the malign influence of older boys who ran with the street gangs of the time. Indeed, Harry and Diana Gould were even able to exercise a little discipline over him, and made sure he attended Mr Crane's class at Glebe school. Both were intelligent and studious themselves, and expected it in others.

They'd not long been married. Harry was an earnest, Irish-born writer in Marxist theory, sometime journalist for the *Workers' Weekly*, and a lecturer with the Workers' Education Society at Sydney University. Diana was a tall, strikingly beautiful English-woman: an accomplished actress, equestrienne and elocutionist who'd come to Sydney as a speech teacher. Shocked by the Depression, she became radicalised, attended Harry Gould's courses, married him, and joined the Communist Party.

To their working-class comrades, Diana and Harry must have

seemed a pair of bourgeois intellectuals, yet their commitment was real and energetic. Diana was much involved with political theatre, putting on the sorts of propaganda plays to which Bill and Marie had taken young Keith. She was also active in the theatre of the streets – arrested and charged with obstruction in 1938 when she stood on a car in George Street to condemn the visit of a German Nazi.

In a world of upheaval, protest and social action seemed the public duty of anyone concerned with the Big Issues of the day. The sorts of issues with which Dad filled his letters. The absolute necessity to defeat the fascists in Spain. The support their own countries were giving murderous aggressors everywhere. *Look at the Lyons government of Australia forcing the waterside workers to load scrap iron for Japan to be made into bombs to slaughter Chinese women and children...*

To say nothing of the Munich Pact in September 1938, when the German-speaking Sudetenland of Czechoslovakia was ceded to Hitler, and Britain's Prime Minister Neville Chamberlain returned with his piece of paper saying he'd obtained 'peace for our time'. To most people, this appeared more a matter of hope than expectation. To the *Workers' Weekly*, it was one more act of fascist belligerence.

Such were the important issues that concerned the comrades looking after Keithy in Glebe – until a matter of more immediate concern thrust itself upon their attention, and the universal and the individual suddenly became one.

The boy was lying on his narrow bed reading at the Gould's flat one afternoon in early December, a month after his 13th birthday, when Diana came into the room and sat silently beside him.

'I've got something to tell you, Keith,' she said eventually, in a voice that was at once sorrowful and studied in the manner of an actress.

He put down his *Triumph*. 'What is it?'

'Your father...'

'Is he coming home?' Anticipation rising.

'No...he's not...It's very sad...' Diana fumbled, trying to find the right words. She was only 24, and had not played such a part before. 'The thing is, we believe...through the Party, we've heard that he's been killed in Spain.'

'When?' A blackness seemed to open in the boy, draining all thought and emotion, and he was left clinging to mere fact. 'How?'

'We don't know exactly. There was the battle at the Ebro River in August, not long after your father had gone to the front and it seems...' She paused and took his hand. 'We're all very sorry.'

He continued to stare at her, wondering what she expected him to do. Did she want him to cry? To throw himself into her arms, sobbing for Dad? Children in books might do such things, but Keith had never been one to show his feelings. Not in front of other people. Besides, his tears had gone as well. His face might have been flushed, but inside was cold and numb.

At last he turned to the wall. So it was true. Quite apart from his own letter, Keith had heard tidings of Dad in articles that Diana or Marie showed him from the *Workers' Weekly*. They featured Bill Young in the thick of the Ebro struggle saying, 'I got four fascist bastards today and I'll bump off a few more tonight.' Big Bill an expert at training with the grenade and rifle. A photo of him under the olive trees. Writing from Barcelona of even the little children raising clenched fists of resistance, and sending his greetings to Party general secretary J. B. Miles, and the comrades back home. One missive ended with an inquiry, too, after his young son, Keith.

Then appeared a brief paragraph in October, saying that no trace could be found of Bill Young or his mate Bill Morcom after the first few days on the Ebro. The last sighting of Dad had been of him filling his water bottle at an old well, tired out after attacking a hill with a machine gun. The International Brigade would keep trying to get information – but in his heart the boy had guessed at the truth. Now, Diana Gould was confirming it. And Keithy realised that he was indeed all alone, with everything that implied.

'He was a very brave man,' she said. 'A wonderful man, who gave his life in the cause of freedom and justice for the Spanish people.'

Yes, he thought. But he was also my father. And he was not here.

The *Workers' Weekly* paid glowing tribute the following week: TWO COMMUNISTS DIE FOR DEMOCRACY ran the headline. AUSTRALIA WILL NEVER FORGET.

*Big Bill Young. Cheeky, cheery Bill, strong enough to upset a couple of [New Guard] troupers at once…His last words when leaving were 'I hate fascism and am glad I'm going to fight it with weapons in hand.'* It was just the sort of thing Dad *would* say.

The following issue carried a reminiscence of Bill helping to set up the bookshop where they'd spent many an evening. In early February a memorial service was held at the Assembly Hall in the city for all the comrades who'd died in Spain, and Big Bill's son took his symbolic place on the stage. Shortly afterwards, the *Workers' Weekly* published a poetic salute to him by 'FR':

> We who are foreigners in our own land,
> We who are strangers to our toil,
> Glad did we spend our dust
> On Spanish soil.

His boy wasn't glad. Nor was Marie, when the tears came.

To their great credit, the comrades rallied to help Keith. A party was held for him on Christmas Eve in a dance hall above a garage in Glebe Point Road, and gifts were sent from supporters everywhere. Presents of clothing and woodwork tools, for he liked to make things. A watch from the District Committee. A ticket for a holiday at the Youth Colony camp in the Blue Mountains from Diana and Harry Gould, and a box of chocolates. Most importantly there was a bicycle, donated by the West Sydney section of the Communist Party – which Diana and Marie made him wheel home, until he'd learned to ride it properly.

The kid made a little speech of thanks from the platform. According to the *Workers' Weekly*, Keith said he would endeavour to grow up like his father – a good Communist and fighter for better conditions for the working class. But those words were suggested by Diana and Marie – telling the comrades what they'd like to hear. His real thoughts were on the cakes and trifles waiting to be eaten at the first party he'd ever had especially for him...and on the holiday at the youth camp.

It was also the first such holiday he'd known, and the happiness Keith felt at his party that Christmas Eve spilled through the summer days at Blackheath. Sleeping in tents. Hiking through the bush. Swimming. Even the accidental drowning of another boy couldn't spoil his enjoyment of the open country: so much so that Marie afterwards sent Keith to stay with her parents at Kingswood in outer Sydney.

They lived in a real bush shack: sapling studs with clapboards on the outside; hessian covered with wallpaper on the inside, which creaked when the wind blew; beaten earth floors; and a log fireplace. Old Mr Barker had been a headmaster, and made sure Keith attended the local school, though he learnt little worth remembering. Sometimes the neighbouring farmer would arrive with freshly killed meat, kerosene for the lamp, and his ukulele, and they'd sit around the fire after dinner, singing the songs of their youth and the last war. The music, as always, remained. Or the men would play dominoes while discussing politics and the prospect of the next war.

Mr Barker's politics were the opposite of his daughter's.

Whenever Marie visited, conservatism and red revolution met head on. Spain was almost lost to the fascists, she'd cry, thanks to our reactionary governments! The next struggle would be on the wider European stage. And for support she'd turn to young Keith – he who had pledged to grow up a good little Communist like his father. But the headmaster was not used to arguing with boys. They did what they were told, and kept quiet. Which led to more argument. More strain. And eventually to Keith's removal to a more tolerant old couple at Corrimal, on the South Coast.

The Blakeneys were a coal-mining family – retired now, their lives given over to playing bowls and growing standard roses. They were well past the appropriate age for handling a headstrong teenage boy. Yet they took Keithy on, getting him to help in the garden, and sending him on his bike down the hill to school, where, curiously enough, Keith accepted the authority of the one teacher who was able to exert any influence over him: the deputy headmaster, Mr Leslie. A solid, well-educated man in a grey suit, he was as free with his cane as any other teacher of the time.

'What's today, children?'

Empire Day? The King's Birthday?

'Today is the first day for a week that Keith Young hasn't had the cane. You can go home five minutes early Keith, as a reward.'

The boy responded to this small kindness, in part because he sensed that Mr Leslie had a degree of sympathy for him and the cause his Dad had served.

'Keith's father was a soldier in Spain, children.'

Yet he was also a very good teacher. He'd been a seaman himself in the Great War, and had several ships sunk under him by enemy torpedoes. A mere question during more tedious subjects such as spelling, and he'd talk for half an hour about his experiences in the sea off Madagascar or the coast of France. It was one way to impart a little geography and modern history. Indeed, the boy even won a book for a talk he gave on current affairs inspired by some of Mr Leslie's lessons; and for the time he was at Corrimal, Keith didn't wag school at all.

It wasn't just Mr Leslie, of course. As 1939 unfolded, the whole world waited as events moved inexorably towards another global war. After Germany occupied Czechoslovakia came the annexation of Austria. Though strangely, as Britain and France began to rearm after years of appeasement, so did policy change for the comrades and readers of the *Workers' Weekly*. From fighting fascism 'with weapons in hand', world peace now became the priority – confirmed when Soviet Russia signed a non-aggression pact with Hitler that August. Britain now was abused for not doing the same! Such were the revolutions in political self-interest. A few days later the Nazis invaded Poland. Stalin secretly prepared to attack Finland and the Baltic States. Britain issued an ultimatum, which was rejected. And on 3 September, Keith sat with the Blakeneys by the radio as Prime Minister Menzies announced: 'It is my melancholy duty to inform you that... Australia is also at war.'

Conflict began to break out everywhere, even on the domestic front. The kid may have stayed at school, but he did a bunk from home. Infuriated by some trivial argument over fetching another barrow of horse manure for the roses, Keith jumped on his bike bare-footed and took off... up the Macquarie Pass towards Canberra, where he had an accident. He spent a few days in hospital; and even when he returned to Corrimal with his mended bike, he didn't stay long. When Keith turned 14 that November, he left school. Any hope that Mr Leslie might exert further influence over his education was gone. And the lad went back to Sydney to find work.

He didn't stay with Marie or the Jepsons. Indeed, he learnt that Ma had recently died of pneumonia. To assert his independence, Keith rented the small attic room of a building in Cathedral Street, down near the wharves at Woolloomooloo. With the country at war he quickly got a job – first as a junior cabinetmaker and, when that didn't work out, with a telegraph company, delivering cables around the city on his bike. The pay was 30 bob a week and it gave him a degree of freedom and was interesting. He always remembered delivering the telegram to the *Sydney Morning Herald* announcing that Winston Churchill had become Britain's Prime Minister in May 1940, and feeling that in some small way he was associated with great events. France would soon fall, and the Battle of Britain was about to begin.

The kid even tried to join the navy – putting up his age, just as Dad had done, and going for the physical examination. He passed it, too. But like his father the boy was found out and his application was returned with a stern letter and a copy of his birth certificate. Still, it was a lesson. He began to drop the name Keith, using his middle moniker William – Billy – which he much preferred. And, pissed off that the navy didn't want him, he decided to pack a swag and go on an itinerant holiday cycling around Australia. Shades of his father there, as well.

A mate called Don – another cable boy, his own age – agreed to join him. Money was short; and about the time Billy turned 15 they quit the telegraph company, put up their ages, and got a better-paid job doing shift work at the Bradford Cotton Mills. When the Christmas break came, they'd saved enough to set off.

Down the Princes Highway, through Corrimal again, industrial Wollongong and the dairy farms of the far South Coast. Doing odd jobs where they could, for Donny was a first-rate mechanic. Into the eucalypt forests of East Gippsland. Sleeping under the bridge at Orbost during a raging storm. On past Ninety Mile Beach and the coal mines of Morwell, until they reached Melbourne, where they stayed a month or so, taking digs, putting up their ages to get adult rates at a metal-stamping factory. Until Billy could bear the boredom no more and they got on their bikes again, revelling in the liberty of the highway. Passing Geelong, freewheeling above the cliffs and vistas of the Great Ocean Road. Beyond Warrnambool and heading towards Portland. When disaster struck.

On a steep hill near town, they hitched a ride by holding onto some pipes hanging over the back of a truck and getting towed along. Which was all right going uphill, but downhill was another matter. The truck put on speed, the front axle of Billy's bicycle came loose and the wheel twisted and locked. He tried to help himself by raising the front of the bike a little and dragging behind on the rear wheel. But another accident seemed inevitable – and the kid was only saved when the truck slowed at an intersection and he was able to drop off.

The bike was a bit of a wreck, however. And so was the trip. He and Donny managed to repair the wheel well enough to go on into South Australia. But at a little town the other side of Mount Gambier, Billy's bike broke down altogether and they had no money to fix it. The lads could only sell the lovely machine for scrap, use the cash to buy food and accept the offer of a lift in a delivery truck back to Victoria.

They worked their way from town to town: helping the truckies; scrounging a meal where they could; sleeping in the truck's cabin because it was winter and the nights were bitter. Donny sold his bike to raise more funds. But that money soon disappeared too – and it was clear such a life couldn't continue much longer.

'We should join the army,' said Don, freezing and wet. 'They'll give us a good feed and a warm uniform. Pay us, too. Five bob a day.'

'Could we get away with it?' asked Billy. The idea didn't worry him, just the logistics. 'I tried to join the navy, but they found out me age and knocked me back.'

'I reckon they'd take anyone,' Don replied. Australian divisions were taking part in the heroic defence of Tobruk in North Africa, and had seen heavy fighting in Greece and Crete. 'Worth a go, at any rate.'

So it was that the two boys found themselves dropped off a truck at Melbourne's Spencer Street Railway Station in the bleak dawn of 23 July 1941. They were cold, hungry and broke, for they hadn't eaten since yesterday. They sneaked a ride on a tram down Bourke Street, until the conductor kicked them off.

The recruiting office was in a tin shed next to the GPO – and it was closed until nine o'clock. There was no help but to stand in the street like a pair of ravenous dogs, without a penny between them to buy a bun or a cup of tea, until the doors opened. Even then Billy and Don had to wait with stomachs rumbling, until the recruiting officer spoke to them.

'How old are you fellers?'

'How old do you have to be?'

'It's 19, if you want to go overseas with the AIF.'

'Oh, we're 19 orright.'

'I'll need your parents to fill in the consent form.'

'We don't have any parents. We're orphans.'

'Both of you?'

'Yeah.'

'Well, I'll need someone to sign it. Have to, if you're under 21.'

Damn! At least there was no talk of a birth certificate. The kid thought quickly.

'We've got an aunt. I could ask *her* . . .'

'Then do it.'

The lads went outside with their forms. Where the hell were they going to get pen and ink in a hurry, for the pains of hunger were becoming acute. They stood debating for fully five minutes, before Billy looked up and saw that the post office arcade was filled with desks and writing materials. Five minutes more and each had signed consent for the other in the name of a fictitious aunt with a fictitious address.

Thus equipped, the two went back into the recruiting office and filled out an enlistment form, being very careful when it came to the question of age. The birth day and month were given correctly; but the date had to be put back four years to 1921. The kid had learned that much at school. And now could they get something to eat? But there was another long, empty delay before they were called back to the table, where the officer examined their documents, laughed, and called to his mate.

'Hey, Fred, look at this!'

They both laughed. But Donny was right. In 1941 the army needed anyone it could recruit. Another grin and a wink. A signature. And the two were sent to the medical officer. Teeth. Eyes. Heart. Pulse. Walk. Strip. Icy stethoscope on winter flesh. Bend. Balls. Cough. Cross your legs. Bang. Reflexes fine. Dress. Passed as Fit, Class 1.

'How long before dinner?'

'What's your rush, sonny? There's one more thing to do. You gotta take the Oath.'

It was well after midday before the morning's recruits were assembled in front of a bemedalled officer, a veteran of the First World War, Bible in hand.

'Before I swear you in to the King's service, I must warn that some of you look rather young for your age. If you are trying to deceive the army, I advise you to fall out now. Otherwise you will surely be discovered and SENT TO JAIL.'

He glared around the room, allowing silence and threat to do its work. The recruits stared back impassively: the kid wooden faced, with only the date 1921 fixed in his brain. *Forget everything else.* Yet the tension grew all too much for one young feller in a sports coat and pork-pie hat, for he suddenly broke ranks crying,

'I'm sorry sir – but I'm only 17!' And fled the room.

Billy looked at the retreating figure, astonished. He'd been thinking how grown up the bloke looked in his flannels and shiny shoes. But the fool didn't even know that, however big the lie, you have to believe it implicitly for the time you're telling it. Never give way! Even the officer seemed bemused.

They proceeded to his Oath of Enlistment.

'Can we get a feed *now*? Please, sir?'

Trouble was, lunch had finished by the time they reached the depot at Royal Park near the zoo, and the cook had gone off duty. But moved by the pleas of two starving rookies, the escort rustled around in the kitchen and produced a couple of bowls and a heap of leftover sausages and mash from the sergeants' mess. The rest of the intake turned up their noses, making noises about 'army swill'. And the old soldiers, watching Billy and Don shovelling food into their mouths, joked and murmured, 'You'll be sorry.'

But the lads kept on shovelling. It wasn't swill. It was the best meal they'd ever eaten. And they weren't sorry. That grub not only filled their bellies now. It fed Billy's mind and imagination over and over again, through the hungry years that were to follow as a teenage prisoner of war.

So the strands of his life spun together, like a hempen rope being turned in Outram Road prison. Every day becoming stronger. Tougher. Able to bear great weight and withstand all weathers. In the end, it needed the whole body of men to carry and lift the ship's cable they'd made onto a waiting truck. Even the kid had to acknowledge it was a job well done. There were those from the beginning who'd said that something worthwhile might come from it. And they were right.

# 6

# BENKI TOBAN

*The Book of Life*
*Lay opened*
*At my page*

A grain of rice had fallen to the floor! The kid could see it quite clearly, sitting at attention in his cell facing the door. A mouldy speck of rice, hiding in a crack, like a louse crawled from the shit bucket. Dirty. Disgusting. And utterly hypnotic.

It must have been there for days, a windfall from his food bowl. It was extraordinary Billy hadn't seen it earlier! Usually, every last skerrick was licked up to maintain the pretence that hunger was being satisfied. Tired after rope making, his head no doubt had been too full of remembered army stews to notice one filthy grain of rice.

Still, there it was – not 12 inches from his knee. And once noticed, it wouldn't go away. He tried to think of other things...of those first days in training as a rookie at Royal Park...of his first good sleep that winter's night after weeks on the road with Don and his bike...But always the kid's mind came back to the bit of rice on the floor, growing larger and more delectable every time he looked at it.

'By George, I'm gunna have that.'

113

Billy was feasting on it already. He felt for his small piece of wire and, leaning forward, prepared to dig the rice grain out of the crack near the *benki* bucket slime.

'No!'

He pulled back his hand, confronting the reality of this thing like a maggot. Not that he had any objection to maggots. Many a time his prison rice had been seething with small white worms, and he always saved them for dessert. They were delicious. And they were clean. Whereas the grain on the cell floor . . .

'No. I'm a white man. I'm not gunna eat in the dirt.'

And to erase the thought, he imagined himself back at Royal Park recruiting depot and the evening concerts in Anzac Hall, when dance bands came from town to fill the place with music. More especially to fill the canteen store with song, and serenade the boy drooling over shelves packed with good things to eat. Jars of boiled lollies and toffee. Chocolates. Biscuits. Iced buns. Cigarettes: roll-your-own or tailor-made. Lemonade. Racks of magazines and comic books. All greatly desirable to a 15-year-old, who'd been welcomed into the army as a lost and penniless kid.

But that was the trouble. Billy was still broke. Another week before payday – and the delights of the army canteen were as unattainable to him then as they were now in memory. The rice, on the other hand, was real. And it was just over there . . .

He stretched out his bit of wire again, prised out the grain and held it in his palm – a tiny, rotten seed that continued to swell in his imagination, until he fancied he was consuming one of Nana Tot's Sunday roasts. Saliva wetted his lips. Digestive juices churned. He carefully wiped away the dirt. And forcing back any vestiges of disgust, Billy placed the rice grain in his mouth.

He rolled it around with his tongue, enjoying the sensation on his palate and letting the flavour, such as it was, linger over his tastebuds. He chewed slowly, fancying a choice cut of beef, allowing his teeth to extract every last morsel of goodness and bliss. Only then did Billy swallow, feeling it travel all the way down his gullet with a sense of replete satisfaction. He even burped.

'White man or not, by cripes, why ever did I hesitate over that?'

The kid felt as content as he had that day he opened his first army pay packet, counted out the 25 shillings and marched into the canteen knowing he could buy anything he wanted. A bag of boiled lollies. *The Phantom*. And two ounces of Wild Woodbine tobacco. The pleasure in his grain of rice was just like that – and just as momentary. As Billy was returning to his tent that day at Royal Park, he was seduced by the siren's call: 'Four bob!'

> I want four bob in the guts! is the cry.
> Four bob in the middle sees 'em fly!
> Sidies, set on this game of swy?
> Come in spinner, and send 'em high!

A pair of copper pennies spun into the air above a huddle of men playing two-up near the latrine block. The polished 'heads' caught the sunlight, sparking like the eyes that followed their flight. Winked. Then fell to the ground in the middle of the ring.

'Pair a heads! Heads it is.'

'Shinies win!'

'You little beauty!'

'We'll let it ride. Eight bob!'

> Eight bob in the guts! is now the cry.

The kid walked over to have a closer look. He'd seen men playing 'swy' often enough before. As a boy he'd been tipped their threepences and sixpences keeping lookout for Thommo's two-up school by the railway arches at Wentworth Park. But he'd not actually chanced himself at the game, beyond playing with buttons. It looked a cinch, betting on whether the pennies came up heads or tails. Still flush with funds from his pay packet, Billy invested a few shillings on the side, and promptly lost it. He invested some more, to get his money back, and lost that too.

By the time word went around that the provosts were coming, the kid had lost all his dough. He went back to his tent with nothing more to show for his first week of recruit training – a week of marching, drilling, blisters on his feet and corporals shouting orders – than a few sweets, a comic and a packet of ready-rubbed.

Yet there were compensations. He got his uniform. For the first week the new recruits had to wear their own civvies: the kid stumbling with two right feet around the parade ground in his working boots, old strides and rough blue serge coat. Thoughts that he would shine with the girls in serviceman's khaki had to be put on hold – as did the free tram rides, which were only available to men in uniform.

With the arrival of new supplies to the quartermaster's store, Billy at last put on his warm winter kit: tunic, greatcoat, slouch hat and marching boots, and legitimately paid no fare to the conductor as he boarded the tram.

'She'll be right, soldier.'

Though without any money until next payday, his excursions into town were limited to strolling up and down Bourke Street, and cadging a drink from a mate – knowing that even if he did catch a girl's eye, he hadn't a penny to spend on her.

Still, his uniform gave the kid a new cachet. It allowed him to stand by the gate and jeer 'You'll be sorry' in his turn at incoming recruits, with all the wisdom of a seven-day soldier. In truth Billy wasn't the least bit sorry he'd joined the army. To his own surprise, he'd taken to it from the start. Whether it was the four-square meals, the emulation of his father or just relief at finding order after the insecurity of those months on the road with Don and the bikes, the boy couldn't say. He knew only that he felt part of a broader camaraderie, such as he'd not known since he sat around Ma Jepson's kitchen table among the market people. A sense of belonging. Of value. And the rising sun on his upturned hat was the badge of that.

Even the discipline Billy accepted – to a point. The shouting drill sergeants: 'Not THAT left foot Private Young! Your OTHER left foot!' Like those artful lessons in free enterprise that old Pop Jepson taught, the kid sensed that much of it might be essential to his survival. And what wasn't could be ignored.

If he was sorry at one thing, it was not having a rifle. Not only had the recruits no uniform that first week, they also had no weapons. And even when their kit arrived, they were still forced to practice drill equipped with nothing more than broomsticks. It was humiliating. Even the corporals acknowledged the absurdity of trying to instil a little realism at bayonet training, when their squad could only charge Adolf Hitler dummies with mop handles.

'Thrust. Twist. Withdraw. Nazi swine!'

Hitler would be terrified.

'God help us, Private Young, try to *look* as if you meant it!'

Only towards the end of the second week did their weapons arrive, as the intake was getting ready to move to the infantry training camp near Bacchus Marsh, west of Melbourne. Most of them were going. Billy's mate Don, with his mechanical skills, applied to go into the motor-transport section. The two 15-year-olds said goodbye at Royal Park, to go their different military ways. They never met again. And often, during those solitary hours in his cell, the kid wondered what happened to Donny. Whether he'd stayed in Australia or been sent overseas as he wanted? If he was alive or dead?

The war had split so many lives: dividing even those men who survived from their companies and from each other. Yet strangely, some lives kept converging. Take Normie Morris, a labourer from suburban Richmond. He was 21 – dinkum – when he joined up a fortnight before Billy. He travelled with the recruits from Royal Park to the training battalion. Learned to shoot at the rifle range. Practised parry and thrust at last with real bayonets (Hitler might have been slightly more worried). Slogged his pack with them on route marches through the bare winter hills of Bacchus Marsh. Normie was assigned to the same outfit as Billy: the third reinforcements of the 2/29th Battalion.

They sailed to Singapore together, where they fought the Japs. They were surrendered as prisoners of war and sent to Sandakan, from where Norm escaped with Alan Minty's group, as Billy was later to escape with MP Brown. They were all recaptured, tried, sentenced and incarcerated together at Outram Road. And Normie Morris was present in the jail one day when the shining coins of Billy's fortune again fell heads up. The kid may have lost more than he ever won at two-up. But when it came to the matter of survival, his luck always seemed to hold...

Encouraged by the rope making at Outram Road, the guards started putting groups of prisoners to other kinds of work about the jail grounds: doing a bit of heavy labouring, clearing rubbish, gardening. It was another chance to get out of the cells and indulge in the perpetual game of pilfering.

The kid was out with such a work party when one of them spotted a treasure – a shard of metal, perhaps, in the dirt. The feller made to retrieve it, but it wasn't easy. Their guard was the small, fat bastard known as Little Hitler – the one who'd bashed Billy on his first day in the jail – and the four-eyed monster Mopoke wasn't far behind. Neither of them looked kindly on their prisoners picking up trifles. In order to succeed, the guards' attention had to be diverted.

There were many ruses, depending on the personality of the guard. In the case of Little Hitler, the nub was his aggression and infallible belief that Nippon would triumph over every enemy. He therefore got a bit stroppy when Alan Minty suddenly stopped and, as the party gathered round, began drawing a map with his foot.

'*Kora!*' Hey! Get along with you. Little Hitler began to flex his scabbard.

Alan stood his ground until he'd finished his drawing. Then, pointing to the outline in the dust, he said, '*Goshu*. Australia.'

Little Hitler paused. He leaned forward and uttered a beam of recognition.

'*Hai! Goshu.*'

Alan indicated the Northern Territory with his toe.

'Darwin,' he said. 'Nippon BOOM-BOOM-BOOM!'

Little Hitler roared with delight.

'*Yoshi! Darwin. BOOM-BOOM-BOOM!*'

Normie Morris pointed to the east coast.

'Syd-e-ney! BOOM-BOOM-BOOM!'

Little Hitler echoed the sounds of bursting bombs. And as Mopoke came up to join in the game, Billy stuck his foot on a town in the west.

'Shirley Temple! BOOM-BOOM-BOOM!'

'*Hai! Shuree Temper! BOOM-BOOM-BOOM!*'

'No, Youngie, you got it wrong.' Alan Minty became serious. The group fell silent. 'Shuree Temper's not over *there*! She's down *here*!' And he targeted Adelaide.

'Oh yeah, so she is.'

'You should have known that, Youngie.'

And as everybody again exploded with 'Shirley Temple! BOOM-BOOM-BOOM!' the feller on the scrounge took his chance and recovered the find.

Normally, this would have been the end of the diversion, and the work party would have continued on its way. But the idiot Mopoke kept laughing and looking at the kid.

'Youngie! Youngie! Ho-ho-ho.' Nudging Little Hitler and gesturing at Billy.

'What is it?' he whispered to MP at the first opportunity, feeling self-conscious and irritated. 'Why are they laughing at me?'

'Your name. Youngie. It sounds like *yagi* in Jap. It means goat – and you are one, too. *Shuree Temper! Boom-boom-boom!*'

It was a foolish enough joke on either side. Yet the irony of Billy's name gave the goat one small advantage – and that can make all the difference in the enduring struggle to survive. For the Japanese did not forget *Yagi*. The gag passed merrily around the Kenpeitai mess. And when next the guards were selecting someone to empty the toilet buckets of a morning – to join the ranks of the trusties and become a *benki toban* – the goat was naturally the first name they thought of.

Ordinarily, Billy would have considered it a shit of a job, in every meaning of the term. But not here. Not only did the work get him out of his cell, it allowed him to visit other blokes' cells: to collect the slopping wooden buckets, to pass on hurried messages, to acknowledge favours that would be returned – even from officers who, in another existence, would barely have noticed Private Young, except to punish him for some infringement. Now it was different.

'Hey, Billy, can you sneak us back a little water in the *benki*?' Thirst was never-ending in the tropical fastness.

'I'll see what I can manage.'

It wasn't very hard for someone who'd been pulling swifties all his life. It took four men, one on each handle, to carry the laden tray outside to the sewerage pit. The oval buckets were emptied into a shallow concrete sump, covered by a lid that looked not unlike a slouch hat and was always kept locked until *benki* time, in case the inmates tried to escape the shithole of Outram Road by, well, climbing down the shithole.

Once emptied, the buckets were rinsed with a hose, and a small brush of palm fronds was used to scrub the tar linings, intended to keep them watertight. That done, the lids were replaced: the large outer lid, and the smaller inner lid for use if you had to sit on the *benki*. It was a simple matter, then, of leaving an inch or so of hose water in the bottom of each bucket. Not too much, in case the guard noticed the weight was heavier than it should be. But enough to smuggle something extra to drink into the cells. And it was of no consequence that it was carried in the toilet buckets. The water would have been drunk whether the *benki* had been washed out or not.

The scrounging privileges of a *benki toban* extended to food as well as drink. Any scraps discovered on the rounds were grabbed and hastily consumed; and on one memorable occasion, returning with the washed buckets, they came across two pails filled with kitchen swill intended for the pigs. It was a chance not to be missed. With a quick glance at his mate on the opposite handle, the kid suddenly stumbled, tripped and fell. Over went the tray. And to shouts of disaster from the guard, 20 empty buckets and their lids were rolling all over the place. There was splendid confusion as everybody bustled about collecting them. But to enable the safe transfer of the pig swill into the *benki* buckets, the guard needed further distraction. This time they used the bloke's known love of martial arts.

'Spike!' Billy spoke quickly to a tall, solid English regular known as Spike Smith. 'Judo.'

'Gotcha!'

Spike had been a heavyweight champion of his army division; and while it had left him a little slow and punch-drunk, he was a master at throwing falls. Being so big, he was also a magnet for every little Nip who fancied himself a master of the black belt. Thus he turned to the guard, shaped up and asked if he was any good?

*'Jujutsu ichiban?'* You number one jujutsu?

Any good?

*'Mochiron!'* Of course! replied the guard. What a question. What a challenge!

The guard removed his sword. Measured his distance. Normie Morris stood as a screen while the scroungers got on with their business.

With a cry of *'Banzai!'* Black Belt launched himself at Spike Smith. He ran. Leaped. Grabbed the big bugger. And suddenly Spike was doing a massive backflip in the air. Up and over he went, like a rag doll. Smacked the ground, bounced once or twice, and groaned. Spike had never thrown a fight with greater conviction.

At length he raised himself on one elbow and observed in his most impressive voice: *'Hai! Jujutsu ichiban!'* Yes! You number one jujutsu!

The fellers went up to Black Belt, shaking his hand and congratulating him on his brilliance. They crowded around, dusting him down and allowing him to revel in the glory of his bout. He smirked and swaggered for several more minutes, until duty called. The guard buckled on his sword and issued his orders. And with the buckets filled, covered and restacked on the tray, the *benki toban* carried them back into the jail, where the lucky recipients were told to look carefully before they had a piss.

Satisfaction all round. Not least in that cell occupied by *Yagi*, the goat. What a buffet of good things came out of his *benki!* Vegetable peelings. Soggy rice. Pineapple skin. Never had fatigue duties been more enjoyable.

He'd known his share of them, known his share of field punishments and buckets filled with potato peelings. In the postprandial glow of the *benki* feast, Billy's mind went back to the last week of his training at Bacchus Marsh – and the rifle that got him into so much trouble.

The kid had grown attached to his new .303 – feeling, as every soldier must, that the weapon was becoming an extension of himself. He was quite good with it, too. The boy who'd never fired anything much beyond an occasional pea rifle while out rabbiting found himself making respectable scores at the range. He was young and silly of course, getting inordinate pleasure from driving his instructors mad by continually calling his weapon a 'gun'.

'Show me again, Corp, the proper way to clean me gun.'

'This not a gun, Private Young. This is a rifle! I've told you. Artillery have guns. Your howitzer is a gun. Your Lewis gun is a gun. This here .303 is a weapon.'

'Thank you, Corp. I understand. Now, about cleaning this here gun...'

Billy could also be rather thoughtless with it, as he demonstrated to the entire training battalion that last week.

A night exercise had been organised, in which the recruits were to surround and capture the 'enemy', positioned on a hill. Surprise was the essence of it – and the key to that, as Lieutenant Trewin briefed his platoon, was absolute silence.

'No talking, men. No cigarettes. We've got to stalk them unawares. You've been issued with blank cartridges to make this exercise seem realistic. But until I give the order to fire, the enemy's not to guess that we're anywhere near them.'

They set off in darkness and drizzling rain up a valley. It was miserable enough, with only an oilskin cape to keep off the wet; but spirits were warmed by the thought that this was real soldiering, and they'd soon be shooting at an enemy.

'Do these blanks go off, Billy?' wondered his mate, forgetting the silence.

'They might. Dunno. Never used 'em before.'

They advanced a little further through the squelching night without speaking.

'Nah,' from his mate at last. 'I shouldn't reckon so.'

'I'll give it a go.'

And without thinking, the kid lifted his rifle, aimed at the clouds, and fired.

'Christ!'

The report shattered the silence. The platoon jumped out of their skins. The blank cartridges sure went off. Worse, from out of Billy's barrel shot a wad of burning cotton, fluttering in the air like a bloody firefly. It could be seen for miles – until it fell a flaming wreck beside Lieutenant Trewin's boot.

'Who did that?' The officer furiously turned to his men as he stamped out the blazing wad. 'What effing idiot...?'

There was no point denying it, for gun smoke was still wisping from Billy's rifle. He stepped forward.

'It was me, sir.'

'Private Young, consider yourself under open arrest.'

Open arrest? What did that mean? He turned to his mate.

'What do I have to do?'

'Oh...you'll be sorry. That's the worst of the lot.'

The kid didn't have long to wait. Within a few short minutes, dummy shells were bursting above their heads like double bungers on Guy Fawkes Night – the artillery pinpointing their position with remarkable accuracy, thanks to Billy's flare. They were surrounded. Shot at with enemy blanks. Captured. And they spent the rest of the sodding night held prisoners in a cow yard, Lieutenant Trewin and all.

It was good practice at being a POW. Good practice, too,

at open arrest. When they got back to camp the kid was put on kitchen fatigues and spent the rest of his time at Bacchus Marsh peeling mountains of potatoes. There came a time when Billy was sick of the sight of them. But now – even after the cornucopia flowing from his *benki* bucket, to say nothing of the filthy grain of rice he'd so enjoyed – he could happily have spent the rest of his life doing nothing else but peeling spuds.

Not that his kitchen fatigues lasted all that long. Another week or so and the hundred men who'd been drafted as reinforcements to the 2/29th were told they'd be packing up and taking final leave before sailing to join their battalion in Malaya.

This was no great surprise. As a rookie at Royal Park, Billy had been sent on a working party to the wharves to help load the 2/29th's gear on board the transport *Marnix*. It was an open secret that the 27th Brigade, of which it was part, was going to fortress Singapore with the 22nd Brigade – and that the ships would return to pick up their reinforcements. There was much excitement at the prospect of exotic travel and service. Seven weeks after enlisting, and the kid was already going overseas! He could scarcely credit it. Even so, it didn't seem a very long period of training.

They were given a week's leave and a ticket home. Billy thought about asking for a fare to Hobart to see Nana Tot and the family. He'd had little contact with them these past three years, beyond an occasional letter after Dad was killed. But if he went there, the army might check up on him, discover his true age and kick him out, as the navy had. He settled instead for Melbourne. Yet it was lonely without the other fellers. And while as yet there was no actual fighting in Malaya, Billy *was* going away on active service like Dad had done, and the people in Hobart were all he had. For some reason he couldn't explain, it seemed ever more important to see them in these final days.

So the kid used the last of his leave pay to buy a passage on the Bass Strait ferry *Taroona* to Burnie. There was nothing left for the railways, however. He jumped the night train to Hobart in his uniform and locked himself in the lavatory when the conductor came to inspect tickets. Indeed, Billy was in there so long that several blokes gathered impatiently in the corridor and started banging on the door.

'Hurry up, feller! We need a piss!'

'Sorry,' when at last he came out.

'What is it, soldier? You got something the matter?'

'I ain't got a ticket.'

'Is that all?'

Even the conductor laughed when he returned and they told him, 'Here's a soldier on his final leave home and he's lost his ticket.'

'Don't worry, son. I'll put you off early. The stationmaster in town's a coot.'

Billy left the train at Glenorchy in the small hours and walked a couple of miles along the track to the embankment behind Nana's backyard. He climbed the fence, crossed the garden and crept into the sleep-out where his uncle lay snoring.

'Uncle Cocky,' he said, shaking him gently and murmuring. 'It's me...'

'Eh? What the dickens...?' The sleeping man roused himself. 'Who the hell is that?' He fumbled for the lamp and as his brain switched on he exclaimed, 'Keith! What are you doing here?'

'I joined the army, Uncle Cock. We're going to Singapore and I thought... We've only got a couple more days, and I reckoned I'd come and say goodbye.'

'By golly, Keith, I don't know what your Nana will say about that.'

'Neither do I.'

Nana had much to say when she discovered him at breakfast,

along the lines of 'Like father like son.' And 'The boy's as big a rum 'un as Bill, but what if he gets himself killed just the same? I couldn't bear that, and I don't know what to do.'

But even 'The Admiral' couldn't bring herself to repeat her action in the Great War, when she'd boarded the troopship and removed her underage soldier. Indeed, she found herself agreeing with the general opinion of a family conference that night that it might be best to let Keithy go. The kid wasn't allowed to attend himself, but he could hear them clearly through the lounge-room door – his uncles Doug and Harold ('Uncle Cocky'), Aunt Ada and Aunt Elsie talking it through with Nana Tot.

'He's not a bad boy – just a bit of a larrikin, that's all. Like Bill. And you know what happened when you stopped *him* going in 1915. Sent him off the rails.'

'The army might be the making of Keith, you know. Help him grow up.'

'But Singapore . . . Malaya . . . What if the Japanese enter the war and invade?'

'They'll never do that, Mother. It's not like China. The Japs couldn't fight a *proper* army. And even if they did, we'd clean 'em up overnight. Singapore's impregnable. No, no – it'll make a man of young Keith.'

This certainly accorded with the kid's own view of things. And with their consent, the latent affection he felt for his family – the need that drove him to visit Nana and say farewell – rose in his breast with renewed force. He'd last left Hobart full of adolescent resentment. Now, the departing soldier had someone to care for – and who cared for him.

Billy had little enough time to enjoy the recognition, for he had to leave the next day to rejoin his unit. He carried in his pocket a train ticket, paid for by his uncles; a one-pound note; and the knowledge that his family in Hobart at least accepted him as one of their own. Love might yet have been too strong a word. But the comfort of that knowledge stayed with him all the way to Melbourne – and from there, on another rail journey to Sydney. At length on 17 September, in the familiar surrounds of Pyrmont docks, the reinforcements boarded the Dutch transport *Sibajak*; and in company with a convoy of four troopships including the liner *Aquitania* and the *Marnix* again, cast off for the voyage to Singapore escorted by HMAS *Adelaide*.

Under the coathanger bridge and through the heads...down the South Coast that Billy had first seen from a ship as a boy with Nana asleep in her bunk...beating through Bass Strait where HMAS *Sydney* took over the escort, and westward across the Southern Ocean towards Fremantle. They were hit by a particularly violent storm crossing the Bight. Almost everyone else was seasick and kept below. But the kid was a good sailor – and thus spent most of his time on guard duty. Which he complained about publicly but privately enjoyed – alone on deck and knowing that this time the promises carried by the adventuring winds would be fulfilled.

*He's not a bad boy...but what if he's killed...I couldn't bear that...*

The words came whistling across the waves, giving the orphan kid solace in the sense they gave him of home and of someone worth fighting for. Though those other words flying around his head on the *Sibajak* – *The Japs couldn't fight a proper army...we'd clean 'em up overnight* – remained to mock him in the depths of his Japanese prison.

If only his family had known that over a mere few weeks the Japanese would have beaten the British armies down the Malayan peninsular and taken Singapore, they might not have let him go so easily. Indeed, for all Billy knew in his isolation, those funny little Nips we'd been told couldn't fight their way out of a paper bag were going on to win the war.

Yet so far he hadn't been killed. He'd known much of death, on the battlefield and in the prison camp at Sandakan. At Outram Road Billy was surrounded by it. The number of mainly Chinese civilian prisoners tortured and killed by the Kenpeitai numbered thousands, though curiously, the military prisoners of war held in the big cell block saw very little of it. Not directly. They knew the death house next door by the rope-making yard, where the condemned were held. In Youngie's experience, however, the *benki toban* never went inside it. The only way the POWs knew there had been another mass execution was at meal times. On such occasions they'd find a browned bit of rice biscuit, scraped from the bottom of the cooking pot, in their food bowls. And they'd know that the cells in the death house had filled – and been emptied that day in a wholesale slaughter, ready for the next abattoir of victims.

The rice biscuit was what? A treat? A salve to conscience? Nobody understood the Kenpeitai mind. Yet to men kept alive by a few mouthfuls a day – for whom hunger had passed beyond a condition of being to a state of bare-ribbed existence – these burnt offerings were like manna, heaven-sent.

Billy might feel sorrow and compassion for those who died. He might one day want to express those emotions in poems of his own, scratched for all to read. But at the time, the boy who'd eaten like a four-course banquet a maggot grain of rice picked from the floor could only look at the biscuit and think, 'Oh good, there's been another mass execution today.' Using gallows humour to cauterise his mind from the horrors behind it. That, too, was self-preservation – not that the POWs ever left the valley of the shadow. It was there constantly, in their hollow forms and gravedigger eyes. Nor could they always keep the spirit of hope alive in laughter.

The kid was summoned one morning to a work party digging out the stump of a tree that had been cut down in the rope-making yard. It was a bugger of a job: the roots were growing deep into the embankment and required much heavy labour with axe and crowbar to remove them. Some of those sent from Sandakan with Billy were there, for they were not yet as weakened as the other inmates. They still had to pace themselves: to appear to be working hard, while conserving their remaining strength.

Dig. Chop. With big, showy strokes. Pause. Wipe the sweat. Another blow. Scrape the dirt busily. Take a breather. So they kept a steady rhythm. All except Bill Fairy, who seemed unable to stop himself. A strong, athletic fellow in his youth – a champion cyclist, so they said – Bill grabbed the crowbar and attacked the tree root like a man possessed, bashing it without cease.

'Hey, Bill, take it easy,' whispered Alan Minty.

'Slow down,' from old Pop New.

But he didn't. He simply murmured, 'Shut up. Let me get on with it,' and kept on hacking away until his hands were ripped and bleeding.

A fine soldier – an acting corporal in Billy's 2/29th and one of Minty's five who escaped from Sandakan and hid in the jungle for months – Bill Fairy was doing his time especially hard at Outram Road. He was missing terribly his family in Melbourne, Alan said. Missing the freedom of the open road. Stabbing and gouging the tree root, it seemed as if he were assaulting with his own bloody hands every Jap who kept him from them.

'Bill, you'll kill yourself, old mate.'

As it turned out, he did. They got the job done: and so, whatever may have been in his mind, did Bill Fairy. His hands didn't heal from the wounds inflicted by the crowbar. They turned septic, so rumour had it, and without medical treatment poisoned his whole system. At length the Kenpeitai sent Bill to the POW hospital at Changi, where he lingered for a few months. He died in early April 1944 of exhaustion and deficiency disease, and was buried in the POW cemetery.

There was no sardonic laughter to shield their grief when word of Bill's death reached his companions at Outram Road. Kenny Bird likely told them of it, when he returned from his own spell in the hospital after biting his tongue. And alone in his cell, Billy found the news piercing his shell of cynicism to breach the vulnerability within.

The religious among them murmured that Bill Fairy at last was free from the shackles of life. But this was something the kid struggled to understand. There was no liberty in the grotesque finality of death, as Billy had seen it: the boy next door in Bulwara Lane impaled on the iron fence railings; the silent, open scream of a soldier's rotting corpse discovered in a jungle battlefield; the absence forever of Dad... Bill Fairy wasn't quite 25, with everything still to live for. He'd left Australia with all the promise and invincibility of every soldier. Now it was gone. And as Billy felt his tears beginning to well, he forced them away by concentrating thoughts on his own leave-taking, and the crackerjack time they'd had at Fremantle before the convoy finally departed.

It was amazing how quickly seasickness cured itself once the *Sibajak* tied up at the wharf. She and *Sydney* were the only ships to berth: *Sibajak* needing to replace a good deal of broken crockery, and *Sydney* to repair a turret jammed in the storm. While the other ships stood off, those aboard *Sibajak* were given a day's shore leave. Indeed, the people of Fremantle put on a parade for them, the kid radiating pride marching abreast in uniform, led by officers and seamen from *Sydney*. And afterwards Billy was gathered up for the day by a decent, middle-class couple and their two children – a boy, and a girl about his own age with whom he immediately fell in love.

Rosalind was slender, beautiful and fair, reminding him of the film stars he'd seen at the pictures but never thought he'd dare approach. Yet here she was with him, out on a picnic in the gardens with her people, laughing and talking and shyly touching hands. It was the first time that Billy had ever been with a girl of this quality; and such is the chemistry of human attraction that he found himself responding quite easily and naturally to her.

He told of his family in Hobart, which gave respectability. Of his father killed in Spain, which won their sympathy. Of the bungled bike trip around Australia, which got them laughing. And of his decision to join the army, which touched their patriotism, though he wisely kept his true age to himself.

It sounded studied, but there was nothing contrived about the kid that day. There was just simple enjoyment in the family's company and kindness, and his heart went out to Rosalind. He held her hand as they strolled around the city sights (though her father kept a close eye on them) and down to the wharf to say goodbye. As he went up the gangway, Billy was aglow with the fires of his first romance.

They burned through the night and into the next day when, lying on his bunk and wondering if he could see her again, a mate came into the cabin and told him to look out the open porthole. The kid stuck out his head and saw that up and down the ship men were squeezing themselves through the portholes like forcemeat through a mincer: hundreds of them, taking another day's unofficial leave.

'I'm having a piece of that,' he said to himself.

Billy had Rosalind's address with promises to write and, being just a kid, slipped through the porthole in no time. The tide was out and the ship had dropped, so that it was easy enough to clamber along the piles beneath the wharf without being spotted by the watch up top. The only hitch was a couple of old First World War diggers on duty at the gate; but they merely waved the fellers through.

Billy fell in with a 2/30th bunch from New South Wales and they went into a nearby pub, where Billy asked for directions to Rosalind's address from the locals. She lived a fair way out, it seemed. He decided to try and find it after a couple of beers with the new mates. But as the afternoon wore on – as two beers became four and then half a dozen – the prospect of getting lost, or of having to confront Rosalind's father if he did find the house, seemed less attractive. Better, perhaps, to stay where he was and hope that he might see her passing in the street. And all the time he was getting more pie-eyed – moon-eyed – until the other blokes were ribbing him.

'Hey, Billy, you're like a lovesick calf.'

'What did ya do to her, Billy? You might of made her pregnant.'

'We only held hands.'

'Oh, you never know…' And they laughed.

'Don't be dopey.'

The kid knew enough to know *that*. Dad had told him the 'facts of life', as he put it. Though it was surprising how many blokes his own age still had no idea. When Billy was living at Woolloomooloo and working as a cable boy, he remembered some of the young toughs talking very confidently about how babies came out of a woman's bellybutton at the hospital. He was able to put them straight on that – even if his teaching was all theory.

In fact he had no sexual experience with girls. Still hadn't. Desire had been there, certainly. He remembered once in Hyde Park seeing a girl in a sweater who reminded him of Lana Turner, and being gripped by one of those sudden adolescent embarrassments that stood up like a crane at Woolloomooloo wharf. Yet his innocence had remained, still unsure at 14 how to respond. When Billy took the girl next door in Cathedral Street to the pictures, he was so shy he didn't kiss her goodnight. Barely even held her hand…

Now, after two years as a prisoner of war, even desire had almost vanished. It was true for all of them. Malnourishment and overwork, augmented by months of brutality, starvation and disease at Outram Road, had seen the sexual impulse decline to zero. It wasn't just the absence of women; it was the absence of carnal need. Children and extra mouths are the last things you want. Food and water for the self are all that matter. In the early days of captivity at Changi, Billy had heard gossip of some homosexual perversion, as happened, so men said, in other jails. But that was long gone. Even the memory of desire brought no arousal. Men of experience could only hope that if... when we won the war, and they returned to health and home and freedom, their sexual drives would also be liberated. Or, in the kid's case, anticipate that he'd at last lose his virginity.

Not that he'd have admitted it to anybody, least of all to those fellers sniggering about his girl at Fremantle...

'Hey, Billy, did ya give her one?'

'That's my business.'

He didn't see Rosalind passing by, of course; and as the boozy afternoon wore on, he wasn't at all sure she'd want to see *him* in this condition. Her father certainly wouldn't! The pubs emptied at six. They went in search of a feed, and it was well after ten o'clock before they made their way through the night back to the ship – sobering up a little more with each step, as they considered the difficulties of getting back on board. For the *Sibajak* would have risen on the incoming tide, and how then would they be able to climb through the portholes again?

Their officers had foreseen the problem. Alarmed by the number of men going ashore without leave, the captain had slipped his moorings, taken *Sibajak* into the outer harbour and anchored half a mile offshore. When Billy and his companions returned to the wharf, they found a motor launch and crew waiting to take their names and service numbers, and ferry them back to the ship. Where, as *Sibajak* rejoined the convoy the next day, the Officer Commanding lined everybody up, roared at them for their disgraceful behaviour and charged and fined them three pounds each for going Absent Without Leave.

Three quid? Less than a fortnight's pay? Worth it: and besides, the kid soon got it back.

Settled by two days in port and calm weather as they steamed up the coast, the men quickly established a gambling school in the saloon. On the second night, Billy had a run of luck at heads-and-tails dice, and won nearly 20 quid. A poker game was in progress across the way and, seeing a spare seat at the table, he joined it.

Billy's luck held. He won the next few hands; and was ready to retire with his substantial winnings, when he was dealt three fours. This could be interesting.

He put in his stake. A quid. Discard.

'Buy two.'

Picking up the cards, he found himself holding the fourth four. Decidedly something worth betting on. He held them close, however, for he didn't like the look of some of his fellow players. There were six of them in the game. In particular, a couple of Queenslanders from the 2/26th were behaving like a pair of cardsharps. They'd chat and laugh away during a hand, then suddenly fall tantalisingly silent. They'd glance at each other and smirk. Start tapping the table. Or, worst of all, lay their hands across the cards with fingers spread, as if sending signals. Three and two. A straight five.

The kid nearly had a row with them. But with such a hand, he thought better of it and played with them instead.

'Bet two quid.'

'Raise yer.'

'Raise again and double.'

The betting went round the table. One of the blokes dropped out.

'Raise again. And bet five.'

'Raise ya. Another ten.'

'Sit.'

'It's too good for me.'

With more than 60 pounds on the table, a second player threw in his hand.

'Your ten. And another tenner from me.'

Billy was beginning to sweat. He'd never gambled anything like this before. Ma Jepson played crib and poker constantly at the kitchen table – but only for matches. New matches, mind you. Ma had a suitcase full of them.

*If you're going to gamble, you've gotta have something worth losing, Keithy.*

*Yes, Ma.* But only a few quid here and there from his pay packet. Never this.

'Raise again.'

The saloon had gone very quiet. Other men came across to watch. A couple stood behind the kid, who held his cards tighter. Even the sharps went silent. They looked at each other.

'And ten.'

The kid felt his blood pumping, brain jumping all over the place. Four fours were good. But plenty of cards could beat them. A royal routine. Four fives would do!

'Raise.'

His nerve was holding.

But it was too much for one of the Queensland sharks.

'I'll see yer.'

He laid out his cards. Full house: three and a pair.

The kid drew his breath. What if he lost?

The second had a straight: queen down to eight, but of different suits.

Billy breathed a little easier, though the third bloke still looked a killer.

But he had a flush: his five cards of the same suit, yet not in sequence.

The kid relaxed. His four fours beat all of them. As the room erupted, he reached across the table and pulled in well over a hundred quid. He'd barely possessed that much at once in shillings.

He flushed himself. Stood. And as he stuffed the money into his pocket, the two sharps jostled him, looking very black.

'Smart-arse. We'll soon get it back off yer, sonny.'

Some hope! Billy spent his winnings royally on sweets, comic books and tailor-made cigarettes. The boy acquired many new friends.

But for the rest of the voyage he stayed well away from the poker game...

Squat in his stagnant cell, Billy the Kid shifted his weight from one raw buttock bone to the other. It was all a gamble; all luck. For him, the chance sound of his name had made him a *benki toban*, and thus better able to forage like a goat for the means of sustenance. For others, like Bill Fairy who'd survived the fortunes of war and captivity, the last roll of the prison dice sent him to an early death.

Some didn't even make it that far. And into the kid's mind came Pat Green, for whom the cards fell all wrong. How disappointed he'd been to miss out on being allotted to the third reinforcements of the 2/29th – and how overjoyed when, after a few blokes failed to return from final leave, he'd been given a deserter's place. Pat suffered badly in the stormy Bight. At first they thought it was a severe case of seasickness, and he spent his time at Fremantle in the hospital ward. But he relapsed at sea again; and as the convoy headed into the Indian Ocean, Pat died.

The whole company assembled on deck as the *Sibajak* slowed to commit him to the deep. Pat wrapped in his weighted shroud on a board beneath the flag. The padre reading the formula words of the burial service – *in sure and certain hope of resurrection* – which Billy thought fantastical.

The board tipped. Pat's unwilling corpse plunged into the sea. And leaning over the side, the kid could see it sinking through the iridescent water like a piece of bait. Or a single grain of rice. Until it disappeared into the funeral depths. *No rising out of there, Pat.*

They resumed their journey – though *Sibajak* parted from the convoy soon afterwards, with the arrival of an escort ship to take her into Singapore. The rest of them were bound for Colombo under separate escort; and there was much cheering and waving and sounding of sirens as HMAS *Sydney* bid farewell and headed back to Fremantle.

Standing on deck with his face to the salt wind, as he loved to do, the kid could see the wakes of the ships widening ever further apart as they turned to follow their separate destinies.

At length they were gone, and *Sibajak* was alone with her escort to steam through the Sunda Strait off Java…and from there through the archipelago, the wind scented with spice island fragrances…towards Malaya and all the hazards of war.

# 7

# POSTMAN'S KNOCK

*Come with me and harvest life,*
*Come before approaching night.*

Of all the low, sadistic bastards who guarded the prisoners at Outram Road, nobody was more cruel than the one they called The Postman. Most Kenpeitai were as vicious. But none took more delight from extending the torment: the torturer playing with his victims for as long as possible, before inflicting pain. It was an art he'd developed to a rare degree.

Sometimes, if you were lucky, there was a warning he was on his rounds. A quick tapping through the stone wall: *The Postman.* Time enough to hide any contraband. To sit up straight on the floor. Hands on knees. Eyes front. Anticipating.

Usually, though, there was nothing. Until, in the dead afternoon, the kid heard a knock on his cell door. One knock. The Postman's Knock. It was a name bestowed, presumably with deadpan irony, from the childhood kissing game – for anything less loving than this Postman's call could not be imagined. One knock. A single, sharp rap on the wooden door. Then stillness again – and the waiting game began.

As a kind of mental reflex action, Billy generally began by

139

wondering if he'd been mistaken. Perhaps it was the wind rattling in the corridor, or a stone falling in the yard outside his window. But no. He couldn't fool himself for long. The kid knew that sound. It might be someone other than The Postman, however; and braving himself to lean down a little, he peeped through the metal ventilation grille at the bottom of the door, hoping to see who was there.

The grille was a useful conduit to the outer world. Bending low you could see figures moving up and down the corridor, and keep track of the brief comings and goings from the cell block. If there was somebody in the cell diagonally opposite, you could even communicate by hand signals across Broadway in a kind of semaphore. And if nothing else, a guard standing at the steps outside the door always threw a shadow across the grille – and you knew at once to be on alert.

But The Postman was wise to this. He never stood by the steps. Creeping soundlessly along the corridor in his rubber thongs, he waited instead by the wall behind the door, where there was no shadow. Hiding. Biding his time. And when he was ready, he merely had to lean across the gap where the two steps rose and swivel the spy-hole cover just below the food slot. Or give his knock. Only ever one knock. Then pull back again into the vaulting, frightened hush.

Waiting. Watching. The kid hoping it was somebody else, but knowing that it wasn't. Knowing, too, The Postman was aware of that. Toying with him. Allowing his nerves to fall prey to the torture of silence. Minutes seemed to stretch into hours. And when Billy thought he could bear it no longer, The Postman raised the tension a notch higher. Into the quiet came the sound of an iron key being inserted in the lock. Slowly. Scratching, as a mouse behind the wall. Every instinct focused on the door as the boy heard the key being turned. Just turned. *Click*. And then nothing again.

Except that there is no nothing. Not while life persists. The emptiness was filled with the kid's own breathing, pulse beating, his head overflowing with doubt.

*What is it? What does he want? What have I done wrong?* the victim would think, classically blaming himself. *Did The Postman see me leaning over? Catch me with the bit of wire? Hear me talking to Brownie in the yard? No. He couldn't have. He wasn't there. But some trustie might have told . . . Oh Jesus! Has he found me pencil and paper hanging behind the vent? No, not that. Please don't let them take that away. It's all I own. Or has he discovered the Morse code cipher on the wall?*

One question tumbled upon another, increasing his sense of guilt. That, too, was part of it. A few would even come to believe their punishment was deserved for some breach of the incessant rules. You could never please the Kenpeitai, or do anything right at Outram Road: and the mind can adapt to all kinds of humiliation.

*Don't be stupid!* The kid's resilience began to assert itself. *It's just The Postman playing his silly games. You know what's coming. Accept it. Concede him nothing. Show him nothing.*

And to deflect the turmoil, Billy concentrated on other things – on those first couple of months in Malaya before the war came, living easy in a fool's paradise, as white men who were soldiers of Empire did in the tropics.

The reinforcements who arrived in the *Sibajak* didn't remain at Singapore, much to their disappointment. The kid was looking forward to this first exotic taste of Asia. But as soon as they disembarked on 5 October, they were trucked across the island and over the narrow Strait via the Causeway, to a training camp near the village of Tampoi, a few miles from Johore Bahru at the foot of the Malay Peninsula.

The camp was designed specifically for instruction in tropical warfare, with exercises in the jungle undergrowth and more open rubber plantations (complete with warnings that the rubber trees were private property and were not to be damaged). There was daily practice at the rifle range; instruction on the new Bren light machine guns, and the rather antiquated Lewis guns from the First World War; constant emphasis on drilling, marching, Physical Training, bayonet and unarmed combat in the training ground known as the Bullring. They did a good deal of trench-digging too, in case the enemy reverted to the tactics of the Great War; and soldiers were required to carry their gas masks at all times. It was solid work – even more demanding for those men from the *Sibajak* who were still acclimatising to the heat. Yet it was necessary after two languid weeks at sea. Besides, many of them were still pretty raw recruits, and much discipline was needed to turn them into effective fighting troops. Especially this lot.

The Australian 8th Division had two brigades in Malaya – the 22nd and the 27th. British colonial administrators, secure behind the privileges of race and rank, generally found more casual – not to say larrikin – Australian ways rather trying. It was quite a relief when their battalions actually left Singapore and moved upcountry to Johore and Malacca. But even their own commanders found these newly arrived reinforcements from Australia to be poorly trained and ill disciplined. In particular, a liaison letter from headquarters considered the group destined for the 2/29th Battalion to be 'outstandingly bad', and advised that they'd not been properly controlled on the voyage over – a reasonable comment for anyone who remembered all those bodies wriggling through the *Sibajak's* portholes at Fremantle and going AWL for the day. It took constant hard work in the Bullring to lick them into proper military shape. And, in fairness to the soldiers, the same letter remarked how quickly they'd improved.

Off duty, though, men had their own privileges to enjoy as Europeans in the Far East. Indian servants looked after their personal needs: washed their clothes and prepared their food. Troops slept not on stretchers but on *charpoys* – wooden bedsteads with strung mattress bases, imported from the Raj. For entertainment, an official gambling marquee offered cards, crown and anchor, and heads-and-tails dice. It was tightly run by a group of officers as a counter to the ravages of two-up; but impromptu swy schools still flourished whenever three or four blokes with a few bob between them gathered out of sight of the provosts.

Leave was not ungenerous. It wasn't difficult to get a pass for a few hours of an evening to go into Tampoi and taste something of the foreign pleasures. A Chinese restaurant served succulent rice and noodles, which Billy loved from the start – though for less adventurous soldiers the cook had also learnt to make bacon and eggs with chips. You could sit at tables playing cards or even mahjong, drinking Tiger beer (for which Billy still had a light head), and walk back to camp past the wall of a village cordial factory, which bore in large letters the sign Fuking and Co.

How delightful! How thoughtful of them!

Not that there was much of that in Tampoi. For real Fuking and Co you had to visit the brothels and stews of Johore. They were out of bounds, but none the less frequented for that. As they were in Singapore. On leave in Lavender Street one night, a few of the older men took the kid with them into a Chinese cathouse for a joke. Past the Mama San they went; and he sat full of bravado in a little theatre filled with smoke and booze, watching a live performance on the stage.

A young woman – she seemed no more than a girl – was up there being shagged by a big black feller. The men below laughed and called out obscenities; the boy was both fascinated and repelled. He'd never imagined such a spectacle. Never seen the sex act before, although Dad had told him the mechanics of it. Yet, however stimulating it was in one sense, he couldn't help thinking how sordid it seemed – the more so when another bloke suddenly clambered over the seats and onto the stage, pushed the black feller aside, unbuttoned himself and completed the deed as the audience shouted their approval. Billy cheered with them, of course. But he was also aware of shame, and wondered what this had to do with those first tender feelings of love he'd experienced for the girl, Rosalind, in Fremantle.

The notion that sex could be brutish, and even dangerous, was not helped by the military doctors in their regular lectures to the men about venereal disease.

'Just stay away from infected women, or you know what will happen to you,' they warned, and passed around photographs of penises covered with syphilis sores or weeping pus – 'custard cock,' somebody called it – all of which left their impressions on a youthful mind.

Sometimes, too, when the kid was on piquet duty he'd be sent with the squad to Johore and the red-light district – to clear men out of the brothels and send them back to camp.

'Go on, you blokes – piss off! You know you shouldn't be here, and the provosts aren't far behind.'

Seeing things beyond the ken of a 15-year-old. Patrolling the filthy back alleys that reeked of scum and corruption, he'd watch the girls come out of the knocking shops and, squatting by the water *tong*, wash themselves from a rusty dipper. It was so squalid. So grubby. And the consequences could be observed when the piquet had to guard the few mongrel men held in a barbed-wire pen at the provost camp: men with VD behaving like animals, stripping themselves half naked and putting on a 'mad act' to get sent home. It was much safer for the kid to think sweet thoughts of his day with Rosalind (though he never summoned the courage to write to her, fearing lack of education would betray him). Better to stick with the known delights of the two-up school and Tiger beer.

Billy indulged both to excess on his 16th birthday. He was well cashed up. A mate, 'Checkie', took the sweep when Skipton won the Melbourne Cup that 4th of November; and the kid cleaned out the rest of them at a swy game down by the main gate. They played 'sudden death' using three pennies, which always gave a result – and the boy spun 11 heads in a row. He could have made a fortune were it not just before payday. Still, his group won enough to spend a profitable hour at the dice tables in the official gambling marquee; and then, spruced up with a leave pass until ten o'clock, a bunch of them went into the village to eat and drink mightily at the Chinese restaurant.

The curfew hour had long passed when the cook eventually threw them out, and they staggered back to camp full as boots. Roaring 'Happy Birthday' into the hot, perfumed night. Hilarious at the sign Fuking and Co, that was not what it promised. Waking half the bloody camp as they crawled under the perimeter wire. And entertaining the piquet no end as they fell in and out of the air-raid trenches in the darkness. At length they fell into the hands of the duty officer, and they spent the rest of the night in the guardhouse. When Billy woke next morning, he was face down on a *charpoy*, his head stuck through the mattress strings, and gasping for air, like a cod fished up in a net. Disgraced again.

Lieutenant-Colonel John Robertson, CO of the 2/29th Battalion, and his colleagues sometimes visited the camp from their headquarters at Segamat to lecture Billy and his cohorts on the ethos and role of the unit – as did officers from the other battalions. They sought to instil a proper sense of pride among their recruit reinforcements in the traditions of the AIF, and the important part the 8th Division was playing in the defence of Malaya – not that there could be any doubt about the outcome. The general view of the hopelessness of the Japanese as fighters should they dare to attack, and the innate superiority of the British forces with their great guns guarding the naval base at Singapore, was pretty much shared by people everywhere, like the family in Hobart. Fortress Singapore was an article of faith. And while it was long recognised that, rather than launch a naval assault, an enemy might attack down the peninsula, not until war loomed did planning for such an eventuality quicken. The RAF opened a string of airfields in Malaya. As for infantry, the British-led III Indian Corps was deployed to the north, the 8th Australian Division in the south.

They seemed at the time so dominant. So superior. So enduring.

The 8th Division's commander, Lieutenant-General Gordon Bennett, himself visited the training camp at Tampoi, and the kid was selected to be in the guard of honour. No superior behaviour there, however. The trick was to pull out your rifle clip a little way, and to snap it shut upon the order 'Present arms' – so that the salute was accompanied by a smart, metallic *crack*. Billy withdrew his clip too far; and even as the General was passing, the thing dropped to the ground and rolled at his feet. The kid was confined to barracks for two weeks.

Part of that time Billy occupied himself by trying to tattoo his forearm with a needle stuck through a cork and dipped in a bottle of Indian ink. A mate had done it. And sitting in his tent on the edge of the *charpoy*, he got as far as his regimental number VX60083, showing true soldierly spirit. He even began on the letters AIF. But then with thoughts of Rosalind before him, he started tattooing a portrait of the girl – until the pain got too much and he had to stop with only the outline of her hair and forehead complete. They remained there, forever on his wasted flesh, to remind.

More fun was to get a day's leave and go into Singapore with a truckload of fellers. It was important to make sure you were wearing correct tropical uniform, otherwise the British provosts (known as 'Redcaps') wouldn't let you cross the Causeway and go onto the island. They were sticklers for this sort of thing. Take off your shirt and the Redcaps would send you back home, with appropriate comments about 'slovenly Australians'. Which had advantages if you were going out with a work party.

On leave days, though, shirts were firmly buttoned on; and once down Singapore's rural roads – through stretches of swamp and jungle, past cultivated rice paddies and small palm-thatched villages known as *kampongs* – what an eye-opener it was to wander through the crowded city. To foray into the bars along Orchard Road, jostling with cooking smells and people speaking a Babel of languages – English, Chinese, Malay, Tamil – and tasting whatever caught your fancy. To venture into the shop-houses of Chinatown or Change Alley and bargain for embroidered cushion covers to send home to Nana Tot, silk napkins for Billy's aunts, and handkerchiefs for his uncles. It was like Paddy's Market again, writ large and exotic, and everything so cheap! These Australian diggers with their six bob a day for overseas service (double that paid the British) felt like lordlings among the masses, and often enough they played the part, too: hiring Chinese rickshaw drivers to run them from one part of town to the other – the passengers urging them to go ever faster, like drivers in their sulkies at the Saturday-night trots.

Sometimes, indeed, they reversed the roles. Late one afternoon, the kid and his mate Bert Cruickshank told their rickshaw men to sit in the back while they got between the shafts themselves, and the pair of wild young colts had a race through the startled streets. It was the sort of lairising Australian behaviour that so upset British notions of colonial propriety. Yet it was good sport while it lasted – half a mile down the road, until they reached a hump-backed bridge over the sluggish Singapore River.

It was not, then, a clean waterway – more like an open drain, collecting the city's waste and effluent from the flotilla of sampans tethered to its banks. But there the lads paused, to laugh and to draw breath; leaning over the side and watching families cook their evening meals on the boats below in the dark, sleazy water. Small fires glowed, and smoke drifted carrying hints of another Asia, when suddenly their nostrils were assailed by an almost overpowering stench. A tropical smell of shit and heat and decay rising from the fetid river. It repelled them. How could people bear to live and eat among this?

The boys' stomachs heaved and they nearly puked over the side of the bridge.

'Christ!' Crookie belched. 'Get us out of here.'

Rousing the bewildered drivers, he and Billy clambered into the rickshaws and told them *chop-chop* to run back to town – to the security of the white man's version of the East.

It was easy enough to believe that life would go on like this. A few commands and you'd be conveyed by coolies back into light and safety and European order. Yet thinking back, Billy realised it was always a waiting game – just as it was in his prison anticipating The Postman. The knock. The silence. The key turning slowly in the lock. Hoping that the next act of this little drama might not take place. Yet knowing that it would.

So, on the world's larger stage, ordinary people might persuade themselves that the Japanese would never dare take on the British Empire, let alone the might of America. But realists knew that Japan had been developing imperial ambitions of its own, almost from the time the country opened itself to Western modernisation in 1868. For the past 50 years, Asia's first great industrial nation had aggressively extended its political and economic power in the East.

First came war with China, which saw the island of Formosa (Taiwan) ceded to Japan in 1895. Then, war with Russia – the first time an Asian nation had defeated a European power – which opened the way for Japan to occupy and formally annex Korea in 1910. While Nippon sided with the Allies in the Great War, a renewed spirit of militant nationalism had arisen in recent years, as it had in fascist Europe, coupled with a form of 'Emperor worship' after the accession of Hirohito in 1926. Manchuria was conquered in 1931. Northern China was invaded in 1937 where, in a particularly savage war against both the Chinese communist and nationalist armies, Japanese troops had killed some 300 000 people in the so-called 'Rape of Nanking'. It shocked Westerners as governments began to realise the extent of the challenge to their own empires from the expanding Empire of Japan. Indeed, Nippon's promotion of a Greater East Asia Co-Prosperity Sphere was not only an economic policy to gain access to raw materials and new markets, but also a direct political appeal to the nationalist sympathies of the colonised people of South-East Asia.

The threat became even more overt in September 1940 – a year after war had broken out in Europe – when Japan signed a pact with Germany and Italy to establish and maintain 'a new order of things' in Asia. The colonies of French Indo-China – Vietnam, Laos and Cambodia – were invaded. And when the United States embargoed the export of scrap metal, matériel, and most importantly oil to Japan, attention in Tokyo turned to the resource-rich colonies of British Malaya, the Dutch East Indies and American controlling interests in the Philippines.

Realists knew these things and made their dispositions. The appointment of Air Chief Marshal Sir Robert Brooke-Popham as Britain's Far East Commander-in-Chief was a sign that Singapore's real defence would lie with the air force rather than the navy. But with war raging in Europe, Malaya had a low priority in London – and less than half of what had been reckoned the minimum number of aircraft necessary to defend the peninsula had actually been sent. Most men on the ground didn't know that. Fortunately, perhaps. Even so, the signs of hostility were sufficiently clear by late

November 1941 for the RAF and the III Indian Corps to strengthen their positions in northern Malaya, and for the two Australian brigades to take up their pre-arranged war stations in the south. To watch. And to await the blow.


SLAM!

The cell door was flung open against the wall. Standing in the frame was The Postman's domineering silhouette. He was not in fact a very big man. He merely seemed so from the kid's perspective on the floor, and the accumulated dread of his arrival. Nor did The Postman look the brute he was. As he walked slowly into the cell, swinging a bunch of iron keys in his hand, window light fell upon his face – a thin, high-boned face, eyes hidden behind his glasses, and teeth smiling through drawn lips.

'*Go-hyaku-ju*.' He spoke Billy's prison number, 510, softly to begin with. Though if the boy made to assent with his own '*Go-hyaku-ju*', then came the sudden shout '*Hanasanai!*'

The Postman stood in front, staring at his victim. Then he stepped to one side, behind the kid's right ear – just out of sight, but all the time talking down and becoming more agitated. The heavy prison keys, on their old-fashioned iron ring, jangling and chattering.

'*Hanasanai*. Prisoner must not talk. Prisoner know that. But *go-hyaku-ju* is bad prisoner. *Horyo*. Prisoner of war. All bad. All dishonourable. Soldier never surrender, and those that do must be punished!'

The Postman spoke in a curious mixture of Japanese, broken Malay and English, getting louder and faster as he worked himself into a fury. Billy could barely disentangle the words, though their meaning was clear enough.

'Prisoner disobedient. Not sit straight. Look at wall. Hide thing.

Talk. *Go-hyaku-ju* not know that Japanese Emperor make rule for own good.'

The keys were swinging wildly beside him, the kid glimpsing their movement from the corner of his eye and knowing what was to come.

*Just do it!* he thought. *Now. And if not now, Jesus, let me hair grow a little longer. Give me head a bit more protection.*

But there was no hope of that. The Kenpeitai kept their prisoners' hair cropped short. Whether it was an attempt at hygiene like the scabies bath, or merely another form of torture, Billy couldn't say. But every month a Japanese trustie would enter his cell and, squatting beside the prisoner, cut his hair with a pair of blunt clippers. It was agony, handfuls of hair torn from his skull, as the guard stood by amused at the operation and ready to bash should the kid show any emotion. Agony, too, knowing that barely anything now lay between his scalp and The Postman's vengeance.

His ritual usually followed the same pattern, like a psychosis. Having talked himself into a state of high excitement, mention of Japan and his Emperor brought a few moments of calm, before the final onslaught.

'Emperor is father. Emperor good. Kind. Japanese people want only peace. Happiness. But *horyo* is bad. Make war. Kill Japanese soldier. *Eibei kichiku*. Enemy devil! Must be taught lesson. *Go-hyaku-ju!*'

He spoke ever more rapidly and violently, the bunch of keys whirling in his hand until, with this last imprecation, he brought them smashing down on Billy's head.

Pain and evil shot through his being. Yet the boy willed himself almost forcefully not to cry out or to move – at least not while The Postman was there. To do so would have risked a second blow, and certainly have shown capitulation. Thus he sat feeling blood running down his cheek, ears ringing, hatred seeding – until the blackguard strode from the cell with a swagger of expiation, pulling the door behind him and locking it. Even then Billy had to wait for several minutes before easing himself, in case The Postman was still lurking outside to spring him again for moving. Only when sufficient time had passed did he feel it safe to shift his aching body upon the floor and staunch the wound with a corner of his filthy shirt, hoping the laceration would heal quickly and not become infected.

It was the savagery and swiftness of the blow that hurt as much as anything, however prepared he was for it. That, and the fact that Billy was almost helpless to retaliate, beyond thinking dark thoughts of revenge in time to come.

So, with the same ferocity after the long wait was over, had war come to Malaya. The kid could remember it as clearly as stars against a tropic sky. Night. And he was on piquet duty at Tampoi when they heard the roar of aeroplanes overhead. A far-off thrumming that grew louder and more insistent until earth and air were shaking, and the heavens were obliterated with shadow as squadrons of aircraft like batwings, eyes alight, flew northward out of Singapore and over the brooding jungle.

Men, awakened by the noise, came running from their tents to see them.

'They must be ours!' they cried.

And the duty officer emerged from the guardhouse carrying a lantern – holding it up into the darkness, as if it might illuminate something, and saying, 'I didn't know the RAF had so many planes.'

It was only when a frantic telephone call to sigs told the news that Singapore had been bombed – and shortly afterwards the ack-ack guns started firing – that men realised they were enemy planes. On the dark horizon they could see the fire-glow of a premature dawn, and illusions of their own invincibility began to falter. Indeed, an officer who emerged shouting, 'The balloon's gone up!'

next morning found a bunch of inflated condoms tied to his tent pole as testament to the fact.

Monday, 8 December 1941. Without warning or declaration, the 25th Imperial Japanese Army landed, and began to advance down the peninsula. At the same time – in 'a day of infamy' – Japanese planes attacked the United States fleet at Pearl Harbor in Hawaii, on the other side of the International Date Line, hoping to keep American forces out of the Pacific long enough to complete the conquest of British and Dutch possessions. Hong Kong and the Philippines were invaded. Italy and Germany declared war on the US, and the conflict became truly global in scale.

In Malaya, the Japanese quickly overwhelmed the defenders in a campaign brilliantly conceived and executed by General Tomoyuki Yamashita. He'd planned to capture Singapore in 100 days: in fact he did it in 70. While his 60 000 infantry were outnumbered by more than two to one, they were well-trained – many of them battle-hardened in China – and supported by tanks, artillery and vastly superior aircraft. Many of the III Indian Corps troops, by contrast, were inexperienced, ill equipped and often poorly led by their British officers. They had no tanks. Their artillery was largely ineffective. None of the Australian battalions in the south had been tested in battle. And with several exceptions it had all, as the kid reflected over and again, been a hopeless disaster.

Soldiers of the Japanese 5th Division had come ashore in southern Thailand, crossed into Malaya, and began moving rapidly down the west coast along the main Trunk Road using some motorised transport but mainly riding thousands of cheap Japanese bicycles. They were followed by the Imperial Guards, consolidating the rear and ready to play their own part as the attack developed. The 18th Division landed at Kota Bahru, seized the important airfields (which were soon repaired for their own planes) and began to advance down the east coast.

The airfields were the key to it. Not only had the RAF less than half the number of aircraft needed to defend Malaya, but half of those in the north were destroyed within the first day or so. True, there were several RAAF squadrons in support, flying Lockheed Hudsons and ageing Brewster Buffalos, but they were no match for the Japanese Zeros in an enemy air fleet four times their size.

Within five days, the RAF had abandoned all its airfields in northern Malaya. The Japanese had broken through the lines at Jitra and the Anglo-Indian defenders were retreating towards Alor Star. A few days later they were again withdrawing further south to the Perak River, along roads crowded with civilian refugees – Chinese and Malay families, plantation owners, mine managers, colonial administrators – all heading for the presumed safety of Singapore.

It was a classic military pincer campaign. Wherever Japanese forces came across opposition, they first attacked it head on with tanks and infantry, which rarely met with sustained resistance. At the same time, other troops began a double encircling movement: a shallow penetration to attack from behind, and a deeper envelopment to set up roadblocks and trap the enemy as they retreated. Moreover, as the Japanese were advancing down both sides of the peninsula, withdrawal by one defending unit meant those in support also had to retreat or risk being cut off. Once the divisions of the 25th Army gained the initiative, they never lost their momentum.

As Christmas came and went, the RAF evacuated all stations north of Kuala Lumpur, taking their anti-aircraft guns and using the few remaining operational planes to protect the convoys still arriving at doomed Singapore with more men. The Perak River was crossed, and Ipoh subsequently abandoned as the attacks pressed further south. The Japanese seized Kuantan on the east coast, and by early new year they were operating out of the nearby air base. Indeed, after a desperate battle at Slim River on 7 January, in which over 500 British and Indian troops were killed and the Japanese captured large amounts of weapons, vehicles and supplies, the decision was made to withdraw to a fresh defence line in northern Johore. And the new Commander-in-Chief, General Wavell, decided to give responsibility for the main element known as 'Westforce' to General Bennett of the 8th Division.

To the Australians, this was one bright spot in what had been a month of disasters. Even as the Japanese were preparing to strike came news that HMAS *Sydney* had disappeared with all hands after a fight with the German raider *Kormoran* off the West Australian coast in mid-November. To someone like Billy the Kid, still in training at Tampoi, this had real meaning. He'd sailed in one of the *Sydney's* last convoys – had marched with many of her crew that day in Fremantle. War was no longer an abstraction for him, even though he had no direct experience of it. Still, as word spread of the Japanese advance, he knew it was coming ever closer.

Within days of the attack on Malaya, both the Royal Navy's capital ships in the region, HMS *Prince of Wales* and *Repulse*, were sunk by torpedo bombers. It was incredible! Fortress Singapore was suddenly vulnerable. All that propaganda about the Japanese being inferior soldiers was exposed as racialist nonsense. The whole of Asia seemed ready to fall to them. In the Philippines, the army led by the US General Douglas MacArthur was bottled up on the Bataan Peninsula. Burma was invaded. New Guinea and the Dutch East Indies were under threat. Hong Kong surrendered amid scenes of rape and horror that foretold things to come in Singapore.

So, as the men at Johore gleaned news out of signals that the defenders were retreating down Malaya like sands before Japanese waves, the appointment of General Bennett seemed like a fighting chance to stem the tide. As it turned out Bennett's 'Westforce' was no more successful in stopping the advance – though several actions by his Australian battalions did slow things up for a few days.

And as the kid remembered the stories on the floor of his prison cell, into his aching head came the faces of those he knew so well: Paddy O'Toole...Bob Shipsides...all those others from the old battalion. They'd been at Muar; had suffered far more than he had from the lunatic Postman's bunch of keys. They'd survived; were still waiting for him. And through Billy's darkness shone his own lantern light of pride in the presence of men whose company he still kept.

The Australians' first major contact with the enemy's 5th Division came near the village of Gemas, on the Trunk Road north of HQ at Segamat. B Company of the 2/30th Battalion (having successfully drawn matchstick lots) laid an ambush where the road crossed a bridge over a creek and ran into a cutting through the jungle. The ambush site was a mile or two forward of the main battalion and, in the pouring monsoonal weather, was perfect for the job.

Just after four o'clock on the afternoon of 14 January, a detachment of around 200 Japanese soldiers clattered over the bridge on their bicycles, talking and laughing, weapons slung over their shoulders. They were allowed to pass through, as a second group of more than 700 cyclists approached the bridge. Once the main body was into the cutting, the bridge was blown and the Australians opened up with grenades, machine-gun and rifle fire. Within minutes the road was strewn with dead and injured enemy, and their abandoned bicycles.

The trouble was that B Company had no wireless. It was in contact with battalion HQ through signal wire laid beside the road – and the wire had been cut early in the action. Once the ambush was sprung, sigs had no way of calling down artillery fire on the enemy that had been allowed to pass and were now between them and HQ, or on others following down the Trunk Road. As the Japanese prepared to counterattack, the company was forced to split into small groups and fight through jungle back to their own lines.

Next morning, the main battalion awaited the Japanese advance beyond a roadblock on a stretch bordered by slender rubber trees and jungle thickets. They had a couple of anti-tank guns positioned forward, although the CO Lieutenant-Colonel 'Black Jack' Galleghan apparently didn't think highly of them. Anti-tank guns hadn't been of much use earlier in the campaign – and besides, he doubted the Japs would use tanks. He soon had reason to change his mind.

As the first of three tanks rounded a bend in the road, his guns began firing, and at least two tanks were hit, one of them set ablaze. More tanks appeared, and in a furious exchange of fire the road was filled with smoke and flame and the flash of bursting shells and mortars. In the course of an hour at least six enemy tanks and armoured vehicles were destroyed, and the enemy crew who survived were retreating up the road. It was a valuable demonstration – though the action was not yet over. Japanese aircraft began to strafe and bomb the Australians; and while a counterattack was mounted, it soon ran into resistance. Japanese infantry and tanks began moving up again, and by mid-afternoon Galleghan decided to withdraw. He left behind the two anti-tank guns, by now bogged in the mud, but also several hundred enemy dead, for the loss of 80 of his own men killed, wounded or missing in the jungle.

This first success was a great boost to morale, and the kid could remember the newspapers being full of it. But in truth it was a mere blip in the sweep of the Japanese advance. And besides, reports had started coming of yet another battle shaping up near Muar on the west coast, involving the Japanese Imperial Guards, the Australian 2/19th and Billy's own 2/29th Battalions.

The Muar River was held by the young and only partly

trained 45th Indian Brigade, supported by an Australian artillery battery. Even as the Gemas battle was raging, the Guards attacked and crossed the river, threatening to cut the road from Muar to Brigade HQ at Bakri, and from there to seize the vital Trunk Road junction at Yong Peng. General Bennett ordered the two Australian battalions to Bakri to try to regain the initiative – and certainly to keep the Yong Peng road open long enough for Westforce to continue its withdrawal south.

Curiously, Bennett told Lieutenant-Colonel Robertson of the 2/29th that there were only about 200 enemy troops. In fact by the time the battalion, less one company and a platoon, took up their positions on the road a mile and a half in front of Bakri on 17 January, most of the Imperial Guards had already crossed the river. The Australians were supported by several guns from the 2/4th Anti-Tank Regiment, although once again the battalion was dubious of their value. Robertson doubted that the Japanese would use tanks: but like Galleghan at Gemas, he was mistaken.

Just after dawn the next day, five Japanese tanks advanced down the road from Muar. All were destroyed by the anti-tank guns, the escaping crewmen cut down by infantry hidden in the bordering jungle. Another three tanks approached and after a furious fire-fight they, too, were put out of action.

But then came tragedy. John Robertson left for a conference at Bakri HQ, riding pillion on a motorbike. As he returned, the bike was attacked by Japanese snipers and the colonel was mortally wounded. He was carried back to his battalion to die.

The ambush was a sure sign that the enemy was now between the 2/29th and Bakri; and all that night, as the Imperial Guards worked their way around the town, their voices could be heard calling, 'You die tomorrow...' Many of *them* died that night, however, in skirmishes with 2/29th patrols, though in the darkness the Australians had learned to rely on the bayonet and hand

grenades, having already injured some of their own the previous
night by misdirected rifle fire.

The 2/19th Battalion joined the Indian units at Bakri on 19
January. Later that morning Lieutenant-Colonel Charles Anderson
ordered A Company to try to contact the 2/29th Battalion further
down the Muar Road, but the attack was repulsed. After almost
a year's training in Malaya, the 2/19th were skilled in jungle and
rubber, and at one point during the battle for Bakri a Japanese force
found itself trapped between two companies. Their own tactics had
been turned on them, and after heavy fighting the Japanese were
routed leaving more than 70 dead. It was one of the few times a
defending force in Malaya had the chance to count enemy bodies.
The first time, too, that Australians came across the Japanese
refusal to surrender: many of the supposed 'dead' suddenly sprang
back to life, began shooting, and had to be killed all over again.

It was a substantial tactical victory. Yet Bakri was still under
threat from the enemy's wider encircling movement and landings
further down the coast. Transport units behind the town came
under attack, and after several hours the survivors dispersed
into the jungle to make their way back to Yong Peng. Late that
morning Brigade HQ was destroyed in a bombing raid. With the
CO wounded and many of his officers and staff killed, Charles
Anderson of the 2/19th took command.

He ordered the 2/29th to wait up the Muar Road for a missing
Indian unit and then to withdraw to Bakri. The Indians reached
their lines by early afternoon, but as the column pulled back it
came under heavy Japanese fire. The battle was fierce. Major Olliff,
who'd assumed battalion command after Robertson died, was
himself killed, and the column was split. Only about 200 made it
to Bakri. The rest took to the jungle, of whom another 200 men
of the 2/29th reached Yong Peng. Some died of disease or injury.
Others were eventually rounded up and taken prisoner. A few even

reached the coast and Sumatra before they were captured.

Next day, 20 January, Anderson decided to evacuate Bakri and cut his way with the remaining Indian and Australian troops back 15 miles to the village of Parit Sulong in an attempt to keep the road open to Yong Peng. A convoy of 50 vehicles carried the wounded, ammunition and the column's dwindling food supplies. Travelling at little more than walking pace they eventually came to a Japanese roadblock. It was cleared after a fight in which Anderson himself lobbed grenades and shot enemy soldiers with his revolver. Pressing on, they came to a second roadblock made from vehicles, tree trunks and a concrete blockhouse. The companies were pinned down by machine-gun and artillery fire, and were unable to attack the enemy flanks through swamp. Thus they mounted a frontal assault, using a 25-pounder gun, mortars and even axes to clear the block and at length put the Japanese to flight.

That night the column passed down a long causeway largely untroubled by enemy aircraft: but they also heard that Parit Sulong was now in the hands of the Imperial Guards, using the familiar tactics of leapfrogging behind them down the coast. Anderson reached the outskirts early on the morning of 21 January, low on ammunition and supplies. His companies attacked and gained the approaches to the bridge after a fierce struggle, but the other side of the river was held by the Japanese in fortified positions.

With his wounded in a bad way, Anderson sent the worst cases in two ambulances to the bridge, with a request they be allowed through to Yong Peng. The Japanese refused, ordering instead that the ambulances remain where they were unless Anderson surrendered. He declined, of course. It was only after dark that two men were able to sneak up and release the handbrakes, allowing the ambulances to roll back into Anderson's perimeter.

During that night more enemy tanks surrounded the diminishing force. Many Indian troops were becoming demoralised. At dawn, as the shelling and aerial bombing grew heavier, and realising he had no hope of dislodging the Japanese, Anderson had little choice but to withdraw. He ordered his vehicles and equipment to be disabled, and the fit and walking wounded to head into the jungle in small groups and make their way east to Yong Peng. It was a nightmare journey of 26 miles through swamp, rubber and all the dangers of the jungle; but over the following days about 400 Indian and 500 Australian soldiers did make it through. A few stayed in the jungle, continuing to fight with guerrilla bands until they were killed or captured. And others simply disappeared among the forest thickets, their fate forever unknown.

About 150 of the most seriously wounded were left by Anderson in the ambulances at Parit Sulong, anticipating the Japanese would care for them. What followed was an atrocity that made even The Postman look virtuous. The injured were herded into a bungalow. Their wounds were kicked. Delirious men were beaten and taunted by their captors until, that evening, they were roped or wired together and systematically murdered. Some were bayoneted to death. Some were doused with petrol and set on fire. Some were taken to the river and beheaded. Only two or three managed to escape the butchery – and it was weeks before Lieutenant Ben Hackney of the 2/29th, for example, was recaptured and able to repeat the story to his comrades. But by that time they were all prisoners of war...

These things Billy the Kid knew only by word of mouth. He'd been to the Muar River and seen something of the country, but that was before the fighting. In the first confused weeks after the Japanese landings, he and a dozen or so 2/29th reinforcements were sent to battalion HQ at Segamat, and from there trucked to guard a small dam on the river near Muar. They were there four or five days, before being picked up and returned to Tampoi, none the wiser for the reasons behind their mission. But that, Billy discovered, was true for so much about army life.

Then the kid came down with a bad case of tinea, and on New Year's Eve he was sent to the 13th Australian General Hospital, not far from camp, until his sores healed. There he heard of the retreat through central Malaya back to Johore. Indeed, the reinforcements had been hard at it preparing a new Base Depot near the Sultan of Johore's palace; and Billy had not long been released from hospital when news came through of the gallant actions fought at Gemas, Muar and Parit Sulong. Charles Anderson was awarded the Victoria Cross for his leadership of the column. General Yamashita described it as the most 'savage encounter' of the campaign. Yet when the extent of the Australian casualties became known, rumours spread like butter under hot sun.

There was talk, for instance, that the 2/29th Battalion would amalgamate with other units. It had over 300 dead, wounded or missing – half its numbers who went to Muar. While D Company was intact, having been deployed elsewhere, and stragglers were still coming out of the jungle, the battalion needed another 540 men to reach full strength: and it didn't have that many trained reinforcements at Tampoi. The situation was even more acute for the 2/19th, of which only about 270 men remustered at Yong Peng, and 690 reinforcements were required.

Such is the strength of a serviceman's identification with his military unit, however, that these battalions were not disbanded. On 25 January, even as survivors were reaching Yong Peng, Lieutenant-Colonel Samuel Pond became the new CO of the 2/29th and began to rebuild. The following day – Australia Day – Billy the Kid was officially taken on strength with other Tampoi 2/29th men. Further reinforcements were brought in from soldiers originally destined for other battalions. Queenslanders, Tasmanians and New

South Welshmen now joined those who'd enlisted for the 2/29th in Victoria. Again, the story was much the same for the 2/19th, which had been raised out of Sydney. Reinforcements were still arriving by ship, moreover, and the kid was among those detailed to go by truck across the Causeway into Singapore and transport them back to the new Base Depot – even though, from a strictly military point of view, these troops may have been more valuable at home. For on the very day that Pond took over the 2/29th, the GOC Malaya, Lieutenant-General Arthur Percival, gave his commanders plans for their imminent withdrawal back into Singapore itself. A delaying action was the most he could hope for before the city fell.

Some of these new arrivals were men of experience and decision. Among the reinforcements who Billy met as they came off the ship was none other than Lieutenant Trewin – whom the kid had last seen at Bacchus Marsh, ordering him on a week's fatigue duty for giving the show away during that night exercise. Don Trewin was destined for a platoon in Billy's own C Company of the 2/29th. And as he came down the gangplank and saw the kid, he cried with some alarm, 'Good God, Private Young, what are *you* doing here?'

'Saving Singapore, sir,' was the best answer he could give.

In truth, none of them could do that. For among the reinforcements sent by their governments were men who, through no fault of their own, were utterly inexperienced and ill equipped for the task demanded of them. Some had come straight off civvy street without ever having handled a weapon. They'd been in the army for barely a month; and of that time, as Lieutenant-Colonel Pond observed, they'd spent a week being kitted out, a week on pre-embarkation leave, and two weeks at sea. Yet they were expected to face the might of the Japanese 25th Army.

Even those reinforcements like Billy, who'd spent time at Tampoi, had no experience beyond elementary platoon training. They knew nothing of company movement and organisation, or how to prepare to face an enemy. Pond thought his new troops would need a minimum of three months to be melded effectively into the re-formed 2/29th Battalion. In fact they had less than two weeks.

There was no option but to use what little time was left for pretty intensive training, to give the new blokes at least a fighting chance. Nor was the range and Bullring at Tampoi available for much longer. As January came to an end and the enemy advanced ever closer, those forces still at Johore began to withdraw across the Strait on to the island of Singapore itself, waiting for the last battle. Rifle and bayonet practice were now conducted every day at the village of Bukit Timah towards the centre of the island, under the very shadow of Japanese bombers.

It was absurd! Nothing could more perfectly demonstrate the ideological collapse of fortress Singapore than the spectacle of its most recent defenders – some of them mere frightened recruits – being taught basic drill, musketry and field craft as their enemies flew unmolested overhead. Sometimes, indeed, the planes were so low they could see the pilots. You couldn't have a piss without Japanese observation balloons spotting you!

Even this, and the knowledge that he would soon be blooded in war, couldn't quite take the juvenile out of Billy the Kid. He was, after all, just 16; and with the insouciance of youth was cementing his trust with the older, now battle-wise men of his new section. Commanders might talk in terms of platoons and companies, battalions, brigades and divisions. But the soldier on the ground knows his section is the unit that really counts – and that those eight or ten men beside him are the ones for whom he fights, and upon whom his safety and self-respect ultimately depend...

Men like Paddy O'Toole, the 'Wild Irishman'. He was only 22, Tasmanian born of a large family, but grew up in Melbourne during the Depression – taking what jobs he could, until the army accepted him. Strong, independent, of larrikin spirit and sport-mad, he was one of those men to whom others naturally turn in times of crisis. When the order came at Parit Sulong to head for the jungle and Yong Peng, he loaded himself with as much ammunition as he could carry, and told others to do the same.

'Load up with ten rounds in your rifles, boys,' he ordered, 'and we'll give 'em a blast. Fire five or six rounds and I'll run a mag off with the Bren gun. Make 'em put their heads down or we're going to knock a few off, and we'll get a hundred yards or so before the next one. And that's how we came out…'

It was also how the 'Wild Irishman' became known as the 'Mad Irishman'. But as Paddy repeated the story afterwards to the new men, encamped now on Singapore in a position near Kranji overlooking the Causeway, the kid sat listening enthralled and ready to do whatever Paddy asked of him. The hero's bandaged flesh wounds only made him the more compelling.

So, one mad afternoon, back at Bukit Timah, where Billy had done well at the rifle range – had even scored fourth placing in a shooting contest – Paddy turned to him and said, 'Bet you can't hit that jam tin.'

'What tin?'

'Over there, near that sergeant yakkin' away. Dare you to take it out.'

Without further thought, the kid unslung his weapon and, taking aim, fired at a rusty can on the ground not two feet from where Sergeant Dobson stood talking to another soldier. It was a good shot. The tin flew up in the air with a *ping* and a rattle – and so did the sergeant, thinking that Japanese snipers were already upon him! Brian Dobson had himself just joined the battalion. C Company as well. As he came back to earth, however, the truth of the situation dawned and he began bawling out the kid.

'Who are you? What's your name? What's your number? What

the hell d'you think you're doing shooting at my feet?'

'I'm sorry, sergeant. I didn't see you there.'

'Didn't see...?'

'No, sergeant. I was looking at the target. I'm very sorry, sergeant.'

Paddy watched on, laughing his head off.

'He thought you was a cow. Sergeant.'

By rights they should both have been charged and sentenced for insubordination, if not outright dangerous behaviour. But there was no time for that. Every able-bodied man was needed at his station. For the last of the British Empire's forces had crossed the Strait on 31 January – a detachment of Argyll Highlanders, who marched with two pipers at their head – and some 70 feet of the stone Causeway was blown up behind them.

Shortly afterwards the divisions of the 25th Imperial Japanese Army moved into Johore, and began making preparations for their final assault across the mile-wide waterway onto beleaguered Singapore.

The first days of February ticked by, one by one. Like waiting – as the kid remembered, nursing his injuries on the cell floor – like waiting for The Postman with his bunch of keys to come knocking all over again.

# 8
# LUCKY 13

*Let's gather all the harvest in,*
*For death is in the fields of life.*

People always said that 13 was unlucky. Ma Jepson thought so, and everyone else felt the same – all except Billy the Kid. Whenever he remembered his few days of fighting on Singapore before the island fell to the Japs in 1942, he knew that – for him – it was the luckiest of numbers.

The first lucky thing was being in the section with Paddy and Bob Shipsides when the shelling got bad: Paddy, the tough young extrovert; Bob, the more taciturn Lance-Corporal. Bob was old enough to be the kid's father (born 1900 – the same year as Dad – Billy remembered), but just as strong as Paddy and as reliable. Solid. Dark, curly hair. No more than middle height, but towering authority. Ready to tell an officer to get stuffed if he thought the order stupid; and while his stripe thereby was always at risk, he was the one you followed, because Bob *knew*. Born at Dimboola. A bushman, like Paddy. And the steel in both of them tempered in the fires of Muar and Parit Sulong.

And there they were when the Japanese shelling across the Strait of Johore began to increase from 5 February. Making light of it. Settling the new men down. Joshing with the fellers about the 2/4th Machine Gun Battalion nearby.

'They're funny buggers that lot, Paddy. Reckon them Vickers bullets are pointed both ends, so's if they don't get you one way, they'll catch ya comin' back.'

Billy was himself number two on the section's Lewis gun – carrying the ammo and feeding it to his number one, Dave Holden. He knew a bit about these things.

'That's not right, is it?'

'Don't worry about them, Billy. They're only Westies. Wouldn't know what they're talkin' about.'

They maintained the comedy of interstate rivalries, even in war. It was only much later, in his first week at Outram Road prison, did the kid realise that the West Australian trustie, Lieutenant Pen Dean, had been among them.

Bob Shipsides would tell Billy that the escalating shellfire was just like penny bungers at a Guy Fawkes bonfire on the night after his birthday.

'D'ya reckon they might hit their own observation balloon?'

'Not that good a shot, son.'

'Make a good target for the RAF fellers though,' remarked Paddy in his dry, laconic way.

They all laughed. The air force barely had a presence for some days. About 50 Hurricane fighters had arrived in crates to replace some of those aircraft lost in Malaya. Not all were actually unpacked, as Billy later discovered. But of those that were assembled, while greatly outnumbered by Japanese Zeros, they at least gave as good as they got – and the kid had watched some terrific dogfights in the skies above Tampoi. But by early February all but a handful had been withdrawn to Java – and enemy bombers now had little opposition as they blitzed the city of Singapore, crowded with more than a million people.

The intensified Japanese shelling didn't go unanswered – though the response was less effective than it might have been. The big guns guarding the sea lanes to Singapore turned and fired inland. The problem was that, prepared for a naval battle, too much of their ammunition was armour-piercing – and not enough was the high-explosive shells that caused real damage to an army on the ground. Moreover, with the Australian 8th Division responsible for the section of coast opposite Johore, General Bennett refused to allow his artillery to aim at a five-storey observation tower in the palace grounds of his friend, the Sultan. General Yamashita and his staff were thus able to use it in relative safety to direct operations.

The offensive was scheduled to begin on Sunday 8 February, two months to the day after the first landings in Malaya. From early morning the Japanese bombardment grew heavier and more insistent.

'This looks like the start of it,' said Bob to the section entrenched with the 2/29th in reserve to the rear. This was the second lucky break, of course. They weren't with the rest of the brigade copping it in the front line by the coast, but were able to see everything from a rise between an arm of the Kranji River and Yew Tree village. 'They're softening us up.'

'Enjoy the show, you blokes,' Paddy observed, as if it were no more than a scene at the Saturday-afternoon pictures. And the kid felt a lot better about it.

At first the bombardment tended to concentrate on the north-east part of the island where the naval base was located. General Percival, with his gift for misjudgement, assumed the naval base would be the first objective of the Japanese, and placed his fittest troops in that sector. General Wavell, on his last visit to Singapore, pointed out that the north-*west* sector was the most likely landing place. The Strait there was only half a mile wide, and the shoreline was fringed with mangrove swamps to screen enemy-troop movements and block the field of fire. Wavell wasn't at all happy with Percival's indecisive personality to command in a crisis. But he let him have his way; and the 8th Australian Division, whose battalions had been replenished by hundreds of new, untried reinforcements, was placed to defend the north-west.

Percival's strategy in fact left the whole island dangerously exposed. With more than 120 000 troops, he greatly outnumbered the Japanese, and his artillery was superior. But unsure where the enemy would attack, he'd placed his forces all around the coast with very little in reserve. His defences were stretched far too thin. By not concentrating on the most likely point of assault, he was weak everywhere. And so it proved. The Japanese took less than a week to conquer him.

For General Wavell was quite right. He understood his opponent's mind. Up there in the Sultan's observation tower, General Yamashita anticipated the naval base would be the most heavily defended point. And perfectly aware of the natural advantages of the north-west coast, this became his principal target. Land there. Move inland quickly. And seize the airfield at Tengah as the first key objective.

So, as Sunday wore on, the fiercest shelling switched to the north-west coast and the 8th Division. The air was filled with the roar and thud of exploding shells. Smoke hung like a sea mist along the shoreline. Officers who'd served in the Great War said it was worse than anything they'd experienced in France.

And for Billy the Kid, exposed for the first time to the full theatre of war, he realised it wasn't a Saturday picture show; not a boyhood game on cracker night – especially not when stray missiles landed closer to their own positions, sending up cascades of dirt and metal. He could feel his nerves tremble like the earth, and his hand tighten on the rifle. Knowing fear, and wondering...

Yet still Bob and Paddy kept up the banter.

'That was close.'

'Not close enough, but.'

'Did you go to that last dance the nurses gave at Tampoi, Paddy?'

'Nah. I was too busy getting shickered.'

Calming everyone down. If they weren't worried, why should you be?

As night fell, and the darkness was lit with the constant fire-flash of artillery and exploding ammunition like some vast tropical storm, even Bob looked at the panorama below and murmured, 'I feel sorry for those poor bastards down there...'

Yet Australian casualties from the opening bombardment were not as bad as anticipated. The two forward battalions of the 27th Brigade – the 2/26th and the 2/30th – were holding about two miles of coast between the Kranji River and the Causeway. To their left, the 22nd Brigade was responsible for eight miles of shoreline: the 2/20th Battalion on the right, the 2/18th in the centre, and the 2/19th, with 600 raw replacements after Muar, on the left – eight miles of swamp and mangrove, defended by 3000 men. Talk about stretched thin. There was on average one man every 15 feet, to face a determined enemy four times their number. For the 22nd Brigade's sector was precisely where General Yamashita planned to launch his first assault. This was where he directed his heaviest fire. But whatever difficulties the terrain and lack of numbers posed to the defenders when fighting started on the ground, the very fact of the mangroves and the distance between soldiers meant that casualties from the initial softening up were relatively light.

At ten o'clock that night, the barrage halted, and a strange silence descended like a cloak upon the battlefield.

'Not long now,' said Bob.

Nor was it. Half an hour later the stealthy shapes of motor launches and barges filled with shock troops emerged from the jungle creeks and waterways on the Johore side, and began crossing the narrow Strait: about 13 000 men all told – 13 battalions of the Japanese 5th and 18th Divisions – to attack the three battalions of the 22nd Brigade and their supporting batteries.

Suddenly the darkness was split by dazzling flares and mortar flashes. The silence was rent by rifle and machine-gun fire, as the Japanese fought their way ashore. And everyone knew how deadly serious and desperate the battle was.

For the natural advantages now worked in the Japanese favour. The mangroves did indeed screen them and block the Australian artillery's field of fire. There were not even any barbed-wire obstacles on the shoreline to hamper the enemy's landing. Gossip had it that several truckloads of wire had been sent to the sector a few days before, but British HQ demanded it be returned intact to Singapore.

In any event, it would have made little difference. By sheer weight of numbers the Japanese soon established themselves on the shore – finding the gaps in the defensive positions and forcing the 22nd Brigade back as the enemy vanguard began fighting its way towards Tengah airfield. So quickly did events unfold that within three hours of the first assault the 2/29th received an order to move immediately from Yew Tree to reinforce Tengah several miles to the west.

Billy left the comfort of his reserve trench and spent the rest of the night moving with the battalion to what would soon be the front line and his baptism of fire. They were in position after dawn: C Company, with the kid in his section, forward of the others among the rubber trees, protected by a little undulating ground, for there was no time to dig trenches. Waiting for their enemy to arrive.

The boy crouched with his ammo and rifle on one side of a rubber tree, Dave Holden and the Lewis gun on the other, listening to Paddy's jocularities *sotto voce*. But in his mind Billy was thinking of Dad and wondering if he'd felt as nervous and unsure the first time he faced fire on the Ebro River in Spain. Hoping that he'd be brave and not let Bob down; not let Paddy despise him.

They heard of some shocking things occurring at Tengah. The Japanese had not only broken through the 22nd Brigade on the Strait, but broken a few spirits as well – especially among those untrained reinforcements. Not surprisingly. As Australian and nearby Indian troops retreated exhausted and disorganised through the 2/29th lines, there were some who in their panic were without weapons or proper uniforms, crying that they'd had enough and were going back to Singapore. Lieutenant-Colonel Pond tried to stop the rot – and even threatened to shoot one officer. Billy the Kid was only glad he'd not personally seen such collapse, for he could not have borne to be like that.

Daylight grew stronger and the sounds of battle came closer. Suddenly Paddy opened up with a burst from his Bren gun.

'Here the little buggers come!' he cried. And among the green shades of the rubber trees, Billy could see figures moving as the Japanese began their usual tactic of trying to encircle their enemy.

Bob responded by firing his Tommy gun, followed by Dave Holden on the Lewis gun. And all at once Billy had no time to wonder how he'd react to his first blooding: he was in the middle of it. Passing another mag to Dave when he called for it. Feeling his adrenalin surging. Aiming his rifle for a shot at the enemy, but they were difficult targets, even for a rifleman who'd come fourth in the shooting contest. The Japs were often camouflaged with bits of foliage tied to their helmets and shoulders. All you could see among the rubber or on the jungle floor was a little bush, which to your great surprise began firing at you and sprinting forward.

Next thing, Billy heard a commotion in the neighbouring section. Crawling under cover of the embankment during a lull in the fighting, he saw that a feller had been shot in the back. The bullet had come out his shoulder, nicking his chin, and the wound was being dressed under fire by the medics.

'Hey, Paddy!' the kid called to the next tree when he returned to his own section. 'They're shooting at us from behind.'

'Up to their old tricks.'

Moments later a bullet slammed into the tree just above Billy's head, and ricocheted with a shower of splinters and bark.

'Christ, Paddy, they must be using dum-dum bullets, the hole's that big!'

The words had barely left his lips when a second bullet hit the tree from behind.

'Paddy, they're up in the trees! Snipers.'

'Another old trick. You hurt?'

'Don't think so.'

'I can't see him…Stay there, and if he has another go I'll get him.'

'What if he gets *me*?'

'You'd better hope I spot him first.'

Within seconds another shot hit the tree above Billy.

'I've got him!' Paddy shouted. 'Got him cold.' And he emptied half a Bren-gun magazine into a rubber tree 100 yards to the rear.

There was a cry and a rustle, and from the branches slumped the bloody carcass of a Japanese soldier, dangling in the arm sling that held him steady in the tree.

'Bastard!'

Billy fired his rifle bitterly into the dappled shadows towards his enemy. Not in anger – and certainly not in fear – but full of indignation that anyone would deliberately try to shoot a nice lad like him! All the same, he knew how fortunate he was that the sniper had not only missed, but that Paddy was there to get him first.

Lucky number three.

The fourth stroke of luck came later that day.

With their bridgehead on the Strait established, the Japanese were landing more troops – about 10 000 men during the course of the day – and pressing further inland. Their grip on the north-west and the airfield was tightening, and by mid-afternoon orders came through for the 2/29th to withdraw from Tengah to a new position near the village of Bulim to the south.

They moved off in orderly fashion along Choa Chu Kang Road, with none of those signs of panic seen among the retreating stragglers that morning. They came under light mortar and machine-gun fire, but the Japanese were really more intent on securing the airfield. Still, there was always a risk.

The Company here was in reserve, bivouacked in more open country. Billy's section found themselves in a rice paddy, the earth soggy with shallow pools from the monsoon rains. Bob had the ten of them gathered in a circle – giving his orders for the evening, allaying uncertainties, making sure everyone had enough rations – when from out of the deepening sky a mortar bomb fell slap in the middle of them. And stuck there. Nose in the ground. Tail fins grinning wickedly in the air.

The kid stared at it, mesmerised by the painted markings. Waiting for the explosion that didn't come. Time and emotion and reason seemed utterly frozen. Until from a corner of his imagination came the thought, 'Shouldn't I be ducking for cover?'

And like a duck, the boy flung himself face down into the muddy water, from which he soon emerged to Paddy's ribald laughter.

'You're a bit late, mate. If it's gunna go off, it would have done so by now!'

A dud mortar bomb. Who would have thought it? And dredged from the sediment of the past came the sounds of Pop Jepson's voice when the woman at the market handed the boy a lead florin for the last of his ferns... *Oh Keithy, she's given you a duddie*. And he remembered, too, the luck that Stiffie Jepson knew how to get rid of it...

It was all luck. *It's there in the turn of the cards, dear.* The kid could still hear Ma saying it – even now in his prison cell – as she sat at the kitchen table in her curls and cardigan telling fortunes from tea leaves or a pack of cards. Laughing privately with Pop when her circus friend, Millie, refused to go out for the day because the Queen of Spades said that she shouldn't.

'What a fool that girl is!'

Ma was never without her playing cards. Crib with Les the Sailor, home from the coastal ships. Poker with friends at night, the cabinet drawer full of new matches, and Millie exclaiming how tinny Ma was! Well, she'd taught the boy to play poker; and with memory of that extraordinary game aboard *Sibajak*, Billy had to admit that so far his cards had been auspicious.

Even when Ma was alone in the house, she'd sit at the table playing patience for hours: turning the cards, red jack on black queen, six of clubs on seven hearts, arranging, shuffling, getting it out, hour after hour, the boy Keithy watching... When, from the grim solitaire of an Outram Road day, came a thought – and with it, one in the eye for the Kenpeitai.

The kid had been wondering for some time how best to use the spare sheets of notebook paper, still hanging with his pencil behind the ventilator shaft. There were three blank pages. One half page had been used to write down the Morse code, but what to do with the rest? Now, with the spirit of Ma Jepson beside him, Billy knew.

That night he withdrew his treasure from the cache and took two pages. Under cover of his blanket he smoothed them straight and began to think how he'd turn them into a pack of cards. There was no hurry. He had plenty of time to occupy.

'Billy the Kid': Billy Young at 15, before departing Australia for Malaya in September 1941. Photo courtesy Bill Young.

Billy ('Keithy'), aged about five, with his father, 'Big' Bill Young, soon after they moved to the Jepson's boarding house in Bulwara Road, Ultimo.

Photo courtesy Bill Young.

'Big' Bill Young, aged 14, leaving school with his bike at Sandfly, Tasmania. He later tried to enlist with the forces bound for Gallipoli.

Photo courtesy Bill Young.

Harry Longley, pictured just after he joined the army in July 1940, aged 17.

Photo courtesy Gerald Longley, Harry's brother.

Joey Crome and his sister, shopping in Sydney, shortly before he left for Malaya in 1941, aged 16. Photo courtesy Bill Young.

Fruit barrow in George Street, Sydney, 1934. Bill says that Pop Jepson didn't have a canopy like this one. Photo City of Sydney Archives file 001/001859.

Battle of Muar: a two-pounder anti-tank gun puts one of eight Japanese tanks out of action during the battle near Bakri, Malaya, 18 January 1942. Photo AWM 068592.

The evil green gates of Outram
Road prison, Singapore, July
1943: Bill Young's drawing of the
day he was incarcerated in the
infamous Kenpeitai jail.

Courtesy Bill Young, from his book *Return to a Dark Age*.

Myles Peace (MP) Brown, in a studio
photograph, before he left for Malaya
and Singapore. He was among the
last reinforcements sent in early
January 1942.

Photo courtesy Judith Gee, Brown's daughter, and
Majella Gee, his grand-daughter.

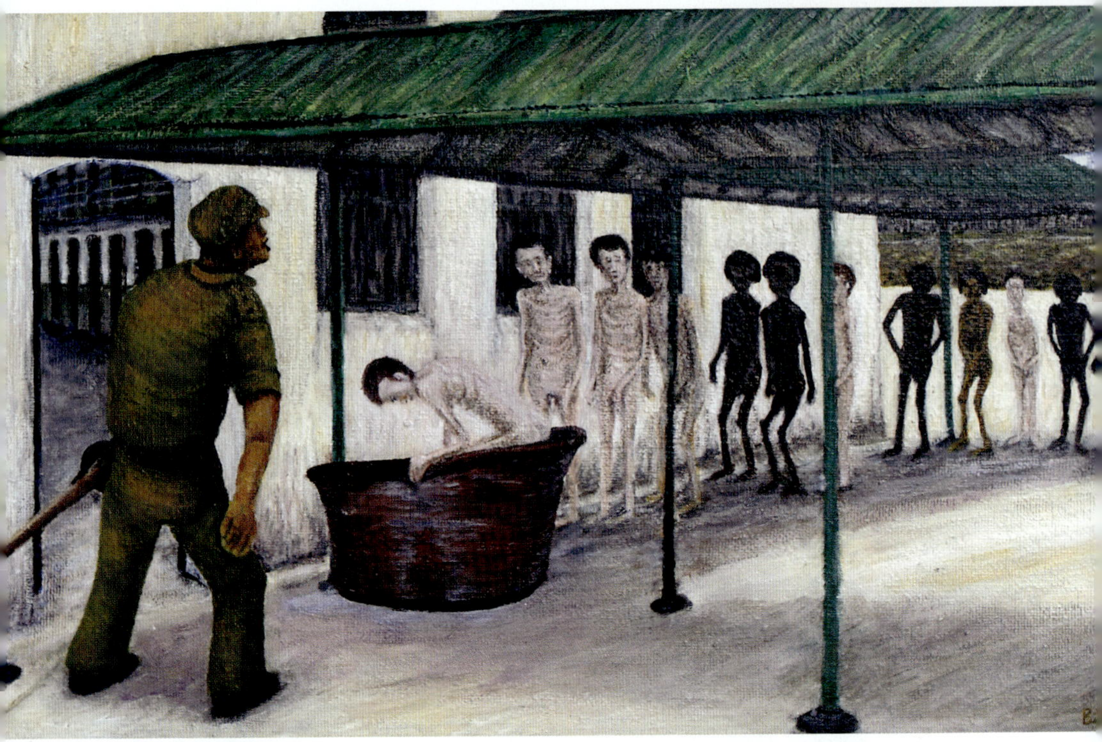

The scabby wash at Outram Road prison: Bill Young's evocative painting of the disgusting scabies-disinfectant bath. Courtesy Bill Young; photo John Feder.

Jimmy Darlington: a photograph of the Aboriginal boxer taken shortly before he sailed for Malaya in February 1941.

Photo courtesy Robert Sweeney of Barraba, NSW, and members of the Darlington family.

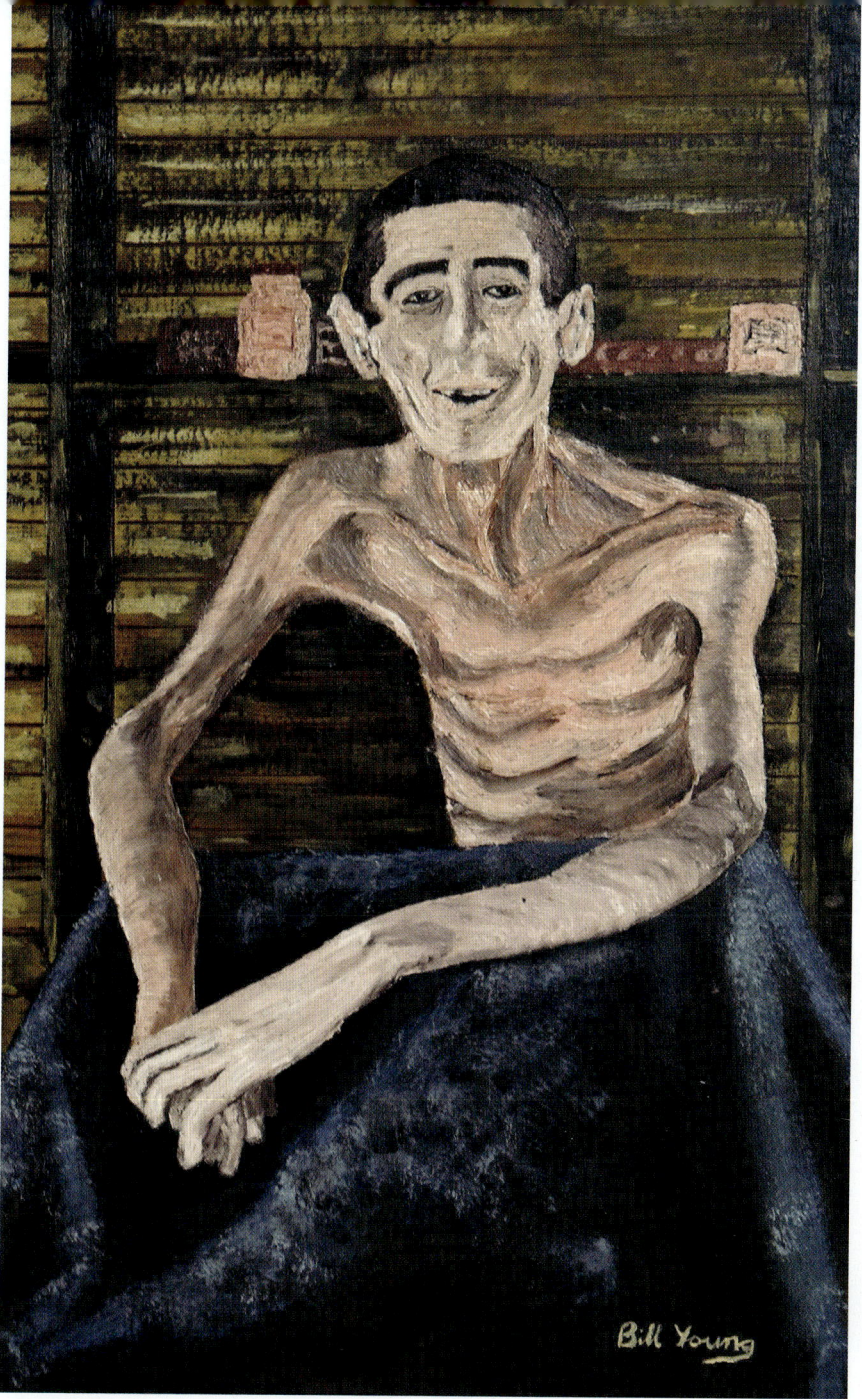

Jack 'Becky' Sharpe: Bill Young's portrait of the emaciated POW, suffering from beriberi, painted from the famous photograph taken at Changi hospital.

Courtesy Bill Young, Ray and Paul Brotherton and members of the Sharpe family; photo John Feder.

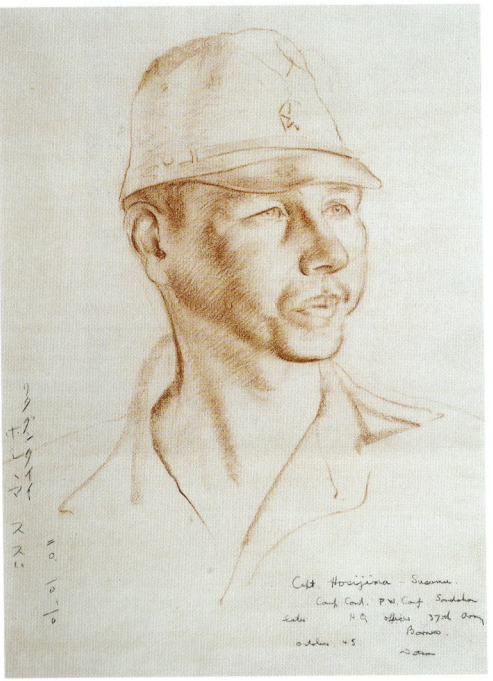

Japanese samurai over Sandakan: Bill Young's imaginative painting of the enemy presence over the Borneo jungle work camp. The Big Tree is shown centre left, the swamp and the Dead End Kids hut lower right.

Courtesy Bill Young; photo John Feder.

Captain Hoshijima Susumi, depicted in red crayon on paper by Douglas Watson, October 1945.

Photo AWM ART22988.

Flying practice: Bill Young's painting of the debilitating POW group punishment on the blindingly white tufa soil during construction of the Sandakan airfield. Courtesy Bill Young; photo John Feder.

'Habbie': Lieutenant John Kerle Tipaho Haberfield. Known as 'Boy' to his family, the Maori pilot was summarily executed by the Kenpeitai among the Palembang Nine several days after the Japanese surrender in August 1945.

Photo courtesy Graham Metzger, his nephew, and members of the Haberfield family. Auckland War Memorial Museum ID 18894.

Postman's Knock: Bill Young's grim picture of himself, cross-legged in his cell at Outram Road prison. It was so narrow he could touch the walls on either side. Courtesy Bill Young; photo John Feder.

The torture of Jimmy Darlington: bashed, trussed with wet ropes in the blazing sun, and made to kneel on sharpened stakes, as depicted in Bill Young's painting of the shocking punishment inflicted at Sandakan airfield in February 1943. Courtesy Bill Young; photo John Feder.

The death cells: Bill Young's haunting image of the *benki toban* cleaning sullage from the filthy floor, as condemned American pilots watch from a cell. Courtesy Bill Young; photo John Feder.

The hospital huts and a burial party at Changi, depicted in a brush, pen and ink drawing by Murray Griffin, 1945. Note the men pulling a cut-down trailer, used as a hearse, past the *atap* huts, and the dead soldier covered by a Union Jack.  Photo AWM ART26480.

Peter's war is over. Billy's poignant drawing of the death of Captain van Hemert in the cell at Outram Road prison, June 1945. Courtesy Bill Young.

The punishment box, known as 'Esau', at the Sandakan POW camp.
Miscreants were kept locked up, hunched in the cage for days – sometimes weeks – and a number died from the treatment. Courtesy Bill Young.

Surviving members of C Company, 2/29th Battalion in their hut at the
rear of Changi jail, September 1945, one month after the war ended.
Note the raised sleeping platforms. Photo AWM 117111.

Liberated POWs at Changi carrying a bucket of rice from the mess.
This had to feed about 250 men – indicating the limited food supplies
available even a month after the war ended.  Photo AWM 019192.

Man's inhumanity: these three Australian POWs on the Burma–Thai
railway were considered 'fit workers' by the Japanese guards. The
stomach of the man on the right is so swollen with beriberi he cannot
fasten his shorts. Secret photo taken by George Aspinall, himself a POW.
Photo AWM P02569.192.

Home: Bill Young photographed in Hobart following his discharge from hospital in November 1945, soon after his 20th birthday. Note he is wearing soft shoes, as his feet are still swollen from beriberi.

Reunion: Bill Young with Nelson Short (left) and Keith Botterill (right), two of the six survivors of the Sandakan death marches, at an RSL club in Sydney during the early 1990s. Photo courtesy Bill Young.

Bill Young, at 85, in a portrait painted by Mitzi Tilley, 2010. The former POW, still a teenager when he returned home in 1945, is amazed he has lived to such an age. Courtesy Mitzi Tilley and Bill Young; photo John Feder.

Each page was about four inches wide by six inches long. Dividing it into seven equal strips and making four cards from each length would give him 28 cards – 56 altogether from two pages. Enough for a full deck with four spares (and he'd still have a blank half page from the notebook left over). The question was, how to do it? Yet even here fortune favoured him. Out with a working party by the pawpaw trees, Billy had found a small green mosaic tile. It was about an inch square and had been thrown up with some rubbish from the air-raid trenches. The kid had kept it among his valuables, for the tile had sharp, straight edges – good for cutting, and now it came into its own.

Sitting cross-legged on the floor, Billy had the tile and a notebook page between his knees. He carefully folded the paper into seven equal strips and rubbed the crease gently along the flat tile for a clean cut. Indeed, the tile was just wide enough to make four cards, the size of his thumbnail, from each strip.

It took days to complete the task – and then to repeat it with the second page – taking great pains not to tear the paper, and all the time keeping an eye open for the guard. With the cards cut, the next thing was to mark them into a deck. This took longer, but then again, time was there to be filled – hours of time as Billy sat drawing his pictures on the little pack of cards. An open heart with a K for king. A shaded clover-leafed club and the number ten. An open diamond with an A for Ace. A black spade and a three. All were shaped as carefully as he could with his pencil stub, sharpened on a piece of brick. He was able to do just a few at a time: the rest of them wrapped for safekeeping in a small length of tape he'd also found among the rubbish and hidden on the twine behind the vent.

Thus, when a fortnight or so had gone by according to the wall calendar, the deck was complete, even to its four leftover jokers. Then Billy could sit cross-legged on the floor playing patience between his knees, just as Ma had taught him. To any guard peeping in, he appeared the model prisoner, contrite in the requisite posture. *Go-hyaku-ju!* But in truth, there was Ma sitting opposite *Yagi* the goat, the kitchen firelight dancing in her eyes, and laughing with old Pop and the jokers. *You fools!*

*It's all in the turn of the cards, dear.*

'Yes, Ma.'

And the skill to take advantage of any opportunity that comes your way.

Which was something – tragically – when it really mattered in Singapore – that General Arthur Percival didn't have.

With Tengah airfield seized, there was a pause in the Japanese advance for much of 9 February. General Yamashita was consolidating his position: ferrying across the rest of his 5th and 18th Divisions – about 23 000 infantry in all – and preparing to attack with his Imperial Guards that night the two battalions of the 27th Australian Brigade guarding the Causeway at Kranji. There was thus a chance for Percival to launch a counterattack during the day, but he was unwilling to move any of his troops from the southern or north-eastern sectors, thinking other landings were likely. It was one more misjudgement. The opportunity passed him by. Men that might have been brought to battle continued to stand idle, and the remainder of the 25th Imperial Japanese Army readied themselves to cross to the island.

In fact, the Allied position was even worse than this. General Bennett didn't visit the north-west sector to see what had happened to his battered 22nd Brigade. Not until the next day was X Battalion formed from several hundred fit men, and the rest of the brigade regrouped. And unknown even to Bennett, Brigadier Maxwell of the 27th Brigade was making plans to withdraw the 2/26th and the 2/30th Battalions inland from the coast that night – precisely when the Japanese planned to attack them.

From late afternoon a heavy bombardment fell on the two battalions. It lifted at about 8.30 pm, and soon afterwards Japanese barges and landing craft surged across the Strait. They were met with fierce artillery and machine-gun fire, and many were driven off. Men of the 2/26th fought those assailants who landed in savage hand-to-hand fighting among the mangrove swamps, and the line was held. The assault, indeed, came close to failing. The valves on the storage tanks at Woodlands oil depot were opened, and two million gallons of oil flowed into the Strait and caught fire. Japanese barges were trapped and incinerated, and a request came through to call off the attack. But Yamashita asked for further reports, refusing at this stage to be panicked. Wisely.

Soon after midnight, even as his troops were holding their own, Maxwell inexplicably gave his orders for the two battalions to retire. The Japanese took advantage of the opening to press home their attack. And still Percival refused to move forces from the southern or eastern sectors. Instead of planning a counter-assault, as someone with Wavell's 'fighting spirit' might have done, he issued his commanders provisional ideas for withdrawal to a final cordon around the city – which were prematurely made known to subordinate officers, who took them as orders to begin preparations, whatever the psychological effect on their men.

Thus, to all intents and purposes, Singapore was lost. By early 10 February, the Imperial Guard had established their bridgehead at Kranji. Japanese engineers easily spanned the 70-foot gap blown in the stone Causeway, and tanks and artillery were ready to drive across and down the last of the Trunk Road, in support of their infantry, towards Bukit Timah – 'Tin Mountain' – less than 600 feet high, but the tallest point on the island: dominating the water reservoirs and the terrified city below.

As for Billy, he spent the night in the field (though his section pulled back a safer distance from the unexploded mortar bomb) getting what shut-eye he could, until orders came through at dawn to move south again towards the village of Bukit Panjang. As daylight came they could see clouds of billowing black smoke, like funeral plumes, from the burning oil depot – and indeed their faces were dark as minstrels with drifting soot.

The companies came under mortar and machine-gun attack and were strafed as they withdrew. There were a number of casualties, including Major Hore, who was wounded by a mortar bomb. But they behaved well under fire, coming to the assistance of a group of Argyll Highlanders who'd been expected to hold a two-mile front with only 150 men after their support failed to materialise. Communications were poor, and the Battalion's own A Company missed the rendezvous. Defences everywhere were weakening under Japanese pressure; and by the late afternoon of 10 February the 2/29th withdrew further to the vital Bukit Timah crossroads and the line now held by Indian, Malay and Australian units.

That night they came under heavy attack from tanks and infantry as the Japanese divisions moved in from Tengah airport and the Imperial Guards struck from the landing at the Causeway. General Yamashita's aim was to capture Bukit Timah by 11 February, a special day celebrating the founding of the Japanese Empire. Which, after a desperate struggle in the darkness, he did.

The kid's battalion moved forward again that morning to a ridge overlooking the main railway line in support of a planned counterattack by the British 18th Division. It wasn't successful. The attackers ultimately withdrew. And after coming under sustained machine-gun fire from the air and ground, in which Captain Bowring of C Company was among the injured, the 2/29th also sought permission to retire. It was refused. The battalion was told to stay where it was. But as night fell, the patrols discovered they were quite alone – and the enemy was closing in behind them.

The CO therefore ordered a withdrawal southward around Bukit Timah to Holland Road.

Retreat. Always, as the kid remembered it now, it seemed to be retreat. No sooner were they dug in to one position, or ready to advance and itching to take on the Nips, than an order came to withdraw. And yet, as he also was aware, sitting on the cell floor in Outram Road with a game of patience and the thumbnail pack of cards between his knees, turning the discards one by one – four hearts, six clubs, three diamonds – Ma looking down as she had taught him, tinny as ever, his luck still held. For it was during this last move that Billy the Kid's war ceased to be part of any wider strategic contest between armies on a battlefield. Instead, it became a personal struggle for survival, in which chance and the support of those few close comrades-in-arms were the only things that helped him win against the odds.

Retreating at night in strange country, under fire and with many inexperienced soldiers, companies became separated. Platoons lost contact with their companies. And sections were cut off from each other. So, during the night of 11 February, the 20 or so surviving men from Billy's platoon found themselves lost in a swamp.

It was, in retrospect, the fifth bit of luck to come the kid's way during the battle for Singapore. He'd stayed close to Paddy and Bob throughout, following their direction as the battalion pulled back towards the city and surviving so far unscathed the onslaught of shell, bomb and bullet where so many others had not. There in stagnant swamp water they were at least protected from pursuit by tanks. Night covered them from air attack – unless you counted the squadrons of mosquitoes that zeroed in on any square of exposed flesh.

'We'll have to stay here,' Bob Shipsides told them. 'I'm not quite sure where we are, and we'll have to wait till morning to get our bearings.'

'And what then, Corp?'

'We'll head for Bukit Timah. We're pretty low on ammunition and they'll have plenty of supplies at the dump there.'

'Righto.'

'We're safe enough here for the time being. Try and get some rest if you can.'

Billy was as exhausted as everyone else, for they'd had little enough sleep these past three nights since the Japanese landing. So he hauled himself out of the slime into a tree and, propping himself in a fork, allowed his mind to relax.

It was certainly true about the ammo. The kid had a few rounds left for his .303, but the bag he carried as number two for Dave Holden on the Lewis gun now held only empty magazines. The kid wanted to chuck it away, but Bob said they'd want it at the resupply depot. So Billy had to lug it with him. He'd also started with three grenades, yet only had one left. Now, in his tree, Billy wondered if he should let it off to drive away the swarms of mosquitoes. But Bob wouldn't appreciate that. The boy yawned and fell into an uncomfortable sleep.

Daylight was breaking when he woke, the dark swamp trees silhouetted against a silvery sky like a stage set. The others were already up and preparing to move out to higher ground to find their bearings. They hadn't far to go. A few minutes and the platoon emerged into a clearing at the foot of a low hill, on the other side of which the sounds of machine-gun and mortar fire could be heard.

They'd just squatted down to eat a breakfast of iron rations, when an intelligence officer appeared – from nowhere, it seemed – wanting to know what was going on.

'The battle is reaching a critical stage,' he said. 'I need someone to go up this hill on reconnaissance to see what the Japs are doing.'

Nobody stirred. The officer grew impatient.

'This is vitally important business!' he exclaimed. 'The outcome could depend upon it. Somebody must go up that hill...'

At last Dave Holden finished chewing and said casually to his number two, 'Come on, Billy. We'll do it for him.'

But the kid had other ideas.

'I don't want to.'

'It's an order, Billy,' from Bob Shipsides.

'Well, I'll go up with Dave if you lend me your Tommy gun.'

'Me Tommy gun?' It was like asking Bob for his wallet.

'I'll feel a lot safer.'

And he could exhibit a lot more bravado. The boy had long admired Bob's Tommy gun as the perfect weapon carried by gangsters in those Saturday picture shows. Now was the perfect opportunity to blackmail his corporal into letting him use it – and it worked.

'Orright. But you look after it, mind. And don't be long.'

Thus, Al Capone and Dave Holden ascended the hill. From the top the view was like a wide shot in some war film: bursts of gun smoke and shellfire in the distance; the stutter of machine guns as Zeros, diving like mosquitoes, strafed retreating men in the country beyond Bukit Timah. Importantly, below them they saw a troop of Japanese mortar bombers preparing to fire. Even more to the point, the enemy saw *them*.

One – two – three...In quick succession a salvo of six-inch mortar bombs was fired at them, getting closer as the troopers found their range. Not duddies either, but live ones exploding in a flower burst of shrapnel. Even Al Capone's audacity began to pale, though Dave Holden was still as casual as they came when he turned and said, 'Come along, Billy. We can always come back later and catch the rest of the show.'

He spoke as if they were merely going out for an intermission ice-cream at the flicks – which the kid found unspeakably funny in the circumstances. And he giggled to himself all the way down the hill. Lucky six.

It was no laughing matter when they reached the bottom. The information they were supposed to have gathered no longer seemed so vitally important. The intelligence officer had disappeared. So had most of the platoon. Only Bob and Paddy were waiting for them with a couple of other fellers – and they were angry and impatient.

'Where the bloody hell have you been?' Lance-Corporal Shipsides demanded, grabbing back his Tommy gun.

'Ya know where we've been – up that flamin' hill.'

'What took youse so long?' Paddy wanted to know.

'We wasn't long. Had to have a look, like that officer wanted.'

'Just step on it,' Bob ordered. 'We've got to catch them up.'

The kid returned to his rifle and bag of empty magazines, and the six set off – skirting grass and swamp, until they found the rest of the platoon (minus the intelligence officer) near a rubber plantation. Gathered together again, they continued to move towards the supply base at Bukit Timah, keeping the Trunk Road and railway line on their right and staying close to the trees and patches of jungle to avoid contact with the enemy. They were everywhere, for the Japanese had advanced a lot further than any of them realised, and it was impossible to escape them altogether. Yet it was here that Dame Fortune dealt Billy one of his better hands.

About mid-afternoon they had to cross a paddy to reach rubber on the other side. The 20 had no choice but to extend in a line, a few yards between each man, and run. But the Japanese now had total control of the air. Unknown to the troops, the last of the Allied planes had left Singapore the day before with General Wavell. As the platoon was crossing the open field, a Japanese Zero came swooping down.

Catching the men in his sights, the pilot opened up with his machine guns, spraying bullets at the hapless soldiers below. Yet in one of those freak chances of war, the dragons' teeth passed between them. No one was hit and the platoon kept running.

The pilot circled like a sparrow hawk and dived again, machine guns blazing. But once again he missed. Once again death eluded them, and with wings on his feet the kid reached the rubber trees with the rest of his platoon.

Seven. Lucky, lucky seven. And eight was not far behind.

Safe among the rubber, the men spread themselves out and lay behind the slender latex trees to catch their breath and count their blessings before resuming the journey. But while the pilot may not have been a very accurate marksman, he could still read a map and quickly radioed back their position. Within minutes came the *crump* of artillery, and shells began ranging overhead.

'Back! Pull back!' Bob cried.

But it was too late for that. The artillery had found them.

Billy was about to move when a shell hit the top of the tree that sheltered him. It exploded in a volley of splinters and metal fragments, killing two men who lay near the trees just behind. The kid himself felt a sudden detonation of pain in his groin. He reached down and pulled back his hand covered in blood.

'Me leg!' he shouted. 'They've got me leg.' And into his mind came memories of Les the Soldier at Bulwara Road, who'd returned from the Great War minus a leg.

'Hang on, kid,' Paddy said as he crawled over to him. 'We're comin'.'

'Dave, you give us what cover you can with the Lewis gun,' Bob ordered during a pause in the fire. 'And the rest of you blokes hotfoot it out of here to Bukit Timah!'

The corporal moved to look at his two men who'd taken direct hits and now slumped bloodied on the earth.

'They've gone,' he said, turning to Paddy with the kid. 'How's the boy?'

'They've taken me leg, Bob!' Billy shook. 'Me whole flamin' leg's gone.'

'No it ain't,' Paddy replied shortly. 'Small bit of shrapnel in ya right thigh. Lucky it weren't a couple of inches further over or it woulda taken out ya middle stump. Mind you,' he added after a pause, 'it would have been two no balls.' And he laughed in his coarse-humoured way, which was precisely what was needed.

Thank you, God, eight times lucky eight!

Paddy applied a field dressing to the wound and once it was bandaged asked Billy if he could stand.

'Think so.'

The kid held onto the man as he hauled himself upright. The leg hurt like hell and his head was clanging, but at least he found he could move.

'Slow going, though.'

'That's all right. Sling your rifle and hang onto me. I'll carry ya bag.'

'We'll get you to the medic as soon as we reach Bukit Timah,' Bob soothed him. 'Have you fixed in no time.'

With the bombardment shifting, they moved off through the rubber trees. The rest of the platoon had gone and the group was now reduced to just the four of them. And for all that Paddy helped him, limping Billy did indeed find the going painfully slow. Darkness had almost fallen by the time they worked back to the Trunk Road and recognised a few familiar landmarks from the vicinity of Bukit Timah, for they'd been there many times in the Johore days.

'This looks like it,' said Bob. 'Safe at last.'

Seeing movement ahead, they walked boldly towards the road in anticipation of friends, supplies, and a doctor for the lad. And once again Lady Luck came to Billy's rescue.

The village was still smouldering after the Japanese attack, glowing embers and ash adding to the Stygian atmosphere of war and night and smoke from the oil depot. There was no moon either, for it was hidden by the pall. Suddenly, a cinder that had blown onto the palm leaf *atap* thatch of a hut by the roadside burst into flame, and the fire lit the faces of a squad of soldiers standing nearby.

'Christ!' Bob exclaimed through his teeth, recognising the distinctive soft caps. 'They're bloody Japs! Quick! Off the road.'

And like four nocturnal rats they scurried to the safety of a large, concrete-lined monsoon drain that ran beside the road. Lucky nine! It was deep enough to shelter crouching men, although the burning hut threw their shadows against the concrete wall. They just prayed that their enemies wouldn't see them.

'That was close, Bob.'

'Ssh, Billy. Silence now.'

'Hope they didn't hear the racket of our weapons,' Paddy remarked. Then he too fell quiet, the stillness filled by the crackle of burning thatch and the laughter of the sentry gossiping up the road. And by something else...

Further along the road they heard a rumble drawing closer. The concrete drain began to echo and vibrate.

'Tanks,' murmured Paddy. 'And plenty of 'em.'

Sure enough, out of the night came five or six tanks, rolling down from the Causeway into the village. They moved in leisurely convoy, not at all prepared for battle, for unknown to the watchers in the drain, Bukit Timah had been in Japanese hands all that day. Most of the island's reservoirs were now under their control. The defenders were withdrawing to an ever smaller cordon around the city. Leaflets had been dropped calling on the British to surrender, as Yamashita prepared his final offensive. The tanks had nothing to fear as they clanked down the road.

'Shit,' Paddy observed, as they realised that their plans for a hot meal, re-equipment and a welcoming rest at Bukit Timah had to be deferred.

'We've got to get out of here,' Bob said. 'The question is, how?'

Yes, indeed. For instead of departure came a number of new arrivals. From one end of the drain crept several Indian sepoys, who told them they'd been abandoned by their officers and left to find their own way to safety.

'I thought youse was Japs,' Paddy whispered. 'Lucky I didn't want to wake the Nips up top and give you a burst.'

'Yes, sahib. Thank you, sahib.'

But hearing movement further along the drain, and thinking the enemy might be stalking them from the other side, Paddy went on alert, Bren gun at the ready.

'Who is it?'

Dave Holden aimed his Lewis gun.

'Only us . . . '

And from the darkness staggered a couple of familiar faces: Sergeant Brian Dobson (he of the tin can fame) and Doug Cameron carrying a Lewis gun. They were also supporting a young officer, new to Singapore, who'd been badly shell-shocked; he was now slumped between them as they hurried stooping along the drain.

'Saw your shadows,' said Dobbo. 'Piece of luck. You too?' he said, noticing the kid.

'Yeah,' Bob remarked. 'And you keep that bloke quiet.'

For the young officer had begun to cry and shake in his distress.

'Billy, look after him.'

They sat the man, tears running down his face and muttering, against the wall. The kid squatted beside him and, despite his own hurt, tried to pacify him.

'It's all right. You'll be okay. Bob knows what to do. He'll see us through.'

'It's getting like Flinders Street Station in here,' Paddy laughed.

'Hush!'

For down the road came yet another sound – a soft, pneumatic wheezing, like the breath of hobgoblins. And all at once above their heads, reflected in the dying glow of the fire, they saw a battalion of Japanese soldiers riding by on their bicycles. Hundreds of them, four abreast – rifles slung over their shoulders, food bags at their sides – silently pushing their way forward to the village, wheels sighing on the road.

'I could take a few of 'em out with the Bren gun,' murmured Paddy as the soldiers passed only inches away from him.

But he thought better of it. Sensibly. No sooner had the cyclists gone than came the flare of headlights through the trees and behind them the distant growl of motorbikes. A large open tourer came into view – a staff car, carrying somebody important – which stopped on the road not far from where the group was hiding.

The despatch riders on their motorbikes caught up, and the listeners could hear voices raised in animated conversation. They couldn't understand the language, however vital the intelligence it conveyed. But that made no difference to the young officer who, on hearing the Japanese words, became more agitated. So much so that Billy alone couldn't keep him quiet, and asked Bob to assist.

'It's all right, sir,' Shipsides said, speaking with his quiet authority. 'Help's on the way. Just settle down. Please.'

The officer seemed to do so for a little, quietly wringing his hands and murmuring to himself. Such a strange reversal of the natural order that an officer should be taking his commands from a lance-corporal and a mere boy.

'That's a good fellow.'

Bob turned away. The staff car drove off into the village and the despatch riders roared back towards Johore.

'This ain't Flinders Street Station,' Bob swore softly. 'The traffic's more like bloody Bourke Street. We've gotta move.'

'Too right,' Paddy agreed. 'Just give us the word.'

'I'm thinkin' about it.'

But as he was thinking, the young officer fell victim to his own torments. He sprang to his feet and with an oath started to climb out of the drain onto the road.

'Come back!' cried Bob, trying to grab him. 'You're going the wrong way, sir.'

But the man was too quick for him, and too desperate. He struggled from Bob's grasp and began running and screaming towards the Japs. Right into the line of fire.

Alerted by the noise, the sentry shouted. Shots were fired, followed by the splutter of a machine gun. A flare went up, lighting the scene with ghostly incandescence. And by its light they saw the young officer, arms floundering like some celluloid extra in a black-and-white film, slowly reach, and double, and fall lifeless onto the roadway.

There would come a time when Billy would see in the eyes of a Japanese warrior, as it happened, one who knew and understood the terrible sadness of war. The dreadful consequence and waste of battle. But that time was not now.

By the flare, which seemed to hang in the sky like a second sun, they also saw more troops coming in single file along the road. It would only take one of them to look over the edge of the drain and notice their furtive shadows flattened against the wall. Just one of them to stop where they hid and decide to have a leak...

Yet they didn't. Billy's tenth stroke of luck in his fight for Singapore. The soldiers passed, the flare also died, and the world returned to the pit of darkness.

For hours they waited, until midnight had interred their troubles. Then, satisfied that all was still, Bob called to the others and they huddled together in the drain.

'This is what we're gunna do,' he whispered. 'Take off your boots and tie them to your belt. We'll crawl over the back of the drain here and tippy-toe across the open ground to the scrub. It's only a hundred yards or so. Once there, we'll put on our boots and work around the hill to the racecourse at the back, using the rubber and jungle for cover. Any questions?'

'What about the weapons?' Brian Dobson asked, ceding his authority as sergeant to Bob's superior bushcraft. 'Leave 'em here?'

'I'm not leavin' my Bren gun behind,' Paddy affirmed. 'Carried it all through.'

'Nor my Tommy gun. Take your rifles, but we'll dismantle the Lewis guns. They're too heavy to lug around with us. Chuck the locking pins so the Japs can't use 'em.'

'And the ammo bag?' from the kid.

'Yes, Billy. We'll leave that.' At last.

They removed their boots and tied them to their belts. The kid and Dave Holden soon had their Lewis gun dismantled, for they were practised at it: Billy gripping the bipod legs at one end as Dave made sure the chamber was empty, pulled the trigger, and twisted the weapon to release the body locking pin, which he shoved in his pocket, to chuck later.

Sergeant Dobson and Doug Cameron were not so skilled, however, for they'd only picked up the Lewis gun when their own men had been lost in the fighting. Dobbo forgot to check the chamber, which still contained one live bullet. And Dougie thoughtlessly placed his hand over the end of the barrel to keep the gun steady – so much easier than hanging onto the bipods, but rather more dangerous. As soon as Dobson pulled the trigger, the gun fired. The bullet went straight through Dougie's hand, hit the concrete drain, ricocheted and struck one of the Indian sepoys in the shoulder. And all hell broke loose.

The Lewis gun resounded through the darkness. Doug and the

sepoy were howling and cursing and calling upon their respective gods for assistance. The sentry yelled. Another flare went up. And in the sudden explosion of noise, Bob cried to the others: 'Out! Now! And run like buggery!'

Billy needed no second command. He and Paddy grabbed the injured Doug Cameron, helping him to scramble over the concrete ledge and out of the drain. They leaped to their feet. And, lifting Doug between them, threw themselves into the night and the distance that stretched forever to the tree line.

Gunfire echoed – rifles and machine guns – and the kid sensed bullets piercing the air around them like the winds of death. Another flare went up. Ghastly. White. The shadows singing. Doug heavy as pain. Billy's thigh wound stabbing, his legs not moving any faster. Stumbling. Gasping. Calling on Dad. His feet cut to ribbons. Until at last the dark sanctuary of the jungle embraced them, and he fell into its protection.

Number 11. Lucky, plucky 11.

Or was it?

A low *coo-ee* from Bob brought the six Australians creeping together. God knew what happened to the Indian sepoys. Yet these six, all from the 2/29th C Company as it turned out, were alive – Paddy even now putting a field dressing on Doug Cameron's bleeding hand.

'I don't think they're following us,' Bob said, alert as ever, 'but it's not safe to remain here. Put on your boots and we'll pull back further into the scrub. First light, we'll head out for the racecourse road and look for the battalion.'

Put on your boots. Sweet Jesus! The kid went to untie them from his belt... but they were gone. Whether they'd come loose in the scramble out of the drain, or fallen off during the flight to the trees, Billy couldn't say. But they weren't there.

'Bob, I lost me boots.'

'Then you'll have to walk without them, boy. Can't look for 'em now.'

'Not unless you want to go back in the morning,' Paddy remarked helpfully.

'No thanks! I'll be all right.'

But he wasn't. By daybreak they were on the move, edging through jungle and rubber in the direction of Singapore, the kid hobbling to keep up. With only socks to protect his feet, he seemed to step on every sharp twig and stone – and his feet, recovering from tinea, were soon torn and bloody. To say nothing of the shrapnel ripping in his thigh.

Their progress was also hampered by the suffocating atmosphere. Oil dumps around the burning city had caught fire, the smoke combining to create a dark, hellish mist. And the six, already filthy from four days on the move, saw by the fitful sunlight they were now blackened from head to toe by droplets of oil.

The oil cloud permeated everything. Or almost everything. Coming out at last onto Racecourse Road, they passed a British officer emerging from his tent, immaculately dressed by his batman in freshly laundered khakis. He seemed to have spent his entire war under canvas.

'I say, you chaps,' he called. 'Where are the Jappies?'

'The Jappies!' Paddy shouted back, the Irish in him igniting at the spectacle. 'I'll tell you where the effing Jappies are, mate. They're not far behind us, and they're comin' right up your arse!'

'How dare you!' the officer cried. 'Australians! What's your regiment? I'll have you charged for insolence —'

'Oh, go and get stuffed.' Bob added his own declaration.

And they kept walking, through the smouldering haze, along a road littered with the desolations of battle. Past shattered vehicles and groups of men wandering, like themselves, in search of their units. Through a devastated *kampong*, the people dead or hiding.

Debris. Confusion. A sense of helpless despair as the Japanese forced the city's stricken leadership to shrink ever further into itself.

Ahead of them they saw a Bren gun carrier coming down the road. It was being chased by a Japanese Zero, guns blazing. The carrier was firing back, but to no effect. As the plane passed overhead it dropped a bomb. The carrier swerved, exploded and upended into the ditch, a fractured wreck of metal and human flesh.

In one small act of defiance, the kid unslung his rifle and took a pot shot at the Zero. But to no effect, either. The plane had gone by the time he pulled the trigger.

'Nice try though, Billy,' Paddy said. 'They'd give you a medal if you hit it.'

Still, the incident carried one more piece of luck. Lucky 12. As they passed the Bren gun carrier, a couple of Australian medics were helping the survivors.

'Where are you from?' Bob asked. 'We've got a couple of blokes need help.'

'There's a Regimental Aid Post up the next track. In a plantation.'

'Good-oh. Thanks.'

They found the RAP without trouble, and before long a doctor had tended to Doug Cameron's severely wounded hand and sent him to surgery in an ambulance about to leave for a military hospital. He then turned to Billy and extracted a small piece of shrapnel – about an inch long – from his thigh.

'Do you want it as a war souvenir?' he asked, stitching the incision.

'Might as well. For good luck.' Billy kept the sliver among his treasures in an empty Log Cabin tobacco tin, safe in his army haversack.

'Your leg will be all right. Not sure about the feet, though. They're badly cut. I've cleaned and washed them with antiseptic. Can you put on your boots?'

'I haven't got no boots. I lost them.'

'Then I'm sending you to hospital as well, until the lacerations heal.'

'I've already been in hospital once. At Johore. Do I have to go *again*?'

'Not unless you want to end up a cripple, you don't.'

'Bob, they're sending me to the hospital,' he whined, as his corporal came into the tent.

'You just do what you're told, Billy,' Bob Shipsides replied. 'It won't be for long. We've got to push on now ourselves, but we'll catch up with you again later – with the battalion.'

His companions departed, leaving the kid to make decisions now by himself. Momentous decisions, as it transpired. The most important decisions of his life.

'We've a couple more ambulances ready to leave,' the doctor said. 'Can you walk on those feet?'

'Dunno.'

'Well, if you can walk, go to the ambulance on the left. If not, we'll put you on a stretcher and carry you to the other one.'

The kid debated with himself. Of course he could walk. Just. He'd been limping like a one-legged man for the past 24 hours. On the other hand, should he be a contrary coot and make them *carry* him to the ambulance?

'Nah. I'll walk.'

He got up and shuffled to the vehicle on the left.

'We're going to the 13th Australian General Hospital,' the driver said. 'Out at St Patrick's College on the Changi Road. That all right with you?'

St Pat's College. That's where the 2/29th Battalion had been quartered when it first arrived in Singapore, so Bob had said.

'Yeah, 13 AGH is fine.'

Better than he could have known. For the other ambulance

195

was going to the Alexandra Hospital, closer to town. And where, the following day, the Japanese were to murder in cold blood 150 patients and staff – one man bayoneted as he lay on the operating table. It was another of those atrocities of the war, to be remembered with Parit Sulong. And Billy the Kid, on the mere turn of a card, might have been there.

Sitting now with his patience cards in the prison cell, he again thanked the angels that guided his choice that day. At lunch time – 1300 hours – on Friday 13 February, he had decided to walk on bandaged feet to the ambulance that took him to 13 AGH. All unknowing, he had chosen life over death; the chance of survival, even in captivity, over the near-certainty of destruction.

Lucky 13.

And even the smallest deck of cards, Billy reflected, as he placed a six of diamonds on the seven of spades – even a thumbnail pack made from two stolen pages of a notebook, has 52 cards. Four times 13.

# 9

# CHANGI

*The trees stood to in silent grief,*
*The flowering scrubs a living wreath.*

There came a morning when Billy the Kid was woken from his unhappy sleep by a bird singing on the high window ledge of his prison cell. He'd been dreaming of Ma's Chester cake, spread with butter and treacle, that was snatched from his lips as he went to eat it...of the salve in Nana Tot's medicine cupboard, good for healing scabby sores, that turned to acid on his flesh...

Restless, hungry, contaminated dreams. As always. When, through his loneliness, he heard the birdsong. Opening his eyes, Billy saw the bird perched against the morning light, hopping between the bars and calling in search of a soulmate.

He lay on the bed boards for several minutes listening, enjoying the company and envying the bird its liberty. It was the first time he'd had such a visitor. The kid couldn't say what sort of bird it was. A bit bigger than a sparrow: a thrush maybe, or a starling, if such birds lived in Singapore. Perhaps it was one of those migratory birds, every year flying to Australia, to build a nest and raise its young? And at once he was filled with a yearning – a homesickness of such intensity that he'd not known for a long time. The smell of soap and roast dinner. The sweep of sunlight and blue gum along the escarpment as far as you could see. Nana Tot stoking the winter fire, and agreeing through closed Hobart doors that 'The army might make a man of him...'

Memory and music and melancholy filled him to overflowing. Two postcards were all he'd been allowed to send Nana as a POW. Two miserable cards written in block letters under Jap supervision: I AM WELL. LOVE TO ALL. BILLY. And in case this tiny bird could fly so far south with a message, he said out loud, 'You can stay as long as you like, little mate.' Though of course it didn't. At the sound of a human voice so close, it took fright and flew away.

Yet the sense of renewal it brought – the elusive hope for his own freedom – remained with the kid. Like another first swallow, it might even have been a harbinger of change. And so it turned out to be.

Some time in early 1944 the Kenpeitai instigated a new regime for the military prisoners at Outram Road. It came without warning or expectation. Alerted by commands and opening doors in the outside passage, Billy assumed it was one of the changeovers during which prisoners were moved to other cells, their old ones searched for contraband. He just had time to retrieve the pack of cards and pencil, when the door was unlocked and he was ordered to pick up his bed boards and blanket, and walk.

*Bango!* Number off every time you leave the cell. The ritual indignity of the strip search (though again never of the naked fist). Prepare to be ushered into new quarters. But this time, instead of being allocated one man to a cell on both sides of Broadway, they were told to share: two men to a cell. And all on the prison's left-hand side. The days of strictly solitary confinement were coming to an end.

Billy's first cellmate was that somewhat punch-drunk English soldier known as 'Spike' Smith, the feller who'd thrown the jujutsu bout. There was no talking, of course, as they entered their cell, but there were plenty of puzzled glances and shrugged shoulders as the men pondered how such a miraculous state of affairs had come to pass.

Nobody ever knew the answer. Wall gossip had it that the Japs were starting to lose the war, and the Kenpeitai had decided on sharing because it would be easier to kill their prisoners if men were grouped close together when the end came. True, the new system required fewer guards, freeing some for the battlefront. And Little Hitler certainly hinted at a grim future as he locked Spike and Billy in their cell that first day, for he drew his finger across his throat, like a blade, and scowled.

'*Suga. Mate!*' Soon. Just you wait! The threat became a standard greeting.

However frightened the Japs thought their prisoners might be at the new arrangements, the effect on the men was quite the opposite. Freed from the dreadful isolation of mind, spirit and body, here was another human being to share the wasted hours. Someone to talk to, side by side on the floor. Whispering. It didn't matter that the other bloke was filthy with his own shit. Reeking of pus and open scabs. So hollowed out with hunger you could count every rib and vertebrae. You were just the same. And while you might seem half dead, the mere fact of another presence was an affirmation that you were – still – half alive.

Once settled in together, the kid asked Spike if he'd like a game of his beloved poker. As a break from solitaire he'd tried playing poker by himself – though gave it up as a bad job when his right hand kept cheating! But Spike didn't play cards; he no longer had the head for it. So they talked instead of the past and their childhoods: similar in some respects, for they'd both had hard working-class beginnings. Yet where Billy had the extraordinary comfort of the Jepsons in Ultimo to remember, Spike had known only brutality growing up as a cockney Londoner, and had gone into the army at a young age to escape it. As had Billy, under different circumstances.

Spike had been sent with the British Army to India, serving from the Plains to the Khyber Pass. He spoke to the kid of his wonder at first eating a banana and a pineapple. Very handy with his fists (as of course was Big Bill Young), he'd been trained in the noble art and soon established himself as regimental heavyweight champion. Spike earned a lot of money for his backers by the number of prize fights he'd won – and even more money by the fights he'd thrown. He was very good at it, as he'd demonstrated with the little Jap guard. *Hai! Jujutsu ichiban!*

The experience had left him with a broken nose, a cauliflower ear, and rather slow-witted – the caricature of an ex-pug. No good for cards. But he had a memory for poetry and taught Billy that favourite of barrack room and music hall, 'The Green Eye of the Little Yellow God': *There's a one-eyed yellow idol to the north of Kathmandu / There's a little marble cross below the town…*

In return the kid tried to teach Spike some of the verses Sergeant Hatfield had scratched on the wall, though with no great success. Yet Spike did respond to those Kipling lines about Afghanistan's plains, for he'd heard of such things in India.

Thus, by stealth, their conversation always came back to the army, and soldiering – and their participation in the military catastrophe that had brought them by separate ways to Singapore, and incarceration together in an Outram Road cell…

Billy was still a patient at the 13th Australian General Hospital with his tinea and shrapnel wound, when Singapore surrendered to the Japanese on 15 February 1942 and he and over 120 000 others became prisoners of war. It was two days after his lucky stars had led him to the correct ambulance waiting at the Regimental Aid Post, and he never ceased to thank them.

Even so, it had been a terrifying journey to the hospital, along roads crowded with retreating soldiers – many without even their weapons, officers vainly trying to rally them. They travelled through the smog of oil smoke, watching the bombed, burning city in the distance, where thousands of panic-stricken civilians – and a good many Australian and British military deserters – clamoured to get aboard the last ships ready to leave the docks. You didn't need to be a General Officer Commanding to know that Singapore was about to fall.

At one point on that 13th of February, Billy's ambulance itself came under attack from a Zero, and the driver turned for protection into a rubber plantation.

'Don't stop!' cried the medical orderly, for there were in the back three shell-shocked patients: men so affected by the constant pounding of high explosives that they huddled together in a corner shivering uncontrollably. 'Don't stop!'

But the driver did – and as if on cue the three jumped to their feet, wrestled open the ambulance door and ran off into the trees. It took the orderly, Billy and a couple of other patients a deal of trouble to find them, lead them back, and try to pacify them – like the young officer in the drain at Bukit Timah.

'It's all right, mate. We're going to the hospital. You'll be fine, now.'

But things weren't at all fine when they got there. The 13 AGH had moved with the general retreat from Tampoi to St Patrick's College on the road to Changi, in the north-east of the island. Outnumbered now by more urgent casualty cases, Billy was told to wait in the entrance hall until such time as a doctor was able to see him. He was sitting there on a box, among a crowd of patients, when a group of women nurses appeared – crying, and kissing the men, and saying goodbye.

'They've told us we have to go to the wharves and board the ships,' they said.

And when a young, blonde nurse hugged Billy and kissed him, he could see the tears in her eyes and feel the damp on his cheek.

'We don't want to leave you fellers. But we've been given orders...'

So they went. To join such ships as *The Empire Star*, which made it to Java – or the *Vyner Brooke*, which didn't. Of the 65 Australian army nurses aboard that vessel when Japanese bombers sank it, only 24 were to come home after the war. Some died at sea. Some were taken POW. And 22 who reached Banka Island were made to walk back into the sea, where Nurse Vivien Bullwinkel was the only one to survive a massacre by Japanese machine-gunners. They could not have known it when they kissed the men at 13 AGH goodbye, but the nurses had much to weep about.

Of course the doctors and male nurses stayed behind; and Billy, admitted at length to a bed, wondered if the hospital cook was among them. He'd last seen the man late one night in the ward at Tampoi. Unable to sleep, the kid had been approached by the feller returning flush with funds from a successful night at the poker table.

'Like a game of cards, digger?' asked the cook, producing a wad of notes.

'I've only got a few dollars...'

'That's all right, son. I'll soon take them off ya.'

But he didn't. Shades of the *Sibajak* saloon! They played for the rest of the night on the hospital bed, and by the time dawn broke Billy had relieved the cook of all his cash. The man was even asking if he'd accept an IOU.

'Forget it,' the boy replied. 'I've got to get some shut-eye.'

There was no sign of the cook at St Pat's, but the fortune that had favoured Billy so far in his war was still there. The next day, 14 February, came the slaughter at Alexandra Hospital, where the kid would have been had he chosen to be carried to the other ambulance. Yet while he witnessed no wholesale massacre, as the Japanese closed in St Patrick's College had its own small share of the butchery.

Alarmed by the sounds of gunfire and shouting in the hospital grounds, orderlies ran out to find half a dozen Australian soldiers lying dead in a heap, the victims of bullet, bayonet or Japanese sword. Rather, most of them were dead. Uncovering a Queenslander called Cookie, blood flowing from his neck after an attempt to decapitate him, they found he was in fact still alive.

God knew what had deflected the blade, but the stroke had cut into the back of his neck without severing any vital artery – and Cookie was taken into the hospital holding his head firmly down on his shoulders. Where the doctors, amazingly, saved his life, though the real nature of his wound was kept hidden. After surrender, the Japanese did not permit survivors of their atrocities to live and bear witness.

Capitulation was not long in coming. Next morning General Percival and his senior commanders met in the concrete bunker at Fort Canning. There was some discussion as to whether they should fight on, but the hopelessness of the military situation and the dreadful death toll among the Chinese civilians made surrender inevitable. The Commander-in-Chief, General Wavell, had given consent before his final departure; and in the late afternoon of Sunday 15 February, Percival and General Yamashita met at the Ford Motor Factory at Bukit Timah.

There was little discussion this time. Yamashita merely demanded to know if the British would surrender by 8.30 p.m. – yes or no. Percival could only agree, although he was allowed to keep a thousand armed troops to prevent looting in the city, until the Japanese occupied it. For the rest, the defenders were ordered to lay down their arms; and over the following days some 35 000 British and 15 000 Australian troops were marched as prisoners of war to the military barracks near Changi.

Over 60 000 Indian and 14 000 Malayan volunteers also became POWs in what was Britain's worst military defeat since the loss of the American colonies 165 years before. Most local Malayans went home; and many Indian troops, influenced by the Japanese success, joined the Indian National Army to fight for independence in their own country. A number of Sikhs, indeed, were used to guard their former imperial masters at Changi and the Singapore work camps.

For Billy the Kid, the first sign that he was now a prisoner came with the appearance of a Japanese soldier as a guard in the hospital ward. The guard was disfigured by an unsightly hare lip – which led Billy to wonder if he might also be cruel and repeat the killings outside. But he turned out a reasonable fellow, whose main concern was to teach his charges to number off in Japanese: *Ichi, ni, san, shi* – the first lesson in what was to become a daily ritual. Apart from that, Hare Lip caused Billy no trouble, until the truck arrived a few days later to take him to the POW camp at Changi.

The 2/29th Battalion was housed on the ground floor of a war-torn building facing the parade ground at Selarang Barracks. Even in captivity, the distinctions between officers and other ranks were maintained, and the men were quartered by companies and platoons. The kid therefore found himself back in the old C Company section – reunited with Paddy and Bob and a number of other blokes they'd brought into the group. Some of them were – or had been – underage soldiers like himself, whom Bob Shipsides gathered and looked after like a mother hen. Among them were fellers like Joey Crome, nine months older than Billy, whose dad managed the picture theatre at Bondi Junction, which the kid knew so well from those Saturday afternoons long ago; and Harry Longley, a farm boy from Yass in New South Wales.

Harry was only just 17 when he joined up in mid-1940, and he transferred as a truck driver to the 2/29th when it was in training at Bathurst. He'd sailed with the battalion to Malaya in the *Marnix*; and ever the adventurer, had written to his parents during those waiting months in Johore asking if they couldn't do something to make the Japs bring on the war more quickly! He'd since seen his fill of it. While Harry was part of Paddy O'Toole's wide circle of mates, and the kid had certainly known him at Johore, it wasn't until they shared the same concrete floor as POWs at Changi that the two became the firmest of friends – always out on the scrounge together.

In the early days this wasn't difficult, as the camp was wide open. Money was still plentiful and it was easy enough to sneak out to the nearby villages and market gardens to buy or barter food and other necessities. Within a fortnight, however, truckloads of barbed wire appeared and the prisoners were ordered to erect their own perimeter fence – some of it, so rumour said, from the very wire British HQ demanded be returned from the 22nd Brigade's shore defences on the Strait of Johore.

After that, scrounging required a degree of skill, which the lads certainly possessed. Every few days they went under the fence, returning with what they could find to share with their group: bananas, rice, yams – though they had to be careful not only of the Japanese, who'd exact retribution on them and any Chinese caught trading with the POWs, but also of their own military police.

The POWs were responsible for their own discipline within Selarang, and the camp was run along strict military lines: parade every day; officers still with their batmen, polished boots and gaiters, insisting on salutes. A hospital was established, together with a library and even a programme of university lectures, though the kid gave them a miss. Work parties were formed to dig latrines, vegetable gardens, drainage pits and a cemetery. There was regulation, regimentation – and the provosts to enforce it. Many troops resented this now that they were all prisoners together – not least the prohibition, imposed by their own officers, against absconding outside to scavenge. Anyone caught was confined to the guardhouse on rice and water.

Billy and Harry Longley once barely escaped capture by throwing away the coconuts they'd collected. By common consent the coconuts should have been taken to the cookhouse: but they weren't, as the battalion cook – a huge man called Two Ton Tony – verified. Undoubtedly they ended up in the provosts' own food store.

These resentments were exacerbated by a growing sense of disillusion among the men that, not only were they captives, but they had in fact been surrendered by their own military hierarchy.

'It's the worst thing that's ever happened to me,' Paddy O'Toole would say – and would go on saying for the rest of his life. 'I feel so ashamed. So ashamed. We were ready up there at Tanglin Barracks to go on fighting, right to the end. And then told to lay down our arms! By our own commanders! I'm disgusted with the army, I really am. We were just gun-fodder. It's all been one big political stunt.'

And while Paddy, like most of them, ultimately accepted the need for camp discipline – realising that, without it, they wouldn't survive – the pettiness still rankled. Especially the seizure of smuggled foodstuffs when, as supplies began to dwindle, the officers were not discernibly going without. Bottles of tomato sauce were still seen on their mess tables.

Thus, in honoured tradition, the rule against scrounging was ignored – which, for the kid, reached a high point on the evening they made what became known famously as 'Changi Surprise Stew'. Billy could still smell it, and his juices gurgled even now as he told the story again to Spike Smith in their Outram Road cell. Food was always the prime topic of conversation.

The group had been playing a game of cards in a shed behind the barracks when one of their number, an ex-shearer's cook called Keith Gillett, came around asking for contributions to his surprise stew. Harry Longley had a yam; Joey Crome offered a bit of palm tree cabbage; Billy donated a spoonful of rock salt, a valuable commodity, for even then salt was in short supply among the men.

And MP Brown from the 2/26th, a bushman mate of Bob Shipsides who'd joined their fraternity ... *What had he given?* Billy couldn't remember. But it must have been something good, because with everyone now having a share in the feast, and a kerosene tin filled with water and put on the fire to boil, Keith produced from a bag his own special ingredient: a dead monkey. It wasn't any old monkey, but the favourite pet of Two Ton Tony. Indeed the cook had written its name, 'Bongo', on a tag attached to the collar around the monkey's neck. Bongo was quickly beheaded and skinned, his carcass put into the stew pot, and the name tag burnt to destroy the evidence.

The men went back to their card game, leaving the surprise stew to simmer.

An hour or so later, Shearer Gillett looked up from his hand and said, 'Go and have a look at how the tucker's going, kid.'

Billy went over to the fire. The stew certainly smelt delicious. But lifting the kerosene tin lid, the boy was shocked to discover the skinned monkey floating on top.

'Oh Jesus!' he shrieked.

The others rose in alarm, asking what was the matter.

'It looks like a dead baby in there!'

Keith examined it. 'Strewth,' he said, 'you're right. But I'll soon fix it.' And grabbing a heavy jungle parang, he quickly cut Bongo up into small pieces.

'Give it a few more minutes,' he added, 'and she'll be ready.'

He was quite correct. The surprise monkey stew was wonderful. The only difficulty arose later that evening, as the meal was being digested, when they heard Two Ton Tony going around the barracks calling for his pet.

'Bongo! Here, Bongo! Where are you, Bongo, little pal?'

They wisely decided to say nothing: partly out of consideration for Tony's tender feelings – and also for their own. Two Ton Tony was a giant of a man, as his name implied, and like most cooks he had a fearsome temper – with fists to match.

Abstentions from Changi 'under the wire' were not only short-term scrounging expeditions: some men had more permanent escape in mind. A few of them were successful. Pen Dean and John McGregor, for example, got away a month after the surrender and spent a few weeks at liberty before ending up in Outram Road. Billy's mate Bert Cruickshank, with whom he'd run the rickshaw race, also tried to make a break for it. Dave Holden apparently was another. Nobody ever knew what happened to them. Whether they were shot by Japanese patrols, or taken by sharks trying to swim the Strait, or lost in the treacherous Malayan jungle, no one could say. But neither Bert nor Dave was seen again.

In these attempts, men had the example of their own Divisional Commander, General Gordon Bennett, who escaped from Singapore on the night of surrender. Bennett had been contemplating it for some weeks; and that evening, after destroying his papers and handing over command, Bennett went to the waterfront with his aide-de-camp and a liaison officer, Major Charles Moses. They found a sampan, and with eight other servicemen headed out to sea. Transferring to a motorboat, they reached Sumatra three days later, where General Wavell's staff at length arranged to fly Bennett to Java and thence to Australia.

He reached Melbourne in early March, to hostile public

opinion. Bennett had not sought permission to escape, nor had he informed Percival of his intention to do so. He argued that he needed to report to Australian HQ on the Malayan campaign and on how to beat the Japanese; but his own battalion and artillery commanders would have been far better placed to do that. They, however, were still languishing as prisoners of war. Safe at home, amid imputations of cowardice, Bennett was sent white feathers and even a pair of running shoes.

Within Changi itself, opinion was divided. Some wished Bennett good luck in his escape and were disappointed only that they'd not been able to do the same. Others, however, felt that he should have stayed with his men – like General Percival, who could be seen sitting outside his Changi quarters with head in hands, contemplating his own tragedy, until such time as he was transferred with the senior allied officers to imprisonment in eastern Asia for the rest of the war. They were but the most distinguished prisoners to depart Changi.

With so many POWs there, the Japanese quickly decided to relieve the pressure by sending men away on work parties: locally to begin with; later to Burma, Thailand, Japan and Borneo.

The first of those to be sent had the awful task of burying hundreds of Chinese men and boys who had been taken out to Changi beach and murdered by Kenpeitai soldiers in the weeks immediately following the surrender, their bodies left to wash up with the tides. Having survived the terror of the bombing, civilians had now become victims of the massacres known as *Sook Ching*, the 'Purge' (or 'Purification by Elimination' to give the full euphemism). The policy had been decided early in the campaign, and General Yamashita issued his orders three days after occupying Singapore. All Chinese males aged between 18 and 50 (and some much younger) had to report for examination, and any suspected of being anti-Japanese or combatants were executed. The number of victims ran into thousands: shot, machine-gunned, bayoneted or put to the sword, their heads displayed in public places as a warning to others.

Billy the Kid was himself soon confronted by it.

A few weeks after reaching Changi, he was sent with a large party to work in the 'godowns' at the docks. The Japanese were anxious to discover just how much booty they'd captured that could be shipped home from Singapore, for the warehouses were full of unopened goods. Indeed, it was here that Billy's mob found several Hurricanes still in their packing crates: engines, chassis, wings, wheels and armaments all ready to be reassembled by the victorious enemy.

There was a good deal of competition to be on the work parties. Not only was there a slight increase in the food ration, the prisoners were also supposed to be paid – ten cents a day for privates, 15 for corporals. They also offered boundless opportunities for scrounging, though you had to be careful. Paddy O'Toole was caught smuggling sugar in his army dixie, and was forced to eat the lot until he was sick. Any grain spilt on the ground earned him another slap across the face.

But this was nothing to the cruelties inflicted upon the Chinese civilians. As they were travelling to the waterfront that first day, Billy saw three heads on bamboo stakes erected in the street. The bloody horror of it left him breathless.

'Oh Christ! Did you see that?'

Three heads! In one sense they seemed strangely inhuman, like death masks, detached from their bodies. In another, they were all too human – the result of what the Japs had tried to do to Cookie at the hospital – and the kid was sick to his core.

And yet just as shocking was the fact that other people seemed quite untroubled by the spectacle. Children were playing on the footpath, men and women hurrying on their daily business without seeming to recognise the atrocity before them. But the mind is capable of all kinds of deceptions; and as time went by, the kid himself became quite sanguine at the sight of severed heads on little stools by the bridge, or hanging from lamp posts like baubles on a Christmas tree. You can become used to anything. Or almost everything. Some matters are too dreadful ever to be disguised from the self.

One lunch break at the godowns, Billy's group was sitting on some bags of rice by the main gate, eating their ration and watching a Japanese guard deal with a truck waiting to enter. From down the road came a Chinese coolie pulling a rickshaw towards the wharf. Unaware of any danger, and apparently not seeing the guard, he passed by on the far side of the stationary truck.

'Kora!'

The guard shouted his customary abuse. As the rickshaw man stopped, the Jap ran around the front of the truck swinging his rifle butt like a club. A few moments later the coolie was dead: his body a smashed and bloody heap on the paving, his rickshaw a broken wreck. They were still there when Billy and his mob left the godown that evening.

'What was it for?' asked the kid, still shaken at the sheer brutality of the episode. 'What did the poor coot do?'

'Nothing,' replied Harry Longley. 'It was to show who's boss.'

The Japanese continued to show who was boss for the duration. Precisely how many Chinese died at Outram Road, for example, would never be known. They were kept in the civilian part of the jail and the military prisoners were only aware of them as the death house filled – and emptied – and the POWs were given their small piece of burnt rice cake as a token.

There was one victim, however, who would never be forgotten. A Chinese-Malay, he was being held in the main block opposite Billy's cell. Nobody knew why he was there: perhaps suspected of belonging to a resistance force. In any event, the man could not bear his confinement. Isolation, starvation, squalor and disease preyed upon his mind until it broke.

He began to howl and call out, '*Lagi nasi! Lagi nasi!*' More rice! More rice! His cries echoed in the stillness until the guard hammered on his cell door – and then bashed him to enforce silence. Yet he went on weeping, '*Lagi nasi! Lagi nasi!*' until the kid and his cellmate heard a new sound, as the Chinaman started smashing his head against the stone wall to try and end his suffering.

'*Lagi nasi!*' Thump. '*Lagi nasi!*' Thump. Through the curdled afternoon. Or so it seemed. In fact it wasn't long before there came the noise of orders being shouted and more guards arriving. And sitting on the *benki* bucket, Billy stooped for a better look through the ventilation grille at what was happening.

The Chinaman's cell door was unlocked and the guard entered. He reappeared with two bed boards, which he formed into a rough cross on the floor of the passageway. The prisoner was dragged out, his head a jellied pulp. And still moaning – *lagi nasi* – he was tied to the boards and crucified there in Broadway for hours. Until his struggles grew fainter...and more fitful...and at last he died.

The mind never becomes inured to that. It was the only killing at Outram Road to which Billy was a direct witness. At a conscious level, when survival is all, the kid might sit on his *benki* watching the man's death – describing it to his cellmate and grateful only that it wasn't him. Wondering if it might mean an extra titbit in the food bowl. Yet always the victim's cries are resonating somewhere through the deepest dreams. There is no *lagi nasi*...nor any scrap of burnt rice cake for tea.

Food. When the worn autobiographical details of who, when and how had been related, conversation in the shared cells constantly came back to tucker. Of the brave Chinese sneaking food to allied prisoners in the first months of their captivity. Yes, and of men stealing it even from the dead.

A few weeks after returning from the docks, Billy's mob was part of a work party 1500 strong under the command of Lieutenant-Colonel 'Black Jack' Galleghan, who had been sent from Changi to construct a road through the jungle to a place called Bukit Batok ('Cough Hill'), on top of which a memorial to the Japanese war dead was to be built.

Men were hostile to working on such a project, though they relented somewhat when the Nips allowed them also to place a smaller cross to their own dead – and even more so when somebody had the bright idea of placing white ants at the base of the wooden Japanese obelisk. (The problem was they forgot to include a termite queen, so the colony didn't survive to eat the monument. Still, the thought was there.)

They set off in early May on a route march through Singapore to their camp in Thomson Road: a journey made memorable by the guard who inexplicably allowed them to spend two hours at lunch time in Lavender Street and its red-lit environs. The girls all came out of the brothels with gifts of food and even money – returning to the men a little of what they'd spent so freely in the heady days before capitulation.

The Thomson Road camp was not so bad, at least not in comparison to what came after. The food was adequate, though it took western stomachs a long time to get used to a constant rice diet. Men slept on the floors of middle-class houses, abandoned by their owners when war came. In fact Billy and his crowd shared a well-to-do modern mansion, with an unexploded shell stuck halfway through the concrete parapet like an architectural ornament. And Brownie was there to serenade them with his mouth organ at evening concerts. Work was from eight in the morning until six at night – clearing jungle, forming the road, digging monsoon drains, laying (extremely sandy) concrete. While it was laborious, and the guard sometimes unpredictable, most men still had reasonable health and the victors' more sadistic tendencies had not yet on the whole been turned on the POWs.

Nevertheless, the boy was never far from the human tragedy of this war for which he had so rashly volunteered.

During a brief *resto* on the way to Bukit Batok one morning, Billy was given permission to slip into the scrub for a piss. And there he stumbled across the body of a young British soldier, killed in the last days of the battle, and laid out by his companions. He was stretched on his groundsheet beneath a tree, still wearing his boots, head resting on a haversack, and arms folded across his chest. The flesh and most of his clothing had rotted; but his skeleton hands still rested on the British Army 'Red Book', the pages of which were open at the burial service.

It was such a peaceful scene. Spangled sunlight glittered through the jungle trees at stand to, and a flowering vine drifted like a living wreath. A bird called from green shadows, as it would from a prison window – and the part of Billy's soul that responded to poetry and song was filled with grief for the fallen soldier and an unutterable sense of futility. He wished the man might be able to stay there forever, in this corner of Eden. But of course he couldn't. The work party buried his corpse beside the road, his helmet for a marker. Though every day, as he passed, the kid would salute his unknown comrade and fix the images in his mind.

Futile it might all have been – and not for many years would he try to express it. But the glimpse was fleeting enough for the 16-year-old. Which was probably as well. The demands of youth, and of life, and of the need to survive in the here and now were too urgent to be denied. Meaning and contemplation could wait their turn.

A fortnight after starting work, the men at Thomson Road camp woke to discover that there were no guards. No one could say what had become of them. Rumour flashed round that the Americans had landed! The Japs had fled! The war was over! It all seemed a bit too good to be true – and so it was. Yet there *were* no guards, and consequently no labour that day. Instead, the kid and Harry Longley decided to visit a nearby Chinese cemetery.

'They reckon the relatives put food on the graves as gifts for the dead,' Harry said. 'We'll go up there for a squiz. Might find something for the living.'

Alas, there was little to eat, although there were plenty of paper messages on the tombstones offering prayers to the gods. They did, however, come across a stretcher lying beside a large open pit, which Harry thought might come in handy.

'We could make a good bed out of that.'

'Too right,' agreed the kid. 'Gets a bit hard sleeping on a concrete floor.'

They were about to retrieve the stretcher, when a truck came grinding up the cemetery hill towards them, a couple of men standing on top of the load in the back with what looked like large wooden clothes pegs clipped to their noses.

'What's that about?' Billy remembering Wingie's stick pegs from Ultimo.

It didn't take long to find out. The truck stopped beside the pit. As it did so, the smell hit the two youngsters: the putrid, nauseating smell of death.

'Faugh!'

The two workmen climbed down from a stack of bodies in the back. And, picking up the stretcher, began using it to carry them to the grave.

'You can forget about sleeping on that stretcher, Harry.'

There were 30 or 40 corpses in the truck: men and women and even children, piled together in the awful anonymity of death. One by one they were dragged out, like the pickings of a rag-and-bone man, carried over, and with scant respect tipped from the stretcher into the pit. Sliding into the darkness.

There was no service here. No ceremony. No flag or words of mourning. Just the workmen plodding back and forth with their mortal loads, watched without much interest by the truck driver and a young Eurasian medico as supervisor.

'What happened?' the boys asked him. 'Has there been another massacre?'

Not really, was the answer. A few were victims of the *Sook Ching* killings. But mostly they were casualties of poverty, disease and injury in the aftermath of war; put out into the streets for collection by the death trucks, like so much garbage.

'We make three or four trips up here every day, sir,' the medico said. 'Things are not good in Singapore. Hygiene. Most necessary for those who are still alive.'

That, and a quick mind. Returning from the cemetery, the two lads were surprised to discover there was still a remarkable absence of Japanese guards about the place. They decided to explore a little further afield, and indeed were on their way back to camp with a fine haul of coconuts when they found themselves passing through a *kampong*. Sitting at a restaurant table directly on the village street, a group of Japanese soldiers were eating, drinking and making merry.

'Crikey!' The kid nudged Harry. 'What are we gunna do?'

In such situations, Harry was always the leader. Always out on point: a fag in his mouth when he could get one, keeping his silence until he had something worthwhile to say. Which he did now.

'Give 'em an "Eyes Right". And keep on marching.'

The two broke into a quick march. Backs straight. Coconuts held by their sides under the left arm, right arms swinging stiffly as if on parade before General Bennett himself. As they passed the Japanese, their heads turned sharply to the right, hands up in the smartest of salutes. Which, to their astonishment, the enemy returned: the soldiers standing and saluting, until the pair had gone by.

The men at Thomson Road were also full of amazement when they heard the tale.

'We couldn't believe it,' the kid said. 'It seems the Nips now will let you go anywhere, provided you throw 'em a salute.'

A number of them put it to the test the next day. It worked. And for the next five or six days thereafter, while 'Black Jack' Galleghan might rail against absconding and threaten the guardhouse, these prisoners of war found themselves at liberty to wander pretty much where they liked around the cafes, bars and whorehouses of Singapore, saluting any Japanese soldiers they came across.

This was the time when the conquering army was being replaced by a permanent occupying force; and the newcomers were uncertain quite what was expected of them. It was to change. But in the meantime the youngsters were out every day, discovering the remarkable generosity of the Chinese towards them.

After surrender, the Japanese had required the British and Australian POWs to march to Changi through the busiest parts of town, as a demonstration to their Asian subjects of just how far these former overlords had fallen; of how contemptible the white man now had become. It was effective propaganda among many of the Malays and Indians. But the Chinese took great risks to help the POWs – no doubt because the Japs seemed to despise them every bit as much as they did the Europeans.

One lunch time the kid, Joey Crome and Harry Longley were passing a poor *atap* hut by a market garden. From nowhere, a small Chinese boy appeared. Tugging at Billy's sleeve, and pointing to the open door he said, 'You eat. You eat.'

The lads glanced about them. The boy disappeared. Nobody else was in sight, save the farmer and his wife watching under their straw hats from the field. No Japs. So they entered the humble room of a subsistence family: a little shrine to the ancestors by the wall; a bowl of cold rice and a jar of pickled shrimps on the table. They were delicious. Without further thought, the three hungry young fellers ate the lot. Only afterwards did it occur to them that the food might be the family's only meal for the day. But it was too late. As they left, and the boy crept around the corner of the hut to see them go, Harry said, 'You thank your mother and father for us.'

'We know what they done,' the kid added. And Joey agreed, aware that the family's lives would have been forfeited had the Japs found out.

As they turned down the road, the lads exchanged looks not just of gratitude, but also of understanding with the couple in the vegetable garden.

During these guard-free days of mid-May, the three friends were often in town together – although after his earlier experience of the squalid brothels of Johore and Lavender Street, Billy left such places well alone. It was more important to satisfy the urge of hunger at the food stalls – and even enjoy a slap-up meal in the house of a Chinese businessman. He was associated with several Australian companies, and had many questions for the boys about their homeland. He was also a Roman Catholic, as was Harry, and the two had much to discuss on matters of faith.

Harry's religion proved a blessing in many ways, as it provided nourishment for both body and soul. During the POWs first Sunday working at Thomson Road, some nuns from a nearby convent asked if any would like to attend their service. Harry was among the few who went. But when he reported back about the feast of banana and pineapple fritters the worshippers had eaten after church, the number of converts who wanted to attend mass the following Sunday was a miracle to behold. Alas, the Japanese guard on duty that day was a non-believer.

The hiatus during the changing of the guard (in itself a wonder) came to an end after a week. On 25 May, as Harry, Joey and the kid were returning to camp, they saw a squad of Japanese soldiers coming along Thomson Road. They clearly meant business. Every so many yards, one of them stopped and went on sentry.

'Quick! Get across the road while we can,' Harry murmured, and the three scuttled over to shut themselves in the house as if they'd been there all along.

They were among the last to be so fortunate. Anyone else trying to cross the road as he returned from the day's liberty was nabbed by the guard and held as punishment in a tennis court guarded by Sikhs. Bob Shipsides and MP Brown were among those penned up for several days, until at length 'Black Jack' Galleghan considered it long enough and demanded that the Japanese set them free.

A solid man of forceful personality, Galleghan was to become the senior Australian officer at Changi when the top brass were sent away. A strict disciplinarian, as many men loathed Black Jack as admired him. Yet he achieved considerable improvements at Changi – for his dominating ways were directed equally at the Japanese. General Yamashita was among several enemy commanders to inspect the prisoners; and on at least one occasion, when certain Japanese soldiers arrived sloppily dressed, Galleghan ordered them to leave the camp and not return until they were properly attired. They obeyed him.

He was that sort of man. A man to be feared by his subordinates. And especially by an underage kid who, running around the corner of the Thomson Road house as Black Jack was inspecting the place one day, collided headlong with the Lieutenant-Colonel, winding him in the gut and knocking him to the ground.

Realising what he'd done from the amount of pips and polished leather about, Billy took off without pausing for a salute. As Black

Jack and his staff officers bellowed 'Come back here, soldier!', the kid disappeared as quickly as he could. And stayed out of sight until the tempest passed.

In the event, he was soon removed from Galleghan's immediate control. Billy came down with his first bout of malaria and dysentery, and was taken back to the hospital at Changi, where he lay on his stretcher, contemplating those freedom days on the scrounge with Joey and Harry Longley, and the rich code of friendship and honour that existed among thieves.

The demands of foraging or solidarity never slackened for a moment, especially not in Outram Road prison. Though honour was sometimes in short supply.

When Spike Smith was sharing Billy's cell, the ex-boxer was usually ordered to help *Yagi* the goat with the *benki* buckets. It was a chance to scavenge outside, where Spike's stolid strength often came in handy – though it could also be a worry.

One morning the two *benki* parties were returning to the cell block – buckets emptied, washed and stacked on the carrying trays – when they were told to go to the kitchen. Prisoners rarely went there, for the cookhouse was strictly out of bounds; but a drain had blocked and the guards wanted the men to fix it.

The trays were put down outside and the prisoners gathered to examine the problem. It was then that Billy noticed a garbage tin close by, half full of cold rice. It was pretty stale, and starting to turn a little green, but still edible. Certainly it shouldn't go to waste on the pigs.

He nudged Alan Minty.

'*Goshu!*'

And Alan began his favourite game with the Nips. Tracing a map of Australia on the floor with his foot.

'Darwin. BOOM-BOOM-BOOM!'

The first bombing of Australia's northern city had occurred on 19 February 1942, a mere four days after Singapore surrendered. And the guards never failed to respond with delight to Alan's pantomime.

'*Hai!* Syd-e-ny. BOOM-BOOM-BOOM!'

Alan pointed to Melbourne.

'Ned Kelly! BOOM-BOOM-BOOM!'

While this was going on, Billy and Spike each took a bucket and, under pretence of washing it at the kitchen tap, began scooping up some of the stale rice.

'Don't take too much, Spike,' the kid murmured. 'The bucket will be heavy, and the Nips will guess.'

'Sure fing.'

But Spike wasn't really listening. By the time he'd finished, the bucket covered and put back on the tray, his *benki* was packed full of cold rice. So that when at last the drain was unblocked and the work party returned to the cell block, the inevitable happened. As Spike lifted down his bucket and began to walk away, he strained a little under the extra weight and the guard immediately became suspicious.

'*Kora! Yame!*' Hey you! Stop!

If it had been one of the long-term guards like Mopoke, he may have been too indolent to notice. But this Kenpeitai was new to the prison: young and enthusiastic.

'*Koi!*' he shouted as Spike kept walking to his cell. '*Kotchi koi!*'

Spike eventually stopped and returned to the group. The others all put down their buckets and tried to confuse them. But the guard would not be distracted. He shouted and gesticulated at Spike, who ultimately removed his *benki* lid to reveal the smuggled rice. The new guard went mad.

'You do this?' he raved. 'You steal rice? *You*!' He began to poke and threaten Spike. 'You very bad prisoner.'

But Spike, thick-headed as ever, protested his innocence.

'It ain't mine,' he said. 'I never done it.'

The guard unclipped his scabbard, becoming angrier and threatening violence to the whole group, as Spike maintained his denials.

'I don't know nuffin' abart it.'

Even his own men became dismayed.

'Oh, Spike,' remonstrated a very pukka sahib who'd been an officer in the Indian Army. 'Oh Spike, you're letting down the side.'

At length Billy the Kid stepped forward.

'It was me,' he said to the guard. 'I took the rice. It was my *benki*.'

The guard looked at the boy, thin as a ring-barked stick. He looked at the bucket. And immediately began laying into Spike for all he was worth.

When he was exhausted, he ordered the buckets outside again, to be emptied down the shit hole and hosed out. The promised feast of cold, green rice disappeared into the sewer.

Back in the cell, the kid asked Spike why he'd lied?

'I told ya not to put too much rice in the bucket. I said the Japs would know.'

But however bruised and swollen from the beating, Spike persisted.

'It weren't me,' he grizzled. 'I didn't have nuffin' to do wiv it.'

Spike had had one fight, and gone one round too many.

For the boy, though, as his mind returned to the narrative of his own past, he knew that the dark struggle was just beginning...

Released from the hospital after his illness, Billy didn't return to Thomson Road but remained at Changi, working for several weeks around the camp – finding himself hitched with a dozen other men like carthorses to a stripped-down truck, and hauling it around the barracks with loads of firewood and supplies. The Japanese required any petrol for themselves.

By early May, with so many men out on work parties, only half the original number of Australian prisoners were still at Changi. Their number was reduced even further during the month when 3000 men were sent to Burma as 'A' Force, to begin building a railway stretching some 260 miles (420 kilometres) from Thanbyuzayat to Bampong in Thailand. Over the next year and a half, thousands of people would die in the most appalling conditions on the railway. But at the time, the Japanese pictured the project as offering much better conditions and plentiful food; and there was no difficulty at Selarang finding enough men volunteering to fill the quota.

It meant, though, that the workload increased substantially on the able-bodied ranks still at Changi, for the officers were not required to labour. Many of the men were recovering from illness, including Billy the Kid, or had been sent back from Thomson Road for disciplinary reasons. Harry Longley and Joey Crome were both returned for some misdemeanour – as were MP Brown, and Bob Shipsides too, who had been reduced to the ranks for having been caught that day the walkabout ended. But it made no difference to his men: Bob was always the Corp, and their leader.

In any event, the number of Australian prisoners still at Changi was about to be halved yet again. In early July the Japanese ordered a work party to build an airfield at a place called Sandakan, in former British North Borneo. The account the Nips gave of the healthy, bountiful conditions was even more promising than Burma; and the AIF officers, preparing the lists for what became known as 'B' Force, added a fair few older men and those recovering from illness. There was also a high proportion of officers and NCOs – one for every three privates – commanded by Lieutenant-Colonel

Alfred Walsh of the 2/10th Field Regiment.

And just in case Sandakan turned out to be not quite as salubrious as the Japanese described it, the staff added many of their known troublemakers – the so-called 'larrikin element' – to the 'B' Force draft. It rid Selarang of them, at least.

Thus, on the morning of 7 July, Billy the Kid with his mates Harry Longley and Joey Crome, Joey's pal Wally Ford (whom everybody called 'Henry' for obvious reasons), Bob Shipsides, Myles Peace Brown, Keith Gillett and nearly 1500 others had an early breakfast, and marched out of the barracks. Paddy O'Toole was not among them, for he was still at Thomson Road – destined to go to Thailand and the railway next year.

For almost everyone on 'B' Force, it would be the last time they'd see Selarang Barracks. The last time they'd be in what, during those five short months since captivity, had become their improvised military home.

Nobody could guess it then, of course. They were off on what had been suggested was the next best thing to a tropical holiday. Into the trucks for those lucky enough to get a seat, or march down to Keppel Harbour and board the ship *Yubi Maru* waiting to take them to pleasant Sandakan.

*Yubi Maru*. It meant a dainty, exquisite, graceful ship.

This one was cramped, stinking, and a rust bucket.

Even the seagulls could not bring themselves to cry farewell.

# 10
# SANDAKAN

*Scratch beneath the layers of those years,*
*Seek to find the reasons for our tears.*

Word spread quickly through the rumour mill of Outram Road in early March 1944. A big group of prisoners had arrived from Kuching. Civilian as well as military POWs, convicted after the discovery of a radio, weapons, documents and an elaborate underground intelligence network. One of the conspirators, Captain Lionel Matthews, had even been executed. More to the point, they were all from Sandakan.

For Billy the Kid – and those like him who'd been transported from North Borneo – this was the most exciting part of the news. It was a chance to catch up on all that had happened in the year since they'd left the camp. Joey Crome? Harry Longley? How were they going? And Bob Shipsides? What had become of him? Billy had last seen him the day of his own escape, when the Japs had laid into him... Was Shippy all right? The others from his hut? Keith Gillett? Wally Ford? Billy looked forward to sharing his cell and having a good natter with one of the new men from Sandakan.

Yet the first of them, when the time came, was not what he expected.

He heard the guard outside. Shouted orders. Numbering. The jangle of keys, and the door swinging open. And there on the step, having completed the indignity of the strip search, stood one of the boy's own officers: Lieutenant Roderick Wells.

The kid's heart sank. Officers, in his experience, were not people with whom you could shoot the breeze. Not your own kind, to share mateship or laugh over old times. On the contrary, they represented authority, and generally kept themselves quite separate. You didn't fraternise with officers. Yet here Billy was to share his cell with this smart young lieutenant – and he wondered how he would manage it.

Besides, the boy had it in for all Sandakan officers. He was convinced one of them had reported Joey Crome and himself to the guards for smuggling tapioca roots into the camp, hidden in bundles of firewood. At a time when men were labouring like dogs on the airfield, tapioca chips made a delicious addition to the diet. He and Joey had carried the slender roots often enough before; yet this time they'd been discovered, bashed and locked in the punishment box known as 'Esau' – forced to sit, cramped, under the sun in a wooden cage five foot long and a mere four foot high. Billy had blamed their discovery on an officer – and the sight of one of them entering his cell brought the anger rushing back.

The kid turned his face to the wall and for fully five minutes said nothing. Yet Billy also knew that they had to live in this cell – to get along together until the next changeover. There was no point in opening old sores. So, when Rod Wells smiled beside him on the floor and said hello, Billy at length nodded and replied, 'Good'ay.'

As it turned out, his cellmate was a good deal more interesting – even enlightening – than Billy could have supposed.

Now aged 24, Rod Wells was the son of a dairy farmer near Shepparton, in northern Victoria. From childhood he'd shown remarkable scientific aptitude for chemistry, mathematics and radio communications. As a boy he'd singed his father's eyebrows by inverting a test tube of oxygen over the pipe his dad was smoking. And he'd nearly blown himself up with a bottle of homemade gelignite. At 14, Rod had assembled his own short-wave radio receiver from bits he'd found, bought or borrowed, making his own battery, the coils manufactured from wire wound about the broken necks of beer bottles.

His dream had always been to take a science degree at university and become a teacher. But the family could not afford that. After fourth form Rod went to Melbourne and became an electrical apprentice in a machine factory – although he continued his studies at a coaching college, eventually sitting his university entrance exam, which he passed handsomely. But war intervened. Enlisting in 1940, Wells was posted to an officer cadet unit after initial training, and from there to the Signals Corps. In fact he was with 8th Division Signals when Singapore fell.

Sent to Sandakan with B Force, he'd used his skills and inventiveness with Lieutenant Gordon Weynton to construct the camp's secret wireless receiver – hidden in a latrine – and subsequently a transmitter. They'd relied on Captain Matthews' underground contacts to find components such as a valve and headphone; but Wells had contrived other parts from whatever he could find. Bits of foil and oil-soaked paper to make a capacitor. String rubbed in burnt cinnamon bark for a resistor. Foil, boracic acid and sodium borate, smuggled from Sandakan hospital, to convert the camp's electricity from Alternating Current to Direct Current. Rod Wells' boyhood experiments with radio at last bore their fruit – until a local betrayed them; the transmitter (though never the receiver) and the whole intelligence network seized; and Wells, Weynton and the others ended up in Outram Road. Among the Sandakan civilians arrested and sent to Singapore was Dr Jim Taylor, formerly the chief medical officer, born in Yass and a friend of Harry Longley's family.

Billy listened to Rod's story, whispered through the soul's midnight hours, and was utterly beguiled. Whatever the social and intellectual distances between the two, they had one thing in common. Both had inquiring, receptive minds: but where Rod Wells had been educated, the kid had not. He sat absorbing these narratives and the wide gamut of the man's scientific interests – radio waves; atomic weights; the measure, known as valency, of the chemical bonds formed in any given element – like a schoolboy being tutored. For the first time since he knew his teacher, Mr Leslie, Billy the truant began to enjoy the prospect of being a student.

More immediately, the story of the radio and the discovery of the underground network Captain Matthews and his team had established with the people of Sandakan helped to make sense of Billy's interrogation after his own capture. For day after day, he and Brownie had been asked questions they found incomprehensible. When was the submarine rendezvous? Where were the weapons hidden? Who else was involved in the plot? The kid was no hero; he'd have shopped his own grandmother if it would have stopped the guard from running a rifle butt down his spine. But neither he nor Brownie had any knowledge of such matters, and at length the inquisitor had discarded them.

Now things fell into place. The group, it appeared, had even made contact with a guerrilla force in the Philippines, and the boy was grateful to Wells for the information – astonished that these officers had concocted such an elaborate ruse to fool the Japs. He'd thought only the Dead End Kids had played such games!

Billy had little to offer the lieutenant in return, however, except to be an object lesson in what Rod, and all the new Sandakan arrivals, would become after a few months at Outram Road. Some of them had been tortured far more barbarously than Billy had been by the Kenpeitai. Chained from a rail, boards placed behind their knees, and jumped upon to tear their limbs in a kind of primitive rack. Forced to swallow raw rice and gallons of water, until their stomachs swelled in agony. Rod Wells was deaf in his left ear where it had been pierced by a bamboo skewer. He'd even been sentenced to death with Captain Matthews, although inexplicably Lionel Matthews alone went to the firing squad.

The new arrivals had suffered all of this: but they'd not yet acquired the haunted look of the Outram Road prisoners. The suppurating sores. The cesspit smell. The shrivelled skin, buried eyes, and stomachs so far beyond hunger as to seem stuck to the backbone. These things would come in time; but so soon from Kuching, the Sandakan men still had a little weight and rude health. The Kenpeitai didn't want people looking too obviously maltreated when they fronted their courts, though nobody cared what happened to them afterwards. Thus the kid could only show his shrunken self like an exemplar to Rod Wells, as if to say, 'This soon will be you.' As it was the first day Billy had seen the skeletons sitting in the courtyard by the scabby bath.

Beyond that, the kid couldn't contribute a great deal to their conversation. He had no knowledge of subjects that would interest a clever man like Rod Wells. Not the tricks of the trade at Paddy's Market. Not cards. And most of his army stories ended in jokes at the expense of the officer class.

Nor did Rod know anything much about Billy's friends. True, he was able to say that Joey Crome, Wally Ford and a few other troublemakers like Mo Davis had been sent to Kuching (along with most of the Sandakan officers) not long before Wells' own arrest in the middle of 1943. But as for Bob Shipsides, Harry Longley and the rest, he had scant knowledge of them. For that, the kid had to rely on the other Sandakan men during his *benki* rounds – and then the surprise was mostly theirs.

'Billy Young!' cried Curly Mills when he saw the kid for the first time. 'But you're supposed to be dead, with your eyes torn out! You and Brownie.' And he fell upon the boy, astounded to see him – if not as large as life, then not yet a corpse.

But within his cell, Billy sat silently listening to Rod Wells' erudition, allowing the active part of his brain to soak up this scientific learning. While in the deeper reaches of his mind, Billy's thoughts were filled with the shadows of those dear mates left behind in Borneo and all that had occurred since they boarded the shit bucket *Yubi Maru* together for Sandakan...

A hellhole of a ship. Originally built for the Australian trade, and sold to the Japanese as scrap metal before the war, the *Yubi Maru*'s holds were now filled with human cargo: the 1500 men of B Force crammed below, worse than cattle, for the 11-day voyage. Officers were in the forward hold; more than 700 men in the centre hold, covered with coal dust; the remaining 400, among them Billy's lot, shoved aft. The space was so crowded they could only sit with knees bunched up, or lie shoulder to shoulder like black Africans on a slave ship, singing 'Ten green bottles', and the like, to Brownie's harmonica, to keep up morale.

Conditions were as bad as any slaver. The vessel heated like an oven during the day, the air funnelled down a canvas vent at the hatch – but it only worked when the ship was moving. Lying idle, the atmosphere below was stifling: saturated with sweat, the stench of vomit, diarrhoea and the nauseating food.

The cooked rice was lowered down to the hold in tin drums, and scooped into men's dixies. But the stuff was so bad it had turned sulphurous green, which the cooks tried to sweeten by adding lime. It tasted foul, and the after-effects were worse: sickness and dysentery. And the only latrines were a couple of four-seater dunnies suspended over the side of the ship's upper deck. They could be reached by climbing a narrow metal ladder out of the hold – the sole excuse for which the Japs allowed prisoners to go above. Yet the runs were so bad, and the queues of men waiting on the ladder so long, that many could not wait...and the contents of their bowels emptied on those waiting below. Consequently, the filth and disease in the hold became ever worse.

'Holy shit!' cried Billy on the ladder one afternoon. 'It's rainin' down on us!'

'Sorry, mate,' came from the feller above. 'Couldn't help meself.'

'They promised us paradise,' Harry Longley observed from the rung beneath. 'But this is the voyage to Hades.'

It was so bad there was even talk of trying to take over the ship. Keith 'the Shearer' Gillett, for instance, had a silver revolver that he'd souvenired in Singapore. It had been broken down for the voyage – the Shearer kept one part, Shippy Shipsides another, and the bullets were distributed among the boys with instructions to keep them well hidden.

'Disguise 'em,' Keith advised. 'Don't let the Jap buggers guess.'

Billy kept his bullet on a string around his neck, like a keepsake.

A feller called Eric 'Mo' Davis – 2/20th Battalion, neat and dapper like many ex-sailors, with a trim moustache – raised the idea of mutiny. Another underage serviceman, Mo had left home at only 13, worked as a boiler man in the merchant navy – including on the *Queen Mary* – before he joined the army, and knew how to hijack a ship. The officers, however, quashed the idea, which was just as well. On deck one day, Mo saw the conning tower of a Japanese submarine that had been tailing them – and realised they wouldn't have got very far.

Yet his knowledge was put to one good effect. Certain there was another hold beneath their deck, Mo and a few of his New South Wales mates prised up the wooden boards to discover crates of tinned food stored below. Soup. Meat and veg. All found in the

Singapore warehouses and destined now for Japanese stomachs. Here was a ticket to food heaven, after the rice that both smelt and tasted of rotten eggs! After each feast the empty tins were replaced in the crates, men hoping the Japs wouldn't notice until they were off the ship. Billy didn't participate in these banquets, as he had a bad dose of diarrhoea – and the thought of eating was for once beyond him.

Conditions aboard *Yubi Maru*, meanwhile, had become even more unbearable. Reaching the west coast of Borneo, they anchored off the oil port of Miri, not far from Brunei. For two and a half days the ship lay there, swinging idly on her chains, the air vents useless and the atmosphere in the holds suffocating.

The kid and Joey Crome were able to escape it a little one evening, by climbing Jacob's Ladder to the latrines and hiding near a storage locker, where the guard couldn't see them. The lights of Miri beckoned across the velvet water.

'It doesn't look far,' Joey said.

'Reckon we could swim it?'

'Oh, it'd be a cinch.'

'In you go then.'

'Nah. You jump first, Billy.'

'You're the kid from Bondi Junction. *You're* the swimmer!'

'It was your idea!'

They were saved from further dispute by a ship's cook emerging from the galley to throw a bucket of scraps over the side. At once the still, midnight sea came alive with frenzied phosphorescence, as hundreds of fish fought for the delectables. The surface became charged with a swirling electric foam, out-rivalling Miri's lights, when from the depths lunged a shadow, and a dorsal fin, and a mouth of serrated teeth. The small fry fled...and so did any thought the boys had of swimming ashore.

Thus at last the voyage continued: up the coast past Labuan

Island and the town of Jesselton beneath the haunting presence of Mount Kinabalu; around the north cape, hugging the land, for the sea boundary with the Philippines and the risk of American submarines was very close; until, on the morning of 18 July, the *Yubi Maru* breasted the red cliffs of Berhala Island and steamed into the harbour of Sandakan.

It was an attractive colonial town of a sort the British built in the tropics to remind themselves of home. The fishing boats and water villages, perched on wooden poles, clustered around the seafront, the Chinese shophouses and alleys behind. The stone church of St Michael's stood foursquare halfway up the hill, above the minaret of the town mosque. On higher slopes, to catch the breezes, the painted black-and-white houses of the European population sheltered among gardens and wide verandahs in mock Tudorish comfort. In the distance stretched the chequered greens of rubber and palm-oil plantations. And beyond that, the jungle ascended to the cloud-wreathed ramparts of Kinabalu, where Dyaks believed dwelt the spirits of the dead.

The prisoners aboard the *Yubi Maru* had no opportunity to enjoy these scenic views. They were kept in the ship for most of the day. Only in the late afternoon were they disembarked and taken to the *padang* – a large, open area found in many Malayan towns – and fed more of the disgusting rice and toilet-coloured 'tea'. Half of them were then escorted to St Michael's church for the night, and the rest, including Billy's mob, returned to the ship.

All this happened under the supervision of Captain Hoshijima Susumi, an engineering graduate, tall for a Jap, who was to be commandant of the labour camp and responsible for building the airfield. He was seeing here, for the first time, those men for whose systematic deaths he would also, in the scales of justice, be held accountable. The native population looked on, though many of the Europeans had already been interned in a former leper colony on

Berhala Island. Some locals were hostile, some sympathetic – but all were intimidated by the occupying army's method of dealing with transgressors. As Billy was leaving the *padang* he saw a Chinese man hanging upside down from a tree – suspended by an iron bar through his ankles – like a side of beef at the butcher. The ways of *Sook Ching* clearly were also known in Sandakan.

B Force left for the camp next morning: the stores and some sick taken by truck, but the rest marching along the gravel road that led to the interior. A few tried singing 'Waltzing Matilda', to keep up spirits. But it was hard slog uphill, made worse for hungry men weakened after days cooped up in the *Yubi Maru* – and even more so as rain set in and the humidity absorbed all their energy. There was no slacking, however. Japanese boots and rifle butts kept the column moving.

At the seven-mile peg they passed a jungle track that led to the site of the airfield, originally proposed by the British. It was a mile beyond that before they turned down a side road to the camp itself, past a boiler shed that generated electricity for the place by water piped from the Sibuga River, another mile and a half away. Then they climbed up a small, steep hill until they reached the gates.

Timber framed and laced with barbed wire, opening inwards, chained and padlocked, the double gate stood behind a guardhouse, with a machine gun on the verandah pointing directly at the camp entrance. On either side, enclosing the roughly five-acre site, stretched a six-foot wire-mesh fence topped with three strands of barbed wire. The wings fanned out from the gates across the summit, and then ran down the sides of the hill to a swamp at the bottom. There, a pair of smaller barbed-wire fences returned below the water, the space between them filled with coils of razor wire, a wooden walkway for the guards and a couple of sentry posts to prevent escape. Electric lights illuminated the whole at night. The camp had in fact last been used by the British to intern

Japanese aliens when war first broke out: now, with the tables turned, the Nips happily transformed it into a prison for their own enemies.

Inside, several rows of raised huts stood parallel on either side of the gates. Soundly built of wooden planks and thatched with *atap*, the huts consisted of three rooms, each able to sleep 14 or 15 men, opening onto a common verandah. These were for the officers. At right angles, running down the slope to the swamp, stood another five rows of huts: similar in design, but of poor construction. They'd been built hurriedly of green *atap* – walls as well as roofs – and leaked like colanders in the downpour. They were also full of lice and rats, and were naturally allocated to everybody else. The open space on the hilltop between the officers' and other ranks' huts was big enough for an assembly ground. It was dominated by a huge Mengaris tree – 'the Big Tree' – its trunk soaring upwards for some 200 feet, supported like a cathedral spire by its buttress roots. The weather-beaten crown, bearing the scars of many lightning strikes, was visible as a landmark above the jungle, as if the spirits that lived within it were telling work-weary prisoners that this was home.

Home. If only. It took days to get the camp into any kind of shape. The malodorous latrines to at least work. The cookhouse, with its rice boilers like laundry coppers, to operate. The boiler, which supplied both power and water under the care of a Chinese engineer, to function properly. Indeed, it was on the boiler shed that Mo Davis, with his experience aboard the *Queen Mary*, had set his sights. And it took days to repair the *atap*, and in the meantime try to escape the leaks by sleeping huddled together or even under the huts (if you didn't mind the mosquitoes), especially lower down the hill where they were raised quite high on timber stilts.

It was in the very last room in the hut at the end of the row closest to the swamp that Billy and his mob took up their quarters.

They quickly became known throughout the camp as the 'Dead End Kids'. Bob Shipsides certainly kept his youngsters together: Harry Longley and Joey Crome; Wally Ford, always with his lopsided grin; Jimmy Finn, an excellent featherweight boxer, tough as a pocket Atlas; and Terry Risely, like Wally and the kid himself, from Tasmania. But there was also a leavening of men in their middle 20s, to offer the counsels of experience. Keith Gillett, of course, who'd been allowed to marry a Malayan girl at Segamat. She was carrying his child – and Keith carried her photograph with him everywhere, showing off her beauty to the boys in the hut. Sid Outram and Jim Donohue from the Wagga district of New South Wales, the closest of mates. Snowy Bryant, another boxer, an inoffensive feller to look at, but with a heavyweight punch like a steam hammer. Cookie, his neck bearing the marks of a Japanese sword, which never failed to fascinate – as did the wounds on the body of George Plunkett, from a neighbouring room, who'd been stabbed 13 times in a Japanese bayonet charge and survived to exhibit his scars to inquisitive youth.

Next to Billy on the sleeping platform was the bloke who would share so much of his subsequent fate: Myles Peace Brown – Corporal Shipsides' timber-worker mate from Queensland. Intelligent like Bob, and largely self-educated, MP had a splendid ear. He spoke Malay and Dutch, and a bit of Jap. He played several instruments: violin, accordion and of course the harmonica with which he would accompany Trevor Dobson on his box drum at night, as Dobbo warbled a favourite song:

> Hi wringle-wrangle,
> Hi wringle-ray,
> He was the finest ram, sir,
> That ever was fed on hay.

Only the clean version. (*The ram it had a tail, sir, it's far too long to tell, it stretched across to Ireland, and rang Saint Patrick's bell.*) Trevor came from a decent-living country family and had no truck with the vulgar verses known to others. (*And when this ram he died, sir, they took him to Saint Paul's, it took ten men and a rouseabout, to carry one of his balls.*)

But there was no time for music or singing to begin with. Those first evenings were given over to the more important business of rat-catching. Not that the kid minded the rats so much. It was the snakes that came after them that he disliked. But to get rid of the snakes they first had to remove the rats. Thus, every night, an arsenal of missiles was accumulated: boots, stones, lumps of wood – anything to hand.

When all was assembled, the room light was switched off. Silence. Until, in the darkness, they heard scratching and rustling in the palm thatch above.

'Ready...'

Upon Shippy's signal, the light was switched on and they let fire at the vermin. They killed quite a few of them too, and eventually won the battle – although in those early days, when food supplies were adequate to maintain the strength of the workforce, men didn't bother to eat the rats they caught. Later, and especially at Outram Road, stomachs were not so sensitive.

And they needed every ounce of strength. A few days after arriving, a work party was called together – including most of the Dead End Kids – and told that preliminary work was to begin on the airfield. The first job was to clear the access track between the camp and the chosen site. They set off in light rain, equipped with parangs to cut the undergrowth, guarded by a Japanese sergeant and his cronies armed with guns and pick handles.

The early going wasn't too bad. The British had established the camp as an experimental agricultural station. The fairly open perimeter was planted with kapok and cinnamon trees (from which Rod Wells got the bark for his radio resistor), rubber, coffee and tapioca plants. The track had been made as a shortcut when the British were surveying the airfield, but war and capitulation intervened. The jungle had returned. And before long, the work party was hacking its way through thickets of vines, thorns and bamboo, until they were exhausted. Rain set in. Thunder rolled. And the path, which had barely been discernible in the undergrowth, now began to run with rivulets of stormwater. Which turned into streams cascading down the slopes, carrying mud and debris, so that the men could barely keep their footing.

Billy slipped and stumbled, afraid he was about to lose his boots in the torrent. He clutched at a branch for support; and was pausing to recover himself, when a crack across the shoulders from a pick handle drove him on. Up the hill. Swinging and slicing back the foliage until he felt his right arm would drop off.

'Yikes!' The kid shouted when at last they were allowed to stop for a breather. The rain had eased briefly and the sun broke through the clouds, turning the jungle into a steam press. 'What's this thing, Harry?'

A dirty, black, blood-sucking thing, inches long, was attached to his forearm.

'It's a leech, Billy. You got any salt?'

As if.

'Well, any matches then, to burn it?'

'After this rain!'

'You'll just have to try to pull it off.'

As they all did, their arms and legs alive with the hateful things, tearing at their skin. Until the rain returned with the pick handles, and leeches were the least of their worries.

It was still pouring when they reached the airfield site. The area, about a mile long and half a mile wide, had been cleared by the British of primary jungle, but much secondary growth had re-established and would have to be cut. It wasn't flat enough for a landing strip, but consisted of a series of undulating crests and gullies, like waves in a rolling sea. The analogy was apt, for water was pouring everywhere, turning the earth to mud. Yet without pausing for anything to eat, the sergeant determined they should immediately start levelling the place. Standing on a rise he pointed to the ground with his pick handle.

'Hill here go in valley over there.' He indicated the next depression. 'All man get *changkol* and basket. Ichi man, ichi yard dig.' Meaning that each prisoner had to remove one yard of earth with a heavy, flat Malayan hoe and use it as fill. 'When finish all man go back to camp. *Yoshi*? Okay?'

Words were simple; the deed virtually impossible. The ground was a deep layer of almost coral-white volcanic tufa. In dry weather it was relatively easy to cut; but in the wet it turned to a gelid mess that defied every attempt to lift it. It was like trying to dig up a milk pudding, the stuff slopping everywhere, sticking to hands and bodies, refusing to go into the bamboo carrying baskets. And even when it did, the bloody goo wouldn't come out again when you tried to tip it into the next gully, however encouraged by the frequent application of pick handles.

As if this wasn't enough, the rain turned into a full-blown tropical storm. Lightning forked across the clouds, striking giants among the forest trees and bringing them down. Thunder exploded, as if the sky gods were cursing this whole damnable undertaking. Men sank to their calves in mud. And the valleys between the mounds became swirling creeks. Every glob of white fill was immediately swept away.

Even the Japanese sergeant came to understand that the day's work was an utter waste of time. He called it off and ordered the work party to head back to camp.

Never, thought the boy, had a prison seemed so inviting.

For the next week or two, day work was mainly confined to improving the access track to the aerodrome, and the night, so far as the Dead End Kids were concerned, to sneaking out surreptitiously on the scrounge, as they'd done at Changi. Here, too, the place was not heavily guarded; and the lads quickly found their best exit was by way of the swamp...

Down the verandah steps in the moonlight and round the back of their end hut they went. Slipping into the dark, oozing water and, holding their breath, wriggling through the hole they'd cut in the wire below the floodlit surface. Gliding like driftwood under the catwalk, though the guards rarely came there. And once safely across to the other side, they'd explore paths leading through the jungle in search of supplies. Skirting past native huts and small Malay *kampongs*, for no one knew who could be trusted and the Japs had offered big rewards to anyone reporting escapees. One evening, indeed, they thought they'd had it. Coming down the track towards them, they saw a bull of a man: head sunk massively into his shoulders, the muscles on his hairy arms flexing.

'He's one hell of a big Jap,' whispered the kid.

Until the penny dropped.

'Oh good Christ! It's a gorilla,' cried Harry Longley, not knowing about orangutans. 'He could eat us!'

They skedaddled back to the swamp. Back to the mosquito-ridden sludge. Wading silently across to the fringe of light, for the water was rarely more than waist height. Then ducking down and swimming beneath the catwalk to the severed wire and doing a quick tug on the safety line that led to the feller keeping nit under the hut.

*We're back!*

Waiting for the reply. One jerk to give the all clear. Two to warn of danger.

'You silly young buggers will get caught one day,' Corporal Shipsides and the wiser heads would warn. 'And then you'll be for it. It ain't just a game, you know.'

Though of course it was to the lads. And Shippy had no qualms about feasting on the bounty they brought back: coconuts, yams, and – best of all – chips from tapioca roots, sliced and toasted by Shearer Gillett on a bit of tin over a little fire out the back.

Some prisoners who made it under the wire had no intention of returning. Within a fortnight 11 men had escaped – six of them Australian Army Service Corps blokes, and the other five Alan Minty's group. The AASC fellers didn't get away for long. Four of them were caught within a few days, and the other two, Herb Trackson and Matt Carr, in less than three weeks. They were the first to be sent by the Kenpeitai, like trailblazers, on the sorrowful journey from Sandakan to Outram Road prison.

Alan Minty's party were more fortunate. They kept their freedom for over five months, though they never moved far from the camp. For most of the time they stayed hidden in a stretch of jungle by a river only seven miles upcountry, protected by a Chinese man called Sin Tshau, who owned a tobacco plantation. From time to time food and medicine were sent to them, once Sandakan's underground support network became established. Even so, their health deteriorated badly. Malaria and beriberi set in; and by January 1943, Minty decided to try to sail home to Australia.

Sin Tshau warned that a voyage during the wet season was not a good idea, but they insisted. Pop New said he had much experience as a sailor. Arrangements were made to buy a boat, with promises to pay after the war. Sin Tshau gave them a map and supplies; and with his son helping to navigate downriver, they set out.

Whatever skill Freddy New possessed as a yachtsman off the summer coasts of England, it was of little use to him trying to steer a Chinese sampan out of Sandakan Harbour during a tropical monsoon. The boat ran aground on a mud bank and stuck fast. It was spotted by some locals who, to earn the reward money, informed the Japanese. The only trip Alan's group made after that was to Sandakan prison – and from there, with the kid and Brownie and Jimmy Darlington in their turn, down the *via dolorosa* to Kuching.

The officers tried to cover up these escapes from the Japanese; but the absentees were discovered during a rollcall – *tenko* – on the parade ground, and the men were kept standing in the sun for hours as the guards counted and re-counted them. Punishments increased. Every POW was issued with a number. Their cigarette ration was cut – and so were the extra titbits of meat and vegetables officially served with the daily rice, though this lasted for only a week. The Nips required a strong workforce to build the airfield, and the basic ration remained much the same: one and a half pounds of rice for those doing heavy labour, one pound for the rest. In a mad bureaucratic mindset, less was given to the sick, which was probably intended as retribution, but it only made them weaker and even more unable to work.

By mid-August, with his appointment as commandant and promotion to Captain confirmed, Hoshijima called another *tenko*; and standing on a box in front of the assembled men, announced they would begin work on the airfield in earnest, for which honour they'd be paid ten cents a day!

Hoshijima actually spoke quite good English, but as a matter of personal dignity always spoke through an interpreter – a small, rather bandy civilian in a peaked cap called Ozawa, who quickly got himself nicknamed 'Jimmy Pike', after the jockey who rode Phar Lap. And when he went on to say that the aerodrome would be built 'even if take three year', titters spread through his audience.

'Three years!' muttered the kid. 'The war won't last three

months once the Yanks get into it.'

'Them Nips couldn't go three rounds with a real fighter given half a chance,' said Jimmy Finn the pocket Atlas, who'd always reckoned the Australians hadn't been given a proper go in Malaya.

Such witticisms infuriated Hoshijima. Quite forgetting his interpreter, he shouted to the crowd, 'I have the power of life and death over you. You will build this aerodrome, if you stay until your bone rot under Borneo sun.'

Which, for most of them, would be the literal truth.

From then on, all energies were directed to the project. The prisoners were divided into work parties of about 50 men, and put to work either making vehicle access to the main Sandakan road, clearing the airfield, or levelling the landing strip. Here were the Dead End Kids, labouring ten hours a day, six days a week, under the cruel supervision of Lieutenant Okahara and his henchmen.

A few minutes breather was allowed each hour, and a brief respite for lunch of rice cooked in a 44-gallon drum. Apart from that, their days were spent hacking at the chalk-like tufa, loading it into baskets, and tipping the fill. Encouragement was not all stick. Okahara tried a little kindness, and for a while awarded the best worker in each section a token for a lunchtime cup of coffee. Billy thought he'd be in that, and the sweat he worked up (augmented by his water bottle) so impressed the guard he won a token. But the wait was long, and the coffee dreadful. By the time he got back to his group, lunch was over – and he had to work all through the afternoon on an empty stomach.

Curiously, for a place with such high rainfall, no provision had been made for drains. Okahara said they were not considered necessary; and the Australians did not disabuse him. The dry season arrived – and the tufa glared so dazzlingly white in the sun that men risked their eyesight. The problem was solved only when someone had the idea of making an eyeshade from two small pieces of bamboo, a slit between them to see through, and tying it around the head with a strip of leaf.

The prisoners were not alone in their undertaking. Thousands of coolies had been sent from Java, and much local labour indentured. Even so, the kid could see that progress was miserably slow. The officers, at this stage, were not required to work – though they maintained a vegetable garden near the airfield to supplement camp supplies and went out on wood-gathering parties. It was during this time that Rod Wells began to collect material for his radio, and furtive contacts were made with local sympathisers. Still, without officers and the sick – already weakened by the *Yubi Maru*, overwork and tropical diseases – the number of POWs in the workforce rarely exceeded a thousand. Indeed, their numbers were nearly reduced quite significantly.

One morning in early September, the camp awoke in uproar. Guards were running in and out of huts – the Dead End Kids roused from their sleep by jabbing rifle butts, and ordered outside to the assembly ground by the Big Tree. The entire force was there, surrounded by Japanese soldiers all fully armed, the machine gun on the verandah of the guardhouse by the gate manned and aimed directly at them.

Gathering his little group, Bob Shipsides ushered the lads as close as he could to the hut nearest the open gate and told them to stand by.

'Something's up,' he said. 'Watch those little bastards. No matter what happens, stick together, take cover, and try to get out if they open fire.'

Thoughts of imminent massacre passed through everybody's mind as Captain Hoshijima arrived with his officers. The interpreter 'Jimmy Pike' got onto his box and read from a paper. He was immediately followed, to the men's great surprise, by their own CO,

Lieutenant-Colonel Alfred Walsh, a person whom they rarely saw.

An artilleryman (and therefore no favourite among the infantry), rather short and overweight, with a shy, almost withdrawn personality, who'd not so far displayed any conspicuous courage in his war, Walsh was not well liked by his officers. Certainly he received little support from most of them. Yet he was to redeem himself this day. Taking the document from 'Jimmy Pike' and standing on the box, Walsh read what was described as 'The Oath'. In it, the men consented to abide by the rules of the Imperial Japanese Army; agreed not to attempt escape, and should any of them do so, 'we request that you shoot him to death'.

There was an audible intake of breath at this from the assembled men – and another as Colonel Walsh went on. 'The Japanese are demanding that I sign this statement on behalf of you all.' He paused, drew himself up straight and added in a remarkably strong, clear voice, 'I for one will not sign such a document.' And to emphasise his contempt, he threw the paper at Hoshijima's feet.

There followed outrage amongst the Japanese. Colonel Walsh was hustled outside the gate and made to stand, as if awaiting execution, by the guardhouse steps. A firing squad was drawn up, and the men could hear the sounds of rifle bolts being drawn. Some of the officers called out, urging Walsh to sign and prevent the inevitable slaughter. But he refused and tension stretched almost to breaking point. Billy could feel the soldiers taking aim at him, and heard the voice of Bob Shipsides in his ear.

'I think this could be it, fellers, so be ready...'

At length, however, a compromise was reached; faces were saved. Colonel Walsh was released and climbed back upon the box with an amended document.

'Men, our captors have threatened to shoot the sick if we do not sign this now re-worded paper. I will read it to you: "If I escape I know I will be shot." I have made it plain to Captain Hoshijima that it is signed under protest, and I ask you to sign it under the same protest.'

Which, ultimately, they did: appending their names on blank sheets of paper, knowing very well that anything signed under duress was invalid – though to make doubly certain, the signatures included a great many Ned Kellys and Bob Menzies. Alf Walsh now stood a hero among the men who'd witnessed his bravery; but within weeks he was removed to a prison camp at Kuching in Sarawak, the Japanese administrative centre of all Borneo.

Work resumed at the airfield. In view of their insubordination over The Oath, men found that punishments and bashings increased: and to speed up matters even further, a network of light rails and metal skips was brought in from surrounding rubber plantations. They certainly made it easier for men to push fill around the site (and were a valuable source of scrap metal for the camp scroungers). But the unstable, undrained nature of the topsoil meant that rails would suddenly veer off or sink and the skips tip over, spilling their contents everywhere.

Still, progress was such that in October the camp was visited by a Major Suga, who advised that the aerodrome was to be ready for the first test landing before Christmas. Another dumpy, absurdly over-decorated individual, wearing rows of medals, a pith helmet, and a sword that he kept fondling, he took much pride in his English and insisted on speaking to the assembled prisoners without the aid of an interpreter.

'I am Major Suga…S. U. G. A.' he announced. 'Commandant of all the prison camp of all the Borneo.'

'Major Sugar?' whispered the kid, who had learnt to spell that much.

'He don't look too sweet,' muttered Harry Longley.

The sniggers this produced were nothing to what followed, as the man resumed. 'The Japanese Government very good, treat you well, so you must have impatience while we get inconvenience for you.'

A breeze of sardonic laughter passed through the ranks, causing the major to lose his temper and shout, 'That is FACT!' Sounding like *that* Anglo-Saxon word.

'I'll say you are,' murmured Joey Crome. And the laughter blew a gale.

Only when 'Jimmy Pike' explained the mispronunciations did Major Suga appear mollified. And standing beneath the Big Tree, he sought to retrieve himself by making a promise to the assembled prisoners.

'All Japanese officer Samurai. All Japanese soldier honourable. You work hard – finish airfield – you be fine.'

It was a promise never intended to be fulfilled.

Even as the 'commandant of all the Borneo' departed Sandakan, the workload dramatically increased. The length of the runway was extended. The daily output demanded was doubled to *ichi* man *ni* yard. Many of the officers and all but the sickest men were required to labour – and the gradations of illness were determined by the boot. Only those unable to crawl away were allowed to remain behind.

Enforcing this was a brute called Lieutenant Moritake, who would have served his masters proud at Outram Road prison. Not that Moritake hit anybody himself. As a rule, that was left to his four large Formosan thugs. They carried wooden clubs shaped like Japanese practice swords – *bokutou* – though the violence with which they laid into anyone not working hard enough was utterly for real. And the punishments were meted out not just to individuals, but to entire squads of men.

'We had "flying practice" today,' Billy would say to a cobber he met on the track back to the camp. 'An hour of it.'

'I seen youse.' The whole 50 of them lined up under the noon sun, staring at the burning white tufa, arms extended horizontally until they almost touched the fingers of the fellers on either side. 'How did ya go?'

'I made it to corporal.' Meaning that twice the kid's arms had tired and drooped a little – and twice 'Mad Mick' the Formosan had belted him across the back.

'I got to sergeant last week,' the other bloke replied. 'Three stripes.'

Painful as these episodes were, the punishment was not entirely one way.

Another of Moritake's bullies was a particularly savage bugger known as 'the Black Bastard.' His favourite occupation was to come roaring down without warning upon a work party, screaming 'Kora! Bakayarou! All man work faster!' and hitting out with his waddy at anyone in his way.

He was thus engaged with a group of men labouring at the tree line, when his practice sword dislodged a hornet's nest hanging on a branch above him. The nest fell on his head. And as the Black Bastard fled, leaping and pirouetting everywhere, he was pursued by the swarm of vengeful hornets. It was a triumph of the dance: a ballet on the theme of cause and effect. Hungry men dined upon it for weeks.

And there were other compensations. Rain started again, and a steamroller was brought in to compact and level the runway. As it approached an especially soggy patch, all eyes turned to watch. The lumbering thing inched towards the soft earth. Tested its weight. Moved forward again. Cautiously. Until it was fair over the bog – and began to sink ever deeper into the quicksand.

'It's as if that steamroller thought it was a bloody submarine,' Billy grinned when he recalled the spectacle during a whispered conversation with Rod Wells in his cell. 'It died of shame.'

Yes. And with much loss of face. What was honourable Japanese solution to such grave problem? Drains, obviously. And in the meantime, several thousand human feet to stamp the runway flat.

The Nips brought in a large excavator, able to dig as much fill with one scoop as ten men in a whole shift. The trouble was that after only a day it broke down – unaccountably – and the best efforts of mechanics to get it going again at the airfield were to no avail. At length it was moved to the boiler shed back at camp, where Mo Davis and his engineering mates were sure they could fix it. And fix it they did. For good. Something to do with sand and the engine. They tinkered for weeks, but the excavator never worked again; and when Rod Wells last saw it, the thing was still sitting outside the boiler shed.

Of course the Japanese guards were sensible enough not to leave the solution to every technical problem in the hands of their prisoners. Some things they undertook themselves, with spectacular results.

There was another Big Tree – a regular monarch of the forest – growing at the very end of the runway, its outstretched arms threatening to pull from the sky any aircraft using the aerodrome. It was decided to remove it, and the Dead End Kids were detailed to dig a number of holes around the base.

They'd no sooner finished than a truck pulled up. Several guards got out, including a couple of Moritake's bashers. Ordering the prisoners out of the way and saying 'Nippon fix', they packed the holes with bundles of old and volatile gelignite. The lads got the hell out of there, and watched from a safe distance as their masters unwound the fuse, took shelter behind the truck and pressed the plunger.

The explosion was immense. The tree rose from a cloud of flame and smoke like some gigantic rocket, trailing stones, dirt and tree roots. Higher it soared – until at last gravity took over. The tree began to disintegrate. Chunks of branches and tree trunk crashed to the ground in a *blitzkrieg*. The guards crawled further under the truck for safety, and for a moment the kid thought they would be spared. But the sky gods would not permit that. A couple of limbs, like large wooden clubs, smashed into the cabin, which, as Billy related it to Lieutenant Wells, dented not only the truck, but also the superior faces of the master blasters.

The kid got even the officer to laugh at that!

Yet for all these delays and small acts of sabotage, work on the first stage of the airfield neared completion. November came, and with it Billy's 17th birthday, which they celebrated on the verandah with a cake shaped from cold rice; a spoonful of molasses acquired from one of the native Dyaks; and a corn-cob pipe Bob Shipsides made, smoking dried pawpaw leaf for tobacco. And there was a sing-song of course afterwards, to Brownie's mouth organ. *Hi wringle-wrangle, hi wringle-ray!*

Oddly enough, Rod Wells told him that 4th of November was the day he received his first broadcast on the clandestine radio headphone – but that was kept very quiet. It amounted merely to a BBC talk on hop-growing in Kent; yet for men starved of news, it was enough to indicate that Britain had not fallen to the Nazis. We'd still win the war, whatever the Japs said! Thereafter, Wells tuned into the news bulletins for a few minutes every day, though the information he gleaned was only dribbled out to the men as 'rumours' well after the event, to maintain secrecy.

There was nothing discreet about the official opening of the airfield. Hoshijima put up a notice to say it would take place in early December, and every prisoner was required to attend. They made a motley spectacle. Boots and clothing had long started to rot in the steamy heat. Many prisoners went barefooted, whatever the risk of sores and ulcers; some wore lap-laps; and the kid had acquired a pyjama jacket, and a pair of shorts made from the bottom half of a canvas kitbag, holes cut out for his legs, and tied with a bit of rope. All of this in contrast to the military finery of the Japanese – and the Malay and Chinese population, many of whom appeared in new clothes acquired from the purloined stores of the Australian POWs.

The locals also came equipped with Japanese flags, which they had to wave rapturously as a bomber, escorted by two fighter planes, droned above the treetops. The fighters peeled away and the bomber came in to land. Every POW was praying it would crash; but the sky gods were not listening that day and the aircraft made a perfect touchdown. Out of it stepped a much beribboned military commander, to whom everyone had to bow. They also had to listen to innumerable very long speeches.

The celebrations continued the following day with a sports carnival, including foot races, such as the prisoners could manage, and a football-kicking competition. But for Billy the Kid, the most memorable thing from that time was the opening of a new hut, built from sawn timber, near the officers' quarters. Most of it was for use as a hospital. While fewer than 20 men had died so far, the numbers of sick were growing fast. But one end of the new hut had been set aside for a chapel, the wall beautifully inlaid with forest woods. There they mounted an arts and crafts exhibition, which the boy found a marvel to see. There were small pictures and models, all made by the prisoners, among them the carved figure of an infantry soldier, standing on a base carrying the word 'Australia'. But the prize went to a man who, scarcely able to move with ulcers, had nevertheless carved a birdcage. Complete with a chain, roof, bars and a door that opened, the cage held a wooden bird that sat silently inside, on its carved swing.

Billy knew the skill involved in making such a masterpiece. He'd seen his Uncle Cocky at work – had even contemplated cabinet-making as a trade for himself. But how, he wondered, could men find the inspiration amid the wretchedness of Sandakan to create such an object of beauty? What was it in the human soul that needed to express itself so exquisitely, even in this miserable camp?

The answers were beyond him. He could only open himself to the experience. As did others, of course. Captain Hoshijima was so impressed he invited the civil governor to visit the exhibition; and he, in turn, was so delighted that he sent a freshly caught dugong to the camp, to be served for dinner. A rare concession, indeed.

Christmas 1942 arrived. Hoshijima gave everyone a day off work at the airfield. The officers' canteen had stocked up on a few treats to share among the men, bartered from the locals or supplied courtesy of the underground assistance group. Some blokes had made a potent brew from fermented coconut milk and molasses, to say nothing of the supplementary trimmings smuggled into the very last hut by the Dead End Kids, including a goodly gift of tapioca chips.

As the men sat outside waiting for midnight, a choir formed by the officers walked through the camp singing 'Silent Night, Holy Night'.

Softly, the familiar melody stole into the tropical air. It rose above the enclosing fences, barbed wire and omnivorous jungle. Here, unlike the carved bird in its cage, these human prisoners could give voice to their song, fervently lifting their hearts towards the stars in distant heavens: *All is calm, all is bright.*

Even the guards stopped to listen. And the boy was moved to tears.

*Unearth the splintered bones, the tattered gear:*
*Uncovered, a scene of massacre appears.*

# 11

# ESCAPE

*The night is as long as a sad sung song...*

Singing. Always, when the dark days came and Billy's thoughts went back to the camp at Sandakan for sanctuary, it was the music in men's voices he remembered first. Carols at Christmas. The choir into which a musical staff sergeant dragooned some of the Dead End Kids: Billy finding he was a decent tenor, learning to sing in parts, and almost aching with their poignant harmonies swelling into the evening. *What a day was yesterday, for yesterday gave me you.*

Work songs to lighten footsteps as they trudged to the airfield. 'Ten Men Went To Mow'. The inherent defiance of 'Waltzing Matilda', which the Japs never understood. Those brittle green bottles hanging on the wall... *And if one green bottle should accidentally fall?*

Why, you'd be there to pick up the pieces, of course. Put them back together as best you could and offer the consolations of mateship. The eternal bond of the Last Post the Japs permitted a bugler to play on Armistice Day. Brownie's harmonica wafting to the Big Tree, where men bloated with beriberi – their testicles sometimes swollen big as footballs – sought relief for the night among the buttress roots. Hearing, in the plaintive melody, the sounds of home. And knowing the fellers cared.

However inhuman the treatment prisoners received outside the camp, or the suffering they endured within it, this was the spirit of camaraderie they ever sought to maintain. The fellowship of song was one of the gentler ways by which they did it.

There were more direct approaches too. The violent fraternity of the ring, for instance. Every few months Captain Hoshijima allowed the men to stage a boxing match. A ring was built under the perimeter lights near the parade ground, and for days men discussed the respective merits of the fighters, and laid their bets. Jimmy Finn. Keith Gillett. The heavyweight Corporal Henry 'Gunboat' Simpson of the 2/29th, ex pug and showing it, went up against the professional Jimmy Darlington.

'It's only an exhibition fight, Jimmy.'

'I know, Gunner. But if you land one on me, I'll bloody kill ya.'

There was a bout in which one of their own wrestlers went several rounds with a Japanese sumo master (who, in his day job, was one of Moritake's heavies). The result, to save everybody's face, was declared a draw.

But the most memorable event was the fight between Snowy Bryant of the Dead End Kids' hut, and Jimmy 'Punchy' Donohue. It was billed as a 'grudge match' – and excitement built up for weeks. Both boxers went into a strict regime. A punching bag was installed under the hut, skipping ropes provided, and men came from all over camp to see the opponents working out.

Gunboat Simpson appointed himself Punchy's trainer, and Keith Gillett took over Snowy's management. He also ran the book, betting heavily on his man, and he seemed set to clean up royally. On the night – as hot and thick with the smell of blood as any evening in the Old Tin Shed at Rushcutter's Bay – Snowy Bryant danced rings around Donohue. Punchy was the younger bloke, but he'd been on the Tin Shed's canvas too often. His eyebrows were split, he seemed to walk on the back of his heels, and was altogether slower than the nimble Bryant.

For two and a half rounds Snowy outclassed his opponent: a jab here, a volley of blows there. Keith Gillett was already counting himself a millionaire. When, just as the bout was ending, Punchy found the resources to land a massive uppercut on Snowy's jaw. Bryant went down – and out for the count himself. The crowd went wild. The Shearer went into bankruptcy and into hiding – emerging a few days later offering to pay one cent in the dollar. After the war.

There was no reneging on any bet at Gunboat Simpson's pontoon school. There, you had to show the colour of your money – minimum ten cents – before he'd let you enter. It was one of the undercover institutions, quite literally, by which men maintained their Australian ethos in captivity at Sandakan. No officer was invited. But often, as the months passed at Outram Road, when Billy found himself sharing a cell with one of the Sandakan fellers, they'd play a hand with the kid's thumbnail pack of cards and remember fondly those games at Gunner's place.

Gunboat's hut, in the row next to the kid, had been built over a hole in the ground where a tree once stood. The pit was wide enough to allow players to sit in a circle betting on a pontoon game: 21. The den was disguised by a wall of blankets and *atap* tacked to the underside of the hut; lit by a shaded electric light let down through the floor above and entered by crawling along a canvas tunnel, with Gunner sitting at the hessian-bag entrance to eye your ten cents.

On those few occasions when the Japs actually paid their promised wages, Gunboat's saloon was awash with money. But mostly cash was very scarce and the Dead End Kids had to scrape hard among themselves to find the ready. Once found, however, the rest was easy. Billy's childhood training keeping nit at Thommo's two-up school, or creeping under a visiting circus tent, paid dividends. He'd be the first to crawl down the tunnel and show his stake.

'Billy the Kid! All cashed up, I see. In ya go.'

Next he had to find the proper place; then, squatting around the ring, he'd pass the ten cents beneath the blanket wall to Harry waiting outside.

'Evenin', Gunboat.'

'Longley...'

Repeat the exercise.

'Joey Crome! You young blokes have come into the money tonight...'

'Yeah.'

Gunboat would have killed them had he twigged. He never did – though he still relieved them of their money. The lights supplied from the camp generator went out promptly at nine o'clock. Game over. If you were ahead, it always seemed to slip Gunboat's mind to pay up, though he never forgot if you were in debt. And the bruiser was such that you didn't argue.

Yet of all the ways by which the Dead End Kids kept up morale, nothing bettered a successful night out foraging under the wire. The rewards were so much greater: but so were the risks of getting caught. Four times, during the seven months he was at Sandakan, Billy ended up in the hands of the guards.

There was the time he and Joey were discovered smuggling tapioca roots in bundles of firewood – for which they blamed an officer, as related; in consequence, they were bashed and locked in 'Esau', the punishment cage by the Big Tree. Once, they followed out the gate a work party emptying toilet buckets into the swamp. The boys got a couple of *benki* buckets, slung them on poles over their shoulders and joined the procession. It looked a pushover. Nobody seemed to be counting them.

While the others went back and forth to the camp with their buckets, the youngsters disappeared down the jungle track to a little *kampong* where they had the luck to catch a scrawny chicken, gather a few coconuts and yams, put them in the buckets, and were back in time to join the last of the returning work party.

This time, however, the Black Bastard was on duty. As the boys neared the gate, he noticed that the numbers were wrong.

'*Kora!*' Hey you!

The pair stopped and put down their buckets.

'*Kotchi koi.*'

'Oh Gawd,' whispered Joey, approaching the guardhouse. 'We're for it now.'

'*Koi!*'

They mounted the half dozen steps to the verandah where the Black Bastard stood and ordered the guard to kick over the buckets. Out rolled the coconuts and one dead chicken. They were dead meat themselves.

Billy didn't see the king hit coming. The blow stunned, and he sprawled down the steps to the ground. But Joey anticipated the Black Bastard and ducked. It was the worst thing he could have done. They almost knocked his brains out by the time they'd finished, and the pair of them spent two days in the hot box.

Yet some things were beyond Billy's experience.

Punchy Donohue (he who had KO'd Snowy Bryant) one night asked to go under the wire with the kid and Joey Crome. No problem. Down to the swamp they went. Beneath the catwalk, where the Japs never came. They waded through the darkling water to the other side and nipped down jungle paths in search of food. They'd filled their haversacks and were heading back to the swamp when they ran into a party of guards returning from an expedition of their own.

'*Kora!*'

Shouts echoed in the forest. Shots were fired as the three prisoners split up: Punchy in one direction, the kid and Joey in the other. The pair could hear the alarm being raised – and were lucky the Japs made so much noise and waved so many torches in the moonless night that they could easily skirt around them. Fortunate, too, they'd been this way so often they had no difficulty finding their way in darkness to the swamp. Once there, things got harder. The camp was alive with activity: lights blazing; the noise and bustle of search parties; and the sentry towers and catwalk over the water now fairly swarmed with guards.

'Jesus!' muttered Joey. 'We've got to be a couple of swamp rats now, Billy.'

Quietly they lowered themselves into the water and, using the coconuts in their weed-covered haversacks as floats, edged their way across...making barely a ripple...ever closer to the catwalk and the circle of light. Where they could see guards sitting, feet dangling over the edge, smoking and laughing about what mincemeat they'd make of the escapees when they captured them.

The catwalk extended forward of the perimeter fence, and it was to one of the piers that the Dead End Kids had attached their safety cord. It acted not only as a communications signal, but also as a guide through the wire on a dark night. And it was towards this that the two clumps of waterweed eddied, carefully, feeling for the lifeline. Holding their breaths...wriggling as eels under water...the weed bobbed beneath the guards. The lads paused to fill their lungs and listen. And when at last came a single tug on the cord – *coast clear* – they ducked beneath the surface, squirmed through the wire and eventually crawled back on land like a pair of emerging amphibians.

All this had taken well over an hour. Billy and Joey were safely back in their room, when one of the officers appeared at the door. Showing little solicitude for the boys' welfare, he curtly advised that the Japanese wanted to see them.

'Donohue has been caught,' he said. 'He's being held at the Big Tree. And unless you present yourselves immediately, he's going to be executed.'

Upon which he turned heel and left.

There was no choice but to go: and with considerable trepidation the two made their way to the parade ground, where they found Punchy, severely bashed, confronted by the interpreter Ozawa known as 'Jimmy Pike', the Black Bastard and his offsider, the sumo wrestler.

'We heard you were looking for us,' said the kid, giving nothing away.

'Can we help you?' added Joey. Not to be outdone.

Three pairs of eyes stared at the youngsters. Two of them burned like cobras. The third – 'Jimmy Pike', temporarily in charge – seemed, if anything, puzzled.

'You men got out of this camp,' Ozawa inquired at length, 'even though my guards were here to *stop* you?'

Billy wondered whether the interpreter wanted an answer? Apparently not; for without further pause he went on, sounding even more bemused. 'You then got back into this camp, even though I had *trebled* the guard to stop you?'

The Black Bastard's hooded tongue flickering, ready to strike.

'This is it,' the kid thought, preparing himself. 'The little snake's *really* upset.'

So he was. But to the prisoners' astonishment, the interpreter's venom was directed not at them but to their guards.

With a brisk order the three were released.

'You may go now,' said 'Jimmy Pike', almost politely.

And as they hurried back to the huts, the lads could see Ozawa remove his metal sword scabbard and start bashing the Black Bastard for having let the escapees slip through his fingers. Talk about loss of face! The Black Bastard recovered by belting his subordinate, the sumo wrestler. Who passed it on the fellow next to him...and so on down the line, until everybody's honour was satisfied. Except for the bloke at the very end. He took it out on the prisoners.

Some oriental customs Billy the Kid highly approved! And yet, when he came to think of his own travail – of his own real attempt at escape – he knew the Japanese were not always as accommodating...

From the day of their arrival at Sandakan – like Alan Minty, Herb Trackson or those officers building their secret networks – the Dead End Kids had been harbouring ideas of escape. Their forays under the wire were not only scrounging expeditions, but under Harry Longley's leadership were also scouting trips. Getting the lay of the land. Looking for likely hiding places. Gathering supplies.

They found a good base camp – a cavern in some riverside rocks a couple of miles upcountry. The lads had been stockpiling supplies: a worn parang, a bit of rice, the odd tin of food. They even had a one-page map of the world, torn from a school atlas Billy found in Singapore. And the escape route didn't look all that far.

'We'll find a boat,' Harry would say, 'and go downriver to the coast.'

'It's dead easy after that,' Billy remarked. 'Look! Just sail round the top of Borneo, past those few islands, and into Darwin. We're practically home.'

'I don't think it's quite that simple. Remember the *Yubi Maru*? It took 11 days to chug that little distance from Singapore.'

'Yeah, but she's an old tub, and three of them days were

anchored at Miri.'

'And then there's the food...'

Which Billy had to admit was a problem. Tins rusted in the humidity. Rice went off. Yams rotted, however carefully packed in the cavern they were. How to keep them from going bad long enough for even a short voyage across three or four inches of coloured map? None of them spoke Malay or the native Dyak lingo. Nobody knew how to ask which were the best foods to gather or how to store them properly.

'We need someone with nous to help us,' Joey Crome proffered. 'Someone like MP Brown who sleeps next to you, Billy. He can talk half a dozen languages.'

'I'll ask him.'

But Brownie would have nothing to do with it.

'Don't be stupid,' the wiser head counselled. 'Even if you found a boat...'

'We reckoned that's where you could help us.'

'The Japs would catch you before you got halfway downriver.'

'We could go overland.'

'Do you realise that many of the upcountry Dyaks are headhunters?'

'Oh.' The boy was trying to remember those stories from his *Triumph* magazine.

'And suppose you reach the coast? There are hundreds of miles of open sea between here and Australia.'

'There are lots of little islands!'

'Yep, and they're all occupied by the Japs. Forget it. You young fellers are better off staying here until the war is over.'

And nothing that Billy could say all over Christmas and New Year would shift Brownie's opinion. Until events conspired to change his mind.

In early February the two found themselves on the sick list and confined to the hut. Brownie had a badly ulcerated leg and the kid was recovering from snakebite. It was Mo Davis's fault. The wet season had arrived and Mo told them that a crocodile had come up from the river and been seen in the flooded swamp. Returning one dusk from a reconnaissance, Billy had his sights so set for any sign of the croc that he didn't see another reptile lurking by the track. Not until he glimpsed the flash of tail and felt the sting on his left ankle.

It hurt like hell. By the time the others helped him across the water and into the hut, the kid's foot was swollen, and the pain intense. He must have passed out, for the next memory was of Doctor Picone – Captain Dominic Picone – cutting the wound and bathing it with Condy's crystals, and the sound of his voice from far away.

'It's the best I can do. If he lives till morning he should be all right.'

He lived. Billy's ankle was still bloated from the venom: but that was a good thing, for the Japs only responded to symptoms they could actually *see*. Malaria, exhaustion, even cancers were invisible. They didn't count, and the sufferers were forced to the airfield to labour on the second stage. But gaping leg ulcers and puffed-up ankles were obvious ailments affecting the ability to work – and for the rest of the week, the kid and Brownie were allowed to remain at the camp.

The boy used his time trying to persuade the older man to join the escape plan – but MP was implacable. The idea was foolish and dangerous, and he kept warning the Dead End Kids against it. Still, by the time they returned to work the following week, Billy got Brownie to at least consider helping their negotiations with the locals.

'There's a Chinese bloke in a *kampong* near the airfield,' the kid pleaded. 'Harry says he'll help us get some of that dried Japanese rice that keeps for months. Wants to know if I'll swap my mosquito net for it. Okay by me, but I don't know how to put it proper, and I thought you might ... '

'We'll see.'

They had no time to see anything for the first few days back at work, other than the dreadful fate that overtook Jimmy Darlington.

The men had finished Wednesday lunch. One of the camp cooks – an older prisoner whom everybody liked – was cleaning out the bucket in which the rice was served, when Mad Mick – another of Moritake's attack dogs – grabbed the pail and began to wash his dirty clothes in it.

'Don't do that!' the old bloke remonstrated. 'We put our food in that bucket!'

Mad Mick's response was to knock him violently to the ground and start kicking. At which point Jimmy Darlington, the Aboriginal heavyweight standing nearby, had his own moment of madness or heroism, and went to the cook's assistance.

'Leave him alone!' Jimmy said. 'You'll injure him.' And he held out his arm to fend Mad Mick away.

The guard took a wild swing at Jimmy, which he easily avoided. And then his professional training took over. Instinctively, the champion retaliated with a right hook that knocked Mad Mick out cold. He fell to earth and didn't move.

Not so the other guards. They came rushing from everywhere, like ants swarming. Jimmy warded them off for as long as he could; but there were too many and at last they forced him to the ground and beat him almost senseless.

Moritake arrived. Ordering the guards to keep the prisoners at bay with their rifles, he directed his henchmen to prepare a torture for Jimmy Darlington that was beyond the imagining of those who witnessed it, though the guards seemed well practised at it. They got pieces of firewood – rubber trees, roughly cut and quartered –

and laid them lengthwise on the ground, sharp edges pointing upwards, making a kind of platform on which they forced the victim to kneel, splinters digging into his bare flesh. A split log was forced behind Jimmy's knees and another into his back over which his arms were bound with thin cord, soaked in water. The rope was tied around the prisoner's hands, looped about his neck and passed behind to his ankles. And there Jimmy Darlington knelt, trussed like a bird, and left to roast in the Borneo sun.

As the cord dried, so it tightened about his limbs, digging great weals and constricting the flow of blood. The kid, watching on, could see his mate's hands and feet begin to convulse and darken.

'They're gunna kill him!' Billy cried. And to create a diversion, those with him also began to shout and throw dirt and sticks to distract the guards' attention.

It had the desired effect. As the sentries rushed to quell the disturbance, a first-aid officer known to the Dead End Kids only as 'Mac', crept from behind a skip with a knife and cut Jimmy's bonds. Everyone knew that this one brave deed saved Darlington's life, though it earned Mac a severe beating from the Black Bastard who caught him. And it didn't prevent Jimmy being re-tethered to the jagged timber scaffold for another two hours. Until, come mid-afternoon, a truck carted the agonised man to the camp, where they flung him into the punishment box.

That evening Dr Picone smuggled him some water laced with morphine, so that Jimmy might at least pass the night in unconsciousness. But the next day Darlington was carried off in the back of another truck and taken no one knew where.

The attack on Jimmy Darlington was so vicious, so prolonged, so outside what the prisoners had experienced from their captors (though they knew from *Sook Ching* of what they were capable) as to change the mood of the entire camp. Hardening attitudes of contempt and a desire for revenge, certainly. Confirming the resolve of those, like the Dead End Kids, who had ideas of escape. Yet also instilling a sense of fear – as Moritake no doubt intended. The methods of *Sook Ching* could as easily be applied to themselves! A few thoughtless moments, and a man's whole world could be turned upside down – as Billy the Kid and his mate MP Brown would soon discover.

Three days later, the pair found themselves working on the far side of the airfield. During the short lunchbreak the kid sat next to Brownie and murmured quietly, 'That Chinese feller Harry says will help us with the dried rice lives near here. We could slip away quick – tell him about my mozzie net – and be back before work starts again. The Japs will never miss us. Will you come with me?'

Brown had been deeply shocked by the torture of Jimmy Darlington. This intelligent man, who'd have nothing to do with escape and constantly advised caution, now understood why the young fellows at least should try to get away from such monsters as Lieutenant Moritake and his servants. He therefore gazed steadily at the kid from the shade of his slouch hat; and to Billy's surprise at last nodded and replied, 'All right. But only to the village. And back. And make it snappy.'

The kid couldn't believe his ears. He'd fully expected another refusal. But knowing never to question a consent, he merely said, 'Thanks, MP.' And glancing around to make sure of their opportunity added, 'Come on then!'

They slipped through the trees fringing the airfield and down the path that led to the *kampong*. The place was only small – a few mean houses, mostly made of palm thatch and raised on stilts, standing in a jungle clearing planted with bananas and pineapples, among which chickens scratched and a pig rooted.

The villagers were not unknown to the prisoners, for they were sometimes allowed to sell fritters and rice cakes beside the aerodrome at lunchtime. This day, however, the man Billy wanted to see was not there. He'd gone away, the pair were told, and wouldn't be back until later.

'*Terima kasih*,' Brownie thanked the people in Malay. And to the kid he muttered urgently, 'Off we go now! Back to the airfield, before it's too late.'

Yet when they arrived they found it was already too late. They hadn't been absent more than ten minutes. Yet in that time the guards had discovered – or more likely been informed by a villager wanting the reward – that two men were missing. As they came through the trees, Billy and MP saw that the Japs had marshalled the whole workforce into their squads, and were counting them.

'Oh, cripes!' the boy exclaimed. 'What are we gunna do?'

Ordinarily, he'd have known exactly what to do: repeat the effrontery shown the night they caught Punchy Donohue. March up to the guards. 'Were you looking for us?' Say they'd gone for a shit. There was always a chance they'd be let go, like Ozawa had done. At most they'd risk a belting. But that was before they'd seen Jimmy Darlington's punishment. Now they knew what would happen to them.

'I'm not going to go back to that,' Brownie said. 'I don't think I'd survive it.'

'Then we'd better make a run for it,' Billy whispered. A few words – a mere puff of breath – and the balance of life over death pivoted upon it. 'Our little hideout's a few miles down this track. We could stay there till we work out a plan. What d'ya reckon? Are you in it?'

Myles Peace Brown looked at the kid. He looked at the workforce lined up and being counted. He weighed the possibility of escape against the likelihood of torture.

'All right,' he said after a moment. 'Let's have a go.'

Swiftly they pulled back into the trees and padded down the jungle path – the kid barefooted with his snake-bitten ankle, the haversack with his few treasures – cigarette paper and the bit of shrapnel from his thigh wound in its tobacco tin – safely on his back. Noiseless. Breathless. Ears straining at furtive green shadows. Knowing the Black Bastard would be after them when the counting was done. Sensing predatory eyes watching from the undergrowth. Vines like hands reaching out to grab. Bamboo whips, and hidden thorns ripping at skin...

They hastened their footsteps from the airfield in the direction of the prison camp. Then skirting wide, the two turned down a track familiar to the kid from his evenings under the wire, and headed further upcountry.

'Not far,' he encouraged Brownie. 'Only a mile or two. This way.'

But the bush, which had given Billy protection and shelter from his enemies when it was all a game, now that he was a fugitive, seemed full of menace. No birds sang, and sunlight didn't penetrate the gloom. He felt like a hunted animal. Yet surely, as time passed, it was imagining. The kid couldn't hear the voices of pursuit. Indeed, as they neared the river, he began to breathe a little easier. Even to feel a little hope. Just down here a bit... around the bend... and he could sense the rush of water already.

Billy turned towards MP and with a grin lightening his face he said, 'We made it! We're almost there.'

When onto the path stepped Lieutenant Moritake and his crew. The Black Bastard. The sumo wrestler. Several Malay policemen carrying rattan canes. And half a dozen recently arrived young Formosan conscripts, known as 'kitchies' – more derisively dubbed 'titchies' or 'boy scouts', because they were comparatively small. There was nothing juvenile in their behaviour, however.

'Oh, Billy... what have you done?' They were Brownie's only words.

The kid was too shocked to reply. Seeing themselves surrounded, with no hope of flight, Billy fleetingly wondered if he should play again the old innocence: 'Can we help you?' But as quickly realised there was no point. The game was over.

It was about the last lucid thought that he and his mate were to have for many days to come. Everything else was subsumed by desperation, as their captors rained blows upon them. Beating them to the ground. Putting in the boot. Billy trying to protect himself as the guards hammered them into utter subjugation. That done, the two were forced to their feet, hands loosely bound in front and, like Jimmy Darlington, a long rope looped about their necks. In single file, the kid behind MP, they were dragged along the track by kitchies pulling the rope at the front, and Moritake's cohorts shoving from behind. The Malay police, having led the Japs to the campsite on local information, took no further part in proceedings.

Stumbling. Bleeding. Bones bruised and throbbing. If Brownie tripped, the neck rope dragged Billy down with him. Burning. Choking like a noose. Until the Black Bastard forced them up again. They were only half a mile along the track, the jungle now seething with hostility, but it took 30 minutes to make that pitiful journey to the clearing where a truck waited. Moritake ordered them flung into the back.

'Ah...Billy...Billy...' MP murmured as the truck jolted them back to camp. But the kid was too preoccupied with his own wounds to respond. Too apprehensive – for the truck had halted beside the boiler shed, and they were shoved outside.

They were still bound together, the rope looped about their necks, as they watched Moritake direct matters from a low embankment by the road that led between the boiler and the generator to the camp gates. It was here that Billy realised his haversack was gone; taken from him during the beating on the jungle path, probably. And he missed it – not only for the comforts it contained, but also for the small protection it might give from the further bashing he knew was to come.

The kitchies were ordered to the woodpile, each to select a stick. The kid reflected that he'd been with the work party that chopped the rubber trees down only a few days ago. The quartered logs were sharp and splintered, like those with which Jimmy Darlington had been tortured.

'*Ichi* man, *ichi* hit,' Moritake commanded, indicating that each boy scout would have only one go at Billy and one at MP.

They took their time selecting the weapons, for their hands were small – titchy – and this prevented them inflicting too much damage. As they swung and struck their single blow at the captives, the rough timber edge cut into their own fingers, hurting them as much as their captives. Billy's knowledge of boxing even came into it, for as he saw one coming he instinctively tried to 'roll with the punch', which helped to limit the harm, but the neck rope also jerked Brownie with him. Several times they fell to the ground, until Moritake's men kicked them to their feet again.

There were no restrictions placed on the Black Bastard and co. when their turn came. There was no time to duck or parry the whirling swordsticks then. Barely a chance to register injury before the next onslaught. Mad Mick...the sumo wrestler...they flogged their prisoners with a ferocity inspired as much by fear of Moritake as it was by hatred of their victims.

When at last it was over, Billy and MP were dragged up the hill and dumped outside the guardhouse to await the arrival of Captain Hoshijima from Sandakan.

The boy lay foundering, as it were, in a sea of pain; his mind numb to everything except the waves of agony that swept over his body, wallowing and trying to drag him under, though his spirit refused to sink quite yet. Billy tried to move his hands, still tied together, but such torpedo stars burst through his left arm that he knew it was broken. Moving his right ankle, too – the one the snake did not bite – sent shocks up his leg. If not fractured,

269

it was certainly out of action.

He turned his head to one side – that, at least, was still mobile – and saw MP Brown lying unconscious beside him: his legs swollen with bruises, his head a bloodied scab, as if his whole face had been ripped away.

'Jesus! What have they done to ya?'

He concentrated everything – and realised that one of their cudgels had sliced into Brownie's forehead and eyebrows, the raw skin hanging like a veil over his eyes.

'God help us...'

The effort cost him dearly. As the afternoon wore on, Billy lay in the dirt unaware of anything except the sensations of grief, until, in the distance, he heard the sounds of singing – *Who'll come a-waltzing Matilda with me?* – as the men returned to camp from the airfield.

Next thing the kid heard a cry, and feet running. He felt arms about him, lifting him up. And opening his eyes he saw the familiar face of his corporal looking at him, tears starting, as Bob Shipsides unscrewed his water bottle and poured the precious liquid onto Billy the Kid's parched lips.

'The bastards!' Shippy exclaimed. 'The bloody bastards...'

But too soon the boy heard the sounds of other feet, as Japs scrambled from the guardhouse verandah and dragged Lance-Corporal Shipsides away, kicking him as they did so. *Bad man! Bad man!* And Billy did not see him again.

So he stayed, as the day dropped into evening; his mind beginning to recover a little and to think of other, happier things, as a release from present hurt. Nana Tot and the family waiting for him in Hobart. The girl Rosalind, promenading in Fremantle. He wished they could see him now... and then was glad they couldn't.

Darkness fell. Billy even fancied he could hear the bugler playing the Last Post under the Big Tree. And Reveille. The plangent strains spoke to him of something good and enduring; of friendships and values that mattered. And though every bone in his body cried aloud, the kid struggled to his feet and stood at some kind of attention. While the guards looked on in amusement and disbelief.

Captain Hoshijima was late. He'd been entertaining guests at 'Newlands', the comfortable, two-storey house overlooking the sea that he'd commandeered from the former Conservator of Forests and his wife, Agnes Keith. Just before the war she'd written a celebrated book about Borneo, *Land Below the Wind*. Now evicted from her home, she was a prominent member of Sandakan's underground assistance group, whose existence the Kenpeitai suspected but had not yet confirmed. Having spent his afternoon drinking in Newlands' pleasant surrounds, Hoshijima was not at all happy at being called back to the camp to deal with a couple of escapees – though it proved of great interest to his colleagues from the secret police, who gave him orders.

It was dark, and Hoshijima pretty drunk by the time he arrived. Billy was hauled up the steps to his office in a wing of the guardhouse. The kid stood beside the desk, trying to prop himself up with his one good hand.

The commandant sat sipping a drink and glowering – saying nothing, but working himself into a state of high agitation. At last he broke out, 'You bad man! You no honour.' And as suddenly he jumped up from his chair, rounded on the kid and peppered him with angry words. 'You very bad man! Nippon treat well. Make Samurai promise. Work hard. Be okay. You sign oath. Run away. Now you punish! Bad man!' And to show his command not only of the English language but of western ways, Hoshijima shaped up like a boxer and began jabbing Billy in the face.

It was extraordinary! The kid's head was reeling. His hands

were still bound and he was backing away on injured feet towards the door, trying to avoid the man hitting his eyes. Yet his brain still registered the fact that the clown was striking him not with the knuckles of a clenched fist but with the extended second knuckles of his fingers. Jab, jab, jab. And all he could hear was the voice of his father – of Jimmy Darlington, Jimmy Finn and of every other pugilist he'd known saying over and over, 'You're gunna hurt yourself if you keep doing that!' Which was taking a victim's identification with his torturer too far. Undoubtedly. The kid was so preoccupied with the man's welfare that he didn't notice Hoshijima take a wild swing at his head. Or know anything else as he was knocked unconscious out the door – to fall down the steps and sprawl beside MP on the dirt.

Billy didn't see it, but the commandant's action was not unobserved. Opposite his office was a small shed occupied by Warrant Officer Bill Sticpewich and his 'technical party', who had made themselves useful to the Japanese by doing small maintenance jobs about the camp. This not only excused their labour at the airfield, but also gave them very favourable opportunities to scrounge.

Sticpewich had seen Brownie lying with the bloodied skin over his face. Through the lighted window and open door he'd witnessed Hoshijima's assault on the kid – in particular, the repeated striking at his face with the fingers. Seeing by night the two victims motionless on the ground, Sticpewich thought not only that they were corpses, but that their eyes had been gouged out.

Such was the basis of the belief about their fate when Curly Mills and the other Sandakan men saw Billy and MP at Outram Road a year later. 'But you're supposed to be dead, with your eyes torn out!' And seemingly, when the wheels of justice finally turned, it would be among the factors that led Hoshijima to the gallows.

In truth, Billy and Brownie were neither dead nor blind. But certainly they were both out to the world when at length a truck arrived – when they were picked up, tossed into the back and driven off towards Sandakan. The flow of air revived them a little during the drive, the boy stirring and hearing his mate groan beside him.

'MP? Where are they takin' us?'

Into town, presumably, as tyres hit a tarred surface and the kid glimpsed the shadowy forms of buildings. Brownie was far too injured to speak. The night was very dark: no moon, and the stars were shrouded. Even when the truck stopped and they were dragged out and flung into separate cages, Billy had no idea of his destination. He could see nothing beyond the outline of bars; feel nothing through his hurt – and a sense of fearful loneliness threatened to overwhelm him. He thought of home and the cribbage board in Ma's kitchen. Of the bright, expectant faces at Gunboat Simpson's pontoon game. And wished with every aching bone that he was back among them again. That this was last night. And that he could relive the opportunity *not* to go looking for that bloke in the *kampong* come lunchtime.

*What a day was yesterday . . .*

Except that, as he lay listening to these thoughts, the kid gradually became aware that he was not entirely alone in the cage. He heard a faint moan and ripples of shallow breathing ebbed from the shadows.

'Brownie?' Billy muttered. 'I think I've got another customer in here.' His brain reverted to the language of Paddy's Market, though who that customer was the boy didn't know . . . or even care as he slipped back into unconsciousness.

When daylight came and Billy woke uneasily to a world utterly changed for them, he saw that his fellow prisoner was none other than Jimmy Darlington. The cage was a little larger than 'Esau' at the camp – about six feet square and high enough to at least stoop. But Jimmy lay huddled in a corner, filthy with his own shit and blood; his body covered in lacerations; hands and feet so black and deeply cut where the wet cords had bitten into him you could see the whitened bones.

He'd lain there untended for three days since his anguish at the airfield, wounded flesh stinking, though fortunately gangrene hadn't set in. Yet when Billy found the strength to crawl across to him and wipe his face with the pyjama jacket, Jimmy was still able to open his eyes and murmur grittily, 'Welcome to the honeymoon suite of Hotel Kenpeitai.'

The kid smiled back, as grim. The accommodation at these headquarters of the secret military police was not all that salubrious: a concrete floor and a tin roof to catch the sun. But he had to confess it was well enough ventilated through the wooden bars. Exclusive: just three or four cages; and only himself, Darlo and MP in residence. The room service was obliging. Three times a day an old bloke delivered a bowl of rice, which the kid fed to Jimmy. The janitor had great delight in turning a pressure hose on them, to clean the occupants down. And the place had commanding views from the top of an embankment down to a wooden colonial building, like a Queensland house: high on stilts, the understorey screened with lattice, and a flight of stairs going up to a red painted door. A door from behind which could be heard the screams of other Kenpeitai guests from time to time.

For several days Billy and his mates languished in limbo – broken bodies beginning to heal from the worst of the bashing, though not the psychological torment. Strange how, when he thought of his flogging, it was the small details that Billy remembered: the kitchies cutting their hands on splintered logs...Hoshijima damaging his knuckles as he jabbed. It was as if the boy's mind was not yet fully able to grasp the enormity of what had happened to himself – it seemed easier to concentrate on *their* trauma. '*You're gunna hurt yourself if you keep doing that.*' Now, though, listening to the screams from the upstairs room, the kid could only imagine this further fate awaiting them, and wondered how he'd endure that.

Sometimes of an evening he would hear the sounds of laughter, as girls and comfort women made their way past his cage to the Kenpeitai house. It only made his anguish worse. Memory took him immediately to the girl walking across Hyde Park in her Lana Turner sweater...to fair Rosalind and the picnic in Fremantle...And the pleasures of what had been, as against the terrors to come, weighed heavy on him.

Billy was forced to confront them on about the fifth day of their incarceration. The previous afternoon they'd been taken from the cages and hosed down – rather more kindly this time – and a Japanese medical orderly attended to their wounds. He was a slight, almost effeminate man – unlike any Nip the kid had so far come across (and Billy wondered how he managed to survive in such a brutal outfit as the Imperial Japanese Army). His voice was soothing, and his touch gentle. He bathed their gashes with yellow Aquaflavine and red Mercurochrome; repaired MP and Darlo's terrible damage as best he could; applied ointment and bandaged Billy's injured ankle; set and placed his broken arm in a sling. It was the sort of treatment the boy received from his own medics as a matter of course: but here, such tenderness was so unexpected that he accepted it with a gratitude he never forgot.

Nor did he ever understand why the Japs fixed them up. Perhaps the Kenpeitai interrogator liked his subjects to be brought before him all fresh? Maybe it was part of the softening-up process? It wasn't benevolence or solicitude for the prisoners, because the inquisition was as cruel as anything the kid had experienced.

Brownie was taken first, and was absent for about an hour. The kid strained himself listening, though there were no screams. Just a look of bemusement on MP's scarred face when he returned – a mere glance that passed between them as the guard pushed him

275

back into his cage and removed Billy from his.

He was led, hands tied behind his back, half-hobbling and half-dragged up the flight of steps to the red door...and into a room that felt like the set of every gangster film he'd seen. It was a small, darkened room, blinds drawn, close and stifling; the only illumination a pool of yellow light spilling from a shaded globe onto a table, behind which the interrogator sat partly hidden among the shadows. The kid had to kneel in front of him, light glancing from the man's spectacles and catching his hands playing with a nut and bolt on the tabletop. Beside them, a length of knotted rope.

Billy had little time to notice anything else. The guard made him sit back on his heels, and the stabbing from the kid's wounded ankle pierced like bayonets. He almost cried out, and involuntarily tried to kneel upright to ease the agony. But the guard, standing behind, put his hands on the boy's shoulders and forced him onto his heels, where he remained, his mind unable to comprehend anything except torment as the interrogator played with his nut and bolt – screwing it up the thread, and unscrewing it, hypnotically.

He seemed to be enveloped in silence and darkness. The thought rather stupidly passed through Billy's head whether the inquisitor had forgotten him, and very gingerly he lifted himself a little to relieve the pressure on his ankle. He waited for the guard to shove him down again...but nothing happened...and he rose higher. He was feeling thus emboldened when the man's questions began to come at him from the shadows. His name...number...battalion...all asked quietly – even purred – in excellent English, and as easily answered.

'And what did you do with all the guns?'

'What guns?'

A nod from the examiner and the guard jerked Billy back onto his heels, spear points thrusting through his sinews. Silence again. Waiting. Ever so cautiously trying to raise himself from the ankle.

'Who did you give the guns to?'

'I don't know about no guns —'

Another nod. This time not a push on the shoulders, but the guard's rifle butt running down the corrugations of his spine. Not hard – not to break bones – but descending rapidly from one vertebra to the next, like sliding down stairs. It was excruciating.

'Ah...God...!' He fell forward onto the desk, then was quickly pushed back to his heels. Shooting starbursts in the blackness...diminishing by degrees...until the ankle throbbed worse than his spine and the kid sought relief by easing himself up again. Carefully, bit by bit, until he was almost kneeling upright at the table.

'What were their names?'

The inquisitor put down his nut and bolt, and picked up the knotted rope.

'I don't know names...'

The rope began to swing – slowly, like a little windmill, at first.

'Which *kampong* did you take the guns to? Who were your contacts?'

The rope turned faster withal – the kid's eyes following it as he would a serpent, knowing it meant mortal danger.

'Where did the guns come from?'

The rope lashed out at him. Billy's reflex was quick enough to save his eyes, but the knot struck him savagely on the cheek, like one of Jimmy Finn's counter-punches, and he fell back upon his ankle.

'What guns? I don't know no guns...'

The deep, breathing darkness again...The guard's hand clamped behind on his shoulder.

'We begin once more. What did you do with all the guns?'

So it went on for what seemed all day, but was probably not much more than an hour. The rope. The rifle butt. The deceptive voice asking questions the kid knew nothing about. The distress as he was held down on his ankle. Until the inquisitor brought the session to an end and departed, merely saying, 'Tomorrow.' Billy was hauled to his feet, taken down the stairs and returned to his wooden cage.

'What was it all about?' the kid asked MP when the prisoners were alone again, sitting as close as possible against their bars to compare notes. 'What guns was that Jap talking about?'

'I don't know,' Brownie replied. 'He kept asking me about a flaming submarine. Where was the rendezvous, and when? I just don't understand it.' MP Brown, who understood most things. The scar tissue on his face was healing a little, the skin starting to grow back. But his ulcerated legs were still purple from the beating and indeed would remain sensitive to touch for the rest of his life.

'He must have got the wrong end of the stick,' Billy remarked. 'Confused us with somebody else. Or been makin' it up.'

'No, sonny...' MP replied. 'It's *us* that got the wrong end of the stick.'

And they continued to get it for the next week, during which they lived in constant apprehension of the examiner. At any time of day or night they could be hauled up to the darkened room – to the shaded light, the meaningless questions and the ever-present threat of rope and rifle butt. The kid knowing that a blow was coming – but not when. The mind forewarned, he suffered long before it was inflicted.

For consolation Billy thought of his haversack and the small securities it held. His tobacco. The bit of shrapnel that might have killed him he had wanted to show Nana. It was not much, to be sure, though it was an assertion of self when all else had been taken from him. But even the haversack had gone now, and he wondered vaguely if he'd see it again? Who could say, when all the time the hands on the table played with his fear and with the nut and bolt...tightening the thread...and loosening it. Over and over.

Then, their visits to the room behind the red door ceased – though the uncertainties didn't. What was to happen next? Was this just a pause in their interrogation? Were they going to take Jimmy Darlington, who, in his wretched condition, had so far been left alone? Nobody could say. Only as time passed, and the guard no longer called, did it seem the inquisitor had probably done with them.

'D'ya reckon he believes us, MP? That we don't know nothing about submarines and hidden guns?'

'He probably reckons you're too dopey to be involved in anything as complicated as that, kid.'

It was a relief, though it led to a host of new anxieties. What was to be their fate now? Would they be sent back to the camp? Perhaps – the thought hitting with all the force of a knotted rope – perhaps they'd be killed? Slung up, like that Chinaman, from a tree? Their severed heads displayed on stools at street corners? After all, no one had heard of the other Sandakan escapees – of Herb Trackson, Alan Minty and his lot – and they couldn't all have got away...Though as one week dragged into another with Billy's head still on his shoulders, fears of an imminent death began to recede. To be replaced by something more protracted.

'D'ya think they're gunna leave us here forever, Brownie, until we rot away?'

'Anything is possible, Billy boy.'

They lay in the open cages for some six punishing weeks, like exhibits in a human zoo, the days broken only by the arrival of food, and the laughing yardman to hose them down. He took particular pleasure in directing the pressure at their private parts – but in the claustrophobic heat Billy didn't complain. Any water was welcome.

Not until late March were the three of them without warning

taken from the Kenpeitai cages, handcuffed and pushed into the back of a covered truck, which drove off towards the waterfront.

They were bundled out on the wharf, in front of a small steamer gathering for departure. Boxes of cargo were being loaded and a few official passengers with their luggage were going aboard. They stood back, however, as the three prisoners were shepherded up the gangplank by armed guards and onto the rear deck – where their handcuffs were replaced by leg irons that locked them to a heavy chain.

'It's like something out of the flaming convict ships,' MP remarked, sitting by the rail overlooking the wharf.

'Well, that's what we *are*, isn't it?'

The kid was spared further retort by the unexpected sight of the Kenpeitai inquisitor, standing on the wharf in a dark trench coat like some cinema detective with a couple of his hoods, silently staring up at them. In the interrogation chamber he'd appeared a figure of power and menace – here revealed, like a cockroach in the sunlight, as a scaly, scuttling creature fit only to be stamped on.

'That mongrel!' MP ejaculated. 'Well, at least he's down there!'

And leaning forward he called the man every filthy name he could think of. There wasn't an obscenity – not a swear word, dredged from a wide vocabulary – that he did not apply, damning the inquisitor to hell. MP spoke calmly, not raising his voice above what was necessary to be heard over the ship's side. And in excellent Dutch – so that no one else, least of all the examiner, knew what he was saying.

After he'd finished, Brownie smiled and did a little Japanese head bow, which the dog returned, and departed feeling mighty pleased with himself.

'By golly, MP, that sounded good! What did ya say?'

'Later Billy, when the bastards aren't listening.'

Sooner rather than later, however, the kid had reason to pride himself on his own vernacular. They heard another truck drawing up on the wharf; shouted commands; the tread of more feet on the gangplank. And over the ship's rail came the faces of Alan Minty and his fellow escapees: Pop New, Normie Morris, Bill Fairy, Bruce McWilliams – all of them from Billy's own peerless 2/29th Battalion, shuffling under guard to join them at the chain.

'Hey! Youngie!' Norm shouted recognition in an unmistakably Australian voice, and the boy's heart surged with the tide.

'Where have *you* come from?' he asked, as the five settled down on the deck. 'We thought you'd got away.'

'Nah. We've been here in the civil prison these two months past.'

'Do you know where they're shipping us?'

'Kuching. Something like that. It's what they said in the prison.'

'Kuching!' Billy laughed. 'That's where Major Sugar lives. S.U.G.A.' At which even Jimmy Darlington managed to crack a smile.

'Kuching...' The kid grew altogether more serious and turned to MP beside him. 'I said I'd get ya out of Sandakan. I told ya we'd escape.'

Brownie replied with some mumble about frying pans and into fires. But Billy wasn't listening. His head was singing like the seabirds.

# 12
# SENTENCE

*Drifting*
*On dawn's returning tide,*
*On a wave*
*Of awakening thought*
*I ride*

Brownie might have considered the ship a frying pan, but if so, she was an elegant one. A mere few hundred tons, sleekly built for comfort, she was called *Treasure* – and had last been owned by Sir Charles Vyner Brooke, third of the 'White Rajahs' of Sarawak. He'd lost her when the Japanese took over the family domain at Kuching; and since then, they'd used her as a coastal vessel for their Borneo possessions.

And very nice she was too, as they steamed out of Sandakan Harbour and headed to the South China Sea. Sedate (though she could put on the knots if she had to), smooth, clean and well provisioned, *Treasure* was indeed a little gem – far different from that hellhole *Yubi Maru*, in which the prisoners had voyaged to Sandakan.

Her delights were not immediately apparent to the eight men chained on the afterdeck, but it didn't take long to discover them. Once at sea, the guards decided they were on vacation, and spent most of their time fishing from the stern – or would, had they not been constantly interrupted. There was only one lavatory on the deck. Each time a prisoner wanted to use it, the guard had to leave his line, unlock the man's foot, wait for him to finish, then chain him again. And – maddeningly – within minutes of returning to his line, somebody else would be calling *Benki*! And the whole business would be repeated.

It was not long at all before agreement was reached. The prisoners would be chained in port. But once underway, they had their liberty – so long as they remained on deck.

'You try funny business, we throw overboard! *Wakaru?* Understand?'

Billy the Kid, who'd seen the sharks that lived in these waters the night they were anchored off Miri, understood only too well. And Brownie thanked them. In Dutch.

'You've never been sworn at properly, son, till you've had it from a Dutchman,' he said.

So they spent their days lounging on the deck enjoying their own little holiday, renewing old friendships and reliving the stories of the time since they'd last met. Minty's lot telling of the six months in the jungle, until their sampan ran aground. The kid speaking of his own recent history, and those comrades they shared from the 2/29th: Bob Shipsides, Harry, Shearer Gillett...Simply to say their names was to reforge the bond, stronger than any steel chain to which the Japs might fetter them.

There were other diversions too. With his freedom of movement restored and mind recovering, Brownie sought stimulation. He found it in Billy's arm sling. The day before they were taken to the wharf, the three prisoners at the Kenpeitai house had another visit from the Japanese medic. He bathed their wounds with more Mercurochrome and bound them afresh. Indeed, the dark red antiseptic was still damp. Bidding the kid undo his sling, and using a wad of cottonwool dabbed with the stuff, MP marked up the inside of the khaki linen into 64 chessboard squares.

'But I can't play chess, Brownie.'

'I'll teach you.'

The armies of chessmen were recruited from any small objects scrounged from the deck. Matches for the pawns, the opposing side wearing red colour patches. Pebbles and twigs for knights, bishops and castles. Royalty was descended from buttons torn off the kid's pyjama jacket and MP's shirt, a scrap of cotton thread to distinguish the king from the queen.

Thus, in the shade of a bulkhead, the two would lie side by side, the sling open on the deck between them, as MP taught the kid his moves.

'No, dopey, I told you...the knight goes two down and one across. Or one down and two across. Or backwards, if you want.'

'I'll never remember it all. Can't we play draughts?'

'Bugger draughts.'

If any guard came sniffing by, it was a simple matter to disguise the game by flicking the sling over Billy's left arm again. Which, when the board was not in use, also made a splendid hiding place for the pieces. The kid even took to leaning on his elbow with the sling undraped, even when they weren't playing chess, just so the guard would get used to the sight.

The boy never really got the hang of chess. But Freddy New could play a bit, and Bill Fairy was pretty good too. Not as good as Brownie, however, who could rarely find anyone to really stretch his intellect and beat him.

The Japanese bandages had other uses. Bruce McWilliams had his foot heavily bound, and he used the bandage to hide a wad of money that had been given to them in the prison by a contact with Sandakan's secret assistance group. Bruce in fact had deliberately cut his foot – had shown the copious bleeding to the guards – who naturally accepted the bandage and his slight limp (even if they never discovered the stash of Straits dollars under his foot).

Billy didn't know about the money either, until their first port of call at Banggi Island, off Borneo's north-east tip. It was a small tropical paradise of coconut palms and white sand, children swimming and playing in the warm sea, their parents watching *Treasure* berth and commence her lading. Supplies were unloaded, and island produce brought aboard. The guards locked the prisoners by their leg irons to the chain, and left to enjoy the township with stern warnings not to escape.

The eight were sitting by the rail enjoying the scene, when the kid was astonished to see Bruce unwrap his bandage and beckon the Malays on the wharf to come closer. Even more startled when he withdrew a bundle of notes and, holding them up to the people, made signs of wanting food and drink. Next thing they were swarming over the side with coconuts – channels cut in their husks to drink the sweet milk – pineapples, rice cakes and banana fritters that melted in the mouth.

'By crikey, Bruce, where did that money come from?' Billy's eyes were as wide as his gob when the five explained the prison contact.

Not for a long time had any of them felt so replete – or so content after the horrors of the past two months – as they did that afternoon. No guests aboard the White Rajah of Sarawak's private cruising yacht had ever enjoyed themselves more.

Still, the incident raised a good many queries in MP's active mind. The loathsome figure of the interrogator was large in his thoughts, for he'd treated the man more harshly than the kid. Once they were joined on the ship by Alan's Minty's five escapees, Brownie was forever trying to understand why *they'd* been sent to the civil prison and not to the Kenpeitai headquarters, like himself, Billy and Darlington.

'I can't work it out,' he'd say to Alan. 'I can only suppose they reckoned we knew something about a conspiracy – and you didn't. All those questions about guns, and submarines, and civilian contacts...'

With the revelation of Bruce's money hoard and some assistance group in the Sandakan prison, a few pennies began to drop.

'Strike me, but that Kenpeitai bastard got the wrong ones!' He laughed sardonically, for there was nothing funny in what had happened. '*You're* the lot he should have cross-examined with his little methods. You knew about secret contacts. Whereas Billy and me copped it – and we were as ignorant as cabbages. Jesus!'

But even this, it emerged, was not the whole story. More than 12 months later, with the breaking of the network, the seizure of Rod Wells' radio, and the arrival of the new Sandakan prisoners at Outram Road, MP began to realise that he and the kid were, unbeknown to them, much closer to the secret group than they imagined.

'Who told you to go looking for the Chinese man in that *kampong* on the day we escaped?' he asked Billy, pondering.

'Harry Longley. He said that bloke could give us some special Jap rice their soldiers eat – cooked and dried, and keeps for months. The feller asked if I'd swap my old mosquito net for it.'

'How would Harry Longley know about him?'

'I dunno.'

'His family is friends with Doctor Taylor, didn't you tell me? From Yass?'

'That's what Harry said. He saw him when we went into Sandakan once, to pick up cement in a truck for the airfield.'

'And Doctor Taylor is now in Outram Road jail with us, for being one of the intelligence network's civilian ringleaders. Well, well, Billy boy. It's a good thing you can't put two and two together... or else you might have told that Kenpeitai inquisitor more than you bargained for, and put all the Dead End Kids in jeopardy.'

'I never thought of that.'

'Course you didn't.'

But such deeper speculations were for another time. At present, the simple idea that the Kenpeitai had got hold of the wrong prisoners was enough to satisfy Brown's curiosity, as they sat on deck digesting Banggi's coconuts and banana fritters. To be sure, the eight prisoners looked enviously at the fish their guards were reeling in, for they were never offered any share of the catch. Their ration was kept to a bowl of rice with at best a smear of fish paste, which the kid thought most unfair. But even so . . .

'This cruise is like a picture postcard,' he remarked. 'Calm seas. Sun shining. Tropical islands off the port bow. Only one thing more would make it perfect. A Yankee battleship on the horizon, to blow this bloody tub out of the water!'

'Perhaps wait until we're *off* it first, Billy, before you wish that on her.'

As it happened, they were the only ones to come under direct attack. On arrival at Jesselton, the prisoners were loaded into a truck and taken to the town jail, where, still chained together, they spent a sleepless night in a small cell being assailed by squadrons of mosquitoes. The air was thick with them, like flights of Zeros. Diving. Strafing. Piercing every defence, and inflicting vast damage on their human targets.

'Yikes, but this is worse than the bombing of Singapore!' the boy observed, fighting off the enemy with his one good arm – but to no great effect. No sooner had he killed one mozzie than ten other kamikaze were ready to take its place.

'I'll tell you this much,' said Brownie. 'We know where the RAF got the idea for its Mosquito combat planes. Right here in flaming Jesselton!'

Strangely, though, such discomforts served to heighten the very real happiness of the voyage to Kuching. Nobody knew what would happen when they got there; but the journey itself had moments of delight that would stay in Billy's mind as counterpoint to the violence he'd endured at Sandakan.

The following night, for example, when *Treasure* berthed at the town of Victoria on Labuan Island, the prisoners were not taken to jail, but secured by their leg irons to a cable stretched on the wharf, while the guards went off pleasure-wards. It was one of those scented, silken evenings, the sunset lingering in the sky, and a peaceful calm settling over the water, when onto the wharf came a group of young Malayan women to bathe at the *tong*. They seemed unaware of the eight men watching their silhouettes around the well in the dusk: laughing unselfconsciously, as they sluiced cool water from the dipper over themselves; bodies wriggling inside their sarongs; rinsing and throwing back their long, dark hair.

Billy looked on, entranced – as were all of them. He felt the stirrings of sexual appetite, though he knew it could not be appeased. But beyond that was a sense of beauty – of the joy of life captured in this little scene – that transcended momentary desire. It was like the time he and Harry were coming along a jungle track and saw three Dyak women walking down to a stream to fill the jars balanced on their heads. A mother and her two daughters – the youngest about ten, her sister perhaps 14. Sarongs about their waists, but the girls naked above: the only time the boy had seen female breasts. It was only a passing glance – transitory and insubstantial. Yet despite their youthful guffaws – 'Did ya see *that*, Harry? What a pair!' – Billy knew he'd also seen something timeless and enduring. And the artist within recognised wonder – and also sadness.

So it was that evening on the Labuan wharf. Chained and scarred as he was, the young prisoner watched the women bathing at the *tong*. The light faded. The moon rose. And he understood that with brutality and ugliness there was also good in frail humanity. A pleasure in the ordinary decencies of existence. Billy rejoiced in it and was filled with a longing for his own people – though God knew when he'd see them again.

This feeling of melancholy persisted all the next day – became even more intense, indeed, as they crossed Brunei Bay and steamed past Miri again. In the late afternoon, the kid was sitting by himself, the chess game put aside, watching the reflections in the water. The sea was smooth as glass – a mirror in which he could see the deep green of the landward mountains, passing clouds, and the infinite blue sky. Like a painting, broken only by the widening ripples of *Treasure*'s wake.

Gradually, Billy became aware that the colours were changing. Dissolving to rubies and saffron as the sun slipped to the horizon. And looking up he saw that the whole western sky was beginning to burn with scarlet and orange flames burnished with gold, glowing across the water. For a few minutes there was scarcely any distinction between sea and land and the heavens, and the boy found himself overcome with a curious sense of dislocation. It was as if his perceptions had turned inside out and he was no longer sure which was reality – and which the reflection. He felt at once utterly alone, yet equally part of some more sublime immensity beyond himself, such as he'd never glimpsed before. Billy knew the sensation would last no longer than the sunset. But he gloried that he was alive to experience it. And thought that, if he did get home, he might one day teach himself to paint, and try to capture – however imperfectly – the splendour of the moment.

If he got home... The prospect drained as quickly as the colours from the sky, and became just a memory. Night swam upon the water. The glass turned to black and the kid knew what terrors lay beneath its surface. They passed through the darkness... and with the coming of dawn *Treasure* crossed the bar and began her slow ascent up the Sarawak River. She pushed against the current – her bows parting the jungle, or so it seemed to those chained on the afterdeck, as she navigated the serpent coils. Until, sweeping a bend, they saw the town before them – and *Treasure*, her engines slowing astern, eased towards her home berth in Kuching.

Home: but only in name. The White Rajahs no longer ruled from their white mansion, *Astana*, across the river. The Rising Sun of Nippon now flew from Fort Margherita and the tower by the town wharf. And the voices of command were not English, but soldiers of the Imperial Japanese Army waiting to escort the prisoners off the ship, shackled again, and transport them to their destination.

There was much ceremony and bowing as the ship's guard handed over their charges. Much counting of the eight, to make sure of their number. A good deal of shoving and prodding to load them into a covered truck – but still no idea of where they were going or what was to happen once they arrived. Keeping prisoners ignorant of their fate, and allowing imagination to do its worst, seemed part of the punishment.

Only by keeping his ears open to the guards did Brownie gather they were bound for the Kenpeitai prison – enough to strike fear into any heart. It was a narrow, two-storey building that seemed originally to have been built as a warehouse. The interior was divided by two rows of columns, about 14 feet apart, supporting the ceiling and upper floor. The holding pen was created by running a cyclone-wire fence around the columns, the cells in the middle separated from each other by timber walls between the piers, so that prisoners couldn't see who was behind them.

'It looks like a bloody big chook house,' murmured the kid as they were herded up the stairs to the first floor.

'Certainly birds,' replied MP. 'Jailbirds.'

Normie Morris laughed. But the shouts of *'Hanasanai!'* No talking! and the jabbing rifles from the guards were enough to force them into silence.

It was here in Kuching, indeed, that the eight were introduced to the regime, designed to strip them of all humanity, that was later to dominate life at Outram Road. *Bango!* The demand they number off constantly in Japanese. *Ichi, ni, san, shi . . .* The strip search every time they entered their cage, just like battery hens, and stepped onto a wooden platform where they had to sit cross-legged, hands on knees, eyes front, in two rows of four, from dawn to nightfall; then use it as a bed to sleep upon.

Which was itself a misnomer. There was barely any sleep. The timber floors and walls, dusty roof beams and filthy window ledges harboured untold thousands of fleas, mites and bedbugs. The moment men lay down, without any sheeting to cover them, the voracious creatures attacked – biting soft human flesh and feeding on their blood. There wasn't a prisoner whose night hours were not devoted to slapping and squashing these enemies of rest. Billy's pyjama jacket, which had begun life with blue and white stripes, now turned crimson with the blood – his blood – from dead insects. The war they waged was remorseless. Not for weeks after the kid's arrival at Kuching was anything done about it – and only then because the guards started coming under assault. When at last the prison was disinfected, the minute corpses of the slain could be numbered by the shovelful. It took days of spraying, however, before the battle could be considered won, and the prisoners able to enjoy a few hours' sleep.

For a long time, though, they were unable to relax at all from the daylight torment of silently sitting at attention. Whenever an officer was about, the guard was on constant patrol around the wire pen. Once the officer departed, the guards (like soldiers the world over) ambled back to the guardroom for a smoke and a chat. Which at least gave the Chinese and Malay prisoners in the cells behind the wooden partitions a chance to stretch their aching bodies. But the Sandakan eight were in the front chamber – exposed behind the wire fence that looked directly at the opening to the guardroom. No chance for them to stir, for the guards could still eat and drink within, while keeping a watching eye on the jailbirds in the first pen.

It was Alan Minty and Brownie who suggested they mount a war of nerves on the guards – as they'd waged a war of attrition against the bedbugs – and the campaign was ultimately as successful. Wherever the guards moved, eight pairs of eyes would follow them and stare. If they lit up a fag, eight noses made a great show of inhaling the tobacco smoke…and coughing. If they fed, eight mouths would open and drool. When they talked, eight sets of ears turned to listen. So that the guards, even from their position of dominance, at length became self-conscious – embarrassed, even – and within a few weeks had a balsa-wood screen erected in front of the cages. To protect *their* privacy!

It was a masterstroke. All at once the prisoners had a degree of liberty. The eight were free to ease cramped arms and legs when the guard was absent. To whisper among themselves. Even to unwrap Billy's sling at any time of day or night (for the lights were never turned off), open the chessboard and marshal the matchstick soldiers in battle order again on the Mercurochrome squares.

The screen also released them to enjoy the rewards of the scrounge. Several times a week they'd be taken down to a small exercise yard, fenced with barbed wire, behind the building. Watched by the guard, they would spend five or ten minutes walking in a circle – apparently aimlessly, but in fact with eyes peeled for anything worth salvaging. A cigarette butt. A small piece of wire Normie Morris picked up. Here, one glorious afternoon, Billy found his pencil stub discarded by the guard. All were carried back to the cell in their fists. For the Kenpeitai regimen had been adopted in detail: while the guards examined every orifice during a strip search, not once did they ask a prisoner to open his clenched hands. Hitherto, such treasures smuggled back to the pen had to be secret. With the screen, they could be shared more openly.

Trouble was, the guard could creep down from his room and spring from behind the wooden screen at any time to catch men unawares, however keenly they kept ears alert for a footfall. The guards, indeed, thought the masterstroke was their own! But within a few days, even this problem was overcome by Normie Morris and his bit of wire. Noticing a tiny gap in the screen boards, he got the other fellers to create a diversion on the way back from the exercise yard.

Up the stairs and past the screen they went, where Billy suddenly fell to the floor, writhing in pain and crying, 'Me foot!'

'What's the matter with your foot?' The others crowded about.

'It's a splinter I think – a whopper. Look!'

The guard was drawn into the melee, stooping to inspect the kid's grubby foot. Touching it. Billy shrieking, and the guard murmuring 'Ah...so...' with evident interest. While all the time Normie stood with his piece of wire, boring away at the weakness in the light timber boards to make a little hole about the size of a nail head.

It took a couple of goes – but the hole became a valuable part of their security. Every time the guard moved from his room behind, the light shining through the pinhole was broken and the prisoners knew somebody was coming. There would be a quick nudge from the nitkeeper, a loud cough to alert the other inmates...and the guard would leap from behind the screen to find his prisoners sitting upright in their rows: hands on knees, eyes front, the sling over the arm (though sometimes, had he looked closely, the wrong person's arm). All of them the very models of penitence.

It became something of a game between them. Cat and mouse. The guards constantly trying to spring them: the men forever outwitting them. In fact the guards never succeeded – not while the

Sandakan eight were there. They could have done so quite easily, of course, by turning out the light in the guardroom. But they didn't think of that . . . and through such a simple oversight the cause was lost.

This had important consequences for the eight's greatest success in their battle of wits. The prison cookhouse stood by a corner of the building, just outside the exercise yard. One afternoon the men noticed that a bucket of cold rice had been placed close to the barbed wire, where the strands had loosened a little by the Chinese cooks banging on them to clean their woks. It was no great matter for the prisoners to distract the guards' attention by falling over or starting an argument – and for the men walking around to quickly stoop as they passed the bucket and grab a handful of food.

Bruce McWilliams even began leaving small amounts of money in the bucket – retrieved from the foot bandage as recompense for the cooks' trouble. Indeed they always made sure the food was liberally sprinkled with rice husks as protection against disease: not nice to eat, but effective medicine. Once, when the cook was standing by the fence, watching and smiling, Bruce quietly asked if it would be possible to acquire some tobacco? Sure. How much? Almost as much money as Bruce still had in the treasury. Agreed. And on the appointed day the remaining wad of notes was exchanged for a plug of Javanese tobacco, dried palm leaf to roll it in and a box of matches . . . all carried to the chook pen in their fists, where they gave huge enjoyment. Almost as good as watching the guards' consternation at finding the chamber reeking of tobacco – for smoking was forbidden. They never found the culprits (or reported their failure to do so to the officer). But whenever a guard jumped behind the screen, there they'd be sitting like eight skinny devotees, with a look of serene contemplation on their faces.

Of course such moments were brief interludes in the deadening stretch of inactivity, boredom and hunger. But they kept the mind alert and were all that remained to shelter the worst moments of fear, when groups of prisoners were taken from the prison to their trial, so Brownie gathered, never to be seen again. Knowing their own fate – and not knowing it. There were times, too, of prolonged cruelty – as when a number of upcountry Dyaks were incarcerated in the cells. God alone knew what they were accused of; but these men of the wild – proud, nearly naked, used only to the freedom of the jungle and longhouse – were forced to perch confined and speechless in the chook house. And their cries through the night were pitiable.

There came the day, about three months after they reached Kuching, when the eight were led to their own judgment. They were handcuffed together, escorted down the stairs and into another enclosed truck, and driven through the apprehensive streets to the court.

The military tribunal sat in the hall of what had been St Theresa's convent school: a large room with a dais at one end, on which sat the presiding officers. Tables and chairs for the prosecutor and staff. Nothing for the accused, who stood in a line, handcuffed to the fellers on either side of him. Brownie was chained to the kid on his right, then Norm Morris, Alan Minty and so on to Jimmy Darlington at the other end, whose hands were still so disfigured and blistered from the wet-rope torture that he could only bear the touch of one iron. They stood for what seemed hours waiting for something to happen, when five civilians – Chinese, Malay, Indian – whom they'd never seen before, were brought in and clipped to Brownie. Thus there were 13 men chained silently, uncomprehending, in front of the chief judge, Lieutenant-Colonel Egami Sobei of Borneo Headquarters when the trial (such as it was) began.

Proceedings were conducted entirely in Japanese, the cases against each of the accused presented without benefit of translation.

Papers passed between the prosecutor and the judges. Questions were asked of the court officials. Whether anyone spoke on behalf of the 13 prisoners, Billy the Kid didn't know. Certainly no one asked him or the others to make any statement in their defence – not that it would have mattered. The hearings seemed merely a formality, designed to approve decisions already made. It was only at the end, when Colonel Sobei had stamped the relevant documents, that an interpreter rose and – in perfect English – announced the verdicts.

He began with the local men. The first: guilty of espionage. Sentence: death. To be executed immediately. A tremor ran through the line of men linked together. The kid could feel it, like a current passing between them, as the words were spoken. He had a sense of unreality – as if this were happening to somebody else, though it disappeared quickly enough as the interpreter continued. The second man: guilty. To be beheaded on the rising of the court. It was all too real. The voltage intensified. And went on mounting as the third, the fourth and the fifth were all condemned to die. Now. And Brownie's sentence was next.

Billy glanced quickly down the line, surprised at the fortitude with which these five men bore their fate. There were no cries or tears. Rather, their heads were bowed already and there was a look of grim passivity on their faces. Perhaps they'd expected nothing else. Or maybe, like the kid himself, confronted with his own mortality, they were still disbelieving.

*Myles Peace Brown.*

Electricity surged through these human conductors, to find its earth. Billy could feel MP bracing himself. Quickly licking his lips. Staring down his judges through eyes still scarred by their torturers. Daring them.

*Guilt of escaping custody, as prisoner of war.*

Every sinew straining.

*Sentenced to eight year imprisonment in solitary confinement.*

And the sense of relief fairly throbbed. When death is before you, any alternative is to be embraced.

*William Young.*

His stomach knot tightened again, but after Brownie not quite so much as before. Surely they wouldn't kill him now? But then he *was* the ringleader...

*Guilty.*

Waiting. Every instinct for life heightened as the boy heard with absolute clarity: *Eight year. Because of your youth His Majesty the Emperor of Japan in his leniency reduce sentence to four year.*

Oh, that nice, good man! Billy could have embraced Hirohito himself. How sweet the air tasted. How alive the dust motes drifting in the sunbeams slanted through windows. The kid revelled in them, and in the futures that now opened before them. Alan Minty: six years. Norm Morris, Bill Fairy, Bruce McWilliams: five years. Fred New: four years. Jimmy Darlington: for striking a guard, six months! Even in solitary confinement, they would *live!*

The sentencing complete, the judges left the court. And Billy watched as the five doomed civilians were unclipped from the line and led away. Departing the stage of life with a dignity and courage he could only admire, hoping his exit would have been as brave. Though at the moment he could only feel gratitude – like every soldier who sees a comrade fall on the battlefield – that it wasn't him.

The Sandakan eight wondered if they'd be sent back to the prison to serve their sentences. But in Billy's clear recollection they were taken straight from the court, loaded into another truck and driven directly to the waterfront, where they were shepherded into a large wooden horsebox standing in the sun on the wharf, beside a cargo ship. The stable doors waited open to receive them – and once inside they were slammed shut and bolted. The prisoners were left in the sweating darkness, alone with the smell of rancid straw, horseshit, and their fears.

'They're not gunna leave us here for years, are they?' the boy cried, utterly disoriented in these surroundings. 'I couldn't stand it.'

Brownie tried to reassure him by pointing out that it was hardly solitary confinement with eight of them packed so closely together.

'P'raps they'll get eight horseboxes,' somebody suggested. And laughed.

'They wouldn't do that, would they?'

Brownie thought not.

'From the look of things, I reckon we're in for another sea voyage.'

'Wonder if it'll be as good as the *Treasure*?'

'Don't get your hopes up, son. Our *Treasure Island* days are over.'

Further talk was stifled by a guard outside banging with his rifle on the horsebox wall and shouting *Damare!* Shut up! And the kid was isolated again in silence and thought. Wondering about Bob and Harry and the others left behind on that fateful day in Sandakan.

A year later, when Rod Wells was sharing his cell at Outram Road, Billy learned that, shortly before his own trial, many of the Sandakan officers had been sent to the POW camp at Kuching, along with several known 'troublemakers'; among them, Joey Crome and Wally Ford. Strange to think that, even on the day Billy feared might be his last, such dear friends were breathing the selfsame air.

Indeed, that late June afternoon Mo Davis was labouring on this waterfront – the sailor removed from his boiler shed and returned to the sea – and was ordered to avert his eyes as the covered truck arrived from the court. Mo knew something was up, and with stolen glances saw the eight unloaded into the horsebox. He watched it swelter for three hours or more on the wharf, supposing those inside would be close to passing out. Craned his own neck as a derrick at last reached down from the ship, hooked the horsebox, jerked it into the air and lowered it down into a hold.

The eight landed heavily on a metal deck, tossed about like dice in a tumbler: covered in manure and straw, though fortunate to find no bones were broken. They had no idea where they were, for darkness still enveloped them, pierced only by a few splinters of light through the horsebox walls, and a curious buzzing noise. They presumed they were on a ship – a fact that was confirmed when they felt the shudder of engines through the flooring and sensed movement as the vessel wound her way down the serpentine coils of the Sarawak River again to the mouth.

It was only when the ship began to heave, and they knew they were in open sea, that the upper door of the horsebox was opened. Electric light flooded in. Peering out, the kid saw they were on the deck of a troopship, surrounded by tiers of bunks – on which lay a company of Japanese soldiers, returning the looks of these pale-faced enemies with undisguised hostility. The buzzing in fact was their conversation.

'By golly, they've got us caught!' Billy exclaimed. 'Like eight flies in a web.'

'Then sit out of sight,' advised Alan Minty, 'and try not to provoke them.'

As it turned out, the elements distracted their attention sufficiently. These Nips were not good sailors. The waves grew rougher. Seasickness took a grip and in the way of that ailment quickly spread through the whole troop deck. Everyone was throwing up – except for the Australians in the horsebox. Having survived the voyage of the *Yubi Maru*, they could weather any storm.

This brought another advantage. Few Japanese soldiers were able to stomach the thought of food, and were only too happy to pass their rice, meat and vegetables over the stable door to the prisoners inside.

'Can we have some more?' And they gave them the lot.

'I'll tell you what,' said Normie Morris, his mouth running with juices, 'this tub may not be as posh as the *Treasure*. But the tucker is twice as good.'

'Only twice?' Billy the Kid digging into diced pork. 'At least ten times, I'd say!'

So they continued stuffing themselves during the three-day crossing to Singapore – for such, Brownie picked up from the soldiers' talk, was their destination. Eating was at least a diversion, for the chessboard sling had long since worn threadbare and been discarded at Kuching – as Bruce McWilliams' bandage treasury had become bankrupt from buying tobacco. And, though they could not realise it, this unexpected cornucopia of food enabled the eight prisoners of war to put on a little weight and prepare their bodies for the ordeals that lay ahead.

For all too soon the ship had entered Keppel Harbour and was tying up at the docks. Too soon the stable door was shut and bolted again. Too soon the horsebox lifted like a toy and dumped upon the wharf. The eight herded like animals into the back of another truck and driven off God knew where.

'D'ya think they'll take us out to Changi again?' The kid wondered.

'Changi? That's home to us now, son,' Alan Minty reminded him. 'That's where the battalion is. And they aren't taking us home.'

No, indeed. Too soon, and they were being forced outside again. Their mob prodded and shouted at by Japanese cowboys. Corralled into a ragged line in front of a high, grubby white wall, topped with strands of barbed wire and broken glass. And a sign saying OUTRAM ROAD PRISON…

Thus, in the wide circumference of memory, Billy's thoughts returned to where they'd begun on the day he entered this place in the middle of 1943. Past and present were now one; and solitary time edged as slowly – and inexorably – towards the future as the shadow of the window bars on his prison wall.

The relentless monotony in the year and a half since then had been marked by small events that assumed an importance out of all proportion. Learning Morse. Making his pack of cards. *Yagi* the goat becoming a *benki toban*, which got him out of the cell for a few hours to scrounge and gather a little news, to keep body and mind together. As men physically wasted away at Outram Road, so did the boundaries of their mental existence shrink. Deprived of food and intelligence from the outside world, they remained in a grey, shrivelled, disease-ridden limbo of ignorance.

Each new arrival was cross-examined for any scrap of information about what was happening beyond the walls...every morsel sucked dry of sustenance, like the flavour from a titbit of gristle. So the Sandakan eight were able to tell Herb Trackson and those who'd escaped soon after arriving at camp all that had happened up to the time of their own arrest. In like manner, Rod Wells, Curly Mills and the rest were able to speak of events until their network was betrayed and they were seized in July '43...

Of how more than 750 British POWs had arrived at Sandakan from Jesselton in April, and been quartered in a new encampment near the airfield. Of how some 500 more Australians – 'E Force' – had been sent from Changi at the same time to labour on the aerodrome; they'd been held at the internment camp on Berhala Island (from which a few successfully escaped). Of how E Force had eventually moved to Number Three Camp, just across the ridge from the main Sandakan camp. In a miserable act of pissantry, however, Hoshijima forbade any contact between men in the two forces – some of whom, like Mo Davis and his mate

'Nutsy' Roberts, were old comrades.

Mo's position of trust in the boiler shed, in fact, made him a valuable link in the secret assistance network: more than most people realised. But when he knocked down a Malayan, Ali Asar, sent to spy on him, Mo was packed off to Kuching with 17 officers and another four Dead End Kids. Apart from Joey Crome and Wally Ford, Terry Risely and Sid Outram (such a redolent name!) were also in town when Billy's eight were sentenced, though what became of them – or of Bob Shipsides and Harry Longley still at Sandakan – no one could say.

Still, these crumbs of news from such close companions were enough for Billy to digest over many weeks. But of wider news from the outside world – and most especially the progress of the war – these prisoners knew virtually nothing.

They were aware of the first Japanese bombing raid on Darwin in February 1942. They knew of the Battle of Midway in June, for the Japs claimed this encounter with the United States fleet a victory. In retrospect, it was the turning point of the war in the Pacific: from then on, the Japanese were gradually forced onto the defensive. Yet of the Coral Sea battle, which saved Australia from any threat of invasion; the heroic fighting in New Guinea; the American landings at Guadalcanal, the Solomons and the islands of the south-west Pacific, the prisoners had little knowledge beyond what Rod Wells had picked up on his clandestine radio before July 1943. They'd have been astounded to learn that by late 1944 the Americans were about to invade the Philippines – the Japanese occupying force now commanded by none other than General Yamashita himself.

Nevertheless, there were indications – even to the inhabitants of Outram Road – that not all was going the Japanese way. As early as 27 September 1943, the dawn was shattered by the sounds of explosions down the hill in Keppel Harbour. The noise breached the prison walls, waking the inmates and causing the guards to rush aroud shouting. When the smoke cleared it was discovered that limpet mines had sunk seven Japanese merchant ships. As none of the Allies claimed responsibility for the raid (Special Operation 'Jaywick' being kept very secret), the Japanese decided it must have been a local conspiracy. Over coming weeks and months thousands of Chinese, Malay and European men and women were arrested by the Singapore Kenpeitai: tortured, imprisoned and executed, as the secret police sought to uncover the plot. So many burnt rice biscuits were distributed among the Outram Road POWs after each mass killing they became a regular part of the diet.

In truth the raiding commandos had sailed from Western Australia in a small wooden vessel called the *Krait*; entered the harbour in three canvas and rubber canoes; attached the mines to the ships; rested on nearby islands during the delayed explosions; and eventually returned safely to Exmouth Gulf. Their leader, Major Ivan Lyon, tried to repeat the exploit a year later in Operation Rimau ('Tiger' in Malay), this time using Motor Submersible Canoes. But the plan went disastrously wrong. The raiders were discovered and either killed or captured by the Japanese. Ten of them would ultimately end up at Outram Road. And when the Kenpeitai were shown to have been wrong in assuming local involvement, they too decided the truth about Operation Jaywick should remain a secret. It was a question of face. Certainly Billy the Kid and his fellow prisoners knew nothing of it, although memory of the early morning detonations remained evergreen.

Yet even as the Rimau operatives were being caught in October 1944, there were other signs the war was turning against the Japs. American bombers were seen in the skies above Singapore. There were dog fights and the sounds of distant explosions – yes, and not so distant. One glorious night, bombs were dropping near the jail. The lights flickered and went out. The kid lay in darkness for the first time since he'd arrived, he and his cellmate listening to the guards running about in confusion. Listening. And laughing. And shouting, 'Take that, ya bastards! See how you like to be on the wrong end of it!' At the same time realising that if one fell too close, they'd be on the end of it too.

The response was an order for work parties to clear the air-raid trenches, built by the British during the early days of the war in the embankment near the outer wall. It was a cow of a job. The trenches were at least seven feet deep, entered by steps cut into the earth at each end and roofed with coconut palm logs covered with dirt. They were long, dark tunnels, filled with rubbish – a perfect home for scorpions – which men had to enter bare-footed, armed with buckets and straw brooms. The kid had never worked with more alacrity, sweeping furiously ahead of himself in the gloom, hoping to God he'd pushed any raised scorpion tail out of the way.

The work was also burdened with irresistible temptation. The pawpaw trees, planted along the embankment, now were laden with ripe, golden fruit. Strictly forbidden to the prisoners, their succulence dripped like saliva with even greater sweetness, until Billy could bear it no more. Bidding Alan Minty distract the guard with another *Goshu! Boom-boom-boom!*, he plucked a pawpaw from a nearby tree.

He was about to sink his teeth into it when a guard began yelling from the roof of the main cell block and the kid realised that he'd been observed. Billy had barely time to chuck the stolen fruit to a feller – was it Kenny Bird? – going down the steps into the tunnel, before a metal scabbard was bashing his shoulderblades: *bang-bang-bang!*

Kenny caught the pawpaw in his bucket, however, and disappeared into the air-raid shelter. Naturally the guards followed him and within less than a minute – no more – he was hauled out and examined for traces of the forbidden fruit.

The Nips found nothing. Not on his person. Not in his mouth, or in the trench. Not a skerrick of pawpaw skin, honey flesh or telltale black seeds. The guards were incredulous. Such a huge piece of evidence couldn't simply disappear! For the size of the fruit increased with every retelling, until it had the dimensions of a watermelon!

'What did ya do with me pawpaw?' Billy muttered to Kenny beside him.

'I eat it.' A sly grin on his lips.

'What? All of it?'

'Yep.'

'Seeds and all?'

'Yep.'

'You greedy bugger.'

Which was the one thing the Japs wouldn't believe. Not this skeleton! But their lack of belief was more about face. Like 'Jimmy Pike' at Sandakan, the guards couldn't admit to having failed in their search, and the prisoners were let go. It was a wonderful example, Billy liked to say, of how one swallow can indeed make a spring – in everyone's step.

That was not his only pawpaw, for they were a prize sought by every *benki* party on the scrounge: a windfall snatched up and hidden in a bucket, to be enjoyed at leisure. Nor was it his only loss. A pawpaw Billy picked up when out with a prisoner called Bluey Rollason, and hid in a garden shed to mature, was unaccountably missing when the kid went to eat it – and Bluey swore he knew nothing about it!

Bluey Rollason had been at Outram Road six months longer than Billy and was a bloke of singular determination. He'd managed to get himself sent out to Changi hospital by acquiring a severe case of sunburn on his midriff. It turned to a festering scab. Once the victim began to shriek and writhe, clutching his side in agony, the Japanese medic easily diagnosed a ruptured appendix – probably fatal – and sent Bluey to the POW camp, where he could die safely away from Kenpeitai responsibility. Surprisingly, Bluey made a miraculous recovery: though he returned to Outram Road after a month or two among friends, minus an appendix to maintain the deception.

Billy the Kid often wondered if he could emulate Bluey and earn himself a little holiday at Changi – or even attempt Kenny Bird's trick at the scabby bath, of biting his tongue until it bled. But the opportunity never seemed to present itself, and the scabies wash had long ceased.

They had one of the Japanese guards to thank for that: an older man of remarkable dignity and military bearing, whom the kid dubbed 'Pop'. Billy had first seen him standing on the embankment by the pawpaw trees, looking down at them by the scabby bath with a look of compassion in his eyes. It was the same look the boy had seen on the face of the orderly who'd treated his wounds at Sandakan.

In physical terms, Pop was altogether different. Tall of stature, he carried himself erect calmly and deliberately – but always with a sense of controlled strength and self-containment. Like one of those samurai warriors of old, MP thought, the brown ribbons of an NCO – a sergeant possibly – on his sword hilt. Yet however skilled he was in the martial arts and ruthless in war, he still seemed to live by a code of honour and decency, never regarding his enemies as less than human. He embodied everything that the swaggering thugs of the Kenpeitai imagined themselves to be, and never remotely approached.

Certainly the commandant of Outram Road, Major Shozo Kobayashi, seemed to accord Pop a respect and authority he gave to nobody else. When the old warrior, having observed the scene, advised that the scabby bath was a disgusting waste of time – that the scabies first had to be cleansed from the cells – Kobayashi listened. Besides, they were beginning to infest the Kenpeitai's own quarters. So the prisoners were issued with buckets of disinfectant and brushes, and ordered to scrub their habitations – thoroughly – every few days.

It took several weeks to complete. But gradually the itches and scratching began to lessen, and the worst of the body sores started to heal. Until there came the evening when Billy the Kid lay down on his bed boards for another sleepless night...And suddenly it was morning – the first rays of the sun touching his window bars and a visitor bird singing on the ledge. Such repose he'd not known since...when? His last night with the Dead End Kids at Sandakan. So ordinary a thing: just one good sleep. But what rare delight it gave when denied for so long.

Again, soon afterwards, he was with a party led up Pearl's Hill behind the jail to a small gully, where a creek ran through the undergrowth. Pop was standing on the bank with that same look of sympathy in his eyes – as if he, too, shared their plight. And pointing to a particular vine he said, 'Eat...good for you.'

So they sat like some primitive jungle ancestors, and ate the green leaves of the forest: which tasted bitter, though in Pop's presence they didn't dare spit them out. In any event, Billy realised, they were undoubtedly beneficial; for he did feel a little better (even if as hungry) and a decent night's sleep came rather more often.

Pop only stayed at the prison for a short while. He was appointed elsewhere about the time that Jimmy Darlington, his six months' sentence completed, departed for Changi, his hands never fully recovered from the wet-rope torture. Billy didn't see Darlo go. The man was taken away in the silence, and the kid one day simply realised that the boxer was no longer among them at Outram Road. But he did see the old samurai leave: the warrior treading his way, stately as a warhorse, between the admiring guards, in full uniform. Brown tunic and jodhpurs. Polished black riding boots instead of the customary rubber thongs. Three stars on his uniform and the blue ribbons of a ranking officer now entwined about his sword hilt.

The scabies mites had also gone, and in Billy's opinion Pop deserved his promotion for that one conquest alone. But there were no more visits up the gully to eat vines – although men began to find themselves more frequently in work parties tending gardens. As the fortunes of war turned against the Japanese through 1944, and shipping and supplies became increasingly problematic, the Kenpeitai had their prisoners dig vegetable plots along the embankment under the pawpaw trees; then around the guards' houses and vacant land further up the hill behind the jail.

Eventually they were out almost every day: hoeing, weeding, carrying the *benki* buckets from the cells to the gardens and ladling the slopping excrement around the vegetables. Being careful not to let the stuff touch the leaves – and even more careful not to let the guards see you pinch a surreptitious bit of bok choy, for the produce they grew was not intended for the prisoners to eat.

There were no such restrictions on other things to scrounge, especially when the pangs of hunger were so great and you saw a black bean or a half-digested lump of yam among the shit you were pouring around the cabbages. Pick it up. Wipe it quickly on your shorts. And put it into your mouth, hoping to Christ you had enough bacteria in your guts already to kill off any new germs. And vowing that one day the mongrels, who reduced you to this animal level, would surely pay for it.

That day came rather sooner than Billy anticipated.

According to the scratches on the kid's wall calendar, it was his 19th birthday, although the records say it was a day later: 5 November 1944. No matter. It was a splendid Guy Fawkes Day. The best ever.

A group of them were out working on the hill: Billy with MP

Brown higher up; Bluey Rollason and a few others lower down in a garden near the officers' houses. From far off came a deep droning sound, interspersed with popping ack-ack guns and puffs of shell smoke in the sky like wayward clouds. The noise approached ever louder, splitting air and earth asunder – and above the skies of Singapore appeared formations of aircraft, flying on myriad wings of death. Exactly as it was that morning Billy had seen the planes flying over Tampoi, and the war in Malaya had begun.

This time, though, they were not Japanese aircraft, but American ones. Squadrons of B-29 'Superfortress' bombers – at least 50 of them on a long-range mission across the Indian Ocean from Calcutta. A few Japanese Zeros were trying to fend them off. A couple of B-29s were actually shot down, but there were far too many of them to stop the raid. For this was no reconnaissance flight – no practice run – but the real thing. Bombs began falling in and around the docks below Pearl's Hill, where the kid had seen one very big Japanese warship brought in for repairs. Now he stood watching the air raid, trying to count the number of planes – their payloads drifting towards the earth in slow motion it seemed, like dark confetti. He felt as if he could reach out and catch them, so unreal did it all seem.

Until, that is, the bombs found their targets and exploded – the confetti erupting in bursts of flame and shrapnel. The wharves and godowns, dry docks, railway yards and surrounding warehouses were ablaze, billowing plumes of smoke again as they had when Singapore burned in February '42. The sky thundered. The very ground Billy stood upon shook. And from disbelief, the boy found himself feeling quite defensive; angry even, as another flight of B-29s came roaring low over the hill and seemingly straight towards them – *as if we were being attacked by the Americans. Just as our Zeros were up there trying to beat them off!*

It wasn't until the bombers veered away and headed for the port that the kid remembered whose side he was on! Besides, he was so exposed on the hillside, with little shelter to find if the bombs *did* reach him. So Billy gave himself to the enjoyment of the spectacle and the dazzling celebration of his birthday. No Guy Fawkes had been lit with brighter bonfires, or resounded with louder bungers!

Even more wonderful was the behaviour of the Kenpeitai guards: they panicked. One moment, there was the lordly Little Hitler – he who had bashed Billy so viciously the day he arrived at Outram Road – parading up and down the vegetable gardens like some overseer from the gods, poking and goading these worthless creatures with his scabbard. Next, as the bombs fell, he and his lot turned tail and fled. All the way down Pearl's Hill beside the prison wall to the main gate. Where they beat on the postern door, were admitted, and locked it behind them.

Pop, the true samurai, would have been ashamed; disgraced by their cowardice. Especially when the prisoners had been left unprotected outside. Or almost so. Those further down the hill found a little cover by the stairs leading up to an officer's house. They were sheltering there when some big Japanese trustie came rushing down, pushed them aside and huddled behind them, sobbing.

Thus, Billy and his mates remained on the hill watching the fireworks – much as he and Dave Holden had observed them that day on the march to Bukit Timah during the first battle for Singapore. The kid squatted down in one of the vegetable patches, munching on a birthday feast of young carrots pulled fresh from the garden, until the show was over.

After which some debated briefly whether they should make a run for it. Agreed the chances of being shot were far too high. And strolled back to the gate and knocked on the postern, wondering who were the jailers and who the condemned, to serve the rest of their sentences.

# 13

# DEATH

*To be alone in Paradise*
*Is to be alone in Hell.*

In the aftermath of the great air raid, the behaviour of most Outram Road guards began to change. Not towards the prisoners, for whom their contempt remained unabated. Even as Billy and his birthday boys re-entered the jail when the bombers had passed, Little Hitler was abusing them. *'Koi! Bakayarou!'* Come, you idiots! As if being locked outside was *their* fault. No difference there. But in Kenpeitai attitudes toward each other, the kid noticed all kinds of shifts. A slightly less confident swagger in the step (though more bashings to compensate for it). Fewer boasts of their own invincibility. Certainly no more bombast about committing harakiri in the honourable samurai way, rather than allow themselves to be taken prisoners of war. As the time approached when they might have to make good that promise, such talk was quietly dropped.

'They don't seem to have the guts for it!' Billy sniggered.

Even the higher military echelons seemed to be turning on each other.

Returning from the gardens, men noticed that a new and important prisoner was being held among the Japanese inmates on

311

the first level. Until then, the phantoms upstairs were all in cells on the same side of the building as the POWs. Now, a guard in dress uniform was posted outside a single cell on the other side of the catwalk. If Billy twisted his head and looked up through the grille of his door, he could see the sentry's polished boots on the iron walkway: for the guard had a chair and was allowed to sit, except when the prisoner was visited by the commandant Kobayashi and others. Then, the sentry stood at ceremonial attention.

Naturally there was much discussion among the POWs as to whom such a distinguished jailbird might be. A person of high military rank, obviously. Billy had once seen him – a man of middle age, his uniform covered in braid and ribbons – being escorted to a formal hearing. But who, or what his crime, nobody could say.

This had gone on for several weeks, when there came a day the prisoners were kept locked in their cells for a full 24 hours. No work carrying shit buckets to the gardens. Instead, the kid and his cellmate – a jolly, recently arrived Chinese resistance fighter called Charlie – heard digging in the embankment outside their window. There followed a fitful night's sleep; and they were woken in the early dawn by marching feet, shouted orders and a scraping of seats. Next thing, a volley of shots rang out.

'Somebody had goose cooked,' Charlie laughed.

As they went out with the work party again later that morning, they saw that the guard had disappeared from the catwalk upstairs. A small section of brickwork had been removed and the earth dug away from the embankment to form a kind of recess. In front of it were several long benches and two ornate wooden chairs for the spectators at the early-morning execution.

'It's a regular shooting gallery,' Brownie remarked.

'Yeah. Like sideshow alley at the Royal Easter Show.'

They never did find out whose row of ducks had been shot down at crack of dawn in this Outram Road funfair. Still, who could doubt the result of the war when the enemy had taken to killing their own!

As 1944 turned into 1945, there were more portents of an approaching showdown. The B-29 air raids continued, and from labouring in and around their jail, the POWs were also sent to work elsewhere in Singapore. Every few days men would be loaded into trucks and driven to various parts of the island – clearing old trench lines, erecting barbed-wire entanglements. The Japanese seemed determined to defend the place even more heavily than the British, and were making use of all available labour to do so – as they'd used every bit of captured British equipment.

One of the first jobs was to clear an ammunition dump. It was part of that vast stockpile of supplies and matériel (and men) that had fallen into Japanese hands. Most of the shells had long since been fired back at the Allies. What ammo remained was fragile and dangerous to handle...lying all over the place, amid lengths of cordite, packing cases, rusty metal and quantities of rubbish.

The task was to clean it up. To one side, artillerymen and experienced blokes from the Army Service Corps were going through what was left of the ammunition: salvaging shells that still looked okay, recovering for future use the cordite and detonators from those that were obviously past it. It was another symptom of shortage – even desperation – among the enemy, but still a delicate undertaking for men greatly weakened. The kid was happy to leave that part of it to those who knew what they were doing. Even so, accidents still happened.

Every lunchtime the guard allowed them to light a fire and boil a brew. If the wood were damp and the fire slow to catch, the simplest thing was to chuck a bundle of cordite on it and *whoosh!* – the propellant would have a cracking good blaze going in no time. You had to watch yourself, though. Stand well back. Make sure the ground about you was clear, as one poor English bloke did not. He tossed a bit of cordite on the fire, but didn't notice there was more of it all around his feet. The blaze caught all right! Before he knew it, a flame was running up his legs, burning his thighs and crotch. And the poor feller took off like a rocket!

It seemed rather funny to the onlookers at first: but not when they discovered the extent of his injuries and saw him carried off to the untender mercies of the prison medics. If he was lucky, he might be seen by Jim Taylor, the Australian doctor from Sandakan, friend of Harry Longley's family, incarcerated in the civilian section of the jail. If luckier still, he might even be sent out to the hospital at Changi . . . the very thought of which revived an idea in Billy the Kid's mind.

As the shells were removed from the ammunition dump, prisoners were issued with *changkols*, ordered to rake the remaining debris into heaps, and to level the ground. It was dreary labour in the monsoonal heat, and during a breather the kid told MP it was time for a change.

'I'm getting out of here,' he muttered. 'I've had enough.'

'And how are you going to do that?' Brownie inquired. 'Escape again?'

'I'm gunna pull Kenny Bird's stunt, and bite me tongue. Get sent to Changi.'

'You'd better be good at it, Billy. Really put on a screaming act.'

'Course.'

'Be a lot more convincing than you usually are.'

'Can you doubt me, MP?'

'Every time.'

'Watch.'

So Brownie watched the kid climb up a pile of rubbish and stand at the top, as a guard came over to see what he was doing.

'*Kotchi koi!*' Come here! Get down.

As the man approached, Billy took a deep breath and, with

a little prayer, bit as deeply as he could on his tongue. The pain burst in his head, and it was not all play-acting as he began shrieking 'Owwww! Ahhh!' and tumbled off the rubbish heap, to fall writhing at the guard's feet. Not all pretend as he jerked and clutched in spasms, blood foaming from his mouth. His face was indeed in agony – though Billy still had one eye open to see what effect his performance was having on the guard. None at all. Disinterest, even. The fellow just stared down at him. With a memory of Cissie's epileptic convulsions in the washhouse at Ultimo, the kid redoubled his efforts: eyes rolling, legs thrashing, mouth spurting blood like a fountain. All to no purpose.

Other men gathered around, calling for assistance as if the kid were in his death throes. But the guard couldn't have cared less. He was either very stupid – or very smart. Either way, he merely had Billy carried to a hut where he lay for the rest of the day, feeling that his tongue had been torn from his face. He howled and banged the wall for a bit, trying to attract the guard's attention and evoke his sympathy. But nobody came, and he was left to suffer alone.

'I think you've got to improve your routine,' MP observed as they were driven back in the truck.

'It's not over yet,' Billy replied. 'Wait till we get to Outram Road. The doctor will send me to Changi for sure.'

But the Japanese medic did no such thing. Billy was carried to his cell, thrown in and left there – for a whole week in solitary, as he was not at the time sharing with anybody else. It was a week during which he even sent back one or two meals half eaten, to show how close to dying he was – without any effect on the Kenpeitai whatsoever. The kid remained alone while his tongue slowly healed, and his mind dwelt on the folly of self-inflicted injuries. By and large his luck had held throughout the war; but in the matter of sickness, he knew, luck passed him by at Outram Road.

Even when he was really ill, Billy found himself ignored.

With food supplies getting lower, the Japanese extended their vegetable gardens by getting prisoners to dig up part of the paving in the jail's rear courtyard. There were a few small sheds nearby where the *changkols* and seeds were stored, and the kid was determined to scrounge inside one of them. At the first opportunity (*Hai! Bob Menzies! Boom-boom-boom!*) he quietly slipped through the door.

There wasn't much to see. Just a few tools and packets and, by the wall, a sack filled with almonds. Billy grabbed handfuls of the dark kernels and shovelled them into his mouth, as if they were the last nuts he'd ever eat. They almost were.

'Did you bring us some?' asked Brownie, back at the garden.

'Nah. I forgot. Ate 'em all.'

'You pig.'

Yes, and the kid was soon as sick as one. Waves of nausea swept through him – from the pit of his stomach, welling up through his body and spewing out his mouth. While at the other end, his bowels opened and he was streaming diarrhoea.

'Oh Jesus...Brownie...help us!' Billy cried as he doubled over on the ground.

'Just what have you been eating?' The older man knelt beside him.

'Almonds. I told ya.'

MP opened the kid's hand and found one or two small, black culprits.

'They're not almonds, you goat. They're castor-oil seeds. It's no wonder you got the shits!'

Once again the boy was carried to his cell and left there, to live or die as the fates decided. On the whole he thought death would be preferable. Billy's only recourse was to lay two bed boards across the *benki* bucket and to sprawl face downwards upon them to vomit his heart out, or squat upright to drain his poor arse.

After several days, the reeking mess was all but intolerable. It reminded him of those first putrid weeks at Outram Road, before his senses adjusted to the pervading stench. And Billy promised, if he did recover, that he'd never eat almonds again.

Of course he also knew that, in the wider sweep of global conflict, his privations were of small consequence. Starvation and sickness and constant beatings certainly mattered to those who endured them. But the entire population of Outram Road prison could perish without making one jot of difference to the outcome of the war. As the kid listened to aircraft overhead – to the ack-ack guns and far-off explosions – he was aware that the battle would only be won by those free people still fighting on land, sea and air. Only through their victory, and their suffering, would his own torment end.

Such thoughts arose from seeing the increasing numbers of Allied servicemen being brought into the prison. There were several officers and militia from the Royal Dutch East Indies Army; British escapees; Indian soldiers; Chinese and Malay resistance fighters; and a number of American airmen captured after the raids over Singapore. The Japanese regarded the pilots and their crews as 'war criminals' rather than POWs, and held them in the Outram Road cell block pending execution.

Into this atmosphere, that February of 1945, came the survivors of the failed Rimau special service operation, who entered the jail for further examination by the prosecutors.

A party of 23 men – six British and 17 Australians – led by the recently promoted Lieutenant-Colonel Ivan Lyon, had left Fremantle on the submarine *Porpoise* in September, to repeat the successful Jaywick raid on Singapore Harbour a year earlier. They captured the junk *Mustika* off Borneo, the nine Malay crew taken aboard *Porpoise*. Lyon's team with their one-man Motor Submersible Canoes known as 'Sleeping Beauties', and collapsible rubber Folboats, transferred to the *Mustika*. After establishing a base and arranging for a submarine pick-up in November at Merapas Island, the Rimau team prepared to attack.

Tragically for them, on 6 October the *Mustika* was waiting off an island south of Singapore when a police launch approached. The Rimau men opened fire, killing all but one of the Malay policemen – who escaped to raise the alarm. Lyon called off the operation. *Mustika* was scuttled with her secret MSCs, and the men withdrew in four Folboats with orders to make for Merapas. For almost a month the Japanese pursued them through the chain of islands, during which four men, including Lyon, were killed. Those who made it to Merapas were discovered only a few days before the submarine rendezvous, and another died in the ensuing conflict. As the survivors fought their way from one island to the next during the following weeks, eight more were either killed or later died of their wounds. Ultimately, only ten Rimau men were left alive in captivity – Major Reginald Ingleton of the Royal Marines and nine Australians. And it was they who ended up at Outram Road in February.

Some Japanese, greatly admiring their courage and audacity, wanted the Rimau servicemen treated as prisoners of war in the normal way. But others, while acknowledging the men's bravery, regarded them as spies and demanded they be executed. Their hand was considerably strengthened when Captain Robert Page of the AIF acknowledged to the interpreter Hiroyuki Furuta that he'd been a member of the earlier Jaywick attack. Furuta had become close to the prisoners and casually mentioned in conversation that there were 20 local men at Outram Road awaiting execution for the raid. Hitherto, the Rimau men had said nothing about Jaywick. But as a Christian, Page told Furuta his conscience could not allow innocent men to die over something for which he had a responsibility.

Thus the truth about Jaywick was made known to the Japanese, and the fate of the Rimau men decided. Apart from anything else, it was necessary to protect the Kenpeitai for having been wrong about that episode; and the prosecutor set about preparing his case accordingly.

None of this, of course, was known to the POWs incarcerated at Outram Road. The Rimau men were paired in cells at the far end of the main block, isolated from everyone else. The Japanese didn't want news of their exploits – or any information about Allied progress in the war – to reach other inmates and further boost morale. Prisoners out to work might glimpse the operatives from time to time, being led from their cells for questioning; but beyond that there was virtually no contact.

Yet still news filtered through.

About a month after the Rimau group arrived, nine airmen from the Royal Navy Fleet Air Arm were brought into the jail. They'd been shot down in raids over oil refineries at Palembang, Sumatra, in January, during which a Japanese tanker had been sunk and many aircraft destroyed on the ground. More 'war criminals'. Obviously.

The nine at first were not held at the far end of the block, but placed in cells nearer the other prisoners. Indeed, on a morning when Billy the Kid was collecting toilet buckets with the *benki* party, an Indian trustie told him that one of the pilots – a New Zealander – was in a cell only a couple of doors from his own.

Here was an opportunity! The guard on duty that day was new to the prison. As the others distracted his attention, Billy nipped back to his cell and retrieved from their hiding place his treasured pencil and the last unused half page of notebook paper. Returning to the work party, he hurried into the New Zealand pilot's cell and found him lying on the bed boards, his neck and arm badly burned and wrapped in dirty bandages.

'I'm Billy,' the kid whispered hastily. 'What's ya name?'

'Habbie...' the pilot answered, clearly in pain. 'That's what my friends call me.'

He was a fine-looking man, with the tanned complexion and dark hair of a Maori.

'Can't stop. Gotta empty your bucket. But listen,' Billy said as he thrust his pencil and bit of paper into Habbie's blistered hand, 'write down any war news ya know...and whatever ya do, don't lose me pencil.'

'But...'

'I'll collect it on the way back.' Upon which he departed with the pail.

God knew what the injured pilot made of this apparition in flimsy shorts, haunting him for information from the outside world. But he complied, and by the time the *benki* party returned he had written his news on both sides of the scrap of paper.

To create another diversion and give Billy time to collect the mail, the *benki* boys pulled the trick of tipping the tray. Empty buckets and lids went rolling all over Broadway. The new guard fussed and shouted as men cried, 'Butter-fingers!' and ran about picking them up, allowing the kid to slip into Habbie's cell with a washed *benki* (still with some water at the bottom) and get his paper and pencil.

'Here you are,' the pilot said, passing the note. 'It's not much, I'm afraid.'

'It's more than we've had,' the kid replied. 'Thanks very much.'

He pressed Habbie's hand as best he dare, given the man's injuries, and waved briefly as he left the cell. 'Good luck to you.'

Safely back in his cell, the note and pencil smuggled past the strip search as usual in his palm, he unfolded the scrap of paper and began to read the news.

The kid was sharing with Alan Minty at the time, and together they deciphered Habbie's scribbled note. His name was Lieutenant John Kerle Tipaho Haberfield, only 24 years of age, who'd been piloting Hellcat fighter planes from HMS *Indomitable* with the Pacific Fleet since December 1943. So much was interesting; but the talking walls ran hot with gossip as the rest of Habbie's war news was relayed down the line...

The Allied armies had landed in Normandy on D Day in June 1944. Paris had been liberated in August, and we'd entered Nazi Germany. Soviet troops were moving from the east. Rommel was beaten in Africa. The battleship *Tirpitz* sunk at her moorings in Norway. And General MacArthur had landed in the Philippines.

It was just the bare bones of it. But for days afterwards, the skeletons of Outram Road walked taller and straighter, for Habbie had indeed given nourishment to the soul. There was less pleasure later on, when the same walls tapped through intelligence that Haberfield with the nine Fleet Air Arm men had been moved to the far end of the cellblock, accused of indiscriminate bombing.

'But the Hellcat's a fighter plane!' the kid exclaimed. 'It don't carry bombs.'

'Makes no difference, son.'

Though it made you wonder just how 'discriminating' the Japanese had been in *their* bombing raids over Singapore in 1942. The flames were still vivid in the memories of everyone who'd been there at the fall and surrendered into captivity.

'Oh, that *was* different, son. Nippon was winning, then. Now, it's revenge.'

No food for the spirit there – and there was little enough for the body, heaven knew. The meals at Outram Road had allowed men to barely exist in the static world of confinement. As the war closed in and the prisoners increasingly were sent outside on working parties, the demands on their physical energies became much greater – and they succumbed more quickly to malnutrition and disease, for it wasn't such relatively light work as clearing an ammunition dump. In these latter days they, the POWs at Changi and a vast conscripted civilian labour force, were sent all over Singapore and Johore to dig trench lines, artillery emplacements, bunkers and tunnels. This was heavy labour with a vengeance: for the Japanese fully expected the Allies to repeat a pincer campaign down the Malayan peninsula and land on the island itself.

Hunger racked every body. Food was paramount in every thought. The rations served at the lunch breaks – a dollop of rice, a sliver of vegetable or meat, and pallid 'tea' – were utterly inadequate to maintain the toil required. Not an opportunity was lost to eat whatever could be found . . . or even taken from the stores of memory.

One morning on the way to the tunnels, the open truck transporting the prisoners broke down in the middle of a wooden bridge over the Singapore River. The kid sat squashed in the back with the others. Stationary. Going nowhere. Heat and humidity rose, sweat trickling down faces and bodies as water drains across the ribs of a washboard. It was then that Billy became aware of a most delicious aroma of hot food. It wafted up from below, like the gossamer drifts of a gourmet dream. Meat frying. Vegetables steaming. Spicy. Seductive. Unimaginably good.

Following the scent, he looked out over the bridge. Along the riverbank was an armada of Chinese sampans and junks, where families sat cooking their breakfasts over small fires: rice and noodles and soups and barbecued chicken and sauce! The fragrance and temptation carried on the smoke seemed overwhelming, when into Billy's head entered the thought, 'But I've been here before!'

And at once came the memory of the night he'd had the rickshaw race with Bert Cruickshank, in those careless days before war came to Singapore. They'd been half a mile down this very road, the drivers perched in the back, until they reached this same bridge.

The same fleet of little boats down there. The same fires glowing and the same smells.

But how different the response! Then, Billy and his mate had been disgusted! They'd nearly puked over the bridge and ordered the rickshaw drivers to run them, *chop-chop*, back to town. What fools they had been in their ignorance, when what they should have done was join the riverboat families at the feast. Never had Billy smelt anything so delectable. Even now, he could barely restrain himself from leaping over the bridge, daring the guards to shoot him!

Wiser thoughts prevailed, of course. But even so, as the truck at last got going and carried them away, his stomach kept dragging him back. And his mind continued to reflect on the transformative powers of hunger and poverty. They could turn any smell, however nauseating it seemed, into the perfume of Elysium. If only he could find a way to bottle it. And sell it. At Paddy's Market. He'd make his fortune!

Well, they'd brought Billy the Kid broke and famished into the army – and into this. Faced with starvation, humanity's differences were forgotten. We were all one. All the same. All looking for that one filthy grain of rice on the floor.

He'd once shared his cell with an Indian – a Muslim, new to the prison, who was very strict about not eating any meat, in case it turned out to be unclean pork. The first time a tiny shred appeared in his food bowl, he gave it to Billy, who repaid the compliment by trying to guess in which direction Mecca lay for the man's daily prayers. The second time a scrap of meat turned up, the Muslim first sucked the juices out of it, before handing over the bit of gristle for the kid to finish. The third time, there were no inhibitions. He ate it all.

The kid was well aware, indeed, that the equality of hunger brought no lasting sense of brotherhood. On the contrary, it reduced everyone to the same base level of instinct. Self. Survival. Suspicion.

Greed. The beginning of every conflict. Sharing a cell – even with someone you liked – there was always a sense of distrust when the *meshi toban* came round at mealtime. Has the other bloke got more than me? Has he a bigger bit of yam? Doubt. Grievance. It was why you took it in turns to get the bowls through the food slot, and pass them over. Why you never told the trustie who was first. It was a way of trying to even things up, to be fair – though you were never free from misgivings. Is his spoonful of rice better than mine? And the best meals were always eaten in the imagination.

For about six weeks or so from early May, Billy's cellmate was an officer in the Royal Dutch East Indies Army. Captain Pieter van Hemert was the most sophisticated person the lad had ever known. He was 40, cultured, unmarried but from a well-to-do Javanese family with interests in the sugar industry, and he had travelled widely through Asia and Europe.

For all his age and urbanity, Pieter and the kid got along very well together. Some Anglo officers might have privately sneered, saying that Pieter was only from the East Indies – 'a wog' – and not a proper officer at all. But not Billy, who even promoted him to 'Pieter the Major'. He had, after all, graduated from the Royal Military Academy in Holland. And he was a leader of distinction. Sent to Burma to work on the railway, he escaped with three other militiamen in October 1942. For almost two years he ensured their survival in the jungle fighting with a brigand-guerrilla band, attacking Japanese outposts, until their betrayal, capture and torture: after which Captain Van Hemert was sentenced to life at Outram Road.

Together in the cell, they would sit for hours, Billy listening as Pieter spoke of these adventures – or spun his traveller's tales from around the world, and told of his rich life at home.

'Ah, Billy,' Pieter would say, 'when this war is over you must come to Surabaya and visit with me and my family. You'll stay with us and we'll dine at the best restaurants on the finest cuisine that East and West can offer...'

Every conversation came back to that. In the beginning was the word, and the word was food. As it was in every ending. They talked about the great meals they'd eaten, and the correct way to cook them. Pieter waxed lyrical on the exotic delights of Peking Duck and the subtleties of hundred-year eggs, preserved in clay and ash until the yolks turned green and creamy, and the whites to a clear, brown jelly. They were something that Billy might once have found squeamish, but not now – not with a stomach inured at Outram Road. Here, among starving men, food was spoken of with the same rapture as sex in a former life, where that other great impulse of existence had not all but ceased to be.

Billy's own experience of haute cuisine was much more limited (as it was of sex), and his contributions to these repasts were confined to the unexaggerated pleasures of a mixed grill from a township café – when he could afford it – on the road with his bike...

'You take five pound of rump steak, three pound of lamb chops, a dozen eggs, ten rashers of bacon, two pound of ripe tomatoes, four pound of mushrooms... and you fry 'em all up together.'

Thus did Billy the Kid and Pieter the Major create these triumphs of gastronomy, until they could see the table spread before them in the cell and smell the food like incense carried through the window bars, as surely as the boy had whiffed it from the cooking fires on the boats beneath the hump-backed bridge. There they would feast until they supposed their bellies full, and imagined they couldn't eat another thing. And burp. And groan. And open their eyes into the dirty light.

Of all the dishes that Pieter served at these banquets, none settled so lastingly in the kid's mind and stomach than the recipe for *Snert* – traditional Dutch pea soup. It may have been the name – for you couldn't deny it sounded like 'snot' – but mostly it was the fondness – the love – with which the man spoke of his home and family, and the passionate bond of meals enjoyed together. It took Billy back to Ma's kitchen at Bulwara Road. Into the soup would go peas, onions, carrots, potatoes, celery... These were the vegetables Pop would bring home from market, though *Snert*'s other ingredients might be a bit more tricky to find in Depression time...

'You must always use good pork, Billy. Gammon or a nice hock. A couple of pig's trotters will do. Streaky bacon. Smoked sausage. When it's all cooked and left to cool overnight, the soup will be so thick you can stand your spoon upright in it.'

'Truly? Even Ma didn't make soup that good.'

'Oh yes. And you serve it with toast or pumpernickel bread. And when you've finished eating it, *snert* sticks to your ribs like cement – and sits in your stomach so heavy, you cannot move for hours.'

The kid sat digesting his *snert* beside Pieter for hours on the prison floor.

There was another reason why Pieter, in particular, had trouble moving for hours at a time. However plentifully he fed the imagination, he was – like all of them – afflicted with the illnesses that accompany prolonged squalor and deprivation: dysentery, pellagra, the debilitating symptoms of beriberi – that wasting, enervating disease caused, Pieter said, by a lack of the vitamin thiamine.

'It's especially common here in Asia, among people who eat only polished white rice, where the husks – a good source of thiamine – have been removed. And white rice is all we are given to eat – little enough as it may be.'

'The Chinese cook at Kuching knew about rice husks. He put 'em on our food.'

'He would, Billy.'

'No rice husks here.'

'Indeed no.'

When Pen Dean had been a trustie at Outram Road, he was sometimes able to get access to Japanese medical supplies – especially the tablets used to treat beriberi – and slip them secretly to men with the food bowls, to help keep the worst effects of the disease at bay. But Dean had been released well over a year ago, and sickness was rife. A few fortunate ones were sent out to the hospital at Changi. Rod Wells, for instance, was transferred in March 1945, and his life almost certainly saved. John McGregor was another, who trained himself not to flinch when a needle was stuck in his eye, and thus convinced the Jap medics he was going blind. But as the months dragged on, other prisoners were left to languish. And to die.

There wasn't one of them untouched by sickness. Billy the Kid – younger than the rest and a little stronger than most – contracted beriberi. Fluid was swelling his ankles and knees, his wrists already so thin he could easily slip his thumb and middle finger around them. Some found their empty stomachs dreadfully bloated, as the men with hugely swollen testicles had sought nightly refuge under the Big Tree at Sandakan. But none of the symptoms of disease, or the awful physical weakness that came with beriberi, prevented the guards from forcing their prisoners out to work.

Even Pieter van Hemert, for whom the disease was affecting more vital organs – his heart and lungs – was sent in the trucks with the labour force. Outwardly, Pieter appeared no more sick than anyone else. No excuse, then, for remaining idle – though after a day shifting dirt in the tunnels, he'd return so exhausted and faint he barely had the strength to sit upright on the cell floor.

Then the kid would try to jolly him along with small bits of gossip, and discussing what they might have for dinner as they awaited the arrival of the *meshi toban*.

'Peking Duck again, d'ya reckon, Pieter? How about a big bowl of thick *snert*?'

'But your favourite is the mixed grill, I think,' said the man beside him. 'How many lamb chops was it? And rashers of bacon?'

'Oh, at least three pound.'

'Mine will be *nasi goreng* tonight, the special fried rice they make in Java, with prawns and egg and chicken satay and vegetables...'

His voice trailed away into remembrance and those hidden valleys where, unknown to both of them, his body fought the last skirmishes of resistance to disease.

They both fell silent, the kid conjuring up a barbecued rump steak the size of a butcher's tray: until at length, when they were permitted to lie down, he'd fall asleep on the bed boards replete and satisfied – and only dreaming that he was hungry.

This had gone on for some days when, in the early hours of a June morning, Billy was wakened by Pieter's laboured, gurgled breathing. There was a liquid sound to it, like gas rising to the surface of some rank pond. At first he thought the man was asleep and snoring heavily. He rolled over under his cotton rag and reached across.

'Hey, Pieter, are ya having a bad dream?' he asked, shaking him gently. But listening to these bubbling pools of distress, he realised soon enough that Pieter was in trouble. It sounded as if he were drowning.

'What is it, old mate? What's the matter?'

Pieter said nothing, his ribcage straining with each breath that welled up; looking at the boy with eyes that already saw through him to the river beyond.

'Here, let me get some help.'

Billy rose and went to the cell door, banging and calling out his prison number 510. *'Go-hyaku-ju! Go-hyaku-ju!'*

'*Nanda?*' What is it? the guard at last mouthed through the food slot.

'My friend. He's sick. *Isha* . . . doctor . . .'

There was a pause as the guard withdrew, uncovered the peephole and, by the jaundiced light, looked into the cell.

'*Dame*. No. He okay.'

'But . . .'

'*Hanasanai!*' No talking! And he went away.

The kid moved to where Pieter lay gasping for breath, the fluid in his lungs broiling. Billy lifted him a little, sat on the boards and leant against the wall, resting the man's head in his lap.

'What more can I do for ya?' he asked.

Nothing. There was nothing that he – or anyone else – could do for Pieter now, except to sit with him as he crossed to the other side. And that sense of helplessness seized the boy, filling him with a great sadness. The sheer indifference of the world to their suffering. The unfairness of it. Loss, and despair, and perplexity . . . All seeped up from the springs of being, like Pieter's watery breath, into the runnels of silence and the yellow cell light that illuminated nothing.

So he sat with his thoughts, until the kid realised that the simmering sounds had ceased. The man's breathing now seemed much more normal. He looked down.

'Ah, Billy,' Pieter smiled weakly. 'The war will be over shortly, and you will come to visit my family in Surabaya.'

'Yes, Pieter. We'll all be going home soon.' Hope guttered like a candle.

He waited for Pieter to respond. But he didn't say anything. And when next Billy looked, he saw that the man had already gone. Pieter's war was done.

How softly – how swiftly – death had entered the prison cell. It was as if, Billy thought, death had come for Pieter wearing carpet slippers. And now both were stolen away. Both released.

No tears. No lamentation. On the contrary, the kid had seen enough of death not to accept its presence – grateful that it had not, once again, come for him. Besides, there was the practical question of what to do next: for as always, survival came first. Billy therefore sat cradling Pieter's head for a little longer, letting his grief drain inwardly. Then at last he got up, lay Pieter down and crossed the hands on his chest, and quietly returned to his own bed boards until morning.

When the *meshi toban* arrived with the breakfast tray, Billy took two bowls of rice as normal and placed the best one – the one with a wisp of green stuff on top – beside Pieter's body. He sat and slowly ate his own mouthful. And when that was finished he reached out and, taking Pieter's share, consumed that one as well. Same with the lukewarm *char*. First drank his own, then his cellmate's.

'Well, Pieter,' the kid murmured, 'we had our feast. Not like we thought, but.'

Not at home on Java. Not imagining it would have been the Dutchman's own funeral banquet.

Only when this was gone, and the *meshi toban* had removed the bowls, did Billy bang on the cell door again and summon up the duty guard, who turned out to be none other than the brave Little Hitler.

'*Nanda?*' Almost spat through the food slot.

'My friend. Dead. *Shinda*...'

He heard the peephole cover scrape and swivel. A pause as Little Hitler eyed the corpse and deliberated. Then came the familiar order. '*Hanasanai.*' No talking.

To reinforce the instruction, he repeated it in Malay. '*Tidak boleh chakap.*' Sounding, to a phonetic Australian ear, like 'Today bully chuck-up'. Unquestionably, pal. And Little Hitler went off down the Broadway, laughing at his own wit.

A short time later, a woven straw mat and a length of cord were brought to Billy's cell. Carefully – as reverently as he could, given his own weakness – he rolled Pieter onto the mat and covered him as if with a shroud. Tied him decently, head and foot, so that he should not come undone again. Said goodbye, as he left with the work party that morning. And when the kid returned, Pieter had been taken away.

From then on, a sense of despond – almost of hopelessness – stayed with him, like a presence always standing just behind, and it was difficult for Billy not to give in to it. On the one hand, it seemed the war was at last coming to an end. By mid-year, a new arrival had brought the news of Victory in Europe: that Hitler was dead and Germany had surrendered in May to the Allies. Surely it couldn't be that long before we'd also beat the Japs in the Pacific! And yet, on the other hand was the constant dread that none of them at Outram Road would be alive to see it.

It wasn't just the fact of Pieter's death, one among so many who succumbed to disease brought on by utter want and neglect. Not just the reaper's casual, uninvited visitation. As the war closed in and Nippon retreated, men began to fear the Kenpeitai would adopt a deliberate policy to exterminate all prisoners. Rightly so, as it turned out. Unbeknown to them, Tokyo had already issued instructions: at the end to 'annihilate them all and not leave any traces'.

It was around this time that crosses chalked in a circle were seen above the cell doors where Habbie and the Fleet Air Arm crews were being held at the end of the cell block near the death house: the certain sign they'd been marked for execution. And far from solitary confinement, the regular POWs now had to share *three* in a cell – squeezed into fewer chambers at the other end of the building.

'What are they doing this for?' the kid asked MP. 'It's not as if they're running out of room. There are hundreds of empty cells in this place.'

'Convenience,' Brownie replied. 'They're herding us into smaller pens like steers at an abattoir. Easier to kill quickly, when the time comes.' The man had spent years working in the bush, and knew of what he spoke.

Billy was happy enough with the arrangements, as such. Any company was welcome, and he especially enjoyed sharing again with Chinese Charlie and Regimental Quartermaster Sergeant Beech. Q, as he was always known, was an older man who'd served decades with the British Army – in India, the north-west frontier – and was ready for retirement when he'd been swept into service again by the war. His stories of military life gave meaning to the verses from Kipling scratched on the prison walls: *When you're wounded and left on Afghanistan's plains…*

From his broad experience Q shared the general view that if – when – the Allies landed to recapture Singapore, the Japanese would certainly kill their prisoners.

And this was the problem. However companionable it may have been sharing three to a cell, the men suspected what lay at the end of it. And that belief affected everybody. Even Charlie became filled with pessimism.

'You know, Birry, every time we go out with *changkol* to dig Japanese tunnel, it as if we dig own grave.'

The kid found it hard not to agree – or to forsake that optimism, innate in every marketeer, that the next opportunity is just around the corner.

'Don't worry, Charlie. It'll be over long before that.'

Wishing, rather than expecting, that were true.

None of this was helped by the attitudes of the guards, whose aggression to the POWs was – if anything – becoming more vindictive as Nippon faced defeat. Even Tokyo now was ablaze with firestorms after B-29 bombing raids. Thus, the ritual slicing of a forefinger across the throat to their captives in Outram Road, and the expletive '*Suga, mate...*' Soon, just you wait...was no longer just a taunt, but carried a real threat of imminent execution. As if they'd already made up their minds.

Which, for the Rimau ten, was certainly the case. The Commander-in-Chief of the Japanese 7th Army had decided in March – with Kenpeitai urging – that the men should die as spies, and the prosecutor, Major Kamiya, spent three months preparing his case. On 3 July the Special Operations men were taken from their cells and lodged at Raffles College, Singapore, where they were tried two days later before a crowded military court on charges of espionage. Kamiya used several arguments against them. The ten were not wearing correct military uniforms when captured: they'd taken off their berets and removed identifying badges from their jungle greens (which looked suspiciously like Japanese army khaki); camouflaged their faces (as commandos usually do); and some had been seen wearing Malayan clothes. The boat *Mustika*, which may (or may not) have had a Japanese flag painted on the stern, had entered Singapore waters, four Malay policemen had been shot and more Japanese soldiers killed in the subsequent fighting through the islands. A notebook had been found containing sketches and shipping information...

As with all these proceedings, where guilt had been decided in advance, the accused had no defence counsel. But unlike Billy the Kid's trial, the interpreter Furuta provided a translation, and the prisoners responded to questions from the judges. Asked if he had killed any Japanese soldiers, for example, Captain Robert Page of the AIF replied coolly: 'I am an officer in the British Army, and I know my aim is good.' Which brought murmurs of admiration from the spectators. The prosecutor's closing peroration, however, was heard in utter silence.

Major Kamiya acknowledged the courage of the ten, describing them as patriotic heroes – identical with Japanese war heroes who'd died in other conflicts. As such, he maintained, it would be disgracing the 'sublime spirit' of the Rimau men to even think of saving their lives. Australia had respected the Japanese killed in the midget submarine attack on Sydney Harbour by giving them proper funerals. The court should accord these ten heroes the same respect.

'Let us not disgrace their spirit by supposing that they may want to be alive. Sending them to death is the only way to send them to an eternal glory.' It was surely one of the most self-serving justifications ever made for seeking the death of an enemy.

The accused listened to this in a state of shock, unaware till then that they had been on trial for their lives. Asked by the Chief Judge, Colonel Towatari, if he had anything to say before sentence, Major Ingleton expressed thanks for being described as a patriotic hero; but while he acknowledged Rimau's operations may have been an unfair (certainly an unconventional) form of warfare, he had not realised until that moment they were considered such grave offences. The other men said much the same, after which Towatari pronounced the death sentence.

Apparently there'd been some trouble obtaining a presiding officer. The first choice, Colonel Yoshida, refused to participate, as he didn't believe the Rimau men were guilty of war crimes within even an elastic reading of the Hague Convention. Towatari was more obliging. But even he must have been troubled; for in an extraordinary act he visited those he'd just condemned to explain that, as a military man, he was acting under orders and had no choice but to deliver the required verdict.

Returned to Outram Road, the ten were taken to the death house and into a single large, barred chamber, like a zoo cage, for the two days that remained to them. Furuta was allowed to visit and bring cigarettes on the last evening; and whatever his own distress at the sentence, he was amazed by the calmness – even cheerfulness – shown by the Rimau men. Furuta tried to obtain clemency for them, but to no avail, since he went to the very officers who had ordered their deaths.

On the morning of 7 July, wearing clean khaki clothes, they were handcuffed, loaded into a truck and taken to the execution ground at Bukit Timah. Bluey Rollason, who was on *benki* duty that day, managed to wave as they were led from the death house – and exchange a few brief words. They were nothing much – merely that they'd been a little better treated... before the guards interposed. The Kenpeitai had gone to great lengths to keep the Rimau men separate from the other prisoners. When the *benki toban* came to collect their toilet buckets, a blanket screen had even been draped at the door. And while the talking walls carried the intelligence that the ten had had something to do with an attack on shipping in Singapore, the details were unknown. But not, as it turned out, the fact they had been killed.

A large crowd was at Bukit Timah to witness the executions, including the head of the army's Judiciary Branch, Major-General Otsuka; the Chief Judge, and the prosecutor; Kobayashi, the military commandant of Outram Road prison, and his civilian counterpart, Mikizawa. All who were present spoke of the courage and steadfastness with which the ten met their end. They stood talking and joking among themselves, smoking a last cigarette, before being informed they were to be beheaded. A last request was granted: that they be unshackled and allowed to shake hands. They wished each other 'Good luck'. In a final speech, Major Ingleton even thanked Furuta for his kindness – though the interpreter, who had hidden among the spectators, turned and fled as Reginald Ingleton was the first to be led away to the place where the swordsmen bowed, and three open pits waited to receive – or release – them into eternal glory. And of course into eternal silence.

There were those among the military echelons who continued to persuade themselves that they'd shown these sublime heroes every respect by the ceremonial nature of their deaths. In fact it was as squalid, bloody and revengeful as these things always are. Not even well done by Nippon's own standards. A couple of trusties heard one of the Outram Road executioners being taunted on his poor swordsmanship. And for all the talk that the ten had been well treated at the end, there were those who had reason to doubt it.

That same day, Bluey Rollason and a couple of others were ordered to clean the cell vacated by the ten. It was one of the few times that ordinary POWs had been allowed to enter the death house. Indeed, they even found a bonus in the cigarettes left over from Furuta's last visit. The guards wouldn't touch them, but the prisoners had no such qualms. As for the work in hand, apart from the muck on the floor from the overflowing toilet bucket, there was a good deal of blood to be washed off the walls. And Bluey Rollason, who had known many Kenpeitai bashings in his time at Outram Road, was quite sure the Rimau men received their share of them.

Death everywhere...

Not long afterwards, Billy the Kid and his mate MP Brown were in a *benki* party that was required to enter the death house and clean out another chamber occupied by eight American airmen. They discovered shit and piss all over the place, for their buckets had not been emptied for a long time. There was soon a good deal more of it, for the fellers pulled the old stunt of dropping the *benki* tray. And as they ran about picking up buckets and lids – mopping the floor while the guard screamed abuse – the kid took his chance to have a few hurried words with the pilots standing by the bars.

They were from the two B-29s shot down over Singapore on the day of the great raid, they said. Amazing they'd lived so long!

The chalk crosses above the cell made it clear they were marked for the sword – like Habbie and the Fleet Air Arm men still held at the far end of the big cell block, and those other aircrew Billy could see watching, like caged animals, further down the death house.

Filth. Disease. Violence. Starvation. The slopping excrement of these human beings *in extremis* was cleaned away by spectres with mop and bucket. Death hovered on carrion wings over all of them.

For nine days after the Rimau men died, a new weapon of mass destruction was tested at a site in New Mexico, and mankind's first mushroom cloud appeared, hideous in the sky. Some ten days after that, the Potsdam Declaration warned that, without unconditional surrender, Japan faced the utter devastation of its homeland. It did not mention the atomic bomb. Nor was the ultimatum accepted. On the morning of 6 August, the device known as 'Little Boy' was detonated over the city of Hiroshima. Three days later a second bomb, 'Fat Man', was dropped over Nagasaki. More than 100 000 people, mostly civilians, died immediately in the two nuclear explosions, and at least as many again from the effects of radiation in the months that followed.

Yet the atom bombs brought the war in the Pacific to an end. On 15 August Japan announced its surrender. Those hundreds of thousands of other soldiers and civilians, who would undoubtedly have died on both sides had the fighting been carried into the Japanese heartland, now were suffered to go on living. Or most of them were. Such are the moral choices made by those who unleash Armageddon.

At the time Billy the Kid was sharing his cell with two Indians – Tamils, one of whom was a coot of a bloke. Swarthy, sullen and riddled with pox, he'd spent some days hostilely staring at Billy across the cell, when he suddenly burst out: 'You say you're a white man…a pukka sahib. Ha! You're as dark as the rest of us. Bastard!'

The jibe stung the kid. Ordinarily he would have shrugged it off. But now he hissed back, 'I am not! Look!' And he pulled up his shorts to show the patch of pale skin around his groin.

The whiteness of his flesh, exposed like some plucked chicken against the rest of him, burnt and filthy from labouring in the sun, was surprising. It certainly shut the Tamil up, who retreated into his brooding self. But what really astonished the kid was the vehemence of his own reaction. In the shared netherworld of Outram Road, racial differences had largely been forgotten. Sloughed off, like fear and even hope, to be replaced by a dull, communal fatalism. All of them cooped poultry awaiting the chop.

Yet the fact he'd responded so angrily to the Tamil suggested that perhaps his old assertiveness was stirring again. And indeed, there was something strange about the second week of August...as if something were going on, but nobody could say what. Small signs on the exchange of human commerce, which a boy brought up at Paddy's Market couldn't fail to notice.

For instance, they'd been kept locked in their cells for days. No work parties (and no *benki* parties either). Then that vicious guard Mopoke had done an extraordinary thing, and offered Billy a second drink one evening from the water can.

'*Lagi?*' More? he asked in Malay at the food slot.

'*Lagi.*' For thirst was constant. And Mopoke obliged, as if trying to ingratiate himself. Smiling, as he'd never been seen to do before.

On the 15th, according to the wall calendar, they were each given a small sip of condensed milk with their evening meal. This happened occasionally – to celebrate the Emperor's birthday or a great victory. What gave it meaning now was the news, tapped through the walls via the Indian food trusties, that the Japanese prisoners upstairs had NOT been given any condensed milk. When Billy considered that he'd heard a plane – one of ours – buzzing overhead that day, without any accompanying anti-aircraft fire, he came to only one conclusion.

'I reckon we've won the war!' he exclaimed to the two Tamils.

And he Morsed the message to Brownie next door, who was too intelligent to share his optimism, and told the kid to calm down. It could mean anything.

Still, that sense of hope reborn quickened in the rest of them. Even the Tamil muttered 'sahib' once or twice, trying to establish himself in Billy's good graces should the white man's order be restored. But as one empty day turned into the next, the silence broken only by the flip-flop of the guards' thongs outside, such expectations seemed stillborn. Nothing happened, and the Tamil resumed his scowling.

Then on the 18th, by the kid's scratches on the wall, the quietude was shattered by the sounds of commotion in Broadway. Stamping feet. Banging doors. Looking through the grille, Billy saw the prison commandant, Kobayashi, and several other Kenpeitai officers all in their black dress uniforms, hurrying past his cell. Between them, guards were hustling the nine Fleet Air Arm men, among whom the kid recognised his mate Habbie – the New Zealand pilot who'd scribbled that little note of war news for him months ago.

Where the Kenpeitai officers were taking them, the kid didn't know. If anything, he supposed they might be releasing the airmen, for they were heading for the door that led to the main gate – not out the other end by the death house where those destined for the blade were always despatched.

In fact the nine – the 'Palembang Nine' as they became known to posterity – were driven out to a beach north of Changi. And there on the sands they were beheaded – without trial, and days after the war had ended – their bodies flung into a boat, which was towed to sea and sunk. The story was put about that they'd been killed while trying to escape; and there may well have been more victims, had these Kenpeitai captains not been stopped by more senior officers, concerned about their own necks when the Allied victors found out.

As they did within a month or so of reoccupying Singapore. General Otsuka of the Judiciary Branch (he who had arranged the trial of the Rimau men) acknowledged the truth. The Kenpeitai officers responsible were arrested and signed confessions – before they cheated the gallows and committed harakiri. It didn't do Otsuka any good. The tribunals still found him guilty of war crimes against other Outram Road prisoners, and he was sentenced to be hanged, as was the commandant, Kobayashi.

But such things were yet to emerge. Within the jail, time – as always – seemed suspended. Nothing stirred the imprisoned silence, except the beating of men's hearts and their fluttering thoughts.

The end, when it came, was as stealthy. Almost anti-climactic. Just the metallic *click* of the key turning in the lock of the cell door, the day after the kid had seen Habbie removed. That one small sound, and then nothing. Billy waited awhile, wondering if The Postman had returned to his rounds. But when still there was nothing, he rose from his squat and gingerly pulled open the door. Nobody behind it. Only a couple of guards standing on the other side of corridor. And most astonishing of all, they were not wearing their swords. They seemed almost naked without them.

Followed by the Tamils, Billy stepped out, and met MP Brown coming from the next cell.

'I'm sure this is it,' the kid said. 'The war's over.'

'Oh come on, Billy. You've been saying that for two years.'

'No. Look at 'em. No swords.'

So convinced was he that he was leaving his cell for the last time, Billy reached up from the stoop and took the bit of card from above the door that had his number 510 written upon it, and his sentence in Japanese. Still the guard did not stop *go-hyaku-ju* from this wanton act of vandalism – but ushered him instead, with the 80 or so other men emerging from their cells, to that end of the building that led to the gate.

The civilian commandant Mikizawa, a rarely seen and somewhat melancholy older man, was standing beside a table on which lay their records. When all were assembled, he spoke to them through an interpreter.

'You are being sent out to Changi.'

Proof positive.

'But of course, you must come back here to complete your prison terms.'

Like bloody hell!

That said, the door was opened and the men exited into the yard by the guardhouse. Where they were handed back their clothes and the few possessions they'd carried when first they entered Outram Road. More: Billy was astounded to be given his haversack – taken from him the day he was arrested and flogged. It must have followed him all the way from Sandakan! And inside were not only his bloodstained pyjama jacket and kitbag shorts, but also the tobacco tin containing the bit of shrapnel the doctors removed from his thigh after the flight from Bukit Timah.

Proof not only that the war was over. Proof of how meticulous the Japanese were in their record-keeping (and it transpired just as meticulous in destroying their records, including those from Outram Road prison, in the hiatus between surrender and the re-entry of the Allies to Singapore).

The prisoners milled about in the yard for half an hour or so, like sheep in a pen waiting for release. Billy had his pencil stub – though not the pack of cards, which he'd left hanging on their twine behind the window wall, and he wasn't going back to get them. Still, he took advantage of the time by getting the fellers to sign the card 510. He didn't get as many signatures as he'd hoped, for Sergeant Adair Macalister Blain scrawled his name in large letters across most of it (but then he was, in civvy life, a politician).

Billy also talked to a few of the American pilots he'd seen in the death house: saying how lucky they were not to have been lopped – and unlucky enough not to hit the warship in the docks that day they bombed Singapore.

'We weren't supposed to hit it, pal. We were told just to destroy the wharves and stop the ship putting to sea.'

Then up the long tunnel through the outer wall they went – feeling rather like fugitives, so sudden and confusing were their changed circumstances. Walking – stumbling – from the darkness towards an arc of light. Out the double gates standing open wide. And into the waiting trucks: the kid still not believing it – wondering if they were not being driven to another day digging in the trenches, or even (in some macabre joke dreamed up by the Kenpeitai) to their deaths. Yet perhaps…it was also possible…they were going home…

Thought and emotion tumbled together like dice thrown into the ring, as they were shaken every inch of the eight miles to Changi, where they stopped outside the prison walls and louring grey clock tower – and for a moment all bets seemed lost.

'Billy! Kid!'

He heard his name being called from out of the past. And turning, he saw Paddy O'Toole beside the truck. Paddy in all his solid, wonderful Irishness.

Paddy's arms reaching out and picking him up – this wretched, ragged stick figure – as if he were no more than a child. Lifting him over the side. Holding him. Rocking him.

And saying with a voice thick through the tears, 'I've come to take ya back to the battalion, Billy. They're waitin' for ya.'

# 14

# LIBERATION

*We suffered because we were weaker*
*Than we ought to have been;*
*We survived because we were stronger*
*Than they thought we'd have been.*

Paddy continued to nurse the kid for some minutes, holding him aloft in his arms and refusing to give him to the medics waiting to take him to the camp hospital.

'No, Billy's coming with me, back to the battalion.'

'But the doctors have got to see him with the rest of these blokes. Now,' the medics demanded.

'I told yer. The fellers want to see Billy first.'

But even the kid began to struggle. 'Put me bloody down, Paddy!' At length he set the stick figure on the ground and allowed Billy to go off with the orderlies to the hospital huts – 'Just so long as you promise to let him visit the moment the quacks have finished with him.'

Paddy mooched off to inform the reception party of the change in plan.

These days immediately following the war were a time of strange interregnum in Singapore: nobody was really in charge. The Japanese had surrendered; but so quickly had the end come that British forces had not yet returned to take over control – nor would they for nearly three weeks. Until then, the privations endured by the POWs remained much the same, despite emergency Allied airdrops of food and medical supplies. And while the jails stood open, most men stayed close to where they were, to avoid the risk of reprisal such as Habbie and the Fleet Air Arm pilots suffered – for there were still over 70 000 Japanese troops on the island with access to arms, some of whom were refusing to accept the fact of surrender.

In the case of the 5500 Australian (and some 6000 British) prisoners still on Singapore island, this meant continuing to live mainly in and around Changi prison, or at Kranji. Most of those Australians who'd remained to build the military airfield, or who'd returned from the horrors of the Burma-Thai railway, had been moved to Changi jail in May 1944. Japanese aircrews required their space at Selarang Barracks. So the interned civilians were sent to a camp at Sime Road, and the POWs took their places – herded into outhouses and prison buildings designed to accommodate 650 people.

The problems of overcrowding, malnutrition and disease became increasingly acute: saved only by the strict discipline maintained by the Australian commander, Lieutenant-Colonel 'Black Jack' Galleghan in such matters as military order, rationing the meagre and often rotten food supplies, elementary hygiene and working the vegetable gardens. Plus the extraordinary efforts of the camp hospital staff who, with only the most basic equipment, limited drugs and their own skills at improvisation and adaptation, performed miracles in saving human life. Even so, by war's end all at Changi were grossly malnourished: better off than the prisoners who arrived from Outram Road – but not by much. Over 80 per cent of them had malaria, many of whom the Japs had refused treatment. There were 500 men suffering beriberi. Even a month after the war finished, the doctors considered that three men out of every four were fit only to travel home by sea ambulance or hospital ship.

The hospital had been moved several times: from the barracks to Changi prison with the men, where it squatted in a series of shophouses (for the officers), and timber and atap huts (for the troops), just outside the walls. Here, Billy the Kid and his fellow Australians were taken from Outram Road to savour as if in a dream those first few hours of liberation. To begin the slow recovery not only of bodily health, but also of memory after years of degradation. To remember what it was to be human again. And to rediscover the simple decencies of civilised life.

Thus it was as a stranger that Billy found himself translated from a stone cell to a hospital hut. Elevated from three floorboards to a timber bunk with a pillow, a mattress and a sheet. Examined by a doctor and an orderly, who did not scream and ignore his plight, but prescribed medication for his beriberi and hookworm from relief supplies dropped only the day before by the Red Cross. Who ordered him to rest. To wash his filthy body with soap and warm water under the showers contrived from a water pipe attached to the prison wall, just outside. To discard his Outram Road rags and to put on the clean tropical kit of an Australian soldier. No boots, though. The kid's feet were so swollen with beriberi he could at first only wear thongs.

Above all, the doctor ordered Billy to eat. To take his meals from the special dietary foods the hospital had been able to conserve for such serious cases of starvation as the men from Outram Road.

'But only eat a little at a time. Don't overdo it. Your stomachs aren't used to tucker, and you'll make yourselves sick.' Which was all very well for *him* to say!

News of their arrival spread quickly through Changi and it wasn't long before the huts filled with men come to visit – to ask after old mates, to say what had happened, or to stare in wonderment at cobbers who'd survived even more reduced than themselves. Like scarecrows congregating to look at skeletons.

'You're even more skinny than we was, when we got back from Thailand and building the Burma railway at Christmas '43,' Paddy O'Toole observed, when he and some of the 2/29th fellers saw Billy that afternoon.

The reception committee could wait no longer, and had come calling on him, Alan Minty and the other battalion men released from Outram Road. And so, in these sentences, they heard the first of that infamous undertaking in which over 80 000 prisoners and coolies died as the Japanese forced them to build 260 miles of railway track through monsoon jungle, over river and mountain pass, between Bampong and Thanbyuzayat, in ruthlessly quick time.

Paddy himself was one of some 7000 Australians sent out with F Force as virtual slave labour for more than seven months. A third of them died of exhaustion, disease and fever. The 2/29th Battalion alone lost almost 250 men on the railway – 150 with a work party led by their CO Lieutenant-Colonel Pond, which laboured on bridges and cuttings in Thailand. The sick and injured – all were forced to work on meagre rations for 14 hours a day (and often longer), digging and carrying up to 500 baskets of earth, as the Japanese made them work faster – putting on 'speedo' – as the monsoon set in.

Pond's Party were rarely in one place for more than a few weeks before being marched to another site: all their equipment, tools, food, medical supplies and tents (plus the Japs' own gear) carried by the POWs – often on the officers' backs, to give the working ranks some respite. Even so, their numbers were dreadfully reduced by cholera, diphtheria, tropical disease and ulcers, malnutrition, overwork and dysentery. By the time the Party returned to Singapore a fifth of them had died. That the death rate wasn't higher was due to the skills of Dr Roy Mills and his medics, and also to the heroism – though he wouldn't admit it – of men like Paddy O'Toole.

Despite his own exhaustion and illness, Paddy used all his resourcefulness to scrounge what extra food and supplies he could for the sick – and also for himself and his mates, of course. Paddy rarely accepted acknowledgment for this, saying gruffly, 'I didn't do it for thanks!' Though he'd become emotional enough as he told Billy of their return to Selarang in December 1943.

'When we got off the trucks we were met by Black Jack Galleghan, as camp commander. "Where are the rest of your men?" he asked Colonel Pond. "That's all we have left, sir." And I'll swear there were tears in Black Jack's eyes.'

'You poor bastards,' said the Outram Road fellers, listening to the story for the first time, that afternoon in the hospital hut.

But when Billy asked about Sandakan and the airfield – about the men from B Force, and the later E Force, and what had become of them – nobody could say.

'Bob Shipsides? Harry Longley? When are they coming back?'

'No one has said, kid. We've had no word from Sandakan. Except from blokes who got away, like you.'

'P'raps they'll pick 'em up direct from Borneo.'

'Probably. I reckon. Yeah.'

The talking went on for hours, as men pieced together the fragments of three lost years: Billy exhilarated, rediscovering what liberty meant. Freedom of Speech! Freedom of Movement! In the congested hospital hut, those mighty principles for which our leaders said the war had been fought were here made manifest.

Yet there came a point when the kid found himself feeling exhausted. Too much freedom of association all at once! Like too much rich food. Others from Outram Road were feeling the same, he could see. And in a moment of quietness, it was suggested a group of them go down to Changi Beach for a little – to allow the high drama of the day to resolve itself calmly, away from any audience.

So they left, a dozen or more of them, to walk through the scrub to the littoral, where coconut palms framed an idyll of white sand, washing tides, and the silver glint of late-afternoon sun. They strolled along the beach awhile, feeling the sand yield beneath them and water bathing their feet. Talking. Remembering. Wondering what it would be like when they got used to liberty, and had to encumber themselves again with the responsibilities of freedom and obligations due to other people.

The kid thought of home... wherever that was. Of Nana Tot and the family in Hobart. Waiting. Expecting. Making plans for his future. And as quickly he put the notion aside. Such things were too complicated at present. It was enough simply for Billy to enjoy the sensations of liberty; to stare at the sea and the panorama of the sunset. Here was freedom. These waves would flow in time to Blackwattle Bay, where he used to play as a boy. The same sun was setting tonight over Paddy's Market, on old Pop Jepson and Uncle Cocky coming home for tea. It was strange, even so, why on this first day of their release these prisoners should choose to be by themselves – and yet not so strange. As Billy would learn much later in life, only those who had been there could really understand.

Day gave way to evening. They stood leaning on a post-and-rail fence by the palm trees, watching a miracle as the world was rinsed with blue and grey, dissolving into the inky night. Stars came out, specks of gold in seams of darkness. Billy absorbed the spectacle with an intensity he could not fathom... until he realised this was the first time in two and a half years he'd actually seen the night sky. The last time had been their final evening aboard the *Treasure* as she bore them to Kuching. Since then, every night had been spent in a prison cell (or the brief interlude of a horsebox) where the windows were shaded and the electric light always turned on.

Billy thought that liberation had come when they walked up the tunnel at Outram Road towards the open gates and the arc of sunlight beyond. But it was not so. Only in the blessed solace of the night did he really begin to feel the shackles of confinement fall away. He'd come to believe escape from degradation was possible only in the blackness behind closed eyelids. Now, all the beauty of the evening opened before him and he felt a sense of tranquillity and of wholeness stir within. A full moon rose, casting her silver pathway across the smooth waters. And Billy the Kid found himself travelling along it – his mind released at last to wonder at a world new found, and his soul to lose itself in the mysteries of the universe.

So they stayed all night. Others came and went – Paddy for a while, some of the other fellers. But those from Outram Road remained through the hours of darkness – alone with their thoughts, yet together as comrades – until the morning sun lifted above the eastern sea and they returned to the hut for breakfast. Free men.


Free. But not wholly so. You never are – least of all in the army, where someone's always giving orders. And certainly at Changi, the military discipline that enabled men to survive years of captivity was just as necessary to preserve the peace during those first weeks of liberation.

Leaflets were dropped advising of interim arrangements, urging the Japanese to cooperate with local Singapore police as civil order was restored. Yet whenever Billy and MP Brown went to nearby villages on the scrounge (for that honourable institution was still equally as important to survival), officers warned them not to seek reprisals or do anything to antagonise old enemies.

'We don't want you starting another war!'

The advice wasn't really necessary. They rarely saw any Japs, and even when they did, the kid gave them a wide berth. He'd spent years planning his revenge, but now that the moment had come, the desire fairly dissipated. He'd make his statements about

Habbie and the Kenpeitai to the authorities investigating war crimes. Yet as for personal retribution, Billy found it enough now to gloat in the knowledge that we had won. He was content to let others bring Little Hitler and Mopoke, Moritake and Hoshijima at Sandakan to their day of reckoning. To renew his identity back in the brotherhood of the battalion. And, since Billy knew the army would never be enough for him, to think more seriously about going home.

Home wasn't just Australia, however much he missed its scent and touch. It was also somewhere specific – with his grandmother and the relatives in Hobart – and he constantly thanked whatever deep, unconscious need had impelled the orphan boy to spend his last few shillings to visit them and re-establish the bond in those final days of his embarkation leave in 1941. He'd had letters and a parcel from them, of course, before war had come to Singapore. But nothing since. Nothing waiting for him at Changi. But now, on army advice, he wrote to Nana to say that he was safe and would be coming home soon. They all wrote: their letters collected for despatch by the first military plane able to fly out.

Even so, quick repatriation depended on the state of the men's health. The prisoners may have been released, but their bodies were still racked by the effects of confinement. Brownie, for instance, suffered severe malnutrition. His legs never properly recovered from tropical ulcers and the dreadful beating inflicted by Moritake's thugs at the Sandakan boiler house. Young Billy was beginning to put on some weight. Even the symptoms of beriberi lessened a little, and he was able to put on a pair of size 14 army boots, which were way too big. But others were not so fortunate.

There was an English soldier called Jack Sharpe in Outram Road jail – a popular, cheery little feller, whom someone with a literary turn had nicknamed 'Becky Sharp' after the character in Thackeray's *Vanity Fair*. At first glance, Becky might have seemed chubby enough, yet in truth his body was swollen with beriberi. He was very sick. And on the morning of liberation, as they walked up the tunnel to the waiting trucks, the kid and Brownie stopped Becky from getting into the vehicle bound for the British POW hospital at Kranji.

'No, no, Becky. You come with us. Out to Changi. They'll feed you better than your own Pommy lot. Look after ya.'

So Becky went with them, and lay on one of the bunks near the kid and MP, too ill to go down to the beach that first evening, or to join them on the scrounge.

Some days after they arrived, Becky was compelled to go to the 'boreholes', as they called the latrine pits drilled in open ground just across from the huts. Becky was sitting there, when he suddenly collapsed. The fluid that had so inflated his body began to pour from every orifice. When Billy and the others reached him, summoned by the alarm of a passing soldier, they found Becky sprawled on the earth, as limp and shrivelled as an empty bladder.

They carried him back to the hut, where the doctors worked around the clock to save his life, which, thank God, they did: though as Becky recovered, he was a man transformed. His flesh seemed to have disappeared. Every rib and bone was visible: a mere frame draped with skin. It was amazing that a human being could survive so depleted – let alone keep his good humour. Which Becky did. Even for the camera.

When at last the British relief convoy arrived, among the first visitors to the hut was a photographer wanting pictures of the POWs for the papers back home.

'Any Englishmen in here?' he asked.

'There's Becky...'

'Mind if I take a snap?'

They propped Becky with Billy's pillow and took a photo of him sitting up under the sheet, appearing more like a corpse resurrecting from the grave – yet with this cheeky, broken-toothed grin and a glint in his eye, staring at the camera as if to say, 'I am yet a man.' And indeed Billy heard afterwards that Becky's picture had been published around the world, famously, as an image of all that the wartime prisoners of Japan had suffered, and endured, and survived. And of the spirit by which they did it.

It was on 5 September that the relief fleet of Operation Tiderace reached Singapore. Paratroops had landed a few days earlier, to begin disarming the Japanese and separating them from the rest of the populace. But late on that Wednesday morning, crowds rejoiced in the sight of some 90 vessels, led by the flagship HMS *Sussex*, steaming into Keppel Harbour to berth at wharves all along the waterfront.

The convoy had sailed from Rangoon and Trincomalee at the end of August: seven escort carriers, two battleships and light cruisers, 15 destroyers, three hospital ships, 14 merchant vessels and dozens of landing craft. They brought the 5th Indian Division to establish the new British Military Administration, to rule the Straits Settlements until such time as civil government was restored. Above all, they carried vast stores of food and supplies: the first priority to begin daily deliveries to Changi and the other camps of meat, pies, soup, lime juice, vegetables and – most especially for European prisoners who'd subsisted for over three and a half years on a rice diet – wheaten bread. The bakeries on the naval vessels laboured to produce enough loaves, which were devoured almost as soon as they came out of the ovens. And such was the demand from the visitors who came aboard the flagship that the cruiser became universally known as the *Hotel Sussex*.

The seamen who took supplies to Changi were shocked at the wretched condition of the men and the miserable rations they'd been forced to eat – even more so when it was discovered the Japanese had withheld Red Cross supplies for months, and only made them available when the food had become almost inedible.

Still, this merely hardened attitudes towards the defeated enemy. When, on that first day, General Itagaki arrived at HMS *Sussex* to sign the terms of reoccupation, he was kept waiting, and upon complaining was told curtly, 'We don't keep Tokyo time here.' Itagaki at first balked at surrender, though he ultimately accepted it and instructed his officers to do the same. Some 300 did not, however; full of sake after a party at Raffles Hotel, they blew themselves up with hand grenades rather than face the dishonour of captivity.

The general was spared the trouble of committing harakiri. A week after the fleet arrived, the Supreme Allied Commander of South-East Asia, Admiral Lord Louis Mountbatten, accepted Itagaki's formal surrender of Japanese forces in the region, at a ceremony in Singapore's City Hall. Immediately afterwards Itagaki was arrested and charged with war crimes – for which, at length, he faced the hangman in Tokyo. He was one of several thousand enemy soldiers brought before the tribunals established to investigate Japanese atrocities during the Pacific war. Australian military courts alone tried over 900 – of whom two-thirds were convicted, and 148 executed.

Of particular moment to the men from Outram Road, 43 Japanese involved with that prison were tried in Singapore for causing the deaths of at least 17 POWs (among them Captain Pieter van Hemert) and 22 civilians, through neglect and ill-treatment. The defendants ranged from General Otsuka, head of the 7th Army's judiciary branch, through the list of Kenpeitai officers, sergeants, privates and trusties who had so abused their victims. Only four were acquitted. Five were sentenced to death, and the rest to long terms of imprisonment.

Such matters, of course, lay in the future on that 12 September when Lord Mountbatten accepted Itagaki's surrender. Thousands had gathered on the Padang by the seafront outside City Hall. It was here that the expatriate civilians had been ordered to muster and march to confinement at Changi after the fall in February 1942. Now, an even larger crowd was there to witness the Japanese capitulation and the victory parade that followed. Billy the Kid, sadly, was not among them. He'd suddenly become very ill. And it was his own fault.

A few days after the fleet arrived, Billy and a mate went down to the wharves on spec, and discovered a group of fellers unloading crates of tinned meat and veg from one of the supply ships. Their eyes lit up.

'Can you spare us some?' they asked.

While the kid was starting to put on a little weight, he was still recovering from malnutrition. Still confined to small, spare meals. Still felt himself starving.

'Couple a cans?'

'You can have the bloody lot, mate.'

So they took a box around the corner, opened the tins with a bayonet, ate every one of them – and were violently sick. It was as if they'd overdosed on food – collapsing onto the pavement, spewing up their entire innards it seemed – until they had to be carried back to Changi and deposited on the hospital bunks.

'I told you silly young buggers,' reprimanded the medic. 'I warned you!'

And there they stayed, all through the victory celebrations.

While Billy missed the Supreme Commander at City Hall, he ran into the official party when the Mountbattens visited Changi two days later. Or rather, they ran into him.

The kid was too sick to attend the main welcome, where Lord Mountbatten spoke to the POWs outside the prison walls. Billy was having a shower instead, mucking about with a bunch of other blokes, when they heard female voices approaching. Women laughing. And around the corner came Lady Edwina Mountbatten and her entourage, as Superintendent-in-Chief of St John's Ambulance, on a separate tour of inspection. Naked bodies went flying everywhere, bare arses disappearing through the doors and windows of the hospital huts. And the women laughed even louder.

As it turned out, this was Billy's last full day in Singapore. It was for many of the patients. Next morning they were loaded into trucks, driven to the docks and taken aboard the Dutch hospital ship *Oranje*. The kid was carried up the gangway on a stretcher, at the foot of which lay a swell new American kitbag, complete with pockets, attachments, an aircraft compass and small gifts for the family, which Billy had acquired over these past few weeks. As they went on deck, a waiting seaman said he'd take the kitbag to be fumigated.

'I'll return it to yer tomorrow.'

Billy never saw it again. There were con men everywhere, of course. But there came a point when an honest scrounge turned into theft – and this was it. He was fortunate only that he'd kept by his pillow the old haversack that contained the tobacco tin with the shrapnel splinter, his signed 510 card from Outram Road, and his pyjama jacket stained with the blood of countless Kuching bedbugs. They were all Billy had left to take home to Nana to show as his war souvenirs.

MP Brown was not aboard *Oranje*. He'd left two days earlier on the hospital ship *Manunda*, returning home at a more leisurely pace via Borneo, to give its seriously ill patients a longer voyage to recuperate.

'They say we're calling at Labuan for a time,' he'd told Billy before he left.

'Remember that night we were chained on the wharf . . . and the girls came down to bathe at the tong.'

'Yeah. The ladies of Labuan...'

Brownie had a wife and infant daughter, whom he'd barely seen, waiting for him at home in Brisbane. Their faces came to him now with particular poignancy.

'If you're going to Borneo, you might see some of the fellers from Sandakan. Harry. The Corp. Joey Crome. You never know...'

'Maybe. Hope so.'

It had been almost a month since their release, yet still nobody had heard anything definite from the men of B and E Force. Talk had gone around Changi of hundreds of deaths at Sandakan and even of forced marches, after a story appeared in the Australian newspapers in early September. But how much was true, and how much 'borehole rumour', nobody could say. The whole place lived on furphies circulated at the latrines. They even made a song about it for the concert parties:

> It's all round the boreholes tonight,
> It's all round the boreholes tonight,
> By the sinking of the Bismarck
> We'll be home before Christmas –
> It's all round the boreholes tonight.

Some joke. But even if there had been a disaster of the kind that had overtaken the men building the Burma-Thai railway, two out of every three of them had come back. So surely there'd be many survivors from Sandakan...

'If I hear anything, I'll let you know,' MP promised.

'Me, too, Brownie.'

So Billy the Kid and Myles Peace Brown went home their separate ways.

The *Oranje* also took its time, to give the POWs aboard a chance to recover something of their health and fitness. The authorities didn't want to give the home folk too much of a shock! The kid was up after a couple of days; and once able to eat properly again, he began to put on fat like a baby. He was still young – not yet 20 – and responded quickly to the improved conditions: a clean ship, proper diet and careful nursing. On average, each man gained an extra stone in weight. The six days it took to thread through the islands to Darwin took on all the aspect of a tropical cruise – marred only by the death of one poor fellow from cerebral malaria. Having survived all the horrors of the war, he was buried at sea only a day out from Australia.

The people of Darwin gave them a tremendous welcome. The returning men were surprised to see the amount of damage inflicted on the northern port during the Japanese bombing raids: destroyed buildings – the hulls of stricken ships like half-submerged corpses in the harbour. Among them lay the troopship *Zealandia* – on which Billy and 'The Admiral' Nana Tot had voyaged from Sydney to Hobart in 1937, before Dad left for Spain. The boy had wondered, then, where the tides would carry them through life. And here they were together again at war's end. Dad dead on the Ebro. The *Zealandia* sunk. Billy somewhat damaged, but not yet wrecked.

Indeed, no. Over the past week several hundred seriously ill men had been evacuated through Darwin by air. But *Oranje* was the first of the hospital ships to arrive; and as the great white vessel drew to her berth, she was saluted with a flight of aircraft overhead, and crowds of people lining the streets to cheer the returning POWs, as they were driven in convoy to a picnic at Mindil Beach.

They arrived to messages of greeting from the Duke of Gloucester and General Blamey, the bands playing 'Rolling Home' and 'Waltzing Matilda'. There were sandwiches, and sausages on the campfire; cricket and tug-o-war on the beachfront; trifles, and iced buns, and proper Australian beer. Another fly-past of a few

Sunderland flying boats followed, dropping streamers – which with coarse good humour turned out to be dozens of toilet rolls, and welcome nonetheless to men who'd spent years without any...

Above all there was the sheer familiarity of the scene. People in the street were speaking with the accents Billy had known since childhood. The girls and women were unmistakably Australian, as Billy remembered them after four years away. Smell. Taste. The touch of the earth, and the sun on his skin. There were coconut palms and bougainvillea by the beach as he knew from the tropics – but also the olive-grey leaves of the gum trees refracted, menthol sharp, against an endless sky. The service clubs were thrown open to them, and they experienced once more the jostle and swill of an Aussie bar. Billy was measured up for a winter uniform with long strides and his two service ribbons, for the day he came ashore in southern ports.

By such means did the kid come to realise that he was almost home.

Billy felt the same as they steamed across the Gulf of Carpentaria and rounded Cape York, to see the sea stained red with plankton skirting the Barrier Reef, ever southwards towards Brisbane. There the bands played 'Old Soldiers Never Die' and 'There's a Boy Coming Home on Leave', as those Queenslanders among the 820 servicemen aboard came down the gangplank onto their native soil again. And men spoke about the horrors they'd endured. The next day, for example, newspapers carried the first reports from Lieutenant Gordon Weynton about the secret radio he'd built at Sandakan with Rod Wells, the betrayal of the underground network, their torture and imprisonment at the infamous Outram Road jail.

As for the fate of those men left at Sandakan, Billy had learnt little more. Not in Brisbane. Not in Sydney. Articles had appeared in mid-September, saying that the prisoners had been marched to a place called Ranau, in the highlands near Mount Kinabalu, and that none were now alive at the Sandakan camp. The day after *Oranje* left Darwin, the big news was that only six of the 2500 POWs had survived, of whom four had just reached Labuan. Among them were Keith Botterill, who'd often sat with the Dead End Kids singing the 'Wringle-wrangle Ram', and Bill Sticpewich, who'd seen Captain Hoshijima knock Billy unconscious out the office door that day he and Brownie had been arrested. But *Oranje* was at sea when the story was published. The kid didn't hear about it – and it was quickly subsumed by other post-war news.

Besides, as the ship slid under Sydney Harbour Bridge and berthed at Pyrmont, Billy found other memories taking over as he was transported back to the haunts of his childhood. Literally so. For his Aunt Ilma arranged a leave pass, and took him to lunch at Romano's restaurant in the city, full of pride and admiration at her nephew's uniform, ribbons, and size 14 boots – though the kid was embarrassed in front of his cousin Wilhelmina when somebody pointed out that his fly buttons were undone.

They didn't speak much of his POW experiences, for relatives had been advised not to ask – and the men not to think – about unpleasant things, for the sake of their mental well-being. Foolishly so, we now recognise. Nor did Billy stay all afternoon. He'd slipped his leave pass through the wire fence for reuse by a few Victorian mates unable to leave the wharf, and arranged to meet them at a pub for a late beer, where they rediscovered all the crush of six o'clock closing: men clamouring outside, fellers at the back unable to get anywhere near the barmaid. They also encountered a new arrangement, to meet wartime shortages.

'We've always gotta look after the diggers,' said some old bloke on the footpath, pushing a couple of empty glasses at Billy.

'What are they for? We don't want your dirty pots.'

'He's doin' you a favour, mate,' said the chap next to him. 'They won't serve you a beer unless you've got a glass.'

As Billy faced the exigencies of returning to this present, civilian life, remembrance of a brutal imprisonment in Sandakan receded from the forefront of his mind. It was natural enough. In any event, Aunt Ilma and the family *knew* where he was – unlike the relations of those 2500 other men, whose ultimate fate was unknown, beseeching government for news of their loved ones. Had any more been found alive? And if not, where and how had they died? The first articles spoke of deaths from malnutrition and disease. Later ones told of unbearable Japanese atrocities. Which was true? This was information that the government, by and large, could not give people. Even as the *Oranje* reached Sydney, Parliament was being told that army investigators in North Borneo were trying to trace individual prisoners' remains – but it was proving difficult. The camp at Sandakan had been burnt down. Evidence destroyed. And most of the graves were unmarked.

The distress of these families was borne upon the kid directly as time went by. From Sydney they steamed to Port Melbourne, where *Oranje* tied up at Princes Pier on 30 September. A crowd of more than a thousand people swept the military police aside, engulfing the returning soldiers in what the *Argus* called 'a tidal wave of emotional humanity'. There were flags, and sprigs of wattle, and cheers, and hugs and kisses. And as Billy was being carried down the gangplank on a stretcher to the cars waiting to drive them to Heidelberg Repatriation Hospital, a radio broadcaster stuck a microphone and tape recorder in his face.

'What's your name, son?'

'Young. Billy Young.'

'Look young. How old are you?'

'I'm 19.'

'Must be one of the crew, eh?'

'No. I'm a soldier – 2/29th Battalion.'

'How old were you when you joined up?'

'Oh... 15.'

He went on to say a little about Singapore, and Sandakan, and Nana Tot waiting for him in Hobart. The interview must have resonated; because after he got home Billy started to receive letters from people all over asking if he knew their husbands, sons or brothers who'd also been at Sandakan, and – desperately – if he had any information about them. He could rarely reply beyond the pleasantries: and certainly, with a dismay that only increased over the years, he could never tell people what they wanted to hear. For he simply did not know.

It was seven weeks before he got home. The kid spent five days at Heidelberg being treated for hookworm and beriberi, which persisted in his lower legs. From there he was flown to Tasmania, where he spent a few weeks in the military hospital at Campbell Town south of Launceston; then went on to the Repat in Davey Street, Hobart. Doctors on their rounds asked if they might examine and press his puffed-up ankles, for they didn't often come across such exotic diseases as beriberi. And Billy's family came to visit him: Nana, his uncles and aunts – rather as strangers at first, yet slowly recasting those links in the chain of relationship that bound them together.

Not long after he arrived, the family gave Billy a welcome-home party at the boarding house run by his Aunt Ada, not far away in Collins Street. Presents were given, among them a triangular AIF flag embroidered for him by Aunt Elsie when he was away at the war – complete with his name, army number, battalion, service medals and wound badges. The lot, in fine needlework.

As it turned out, he'd come bearing gifts for them as well. They sat rather formally on upholstered chairs in the lounge room, looking at Billy's bloodstained pyjama jacket, his bit of shrapnel, and *go-hyaku-ju's* signed prison card 510, without really comprehending. Instead they lamented the loss of the American kitbag with its more interesting presents. It felt a little awkward and strained. The kid reached into his pocket, pulled out a packet of cigarettes, and lit up. At once all conversation stopped, and Billy felt the family eyes upon him. Unease turned to embarrassment.

'What is it?' he stammered. 'Don't you like me smoking?'

'Oh no, Keithy,' for the old name stuck. 'You go right ahead. Don't mind us.'

Silence fell again, like a lead curtain. Staring at him.

'Would you like one?' he asked eventually, proffering the packet.

'No, no, son. We couldn't take your last cigarettes.'

'They're not me last. I got plenty. Look!'

He upended his haversack, and a whole carton of Players tipped onto the floor.

His uncles fell upon them with cries of delight. 'Tailor-made!'

'There's more where they come from.'

Within moments the room was filled with the blue fog of tobacco smoke, and the atmosphere transformed into one of happy, noisy reunion.

'Tomorrow's ration day, you see, Keithy. We've all run out of cigarettes. And we don't get our next lot of coupons till then.'

They went home with enough fags to last them a week.

Thus, by degrees, Billy was reintroduced to post-war society. He remained in hospital until the third week of November, when he returned to the depot. But he was anxious to get out of the army as quickly as possible to start his new life. He'd been fined ten days' pay for going AWL to belatedly celebrate his 20th birthday, for God's sake! The kid was discharged on 11 December, and went home to live with Nana again in the red-brick house at New Town.

The whole business of liberation and readjustment, however,

was not as easy as he'd thought. As time went by, Billy discovered the paradox that freedom was both more than it seemed, and less than it promised. More, because without the daily orders and routines of military life, he was thrown upon his own resources to motivate and discipline himself. If he wasn't careful he could become as aimless as his dad had once been before his conversion to Communism. And less, because this necessarily meant restrictions. You weren't at liberty to do whatever you wanted: for even the most independent little boat must be rigged and steered, if she's not just to drift upon the wide sea.

The restraints on freedom came in all kinds of ways. Small things, for instance, like table manners, or the rules of basic hygiene. Billy had spent so long in a dehumanising prison that he was constantly at risk of slipping back into the old ways and shocking Nana. Forgetting. He could barely speak to his family about it, beyond a few jokes. How could he tell them of picking a grain of filthy rice from a crack in the floor and eating it? Or of lying for days in a cell smeared with his own shit, and not a scrap to wipe himself? Yet how hard it was, always having to meet other people's expectations of normal behaviour. Please pass the salt. Use a fork. Wash your hands when you've been to the bathroom, Keith. Change your socks. Don't spit on the floor. That wasn't normal in Outram Road!

Yes, and there were the big things. Billy hadn't been home a fortnight before Nana was saying it was time he thought about a job. He began a returned-serviceman's trade course at a cabinet-making shop, but it was too soon. Too many dark memories were lurking unexamined beneath the consciousness. Too many frustrations unexpressed. Too many conflicts unresolved between the prisoner of war and the civilian. And there was no one with whom to discuss it, beyond the doctors' advice to 'just put it behind you, son...don't think about it'. A few months into the job, Billy one day smashed a hammer into the piece he was making; he was fortunate that his employer – a returned man himself – at least understood.

The kid went back to hospital – to the Claremont Convalescent Home, and was there when Lady Mountbatten came on a State visit that Easter of 1946. Billy reminded her that the last time she'd seen him was at Changi, as she'd come around the corner, with the fellers still under the showers. Lady Edwina laughed. Again. She remembered it too. And she went on to remark that the spirit, good humour and cheerfulness of the Australian ex-POWs was the same as always!

Perhaps. But each man also had his own torments to deal with, and each would do so in his own way. The war had changed them, and trying to reconcile that past with this present took a long time. Some never made it – never properly came out from behind the prison bars. In the case of Billy the Kid, it was several years before he felt sufficiently free to begin to settle down, and follow his Uncle Cocky into the building trade. He'd made several trips to Melbourne, gone to a battalion reunion, seen old Pop Jepson and Dad's fiancée Marie, for one last time, in Sydney – trying to draw together the strands that had woven the fabric of his youth. The kid was now a man, and he sought to make sense of it all.

For the army – as the man who'd enlisted as a barely literate teenager now recognised – the army and the battalion had become his schoolroom. And the men – those brothers-in-arms with whom he served – had been his teachers.

He went on a fishing holiday just out of Coff's Harbour with his mate MP Brown, and they spent much time talking about Outram Road and Sandakan: for the shadows of these places lay deep across both their lives, and for the most part they were unacknowledged to anybody else. It was Brownie, in fact, who confirmed for Billy that neither Bob Shipsides nor Harry Longley had survived the atrocities of North Borneo. Nor had Joey Crome and Wally Ford – two of those dear Dead End Kids who'd been sent to Kuching, and from there to Labuan.

Bill had guessed it, of course. But as to the how or the why of it, Brownie didn't know. And it would be years before Billy heard any answers from the six who came home from the Sandakan death marches:

> *Where jungle canopy blocks sunlight from the ground,*
> *Where towering mountain peaks lie covered in cloud,*

Six. Only six survivors from two and a half thousand men.

And while, in the aftermath of war, the lives of those who came home flowed down many different channels – and indeed for decades the very name Sandakan became almost forgotten by another generation of Australians – for those few who knew or who remembered, it burned as one of the most appalling tragedies of the Second World War.

> *Where foul black swamp and deadliness abound*
> *There, falling leaf and twig became their shroud.*

# 15

# AFTERMATH

*You cannot tell a battlefield*
*Once the dead are buried...*

The newspaper articles published in the first months after the war contained merely hints of the Sandakan story. A few more details were added in reports of the war-crimes trials the following year. The tribunal that condemned Hoshijima at Labuan, for instance, heard about eye-gouging – apparently a reference to what Bill Sticpewich saw when Billy the Kid was jabbed in the face and knocked out of the commandant's office on that evening of his escape.

The Sandakan disaster was further fleshed out in an ABC broadcast written by the journalist Colin Simpson in 1947. The previous year he and a party had travelled the route of the death marches with Major Harry Jackson of the British-Australian Reward Mission: interviewing the survivors, Japanese guards, and above all the Borneo people who'd helped the prisoners of war. The purpose of Jackson's mission, indeed, was to identify and recompense those locals who'd assisted. His 90-page report to the government, outlining the story in full, was supposed to have been tabled in Parliament – but it does not appear to have been. Perhaps it was felt that it would be too upsetting to be seen by the relatives of the dead. Harry Longley's brother Gerald, for example, was curtly sent away empty-handed when he first approached the Australian War Memorial in the 1970s seeking information.

Major Jackson's report instead lay in the archives – along with more sensitive material relating to an abortive Sandakan rescue mission, Operation Kingfisher – until released to the public (including Gerald Longley) under the 30-year rule. Only then, and in the decades that followed, did historical researchers really expose in all its horrid substance the calamity that was Sandakan.

Following the arrest of those POWs and civilians involved with Sandakan's underground network, and the departure of most of the officers for Kuching in late 1943, conditions at the camp – hard as they'd been – began to deteriorate into the ultimate catastrophe. The evening singsongs and concerts that Billy the Kid had known and which helped to make life a little more bearable, the boxing matches and Gunboat Simpson's pontoon school, all ceased in time to be. Under an evermore sadistic regime, existence descended into a mere brute struggle for survival.

There were then less than 2500 prisoners: about 1800 Australians from the amalgamated B and E Forces in the main camp, and over 600 British in the No. 2 compound a short distance away. They were expected to maintain the same work rate at the airfield, yet the rice ration was cut by a third from 17 to 12 ounces a day – and then reduced to eight from June 1944. It was supplemented by a few vegetables like tapioca, taro and swamp cabbage, and scraps of meat when the Japs permitted. The punishments for being caught outside the wire or with foodstuffs were severe: beatings, log torture, confinement in the cage for weeks at a time, such that some men died. And not just from the enemy. The historian Lynette Silver says that the Australian camp master, Captain George Cook, asked Hoshijima to build another punishment box, and had his own starving men caged for stealing food. Eight, confined at his request 'for the duration' of the war, were dead within a few months.

Malaria, beriberi, dysentery, hunger and exhaustion also took their toll. The death rate, which until now had remained relatively low, began to rise. By late 1944 there were just over 2400 prisoners, of whom more than 600 were sick – though that didn't deter the guards forcing as many as possible into work parties to repair the airfield after Allied bombing raids began in October. Hoshijima had a large POW sign made for the camp, but it wasn't always seen by the pilots. Only after several prisoners were accidentally strafed did he have it moved to a more prominent position. Still, with the war obviously getting closer, hopes rose among the POWs that they might soon be free – especially when a major raid on Christmas Day finally put the airfield out of action.

The Japanese, however, were resolved to rid themselves of any threat the prisoners might pose – even if it meant mass murder, to quote Major Jackson's report. By early January 1945 all work stopped at the airfield. So did the rice ration, though 90 tons of rice were stored under Hoshijima's house, and the POWs were reduced to their own reserves of three ounces a day. Supplies of Red Cross drugs and bandages were deliberately withheld from the prisoners, as were 160 000 anti-malarial quinine tablets. The death toll rose accordingly: 65 Australians alone in January. And orders were given for the fittest prisoners to prepare for the first of three death marches – over 150 miles up a dense jungle track to the village of Ranau in the highlands, beneath Mount Kinabalu.

There were 455 men – some 335 Australians and 120 British – in the first march: among them Keith Botterill, who'd joined the Dead End Kids' singalongs, and Bill Moxham – two of the six who survived from those who'd been at Sandakan at the beginning of 1945. The first group of 50 men set out on 28 January, apparently believing they were headed for some fabled 'land of plenty'; the rest in eight similar parties, under Japanese guard, over the following days. They'd been chosen for their strength, but that was a relative term. Not one could have been considered 'fit' for such a march: malnourished, weakened by disease, and dressed in rags, only one in ten had leather boots. Some were given Japanese cloth-and-rubber footwear; but they were useless in knee-deep mud and water, for the wet season was upon them, and were mostly discarded. Despite ulcers, stones and jungle thorns, bare feet gave a better grip – especially as men had to carry not only their own supplies meant to last four days (later eked out to eight), but up to 60 pounds weight each of Japanese ammunition, rice and equipment.

The going was made even worse by the route chosen to cut the track. The local Dusun people as a whole loathed the Japanese; and ordered to map a *rentis* or path through the jungle to Ranau, had selected the steepest and most difficult terrain – up saw-toothed mountains, over swamps and rushing rivers – never thinking that European POWs would be forced to march along it as coolies at the point of an enemy gun.

Within days of entering what became known as the 'green cage', the first deaths occurred. Some prisoners collapsed and died where they were of exhaustion. Others, too weak to go any further, said goodbye to their friends, left messages for their loved ones, were given a last cigarette, and were shot by guards bringing up the rear (who often robbed them of what little they had left). Several men sought to escape into the jungle; and while a few were rescued by local people, none from the first march lived long enough to return home safely. Snakes, crocodiles and all the deadly perils of the wilderness got them. Many probably expected nothing else but a quick death as free men.

'Bugger this!' Gunboat Simpson is reported to have said during the second march – before he simply walked off into the jungle, and was never seen again.

However that may be, when the first five groups of prisoners reached Ranau after some 15 days, about a quarter of their number had died. As had many in the last four groups who reached the village of Paginatan, below Ranau, where they remained for the next month. During that time, deaths from disease and exhaustion multiplied rapidly at both places – as if the human body, having survived the extremes of the track, could withstand nothing further. By late March, only some 60 men were still alive at Paginatan. And by the end of April, of the 160 POWs who had reached Ranau less than 60 were also living. In other words, almost three-quarters of those who left Sandakan at the end of January were dead.

The death rate was exacerbated by the brutality of the Japanese and Formosan guards under the command of a Major Watanabe. Debilitated as they were, men were forced to go on food and wood-gathering parties; and 50 of the least unwell were ordered as pack animals to carry 50-pound sacks of rice each down the steep, 26-mile track to the Japanese base at Paginatan, and walk back again. It was a five-day trip, and claimed many lives. But for those like Keith Botterill who survived the five journeys, the opportunity to filch a little rice on the way was worth it.

For the rest of those in the camp at Ranau under the clouded ramparts of Kinabalu, the mountain that is sacred to the spirits of the dead continued to claim its own. While the local people did try to help these poor, miserable wretches where they could with gifts of food, the penalties for stealing rice and certainly for escape were barbaric. Gunner Albert Cleary, recaptured after an attempt at escape, was beaten, tortured, tethered to a tree for days, and cut down only at the end, where he died in the arms of his mates. A memorial cairn to them all now stands on the site, with a stone for every one of the prisoners who died on the marches. And in May, Keith Botterill's best friend, Richie Murray, heroically took sole responsibility for a group raid on a Japanese food store. He, too, was tied to a tree – albeit briefly – before being bayoneted to death.

This atrocity took place at a new campsite. The first Ranau compound was not far from the airfield; but when Allied bombing raids began in late April, the Japanese moved the POWs about a mile away to what became known as the Number 1 jungle camp. By now, only 56 of the 455 prisoners who had left Sandakan still lived. But even this was not enough for their murderers. During the terrible month of May the majority died; and by 10 June perhaps only 20 were alive. On that day, ten who were too sick to move were carried from their hut and shot; the rest were sent to a Number 2 jungle camp, by the river about five miles from Ranau – there to await the arrival of the second march from Sandakan. But when the survivors of that expedition reached them on 28 June, only six still breathed.

In the five months following the departure of the first march, Japanese ill-treatment and Hoshijima's policy of deliberately withholding food and medical supplies from the POWs still at Sandakan had resulted – as was no doubt intended – in a dreadful death toll. Over that time about a thousand prisoners died at the camp. Among them, in late March, was Snowy Bryant who had fought Punchy Donohue in that memorable bout. He was followed to the grave a few days later by Bob Shipsides – the Corp, who'd been like a father to Billy the Kid; who'd held him after his flogging, crying 'the bastards!' It was said that Bob's family always kept a night-light in his room, for the time he'd come home.

But death was taking almost all of them. Keith Gillett, who'd promoted Snowy Bryant, died from beriberi and malaria at Ranau in March; and Punchy Donohue himself succumbed at the end of May. Unbeknown to any of them, Joey Crome and Wally Ford – who had volunteered to go from Kuching to Labuan Island to help build an airfield with 300 British troops – had both died from disease and malnourishment. They were at least spared a worse tragedy. In March 1945 the 112 Labuan survivors were taken ashore at Brunei. By 10 June, after several moves, the 40 or so who still lived were taken up a jungle track not far from Miri and machine-gunned; Miri, where Billy and Joey Crome on board the *Yubi Maru* had seen the monster rise from the deep, and rip the peaceful night asunder.

Harry Longley was still alive at Sandakan, however, when Hoshijima was relieved as commandant in mid-May by a Captain Takakuwa, with orders to march the fewer than 900 remaining POWs to Ranau, and to close the camp down. The large POW sign, one of Hoshijima's few decent initiatives, was immediately removed. The Allies, believing from this and false local intelligence that the prisoners had already gone, resumed their bombing raids, causing many more deaths.

By 29 May there were just over 820 prisoners living at Sandakan. That morning, the able-bodied were assembled with their few possessions, and the camp set on fire. The sick were carried from the hospital huts and dumped outside, and the buildings were also burnt to the ground. Ammunition dumps were exploded. And as the infernal night descended, a total of 536 POWs – 439 Australians and 97 British – some merely hobbling on crutches, set out to march to Ranau in 11 separate groups. Harry Longley was with them – as was Doctor Picone, who had saved Billy's leg after the snakebite, and the camp master Captain Cook. Believing an Allied invasion was imminent, the Japanese left the rest of their mates – 288 sick men unable to move – lying on the open ground under the tender supervisions of Lieutenant Moritake and his crew.

For those on the march it was of a policy of extermination, as the Japanese well knew, for they'd lost hundreds – perhaps thousands – of their own soldiers making the overland trek from Sandakan to Jesselton. The first deaths in the 'green cage' among the POWs of the second march began soon enough, for these men were in even worse condition than those who undertook the first trek. Any who weakened or fell behind were killed – 35 massacred at one river crossing alone. By the time the column reached the jungle camp at Ranau a month later, over 350 men – two-thirds of those who had set out on the second death march – had already perished. Yet, remarkably, two men who escaped into the jungle during the second march survived...and returned home to tell the infamous tale.

The first was Gunner Owen Campbell. Taking advantage of a diversion on 7 June when the column was strafed by Allied aircraft, he slipped into the jungle with four others, after first rifling Japanese food supplies. The party split after some days, for Campbell's mate, Private Ted Skinner, was suffering badly from dysentery and could no longer keep up. Indeed, a few days later Skinner took his own life, in a noble act of self-sacrifice, so as not to hold his friend back, and Campbell rejoined the other three by a riverbank. Yet within a week all but Campbell were dead – two shot by a Japanese soldier hidden in a fishing canoe they tried to hail, the third to sickness. For the next 12 days Campbell wandered alone in the jungle: weak, delirious, shot through the wrist by a Jap as he tried to cross a river on a log, in constant fear of attack by wild creatures.

At length he was picked up by two Dusun men in a canoe, who took him to their *kampong* where the headman, Kulang, was away on a secret mission with an Australian Special Operations group working behind enemy lines. The villagers tended Campbell – bathed, fed, clothed and hid him – until Kulang returned, and eventually led him to the commando camp. After an emotional reunion with his fellow countrymen, arrangements were made to take Owen Campbell downriver, where he was picked up by flying boat on 24 July and – after almost seven weeks of endurance – flown to the Allied base on Morotai Island.

At about the same time that Campbell escaped, Bombardier Richard Braithwaite also made his successful run for it. Noticing that he was briefly out of sight from the guard as they crossed a small creek, Braithwaite slipped into the bush and hid beside a log. A malarial cough gave him away, but while a Japanese soldier saw him and unslung his rifle, amazingly he didn't shoot, but passed on up the track. Braithwaite didn't return the compliment. Seeing a lone enemy soldier pass by a little later, the POW battered him to death with a branch – astonished at the strength he found in the pent-up fury from years of torment.

For the next six days Dick Braithwaite roamed the jungle, at constant risk from snakes and scorpions, until he was picked up by a fisherman called Abing, and taken to a *kampong* near the Sapi River. Like Campbell, he was fed and hidden by the villagers at great risk to themselves, for many Japanese were in the area. From there, he was taken by canoe to Liberan Island and picked up by an American PT boat. By 15 June – just over a week after he'd escaped – Dick Braithwaite was telling his astounding story to Allied commanders: astounding not just because of his survival, but for what it said about the Special Operations' own intelligence failings.

When bombing resumed at Sandakan in early May, the POW camp had not been abandoned as thought. There were still over 800 prisoners there – and when the second march left at the end of May, more than 280 sick men were left behind. Yet despite Braithwaite's news in mid-June, no attempt was made to save them. An earlier rescue plan, codenamed Operation Kingfisher, had stalled through a combination of bungling, bad luck and faulty intelligence, and was ultimately abandoned. Indeed, the regular forces were not even properly informed when Braithwaite told of the true position. Bombing raids on the Sandakan campsite continued until late July when, Lynette Silver says, the RAAF learned by chance that prisoners were still there. One great tragedy of the Sandakan story is that the remaining POWs were finished off not just by their Japanese enemies, but also by the inadequacies of their own Australian command. The resulting attempt to secrete the truth about Kingfisher in bureaucratic files, and to wrongly blame the US General Douglas MacArthur for its failure, may help explain why details of the Sandakan story were withheld from the prisoners' relatives for so long.

Whether a rescue attempt would have succeeded – or whether it was too late – can be endlessly debated. By the end, the Japanese were determined to 'annihilate them all'. And so they did. When the expected Allied invasion failed to materialise, the sick left at Sandakan huddled behind a barbed-wire enclosure, seeking shelter under humpies erected in a grove of rubber trees. Deprived of medicine and all but mere scraps of food (while the Japanese guards had plenty), however strong the bonds of mateship, their bodies could take no more and their souls departed. Trevor Dobson, who had sung of the 'Wringle-wrangle Ram', died on 10 June. The previous day, 75 men had been trucked to the start of the Ranau track and ordered to begin a third march. Some were shot even as they disembarked. The rest were never seen again.

As if starvation and medical neglect were not sufficient forms of murder, the men still at Sandakan were beaten and tortured to exacerbate the process; and in one unspeakable act of Christian mockery, Moritake crucified a British prisoner accused of stealing pig meat – his body mutilated and his corpse left to decompose nailed on a cross. By 12 July only 53 were alive – and the following day, 23 who could still walk were taken to the airfield and shot.

Moritake, sadly for the hangman, died of malaria a few days later, and was succeeded by a Warrant Officer Murozumi. By early August, when they had been given no food for a week, only five prisoners – four Australians and one Briton – still lived. And on the

15th – the very day that Hirohito announced Japan's surrender – Murozumi took the last Sandakan survivor from the compound and beheaded him. He was Private John Skinner, brother of the man who had bravely committed suicide so that Owen Campbell might have a chance at escape.

The story was every bit as horrific for those at Ranau – except that four managed to escape successfully by the end. A total of 183 prisoners from the second march reached the Number 2 jungle camp on 28 June: 142 Australians and 41 British. They were all exhausted and debilitated – but even more shocking was the discovery that only six were still alive from the first march. It was clear what their own fate was to be.

The two groups were kept separate at first, and for some weeks men had to find shelter in the open until a hut was built. The rice ration was only two ounces a day; and there were no medicines for the sick available to Dr Picone and Dr Oakeshott. Yet still men were forced to trudge miles carrying wood, water and food for the Japanese, beaten and kicked when they fell behind. Not surprisingly, they died in ever greater numbers.

Among them, on 5 July, was Billy's dearest mate, Harry Longley. He had survived the second death march; but on that day, carrying a load along the track, Harry could go no further and collapsed. He, who had so loved life to the full.

Keith Botterill and Nelson Short, who were with him, picked Harry up and sat him against a tree. They found a cigarette stub in a pocket, lit it up, and placed it in Harry's mouth: for he'd rarely been seen without a fag hanging from his lips.

Then – as they told it to Bill Young years afterwards – they had to leave him. Shortly afterwards came the sound of Japanese shots.

'Harry's had his last cigarette,' they said. The last for many of them.

By the middle of July, when the men moved into a new hut, only

72 were still alive. Actually it was a few more than that, because four of them – Botterill, Short, Bill Moxham and Frank Anderson – had escaped two days after Harry died. Stealing food from a Japanese rice dump, they made a bolt for it on 7 July: through Ranau and down the track that led to Jesselton. For days they hid in a cave, hoping Anderson's dysentery would stop. Later they moved to a deserted hut, five miles from Ranau, where they were discovered by a headman called Barigah. Showing extraordinary courage, Barigah and his people brought the escapees food and water; warned them of Japanese approaches; built lean-to shelters to hide them in the jungle; and, after Anderson's death, eventually brought news on 13 August that Australian Special Operations men were in the area.

Moxham wrote notes to the commandos saying the three POWs were alive, as were others when they'd left the jungle camp. At length Barigah returned with food and medicine, and a guide to a rendezvous point 12 miles off. It was a slow journey that took days, the men unable to bear the pain of being carried on a bamboo stretcher, and so weak they could scarcely lift their feet. It wasn't until 24 August that they were found by Private John 'Lofty' Hodges slumped over a log – so filthy and emaciated the commando initially thought they were dead.

'How're ya going, boys?' They were the first words from home that Botterill, Short and Moxham had heard since their escape six weeks earlier. And knowing that the war was over and they now were safe, the three wept.

They were taken to headquarters and joined the fourth survivor from the Number 2 jungle camp, Warrant Officer Bill Sticpewich. After having been restored to some health, in late September the four were flown to Labuan – from whence the story of their astonishing endurance became known to the world. Whether any more could have been saved remains one of those tantalising unknowns from the war. The Special Operations team in the Ranau area had by 12 August been ordered to stop all activities so as not to aggravate the danger of the surviving POWs being killed. Yet it appears the last of them were not murdered until 27 August – 12 days after the war had ended, and three days after Botterill's group were found. It was another operational disaster.

The 72 remaining prisoners at the jungle camp had moved into their hut on 18 July. Measuring only 18 by 30 feet, built of bamboo with an atap roof, raised floor and open sides, it at least gave some protection from the pouring rain. Those with the worst cases of dysentery lay beneath the platform floor, with a reeking latrine pit some yards away. But this small concession to hygiene made no great difference. Those who didn't die from disease were carried off either by exhaustion from carrying heavy water buckets and supplies for the Japanese or from the violence of the guards, whose hatred of the prisoners seemed only to increase. The task of burying the dead in the little cemetery was almost overwhelming, and by 26 July only 42 were still alive: 35 Australians and seven British.

Two days later Sticpewich made his break. The warrant officer had maintained his usefulness to the Japanese (and access to scrounge their supplies) – had supervised building the hut, and kept the camp records – such that some POWs regarded him with suspicion, even hostility. Yet he was never fooled by the Japs. Warned by a guard that commandant Takakuwa had received orders to kill them all, he determined to escape and advised Captain Cook to do the same. Cook refused, as did Dr Picone, Dr Oakeshott and some others who were too sick. But Cook promised to bury the camp records in a tin at an agreed place if his own survival was in doubt, for they gave crucial details of POW burial sites, even if Sticpewich had been made to falsify the causes of death. It now appears that Cook didn't do so, but instead gave the records to the Japanese who destroyed them. Certainly the tin has never been found.

Sticpewich and Herman Reither escaped on the night of 28 July and hid in jungle near the camp until the hue and cry died down. Discovered by a local man named Ginsaas, they were sheltered in a hut – and eventually moved to the *kampong* Samang and hid in a house. Tragically, Reither was wounded and suffered dysentery so badly that he died on 8 August – only one day before local agents working for Special Operations found Sticpewich.

Even then it might have been possible to save more POWs. On 9 August, 15 of them apparently were still alive at the jungle camp. At the beginning of the month their numbers had been reduced to 32. Among the dead was Jimmy Finn, the last of the Dead End Kids – the 'pocket Atlas' for whom the burden of the world had ultimately proved too great. And perhaps it was as well. On 1 August Takakuwa called a conference and announced the time had come to implement orders and dispose of the final prisoners. Thus, 17 of the sick were immediately carried up the hill to the cemetery and shot.

In his 1947 report Major Jackson says the remaining five officers and ten other ranks were also then killed; but Lynette Silver states they were seen alive during the intervening weeks. Not until 27 August were the other ranks taken about half a mile from the camp, sat down and told they were to be shot. They were given food, water and cigarettes – a generous gesture – then one by one led away and executed.

As for the officers, among whom were Captain Cook, Dr Oakeshott and Dr Picone, they were told they were to go to Ranau for interrogation. As they were waiting unsuspecting by the track on a hillside overlooking the river and campsite, the guards suddenly opened fire and killed them all.

It was a barbarous end to one of the most atrocious stories in the litany of man's inhumanity. Hoshijima and Takakuwa were among some dozen Japanese executed for the Sandakan-Ranau murders, and over 60 others were sentenced to terms of imprisonment by the war crimes tribunals. Many others fled and were never brought to justice. Yet nothing could ever expiate their guilt, or assuage the memory of those two and a half thousand souls on their collective conscience.

*From Sandakan they came away*
*Stumbling on until they fell;*
*There along the track they lay,*
*Leaving only six to tell*

Bill Young did not learn the full horror of the Sandakan story until perhaps 40 years or more after the war. He'd see old comrades from time to time, and they'd share what knowledge they had: Brownie, of course, until he died too early – electrocuted in an accident – in 1954; Alan Minty and some of his group, though Normie Morris, too, died young. He even came across one of the Dead End Kids – Terry Risely – quite by chance in Hobart in the early '50s.

'Youngie! But you're supposed to be dead.'

'You too, mate.'

Terry, it transpired, had been sent to Kuching with Joey Crome and Wally Ford. Unlike them, however, he'd not gone to Labuan, and so survived.

Yet such meetings were rare, and became even more infrequent as the years went by. It was not until the 1980s, when Bill Young's life seemed to be falling apart, that he actively sought the company of returned servicemen – met the Sandakan survivors Keith Botterill and Nelson Short, Dick Braithwaite and Owen Campbell, who had also assumed him to be dead – and by understanding from them what had really happened, began to confront the shadows that, he realised, so haunted him.

To that point, Bill Young felt the war had left him largely unscathed – except in one important respect. But mentally, at least, he seemed unburdened by the past. He was seldom troubled by nightmares – for he'd been a kid, and right to the end regarded the war as a rather heightened version of a boyhood game. Indeed, once he'd come through the first difficult year or two of adjustment to civilian life, Bill settled down to responsibility and began to establish himself as a successful young builder about town. At one time he even became a counsellor: understanding only too well the internal conflicts that beset so many returned servicemen, though nonetheless shocked when they sometimes resolved themselves in suicide. All through his POW years, Bill had not known one man who'd sought to escape that way. Survival, then, was everything. But now they were home... The tragedy was not merely that some could contemplate no other way out, but that Youngie felt so helpless to prevent it.

As for himself, Bill sought to put those years behind him, as the doctors advised. He didn't join the Returned Services League. He rarely went to reunions. Never attended Anzac Day. He seemed to be doing fine. Apart from this one thing...

For Billy the Kid returned from his war essentially impotent. The years of malnutrition and overwork at Sandakan – of untreated disease, filth, starvation and ruinous isolation at Outram Road, during this critical time in his physical and psychological development – had taken their toll. As had the scenes of squalid sex he'd witnessed as a soldier, far too young, in the brothels and back streets of Johore and Singapore, which left a lasting impression on his mind. It's true that, as hunger and sickness gripped men in the POW camps, their libido tended to disappear almost completely. The body shut down any impulse not necessary for survival: and that was the first of them to go. For most men, as health and liberty was restored at war's end, so was this most basic instinct. Many a liberated digger emerged from the brothels with a grin on his face, saying, 'I can still do it!' To say nothing of the baby boom they fathered when they got home.

Yet Billy was not one of them. His sexual drive never returned. He'd gone to war at 15 a virgin; and came home a man of 20 still a virgin, and indeed unable to function in a normal, sexual way. It wasn't through lack of desire; merely the confident ability to perform. Nor was he unique. 'What sex life?' ask numbers of soldiers returned from more recent conflicts, suffering what is now recognised as post-traumatic stress disorder. 'But this is something I don't even tell my doctor.' And such war wounds are no less painful or enduring for not being visible to anyone else – or even able to be much spoken about. These are not matters to which most men will admit, for they go to the essence of one's perception of self. The world's perception, too. 'I wouldn't admit to it either,' Bill Young observed during the interviews for this book. 'But I'm in my 80s now, and I've nothing to lose.'

In his own case, Billy spent several years after he got home being treated for impotence – a brave thing to do at that time – and with some success. He gained a little experience. At the age of 26 he married, and the prospering couple raised four children. But by the late 1970s the marriage had failed – and Bill Young acknowledged that responsibility for the marital breakdown lay with his own lack of sexual energy. 'It's the one thing I can't forgive the Japs for: they took this part of my life from me.'

However that may be, he sold the holiday home, relinquished almost everything to the family and, keeping $10 000 for himself, left for Sydney in his mid-50s, to establish a new life. There he bought a caravan instead, and spent a couple of years travelling around Australia – thinking, odd-jobbing, trying to let the scars heal. For company Bill started going to the RSL clubs; and back in Sydney he became a regular member, finding much support in the friendship of old comrades-in-arms – gravitating naturally enough to 8th Division veterans – and beginning, through anecdote and shared experience, to exhume those memories of a kid's war he thought had long been safely buried.

It was not without difficulty. The suffering, as well as the camaraderie of battle, may be universal in many ways. A glance – an inflection glimpsed through the telling of some amusing story – is generally enough to convey, to those who *know*, the horror that lies behind it. Yet every encounter is also particular: and as Bill Young listened to men talk of life at Changi, or discuss endlessly the details of incidents that occurred as they laboured on the Burma-Thai railway, he knew he could never intimately be part of that conversation. Few of them knew anything about Sandakan or Outram Road, nor could they share it. He didn't even have his war souvenirs any more. A box containing his bit of shrapnel and 510 prison card had been stolen; and, apart from a few photographs, much of the memorabilia left behind in Hobart disappeared over time.

Only when he met Keith Botterill and Nelson Short did Bill begin to feel he was with those who really understood. Indeed, as they made contact with the children and relatives of those who'd died in the death camps and who still wanted to know what had happened to their loved ones, a support group known as The Sandakan Family was established – which continues to this day into the second and third generations.

As memory, so long repressed, rose to the surface of consciousness, Bill Young decided to write a book about his war. It was his Sydney landlady's idea. The widow of a returned serviceman, Marjorie had become friendly with her boarder in a platonic sense: going out with Bill to various RSL functions, and thus saving him the dilemma of people trying to pair him off with other women in relationships he knew he couldn't fulfil; being something of a shield. And listening to Billy speak of how he joined the army, broke and starving, at 15...of Johore and the battle for Singapore...of the *Yubi Maru*, Sandakan and Gunboat Simpson's pontoon game...of Jimmy Darlington, who had tragically died with his wife in a fire in 1976...of escape, capture and the sheer luck that helped *Yagi* the goat survive two years in Outram Road prison...

Marjorie suggested he should buy an electric typewriter and put it all down on paper. This he did, though the typewriter soon gave way to one of the early personal computers, which contained for him the very great benefit of a spell checker. Billy the man had retained his boyhood love of books, and read widely: science and practical technology, building on the foundations of an interest laid by Rod Wells during those whispered tutorials in their prison cell; Japanese history and culture, trying to understand how the barbarity he'd known during the war had emerged from such a civilised people? Or why, even now, their government refused to formally apologise? Billy found no answers to such questions: still, he discovered that the pleasure of reading books was very different to the labour of writing them. For a market kid who'd spent much of his time playing truant and who left school as soon as he could, spelling was a matter of hit and miss. Hence the advantage of the computer. And for the self-educated adult, grammar, syntax and punctuation – as Bill put it himself – seemed foreign vegetables.

Yet as he worked on his story at nights, home in the rented room from a day's casual work renovating bathrooms and kitchens – as Bill remembered that terrifying night hiding in the drain when Bukit Timah burned...the sight of severed heads on poles in the streets of Singapore during the *Sook Ching* massacres...the look on Moritake's face as he and Brownie were beaten senseless by swordsticks outside the Sandakan boiler house...the inquisitor's knotted rope...the words *Sentenced to be executed* echoing beside him in the Kuching courtroom...the awful weight on his soul of the Outram Road silence...the death of Pieter the Major, so lightly, alone on his lap...the thought of eating a lump of half-digested carrot picked from the shit bucket – as such memories welled up from the depths of his being and spilled with all their awkwardness onto the page, Bill Young realised what a heavy burden he'd been carrying unacknowledged all those years. Merely to express them – as so many others could not – was to find that yoke considerably lightened.

And something else. War and its aftermath had come at great cost to his personal life. Yet in these latter days it offered Billy certain compensations. As he became more truly liberated through the telling of his story, he found himself able to satisfy deeper artistic needs. The boy had always been drawn to singing and poetry. He still sang. Now, as the lines scratched by Sergeant Hatfield on his prison walls came back with remarkable clarity, Bill began to write his own verse.

Entirely self-taught, he also began to paint – at first using a computer programme, later moving to brushes and oils – trying to capture something of that intensity he'd felt as they'd steamed into the painted sunset that evening aboard the *Treasure* across the Bay of Brunei. Indeed, when Billy's book was self-published in 1991, it included many of his poems and illustrations. Flying practice and the sweat box at Sandakan...the black wooden doors of Outram Road...the skeletons at the scabby bath...Habbie lying broken in his cell...

He called the book *Return to a Dark Age*, complete with his own epigraph: *Sometimes when crimes have been committed, it is necessary to go back and mark the spot. This I have tried to do.*

Whatever else may be said of it, his expression is raw and powerful, and the voice struggling to be heard utterly genuine; at times, profound. And it is Billy's *own* voice speaking out to the world, where he might so easily have turned inward and bitter upon himself. It was the making of him.

For his voice is still able to be heard among those keeping alive memory of Sandakan and Outram Road, when the voices of other veterans are becoming fewer and fainter. Reasserting, for as long as traces of ink may be read upon paper, those bonds that were made among the men of the 2/29th Battalion – the whole 8th Division – in the fires of war, and affirmed throughout their imprisonment. In 2004, indeed, Bill Young was awarded the Medal of the Order of Australia for his services to preserving and recording the nation's military history.

'We depended on each other for survival,' Paddy O'Toole used to say, 'and grew together as one big family of brothers. I just love all those guys; I just love every one of them. And that's a big word. Love is a big word.' It is true nonetheless. And continues to be true, though Paddy died on the very day in January 2009 that the battalion remembered the anniversary of the Battle of Muar.

Bill's book *Return to a Dark Age* and its successors opened many doors for the man: leading to invitations for him to speak at reunions and services of remembrance. At schools, where Billy the Kid tries to remind the youngsters that there is nothing 'kid's stuff' about war. They don't believe him, naturally. We're all invincible at that age. As he was himself. And it led to several return visits to Singapore and Borneo, where his verse has charged many an Anzac pilgrimage.

*The boiler's dry, the fire's out,*
*The years have laid the ghosts about,*
*With only now and then a sigh –*
*A whisper from the past – of Why?*

Much has changed at the Sandakan campsite. The dead have been reinterred in a beautiful war cemetery on Labuan Island, where they lie beside the mates from Ranau – their names recorded on the Roll of Honour, the individual remains, for the most part, only 'Known Unto God'. The swamp has been drained and a housing block built where the huts of the other ranks and the Dead End Kids once stood, which is no bad thing: a better life, after all, is the reason the Sandakan men ultimately went to war. Children play and lovers court in a park of remembrance, created in the open space at the crest of the hill where the prison gates and parade ground once were. Where Corporal Shipsides poured water onto the lips of the beaten kid outside the guardhouse, before they kicked him away. But the boiler is still there down the slope, rusting and monumental with the past. And standing by the memorial stone at the site of the Big Tree, as the dawn birds stir and light breaks through the canopy on Anzac Day, it is easy enough to feel the spirits of Harry Longley and Bob Shipsides, and their two and a half thousand brothers move across hallowed ground.

*Ah, Billy, what have you got us into?* He can sometimes hear MP Brown saying it over and over again, during the years of ordeal that followed their escape and recapture. The swordsticks and fractured bones. The cages. The crushing silence on mind and body, sitting cross-legged for 12 hours a day in a solitary prison cell.

*If only we'd stayed at Sandakan we would have been all right.*

When of course they would have been dead, too.

It was all luck. All in the turn of a thumbnail pack of cards. All in the roll of a dice. That the shrapnel fragment hadn't struck the kid a few inches higher. That he'd chosen to walk to the correct ambulance. That they'd seen Jimmy Darlington's torture and decided, when their own time came, to make a run for it.

*Billy, what have you done?* As Moritake's thugs stepped onto the jungle track.

But whenever Bill Young hears those words, his mind is also taken immediately to another summer's day, a year or two after the war, when he and Brownie went on their fishing holiday at Sawtell, near Coff's Harbour.

They were walking down the road from the railway station, talking of such things, when he suddenly turned to MP and said, 'You owe me a beer.'

'What for?'

'Well...I saved your life.'

There was a pause as Myles Peace Brown cogitated. You never had the last word with him. At length he looked Billy the Kid square in the eye and replied:

'Inadvertently.'

# CHAPTER NOTES

NAA refers to files held at the National Archives of Australia, AWM to the Australian War Memorial. Unless otherwise stated, Silver refers to *Sandakan: A Conspiracy of Silence*.

## CHAPTER 1

*Truck:* Details based on author interviews with Bill Young 2007–2011, transcripts deposited at the Australian War Memorial and National Library of Australia. The conversations have been re-imagined.

*Chronology:* As the Japanese destroyed the Outram Road prison records, dates are imprecise. Silver, 96, says the Sandakan eight were sentenced at Kuching on 26 June 1943. Bill's firm recollection is that they were taken straight to the ship. Mo Davis saw the horsebox loaded 'about a fortnight' after he arrived at Kuching in mid-June (Silver, 119), which is consistent with Young. But McGregor, 9, states they arrived at Outram Road on 23 August, as does a schedule compiled by Rod Wells immediately after the war (NAA B3856 144/1/358). As the voyage to Singapore took only a few days, there is a discrepancy I can only reconcile by assuming Bill entered Outram Road some time in mid-1943, probably July. McGregor, 190, was transferred to Changi on 19 July and Wells didn't arrive until March 1944. These lists were compiled largely from memory and are incomplete. They include only British and Australian POWs: a New Zealander (Haberfield), Indian, Dutch, American, Chinese and Malay military prisoners are excluded, as are the Rimau ten. The dates of most other events at Outram Road are also approximations.

*Deaths at Outram Road:* McGregor, 132, and Dean, 95. Dr Taylor witnessed at least 1400 civilian deaths: Nelson, 173, and Firkin, 112.

'*The devil's Kenpeitai*': Tanaka, 26.

*Commands:* I am very grateful to my friend Shuji Yamazaki for his kind assistance with Japanese words, phrases and cultural advice, and for reading what I know must have been a confronting manuscript. I have first used the full command e.g. *Zentai tomare!* [roughly: Squad, halt!], although John Hook, who was an interpreter at the war crimes trials, advises that usually the word *Tomare!* alone was used for POWs, which I adopt thereafter.

*Cell block:* Young interviews, also Young, *Return to a Dark Age*, 139–45.


## CHAPTER 2

*Solitary cell:* Young, *Return*, 145–9, and interviews.

*Bed supports removed:* McGregor, 179.

*Verse: The Young British Soldier* by Rudyard Kipling. Bill remembers this as one of the poems on the Outram Road wall.

*Letter:* Written by William John Young to his mother from Altozona, Barcelona, 10 July 1938. Copy in Bill Young's possession. The letter to his son is lost.

*Hay Street:* Now known as Clarendon Street. *Family background:* Young interviews.

*Adora:* Bill Young's birth certificate names his mother as Adora Young, formerly Shaw, born in England and aged 22 in 1925. There is no will by a person with the name Adora in the Archives Office of Tasmania, nor is there any death of a woman named Adora recorded in the Tasmanian or NSW Registries of Births, Deaths, and Marriages between 1925 and 1978. The searches included the surnames Young and Shaw. Whether Adora died when Bill was an infant, or whether she moved away with her first child, Kevin, (perhaps to take another name) cannot be ascertained. Certainly Bill was told as a boy that his mother had died and he grew up with this belief – although in later life he is aware of other possibilities. The birth certificate states that Adora married William John Young in Sydney on 4 May 1925. No record of that marriage was found in a search of the NSW Registry.

*Dean:* Bill remembers that Penrod Dean first spoke to him through the
cell door about a week after he arrived at Outram Road.
*Kranji:* See Dean, 15–17 for the 2/4 Machine Gun Battalion deployment.

## CHAPTER 3

*Dean's escape:* Penrod Dean and John McGregor, also of the 2/4
Machine Gun Battalion, escaped from Changi to southern
Malaya in mid-March 1942. They were recaptured on 6 April,
taken back to Singapore, and entered Outram Road prison on
24 April. See Dean, 34, and McGregor, 31.
*Attack on guard:* McGregor, 135–9.
*Sewing Machine:* McGregor, 149–51.
*Food trustie and Australian officers:* Dean, 102.
*Vitamin B tablets:* Dean, 108–9.
*Scabies Bath, Ken Bird:* Young, *Return*, 149–56, interviews.
*Bulwara Road, Paddy's Market, Mullet:* Young interviews.

## CHAPTER 4

*Morse code:* Young, *Return*, 173–4, interviews.
*Education:* Young interviews.
*Madam Will You Walk?:* Adapted from a traditional Cheshire song,
'I Will Give You the Keys of Heaven', available on the Internet.
*Tongue biting:* Young, *Return*, 156–7, interviews.
*Depression, Dad converted:* Young interviews.
*Communism:* See *CPA Growth During the Depression*, at www.
greenleft.org.au.
*Newtown eviction: Sydney Morning Herald (SMH)*, 20 June 1931
*Trades Hall fight: SMH*, 5 June 1931.
*Left Wing Bookshop:* Young interviews. See also *Workers Weekly [WW]*
tribute to Big Bill Young, 20 December 1938. It was in Pyrmont-
Ultimo.
*Marie:* Young interviews. Irwin Shaw's *Bury The Dead* was reviewed in
*WW*, 27 April 1937. Bill remembers seeing the play with Dad
and Marie shortly before he left for Hobart, and his father for
Spain.
*Evictions:* Young interviews.

*Hatfield:* Eric Edward Hatfield, Mentioned in Dispatches for his
'Gallantry and outstanding services as a POW' with the guerrilla
group in Malaya (March 1947, Citation AMF 21/A-Z 26, which
incorrectly states he was a POW in Europe). His promotion to
sergeant was not confirmed by the AMF. Details of his escape
from Changi, service with the guerrillas, capture and execution
are in sworn statements to the war crimes investigators by Sgt
Picozzi and others, October 1945 and March 1946 (NAA File
B3856 140/11/898). Dean, 101–2, writes of seeing Hatfield
before his death.

*Execution:* Hatfield was beheaded 6 December 1943, NAA file above.
Also *Sydney Sun*, where Hatfield worked as a journalist,
21 October 1945, interview with Picozzi, where Hatfield is
described as a sergeant.

*Hatfield poems:* Young, *Return*, 164–6.

*Not Understood:* Thomas Bracken (NZ 1843–98). *The Quitter:* Robert
W Service (UK/US 1874-1958). Both are available on the
Internet.

*The Triumph:* Young interviews. *Signs.* Ibid.

*Spain, Numbers:* Inglis, 213; *SMH*, 23 April 1983, *Good Weekend*,
'The 50 fighters nobody wanted to know'. Also Wikipedia
article on Spanish Civil War.

*Hobart:* Young interviews. *Coal bunker: SMH*, 23 April 1983, *Good
Weekend.*

# CHAPTER 5

*Rope making:* Young, *Return*, 177–9.

*Pustules:* Young interview.

*Pig sty, civil servant:* Young, *Return*, 178–9, interview.

*Notebook:* Young interview.

*Morse:* Young interviews. Bill now believes Chris Neilson wrote the code
for him, as he taught both McGregor and Trackson: see Nelson,
171, and McGregor, 174.

*Boyhood:* Hobart, Sydney, Corrimal, Young interviews.

*Letter:* W.J. (Big Bill) Young 1938, see Ch 2.

*Harry and Diana Gould:* See *Green Left Weekly*, 3 August 1994, interview with Diana two years before she died. Available on the Internet. Also photo of Diana in *WW*, 6 January 1939, with a dog called Karl [Marx?]. Harry was author of the *Marxist Glossary*.

*Big Bill in Spain:* See articles in *WW*: *inquiries after Keith*, 26 August 1938; *clenched fists, rifle practice* 13 September 1938; *'fascist bastards'* 11 October 1938; *photo* 25 October 1939; *death* 13 December 1939; *bookshop* 20 December 1939; *memorial service* 7 February 1939; *poem* 17 February 1939.

*Christmas party:* See articles in *WW*, 7 and 20 December 1938, 3 January 1939, including bike, holiday ticket, and Keith's speech.

*Sydney 1940:* Work and attempted naval enlistment, Young interviews. Christina 'Ma' Jepson died Sydney, 16 September 1939, aged 65.

*Bike ride:* Young interviews.

*Enlistment:* Young, *Return*, 2–11, and interviews. 'Martha Young' (the only female name that Billy says he could then spell) still appears as his next of kin on his service papers.

## CHAPTER 6

*Grain of rice:* Young interviews.

*Four bob in the guts!:* Young poem in *Return*, 12–13; also recruit at Royal Park.

*Boom-boom-boom!:* Young, *Return*, 180–1, and interviews.

*Benki toban:* Young, *Return*, 180, and interviews.

*Pig swill and judo:* Young, *Return*, 181, and interviews.

*Night exercise:* Young interviews, and *Return*, 14–15. Service papers show he went to Bacchus Marsh, 7 August 1941.

*Hobart:* Young interview. Formally to 3rd Reinforcements 2/29 Bn 14 September.

*Sibajak:* Formerly in the Dutch East Indies service. Young sailed in Anzac convoy US.12b (Gill Vol I, 434 footnote).

*Rice Biscuit:* Young interviews. Cpl Bill Fairy died Changi, 5 April 1944 (Lack, 281).

*Fremantle:* Young interviews. Service papers show he was fined £3 for breaking ship on 27 September. Bill cannot remember the name of the girl; I call her Rosalind.

*Sexual drive:* Young interviews, also experiences at Johore and Lavender
    Street. The suspension of libido under extreme conditions is a
    common phenomenon. It is said some women cease to menstruate.
*Poker:* Young interviews; also Pat Green. The *Sibajak* reached Singapore
    5 October.

## CHAPTER 7

*The Postman:* Young, *Return*, 163–4, and interviews.
*Liaison letter:* 'Standard of training and discipline of reinforcements
    from Australia', 9 December 1941 (AWM61 S54/1/1902).
*Johore and Tampoi:* Young interviews.
*Singapore bombing:* Warren, 203.
*Malayan campaign:* Warren, Chs 3–12 for full description; Maj-Gen
    John Coates in Dennis et al, 375–80 for excellent short overview.
    Bill's view: Young, *Return*, 16–20.
*Gemas, Muar Road:* Warren, Chs 10–11; Coulthard-Clark, 197–9;
    Christie (Capt Bowring), 39–55; (Dr Brand) 63–84; War Diaries,
    2/30 Bn, 2/19 Bn, 2/29 Bn, Jan 1941.
*Anti-tank gun scepticism:* Warren, 156, 164.
*Body count:* Warren, 168. Some put the body count at 140; 2/19 War
    Diary says 67.
*Sumatra:* Christie, 58–62.
*Yamashita:* Warren, 177, also *casualties*.
*Pond, reinforcements:* Christie, 97–101. *2/19 casualties:* War Diary, Bn
    website.
*O'Toole:* Lack, 19, 30, 73; Young interviews. *At Parit Sulong:* Lack,
    102.
*Withdrawal to Singapore:* Warren, Ch 12. *Argylls: Ibid*, 200.

## CHAPTER 8

*Fall of Singapore:* Warren, Chs 13–16; Christie, Ch 7; Coates in Dennis
    et al.
*Air force:* Warren, 203–5. *Tower: Ibid*, 217.
*Wavell:* Warren, 213. *Yamashita: Ibid*, 216. *Shelling: Ibid*, 221.
*Allied strength:* Best estimate: Warren, 301.
*Brigades:* Warren, 222. *Japanese numbers: Ibid*, 230.

*Barbed wire:* Young interview.
*Tengah:* Warren, 228; Christie, 103.
*Panic:* Warren, 229–30; Christie, 105 and interview.
*Sniper, Pack of cards:* Young interview.
*Percival:* Warren, 230-31. *Cordon:* Ibid, 235.
*27 Bde, Maxwell:* Warren, 234–5.
*Bukit Panjang, confusion:* Christie, 107–10, Young interviews.
*Swamp, wound:* Young, *Return,* 26–7, and interviews.
*Bukit Timah, drain:* Young, *Return,* 28–31, and interviews.
*RAP, ambulance:* Young, *Return,* 32, and interviews. *Alexandra Hospital:* Warren, 261.

## CHAPTER 9

*Sparrow:* Young, *Return,* 161, interviews.
*Sharing, Spike Smith:* Young interviews, and *Return,* 184, where Bill calls him 'Spike Jones' after the bandleader.
*The Green Eye of the Little Yellow God:* By J. Milton Hayes, (1884–1940), on Internet.
*Deserters:* Warren, 249, estimates that by 11 February hundreds of soldiers, the majority of them Australian, were at the docks and in the streets of Singapore. By the end, on 15 February, they numbered thousands. In additional comments to the 2/29 War Diary, Lieut-Col Pond remarks, 14, that up to 40–50 men left the battalion deliberately or when temporarily detached, made no effort to rejoin it, and spent the final days at large in Singapore. An Australian officer estimated that, as morale deteriorated, only about two-thirds of those fit to fight were manning the final perimeter at Tanglin Barracks (Warren, 262). The British have criticised Australian deserters, but their own troops were also involved, as Bill Young witnessed. Coulthard-Clark, 204, and Coates in Dennis, 381, note that Australians made up about 13 per cent of the ground troops yet sustained over 70 per cent of the battle deaths. They pulled their weight. It was a failure of Allied leadership at the highest military and political levels, and the brilliance of the Japanese campaign, that led to Singapore's collapse. Warren, 263, points out that

stragglers are the consequence of lost battles, not the cause.

*Ambulance, Cookie:* Young interviews.

*POWs:* As in other areas of military history, exact numbers are difficult. Warren, 301, estimates the number of Singapore POWs at 120 000, Coates in Dennis at 130 000. Almost 18 500 Australian troops took part in the Malayan campaign, of whom approximately 1800 were killed and 1300 wounded. Many were lost in the jungle fighting, and some escaped to Sumatra and Java. Approximately 15 000 Australian POWs were sent to Changi, Dennis, 477.

*Nurses:* See Dennis, 128, and AWM website captions to photos of Vivian Bullwinkel and nurses. Walker gives a full account of the Australian hospitals in the Malayan campaign and the fate of the staff. *13 AGH moves:* Walker 511, 519.

*Surrender:* Warren, 263–6.

*Changi:* Early days: Christie, *History* 119–26, and interview.

*O'Toole:* Paddy's comments in Lack, 121.

*Bongo:* Young, *Return*, 47.

*Bennett escape:* Warren, 267–8. Moses became General Manager of the Australian Broadcasting Commission.

*Percival:* Warren 272–3. In August 1942 officers at Changi above the rank of colonel were transferred to Formosa (Taiwan), then to Manchuria and other parts of north Asia. At this time, Lieut-Col Frederick 'Black Jack' Galleghan became the most senior Australian officer at Changi.

*Sook Ching:* Warren, 278–9; also an article on the Singapore massacre by Professor Hayashi Hirofumi in the *Asia-Pacific Journal*, 13 July 2009, available on the Internet. The Japanese acknowledge a minimum 5000 victims of the purges; in Singapore the number is put at more than 50 000 people: Warren, 279. Yamashita was hanged for massacres at Manila, over which he had no direct control. His real war crime was ordering the *Sook Ching* killings: Warren, 287.

*Sugar:* Lack, 133.

*Heads, rickshaw driver:* Young, *Return*, 40–2. Photos on Internet – search *Sook Ching*.

*Crucifixion:* Young interviews.

*Thomson Road:* Christie, *History*, 123–6; Silver, 26–7.

*Dead soldier:* Young, *Return*, 43–4.

*Guard changeover:* Young, *Return*, 45. Bob Christie's diary records that the hiatus lasted 17–24 May (see Christie, *Surviving Captivity*, 67).

*Chinese family:* Young, *Return*, 45, and interviews.

*Conversions:* Young, *Return*, 44. *'Black Jack':* Ibid, 46; Christie interview.

*Spike and the benki:* Young interviews.

*'A' Force:* Dennis, 129, 477; Silver, 31.

*'B' Force:* Silver, 31–5; Young, *Return*, 48, and interviews. Silver, 32, states 143 officers and 312 NCOs (warrant officers, sergeants, corporals and lance-corporals) were among the total 1494 men who embarked for Sandakan.

## CHAPTER 10

*Wells Background:* Interview with Mrs Pamela Wells. *Radio:* Speech by P. Wells, 'Sandakan's Secret Wireless', March 2004 at Sandakan memorial, Bendigo; Silver, 86 ff. See also caption to Wells' photo AWM P03863.001.

*Sentence:* After the war it was discovered that Wells had been saved from execution by a typographical error. The Japanese authorities at Saigon approved the two death sentences on Matthews and Wells, but the cipher clerk wrote 'one' by mistake: thus, as the senior officer, Matthews alone was executed (Silver, 156). Eight Chinese and Malay civilians were also executed. *Trial:* Silver, 150–4.

*Torture:* Pam Wells interview, Silver, 132–5.

*Yubi Maru:* Young, *Return,* 48–51; Silver, 36–40.

*Mutiny:* Young interviews, Silver, 40. *Mo Davis:* Silver, 9.

*Tinned food:* Silver, 39, and Young interviews.

*Miri:* Young, *Return*, 51.

*Sandakan, Hoshijima:* Silver, 42 ff.

*Camp:* Young, *Return*, 54–6, Silver, 44–9. *Plunkett:* Silver, 25, 78.

*Wringle-wrangle Ram:* Young interview. See also a version *Wattle Flat Ram* at http://warrenfahey.com. The song was adapted from an old English original.

*Snakes and rats:* Young, *Return*, 58, 66; *Gorilla*: Interviews.

*Escapes: AASC:* Silver, 54–5; *Minty:* Silver, 91.

*Hoshijima speech:* Silver, 59.

*Eyeshades:* Young Interview. *Drains:* Young, *Return*, 69.

*Walsh:* Young, *Return*, 87; Silver, 62.

*Skips:* Young, *Return*, 69; Silver, 69.

*Suga:* Young, *Return*, 61; Silver, 65.

*Flying practice:* Young, *Return*, 67; Silver, 67–8.

*Black Bastard:* Young, *Return*, 68. *Steamroller:* Ibid, 70. *Excavator:*
     Silver 71; the remains are still visible at Sandakan near the boiler.

*Gelignite:* Young, *Return*, 70; Silver, 70.

*Birthday:* Young interviews. *Broadcast:* Silver, 88.

*Airfield opening:* Silver, 77. *Exhibition:* Silver, 83; Young, *Return*, 81.

*Deaths:* Silver, 73, says that by mid-November there had only been 14
     deaths, most from dysentery.

*Dugong:* Young, *Return*, 83. A dugong was also served as a mark of
     respect when a ship called at Sandakan in August 1942, carrying
     the ashes of Japanese submariners killed in the attack on Sydney
     Harbour on 31 May (Silver, 74; also on Internet e.g. www.1942.
     com.au/midget-sub-sydney.html.).

*Christmas:* Silver, 84.

## CHAPTER 11

*Singing, boxing, pontoon:* Young, *Return*, 76-81, and interviews; Silver,
     78, 80–2.

*Benki:* Young, *Return*, 91–3.

*Donohue:* Young, *Return*, 89–91, and interviews; Silver, 79.

*River cavern:* Young, *Return*, 101–2, and interviews; Silver, 79.

*Snake, Brown:* Young, *Return*, 98–9.

*Dried rice:* Called *Hoshiii* in Japan. The rice is cooked, dried, and keeps
     for a long time. Apparently it was among the rations carried by
     soldiers in the field.

*Darlington:* Young, *Return*, 93–6, and interviews; Silver, 93–4, gives
     date as Wednesday 17 February 1943.

*Escape, bashing, Shipsides:* Young, *Return*, 103–6; Silver, 94–5, says it
     occurred three days after Darlington's torture.

*Kitchies:* Silver, 97, says they were aged between 16 and 20, recruited
into the Bushido Youth Corps. Main body arrived at Sandakan
about April 1943, but Bill remembers that six (perhaps an
advance party) were present at his capture and beating. Name
possibly derives from *kichigai* ('crazy people'), or perhaps *kichi*
(military base). 'Titchy' is Australian slang for 'small'.

*Waltzing Matilda:* A. B. Paterson (1864–1941).

*Hoshijima:* Young, *Return*, 106–8.

*Sticpewich:* Young interviews; Silver, 68. Sticpewich was one of only
six prisoners to survive the Sandakan death marches of 1945.
*Report of eye-gouging.* See e.g. *Canberra Times*, 12 January
1946, Hoshijima's trial; also Darlington's torture; also statement
by Keith Botterill in Young, *Long Ago in Borneo*, 22, referring
to Hoshijima poking Bill's eyes and Young's and MP's 'deaths'.

*Kenpeitai HQ, medic:* Young, *Return*, 109–10, and interviews.

*Interrogation:* Young, *Return*, 111–14, and interviews; Silver, 96.

## CHAPTER 12

*Treasure:* Silver, 96, Young interviews.

*Minty:* Young, *Return*, 115–16. *Voyage:* Young, *Return*, 117–24, and
interviews.

*Chess board, bandage:* Young interviews.

*Longley, Taylor:* Dr Jim Taylor grew up in the Yass district and was a
friend of the Longley family. An undated card from Harry sent
from Sandakan as a POW says: '...have seen Jim Taylor, he is
fit and well, best wishes to all, Harry.' Courtesy Harry's brother,
Gerald Longley.

*Jesselton, Labuan, sunset:* Young, *Return*, 122–5, and interviews.
Jesselton is now called Kota Kinabalu, capital city of the
Malaysian State of Sabah.

*Prison:* It is unclear where the prison was. Bill thinks it may have been
near the Batu Lintang barracks (now a teachers' college) where
other POWs were held. He remembers hearing distant shots.

*Chief judge:* Bill remembers him as Lieut-Col Egami Sobei, who also
tried Matthews' group: Silver, 151. *Trial:* Young, *Return*, 131–4.

*Horsebox:* Young, *Return*, 135–6. See also note under *Chronology*

Ch 1. *Sandakan movements:* See chronology in Silver, 318–21.

*Jaywick:* For a good short history see Gill, Vol II Ch 11 'The Mission of
    Krait', 317–25. *Rimau:* Ibid 544–6, 691–2 (see note Ch 13).

*Bombing:* Young, *Return,* 185.

*Pawpaw:* Bill now thinks the other prisoner was Ken Bird. In *Return,*
    187, he names Bluey Rollason, similar in stature to Bird;
    but in an interview Rollason said it wasn't him, though he
    acknowledged taking Bill's pawpaw from the garden shed. Alan
    Minty also got a bashing for stealing a pawpaw. Bluey spoke
    of the sunburn and fake appendicitis, which got him a spell at
    Changi hospital.

*Pop:* Young, *Return,* 169–72; also scabies disinfectant and vines.

*Vegetable garden:* Young interviews.

*B-29 raid:* Young, *Return,* 205–7 and interviews; Rollason interview.
    See Internet e.g. www.pacificwrecks.com/60th/1944/. It says of
    Twentieth Air Force: 53 of 76 B-29 bombers dispatched from
    Calcutta attacked Singapore on 5 November, putting the dry
    dock out of operation for three months. Two B-29 bombers were
    lost, and seven attacked a refinery on Sumatra.

## CHAPTER 13

*Japanese officer:* Young, *Return,* 189–92.

*Ammunition dump:* Young interviews.

*Tongue:* Young interviews.

*Castor oil seeds:* Young, *Return,* 201.

*Rimau:* Gill, Vol II 543–5.

*Page:* McKie, 262; *Silver, Rimau,* 200.

*Habbie:* Young, *Return,* 202–4, interviews. A photograph of Lieut
    Haberfield (known to his family as 'Boy') and a short article on
    his life will be found in the Cenotaph Record of the Auckland
    War Memorial Museum website at www.aucklandmuseum.
    com. He was of the Ngati Moemoe people. My thanks to
    Graham Metzger, Alison Simmons and members of Haberfield's
    family for their assistance. See also notes to Palembang Nine,
    Ch 14.

*Tunnels:* Young, *Return,* 217; McGregor, 194, who says the prisoners were dressed in Japanese khakis for the work parties.

*Bridge:* Young, *Return*, 199–201, and interviews.

*Pieter:* Young, *Return*, 195–7, and interviews. The Dutch website www.wereldoorlog2.com says Capt Pieter Lodewijk van Hemert was born at Sumenep, on Madura Island off Surabaya, East Java, 1 March 1905, and died in prison at Singapore 17 June 1945. He graduated as an infantry officer from the Dutch K.M.A. (Royal Military Academy) and returned to the East Indies in 1926.
The site www.onderscheidingen.nl says Capt Van Hemert was posthumously awarded the Bronze Cross in 1947. His remains are interred in the field of honour at Surabaya, grave B377 (www.ogs.nl, War Graves Foundation).
A file from the Foundation for the Administration of Indonesian Pensions has a 1949 application by Pieter's sister Louise for a rehabilitation benefit. She states that Pieter then had a brother and a sister living in Surabaya, and three sisters in Holland. Bill recalls Pieter telling him that before the war, some members of his family escaped from Java to Europe.
The Dutch veterans' website www.veteranen-online.nl contains a report by Ernest Ferdinand Portier, one of the militia soldiers who escaped from the Japanese in Burma with Capt Van Hemert. It gives a full account of the nearly two years they spent in the jungle before they were recaptured and sent to Outram Road in October 1944.
I am deeply grateful to my friend Anny de Decker of Ieper, Belgium, who researched this material and provided a valuable translation. See also the note under *War Crimes* in Ch 14, where Van Hemert is named as one of the victims for whose deaths at Outram Road the Japanese were put on trial.

*Wells:* Statement in affidavit NAA MP897 156/19/152. *Needle:* McGregor, 196–8.

*Annihilate them all:* Silver, *Rimau*, 217; also Silver, *Sandakan*, 215.

*Three in cell:* Young, *Return*, 214–5, and interviews.

*Rimau trial:* McKie, 266–9; Silver, *Rimau*, 203–13. *Kamiya:* The two vary in the prosecutor's closing words, though the sense is the same. I use Silver.

*Execution:* McKie, 272–6; Silver, *Rimau*, 214–16, who reports the taunt
    to the executioners.

*Rollason:* Silver, *Rimau*, 214, Rollason interview with author. A
    statement by an American airman held at Outram Road,
    T/Sgt John MacDonald Jr, to the Judge Advocate General's
    Dept in January 1946 speaks of the ten Rimau men executed
    in July 1946. He says they were given cigarettes, sweetened
    condensed milk, large amounts of rice and vegetables before
    their executions. He also spoke to three Australians – named
    as Jim (MP) Brown, Rollason and Bill Hughes – who had to
    clean up the cell afterwards. They said it was covered in blood.
    They also had to wash the ten suits of clothes the men wore,
    and these were 'completely soaked in blood'. MacDonald also
    mentions Haberfield, though he confuses the date of the death
    of the Palembang nine (giving it as May, not August). Copy of
    statement provided by Bill Young.

*US Airmen:* Young, *Return*, 212–13, interviews. See MacDonald
    statement above under *Rollason*.

*Tamils:* Young, *Return*, 218, and interviews.

*End of war:* Young, *Return*, 218–21, and interviews.

*Palembang Nine:* A memorial to the victims is at St Bartholomew's, the
    Fleet Air Arm church at Yeovil, Somerset. An account of them
    will be found under 'The Palembang Nine' 1 March 2007 on the
    website www.cmwarstories.blogspot.com, which includes photos
    of Haberfield and his late sister Mrs Koa Murdoch. See also
    notes to *Habbie* in this chapter.

*Release:* Young, *Return*, 220, and interviews.

*O'Toole:* Young, *Return*, 222, and interviews.

## CHAPTER 14

*Changi:* Medical conditions of prisoners at end of war: Walker, 665–7.
    Of the 5557 AIF prisoners on Singapore Island on 8 September
    1945, Walker says 4609 were at Changi, 740 at Kranji and
    208 at Adam Park and Tanjong Pagar. He notes that 'gross
    malnutrition was the rule'; 80–85 per cent had malaria, and 500
    (ten per cent) of the men suffered beriberi.

# CHAPTER NOTES

*Japanese forces:* There were some 50 000 Japanese army and air-force personnel, and nearly 27 000 naval personnel at Singapore and Johore at the surrender, plus another 26 000 in central and northern Malaya: Warren, 299.

*Hospital:* Walker, 564, 569. The main Australian POW hospital was at Changi, the British one at Kranji on the Johore Strait, near the site of the present war cemetery. A preliminary medical report issued in early September said the men were wasted and exhausted, readily fatigued, had low resistance to disease, and were either temporarily or permanently unfit for service: Walker, 666.

*Burma-Thai Railway:* Dennis, 129. 2/29 Bn. Christie, 129–42: Lack, 145–210 for individual stories. *O'Toole:* Lack, 160, 171, 193, 199. *Pond's Party:* Christie, 153–74; Mills, esp. 132-5. The 2/29 Bn lost 249 men on the railway: 36 with A Force in Burma, 213 altogether with F Force. A total of 72 2/29 men died with B Force at Sandakan and Ranau: Christie, 212.

*Changi beach:* Young, *Return*, 222, and interviews. It remains the most memorable evening of his life.

*Scrounge:* Young interviews. Bill remembers the leaflets; also the POW card sent to Hobart.

*'Becky' Sharpe:* Young, *My War in Pictures*, 85, and interviews. Private John 'Jack' Sharpe served with the 2nd Bn Leicester Regiment. He escaped from the Thai-Burma Railway, was recaptured and entered Outram Road in August 1942, McGregor, 8. Copies of the famous photo of him are at the Imperial War Museum, London, and also the Changi Museum. For years Bill Young thought Sharpe had died on the way home to England; in fact he survived, married, had two children, and lived until August 2002. See article with photos 'I Will Walk Out On My Own Two Feet', 1 December 2006 on the website www.cmwarstories. blogspot.com. My thanks to Ray and Paul Brotherton and members of the Sharpe family.

*Operation Tiderace:* Warren, 299. Also numerous Internet sites including Wikipedia, www.Fepow-community.org.uk. *Itagaki.* See e.g. www.encyclopedia.com.

*Hotel Sussex:* See letter by Guy Howard Bedford, who served on *Sussex*, for an excellent eyewitness account of the first fortnight after

the convoy reached Singapore: www.britain-at-war.org.uk/
Liberation-of-Singapore.

*War crimes:* See Dennis, 641. *Outram Road.* Trial records from August–
October 1946 compiled by Stephanie Beckman: see 'Singapore
Cases – Otsuka' under war crimes at http://socrates.berkeley.edu.

*Return to Australia:* See e.g. *The Argus* Melbourne, 20 September–1
October 1945.

*Sandakan:* First reports, see e.g. *The Argus* and *Canberra Times,*
1 September 1945, Owen Campbell's rescue; *Hobart Mercury,*
17 September, and *The Argus,* 22 September, six known
survivors; *The Argus,* 28 September, Parliament.

*Hospital:* Casualty form, Young service papers; interviews.

*Lady Mountbatten: Hobart Mercury,* 22, 25 April 1946. Young interviews.

*Post-war life:* Young interviews.

*Brown:* A letter in MP Brown's service file from his former wife, Valeria,
then at Wacol, Queensland, dated 1 November 1954, says that
he was recently deceased. He had never sent for his ribbons
or medals, and Mrs Brown asked if they could be sent to their
daughter, then aged 13. Valeria Rose Brown died at Ipswich,
Queensland, in October 1994. Brown divorced and remarried
after he returned to Australia. He died in Brisbane after an
accident involving an electric lawnmower. My thanks to Denise
Juler, Judith (née Brown) and Majella Gee for their assistance.

# CHAPTER 15

*Death Marches:* I have relied on Jackson; Silver Chs 9, 11–14, and
Wigmore's excellent summary, 593–604. I commend them to
interested readers. Major Jackson paid just over £290 ($580) to
Borneo people for services they rendered to Australian POWs at
Sandakan and on the death marches.

*Numbers:* The death toll varies; 2500 is an upper limit. Based on
extensive record research, Silver, 335, gives a figure of 2428
deaths (1787 Australians, 641 British) from the time the officers
left Sandakan in late 1943. Another six POWs of course
survived the marches.

*Burial:* The bodies recovered after the war at Ranau were taken to

the beautiful Labuan War Cemetery, which also contains the
remains of the POWs killed at Miri and on Labuan itself (among
them Joey Crome and Wally Ford). The remains of the POWs
who died at Sandakan were first interred in a war cemetery
near the airfield; but in 1949 they were also taken to Labuan
War Cemetery where all their names are commemorated and
headstones honour the remains whose names we know or the
great majority who are 'Known Unto God'.

*For the duration:* Silver, 167; also Botterill in Young, *Long Ago,* 21.

*Gunboat Simpson:* Silver, 224, Young interview.

*Cleary:* Murdered in March 1945, Silver, 199-201. A memorial cairn
stands on the site of his torture, with a stone for every man who
died on the death marches.

*Richie Murray:* Killed 20 May 1945, after taking sole responsibility for
stealing rice, a few sweets and hard tack biscuits, Silver, 210.

*Shipsides:* Silver, 216, Young interview.

*RAAF sheer chance:* Silver, 231.

*Kingfisher:* Silver, esp 301–11. She quotes a senior intelligence officer,
Denis Emerson-Elliott, 312: 'The intelligence was a disaster. The
bungling on the planning side was dreadful, so [General] Blamey
decided to blame MacArthur.'

*Crucifixion:* Silver, 235; Jackson, 72.

*Longley:* Silver, 250, Young interview.

*Orders not to undertake further activities:* Silver, 252, 261.

*Cook and records:* Silver, 251, 260 where she says Cook handed the
records to the Japanese who destroyed them on 27 August.
*Tin not found:* Ibid, 270.

*Finn:* Silver, 259.

*Last 15 Ranau deaths:* Jackson, 69–70 says 1 August; Silver, 258–9 says
27 August based on intelligence and Special Operations reports.
I thank Lynette for her kind assistance, especially with this
chapter, and for her advice on the whole Sandakan story since I
travelled with her party to Singapore and Borneo for Anzac Day
2009.

*Retribution:* Figures from Silver, 380–2. Hoshijima and Takakuwa
hanged Rabaul 6 April 1946: Silver, 273; report in *SMH* 8 April.

*Later life:* Author interviews with Bill Young 2007–11.

*Darlington:* Jimmy Darlington returned to Barraba, NSW, and became a
local institution, still putting up his hand into middle age when
Sharman's boxing troupe came to town. 'You do the writing,
I'll do the fighting,' he'd say to a mate. Jimmy became a heavy
drinker, and tragically died with his wife, Molly, in a caravan fire
on a property 30 miles from Barraba in June 1976. My thanks
to Richard Chapman, Vicki Chin, Vic Gillies, Max Kelly and
Robert Sweeney for their help.

*O'Toole:* 'Love is a big word', Lack, 199.

*The Big Tree:* The Sandakan commemorative stone is near where the
Big Tree once stood. It burnt down after the war in mysterious
circumstances. According to rumour, certain NCOs were said
to have hidden jewels in the tree, the proceeds of the official
gambling casinos run at the base camps before the war (see
e.g. Billy's birthday Chapter 7). It is unknown if any stash was
recovered from the ashes, Silver 293.

*Inadvertently:* Young interview.

# REFERENCES

Battalion War Diaries, 2/19 Bn (AWM52 8/3/19 Jan-Feb 1942); 2/29 Bn
(AWM52 8/3/29 Dec 1941-Feb 1942); 2/30 Bn (AWM52 8/3/30 Jan-
Feb 1942). Available online.

Bedford, Guy Howard, *Liberation of Singapore,* letter written while serving on
HMS *Sussex*, available on the Internet at www.britain-at-war.org.uk

Christie, R. W. ed., *A History of the 2/29 Battalion – 8th Australian Division
AIF* (High Country Publishing, Stratford, Vic., 1983).

Christie, –, Lack John ed., *Surviving Captivity, The campaign and POW diary of
Bob Christie 1942-1945* (Australian Scholarly Publishing with 2/29th
Bn AIF Assn, Melbourne, 2010).

Coulthard-Clark, Chris, *The Encyclopaedia of Australia's Battles* (Allen &
Unwin, Sydney, 1998).

Daws, Gavan, *Prisoners of the Japanese, POWs of World War II in the Pacific*
(William Morrow, 1994; Scribe, Melbourne 2004).

Dean, Penrod, *Singapore Samurai* (Kangaroo Press, Sydney, 1998).

Dennis, Peter, et al ed., *The Oxford Companion to Australian Military History*
(OUP, Melbourne, 1995), esp John Coates on Malayan Campaign
375–81.

Firkins, Peter, *Borneo Surgeon, A Reluctant Hero, The Story of Dr James P
Taylor* (Hesperian Press, Victoria Park, WA, 1996).

Gill, G. Hermon, *Royal Australian Navy 1939–1942* (AWM, Canberra, Vol I
and Vol II *1942-45*, Navy series of the official history of Australia in the
War of 1939–1945).

Inglis, Amirah, *Australians in the Spanish Civil War* (Allen & Unwin, Sydney,
1987).

Jackson, Major Harry, *Awards to helpers British North Borneo, Major Jackson's
report* (NAA MP742/1 Control symbol 328/1/32).

Lack, John, *No Lost Battalion, An Oral History of the 2/29th Battalion AIF*
(Slouch Hat Publications, McCrae, Vic., 2005).

McGregor, John, *Blood on the Rising Sun* (Bencoolen, Perth, undated c. 1980).

MacDonald, T/Sgt John, Statement to Judge Advocate-General's Department,
January 1946. Copy provided to author by Bill Young.

407

# REFERENCES

McKie, Ronald, *The Heroes* (Angus and Robertson, 1960).

Mills, Dr Roy, *Doctor's Diary and Memoirs – Pond's Party, F Force, Thai-Burma Railway* (Self-published, New Lambton, NSW, 1994).

Nelson, Hank, POW *Prisoners of War, Australians Under Nippon* (ABC Enterprises, Sydney, 1985), from the ABC radio series with Tim Bowden.

New Zealand War Memorial Museum. See Cenotaph Database and search John Kerle Tipaho Haberfield at www.aucklandmuseum.com for details of Habbie's service, photo and short biography.

Silver, Lynette Ramsay, *Sandakan, A Conspiracy of Silence* (Sally Milner Publishing, Bowral, 1998).

Silver, –, *The Heroes of Rimau:Unravelling the mystery of one of World War II's most daring raids* (Sally Milner Publishing, Bowral, 1990).

Smith, Kevin, *Borneo, Australia's Proud but Tragic Heritage* (Self-published, Armidale, 1999).

Tanaka, Yuki, *Hidden Horrors, Japanese War Crimes in World War II* (Westview Press, Colorado, 1996).

Walker, Allan S, *Medical History of Australia in the War of 1939-1945, Vol II Middle East and Far East* (Australian War Memorial, Canberra).

Warren, Alan, *Singapore 1942, Britain's Greatest Defeat* (Talisman, Singapore, 2002).

Wigmore, Lionel, *The Japanese Thrust* (AWM, Canberra, Vol IV Army series of the official history Australia in the War of 1939–1945).

Young, Bill, *Return to a Dark Age* (Self-published, Sydney, 1991).

Young, –, *My War in Pictures, My Thoughts in Verse,* (Self-published, Sydney, undated).

Young, –, *My Little Book of Po-Ems and Other Gems* (Self-published, Sydney, 2006).

Young, –, *Long Ago in Borneo* (Self-published, Sydney, undated). It contains extracts from Major Jackson's report, a report by Dick Braithwaite on the Sandakan death march, a statement by Keith Botterill to the war crimes tribunal, and an article by Bill on B Force.

# ACKNOWLEDGEMENTS

This work began when Win Adams visited my market stall in Canberra and suggested I write a book about her husband's cousin Bill, as mentioned in the introductory Author's Note. I begin these acknowledgements by again thanking her for the idea. I've also written of my deep gratitude to Bill Young for his enthusiastic agreement and constant support. It is evident on every page of the book, but I acknowledge it once more here, and thank him for permission to use his poems and pictures.

Many other people assisted me with advice, leads, recollections and by reading the manuscript in whole or in part. I thank them all for their friendship and guidance, though naturally any errors remain my own: Professor Richard Braithwaite, Ray and Paul Brotherton, members of the Sharpe family, Sheila Bruhn (née Allen), Leslie Bunn-Glover, Richard Chapman, Vicki Chin, Bob Christie – secretary of the 2/29 Battalion Association, Dr Alan and Susan Cowan, John and Esther Davies, Anny de Decker, Russ Ewin, Vic Gillies, June Healey, Denise Juler, Judith (née Brown) and Majella Gee, John Hook, Max Kelly, Dr Graeme Killer, Veronica Kong, Associate Professor John and Sue Lack, John Lewis and Eric McDonald of Sandakan Families, Gerald Longley, Dr Peter McCawley, Dr Michael McKernan, Jane and Paul Mangion, Graham Metzger and members of the Haberfield family, David Mills, Professor Hank Nelson, Ced Pratt, Herbert 'Bluey' Rollason, Keith Rollason, Dr Rowley Richards, Jen Sanders, Lynette and Neil Silver, Alison Simmons and her daughter Amy Roberts, Margaret and Ron Simpson, Joanne Smedley, Robert Sweeney, Dr Keiko Tamura, Jane Tanner, Barry Tinkler, Herb Trackson, Pam Wells, Shuji Yamazaki, Scott Young.

I am grateful for the support and encouragement of artsACT,

and the publisher, Penguin Books, in particular Bob Sessions, Anne Rogan, Cathy Larsen and Adrian Potts, and also Suzanne Wilson, who has given me her editorial wisdom and advice over nearly two decades.

I also thank the directors and staff of the following institutions, whose assistance with my inquiries and research has – as always – been unfailing: Australian War Memorial, House of Representatives' Table Office, National Archives of Australia, National Film and Sound Archive, National Library of Australia, New South Wales and Tasmanian Registrars of Births, Deaths and Marriages.

Finally – first, last and always – is my dear wife, Gillian, whose patience and commitment have been constants throughout my writing career.

# INDEX

411

# INDEX

# INDEX

# INDEX